Fourth Edition

THINKING
for
YOURSELF

Developing Critical Thinking Skills Through Reading and Writing

Marlys Mayfield

College of Alameda

Wadsworth Publishing Company
I(T)P® An International Thomson Publishing Company

Belmont, CA • Albany, NY • Bonn • Boston • Cincinnati • Detroit • Johannesburg •
London • Madrid •Melbourne • Mexico City • New York • Paris • San Francisco •
Singapore • Tokyo • Toronto • Washington

English Editor: Michael Llwyd Alread
Editorial Assistant: Royden Tonomura
Production Editor: Karen Garrison
Print Buyer: Barbara Britton
Permissions Editor: Robert Kauser
Text Designer: Wendy Calmenson
Copy Editor: Polly Kummel
Compositor: Thompson Type
Cover: Rob Hugel
Cover Photograph: © Sylvain Grandadam/Tony Stone Images
Printer: Quebecor Printing/Fairfield

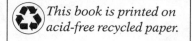

Printed in the United States of America
5 6 7 8 9 10

For more information, contact Wadsworth Publishing Company, 10 Davis Drive, Belmont, CA
94002, or electronically at http://www.thomson.com/wadsworth.html

International Thomson Publishing Europe
Berkshire House 168-173
High Holborn
London, WC1V 7AA, England

International Thomson Editores
Campos Eliseos 385, Piso 7
Col. Polanco
11560 México D.F. México

Thomas Nelson Australia
102 Dodds Street
South Melbourne 3205
Victoria, Australia

International Thomson Publishing Asia
221 Henderson Road
#05-10 Henderson Building
Singapore 0315

Nelson Canada
1120 Birchmount Road
Scarborough, Ontario
Canada M1K 5G4

International Thomson Publishing Japan
Hirakawacho Kyowa Building, 3F
2-2-1 Hirakawacho
Chiyoda-ku, Tokyo 102, Japan

International Thomson Publishing GmbH
Königswinterer Strasse 418
53227 Bonn, Germany

International Thomson Publishing Southern Africa
Building 18, Constantia Park
240 Old Pretoria Road
Halfway House, 1685 South Africa

Library of Congress Cataloging-in-Publication Data
Mayfield, Marlys, date
   Thinking for yourself : developing critical thinking skill through reading and writing /
Marlys Mayfield. — 4th ed.
      p.   cm.
   Includes bibliographical references and index.
   ISBN: 0-534-51858-3 (alk. paper)
      1. English language—Rhetoric.   2. Critical thinking.   I. Title
PE1408.M3933   1996   96-8677

Brief Contents

Contents

PART I
BASICS OF CRITICAL THINKING

Chapter 3 Facts: What's Real? 75

Chapter 4 Inferences: What Follows? 104

PART II
PROBLEMS OF CRITICAL THINKING

Chapter 5 Assumptions: What's Taken for Granted?   144

PART III
FORMS AND STANDARDS OF CRITICAL THINKING

Chapter 12 Deductive Reasoning: How Do I Reason from Premises? 350

PART IV
CREATING WITH CRITICAL THINKING

Foreword

Marlys Mayfield's book docs not preach critical thinking; it practices it. Engaging to read, it contains an abundance of examples showing the richness and complexity of the thought we exercise every day. These examples are then successfully linked to the course material in such a way that it soon becomes quite evident how mastery of these few concepts can powerfully affect the discourse in almost any field—evidence often sought but not often achieved in the teaching of critical thinking.

The book is also about the writing process—about the courage to keep questioning even at the risk of not getting the assignment done neatly and on time and about the truths that can show up on the page unexpectedly when that courage is exercised. It is not a book about how to write an "argumentative essay," "convince" an audience, or "defend" one's conclusions but about how to use the writing process to test one's own convictions and make sure they are worth promoting. It is not, in short, about how to *sell* the truth but about how to find it.

Thinking for Yourself begins where the effort to find the truth must begin: in observation. And by thus grounding critical thought in perception, the text manages to promote self-confidence even while leading toward self-scrutiny—a delicate accomplishment that is crucial to the successful teaching of critical thinking.

Indeed, throughout the text, the underlying approach continually proves both psychologically astute and morally appealing, for it takes as the touchstone of critical thought the perceptions and opinions of the individual thinker. It recognizes that the point of instruction in this area is not that students should come to doubt their powers but that they should come to know where they are responsible for the exercise of these powers and to understand how they may improve this exercise.

Thus in Part I, after developing care for what one observes (Chapter 1), Mayfield encourages similar precision in the choice of words for talking about these observations (Chapter 2). Only then are facts discussed (Chapter 3), the placement of this topic subtly making the essential point that "facts" depend on words and perceptions. Inference (Chapter 4) is carefully distinguished from fact, and the groundwork is laid for the discussion of inductive argument.

Of particular value—and rarity—among critical thinking texts is the acknowledgment in Part II of the role of feelings and intuition. The text here appeals to the practical and makes immediate connections with most domains. And in such appeal, as well, the text is culturally accessible, honoring not only the intelligence and inspiration of those from diverse backgrounds—where ethnicity, gender, social class, or geographic region have an effect on cognitive styles—but also the styles and perspectives of managers and employees—and indeed of all those whose hands-on experience of the world makes them skeptical of mere bookishness.

Having thus firmly established the locus of critical thinking in the individual writer as perceiver and doer, Mayfield then pursues formal thought. Her chapters on formal argumentation and research successfully build a bridge into academic competence. And in Part IV, Mayfield demonstrates how critical and creative thinking can combine to produce innovative solutions for practical problems. This section can be used separately as a resource at any time in the study of the book or elsewhere.

To have been drawn into this book and worked through its exercises—which come as naturally as responses in a conversation—is to have learned what cannot be unlearned: how to think more carefully, not only in class but wherever else it matters.

Nancy Glock
California Community Colleges

Preface

"Wait! Wait! Listen to me! . . . We don't HAVE to be just sheep!"

Used with permission of Chronicle Features, San Francisco.

HISTORY OF THE TEXT

Critical thinking occurs when we wake up and take initiative. Sometimes the need to think critically begins with the momentous, and sometimes with the ordinary, but inevitably it begins with a discovery that we have been asleep.

This book originated through some acts of waking up. Its germination began with a nagging dissatisfaction with the way I had been teaching English composition for fifteen years. Like my colleagues, I knew that writing was clear when thinking was clear. And so, I wondered, why not focus primarily on the thinking process instead of the writing process? Why not use writing to show how we think, instead of thinking so much about how we write? It seemed to me that this approach would do more to improve writing in the long run. The problem then was that none of us knew how to teach thinking or even if that were possible.

In 1980 I learned it was possible to teach thinking when I heard of new curricula designed to teach thinking as a skill. My studies began under Arthur Costa, who led me through the teaching instruments of Reuven Feuerstein. By 1982, I was offering two experimental college courses. The first was a remedial one in thinking skills. The second was an English course designed to meet the new critical thinking study requirement mandated by the California state universities. My course combined the teaching of critical thinking skills with those of reading and writing, an innovative course idea at a time when critical thinking instruction was the customary province of philosophy departments.

This book is based on the material I developed for that course. I wrote it chapter by chapter, based on whatever my students showed me they needed to know. What they needed sometimes surprised me, such as the difference between facts and inferences and between reasons and conclusions; the meaning of assumptions, opinions, and evaluations; and the significance of viewpoint. During this period, I was also working with Wadsworth Publishing's editors and reviewers, whose suggestions continued to shape the book's content and organization. The result, published in 1987, became a unique text serving two purposes:

- To teach English composition by emphasizing the thinking process.
- To teach critical thinking through writing.

Validation for the effectiveness of combining critical thinking and composition appeared in the 1989 uniform agreement of the University of California system, the California state universities, and the community colleges to require students to take a course with the two in combination.

Subsequent editions have included new multicultural readings as well as new chapters on research and problem solving. This fourth edition represents another extensive revision based on feedback from my own students, from colleagues, and reviewers. It includes many revised assignments, new methods for peer evaluation of writing exercises, new student writing examples, new charts, readings, photographs, and cartoons. The argument chapter now appears in the middle, instead of at the end, of the text; the fallacies have been reclassified in more groups, more accessible for learning.

In each edition, the guiding purpose has been to provide more flexibility and teaching options. The text is meant chiefly for use in either first or second semester English courses. It contains enough materials for two semesters of work, yet, with omissions, can serve for either course alone. Instructors of subfreshman English could adapt the first nine chapters to serve as a full text. Philosophy instructors can use the text with or without the composition writing assignments. Instructors who wish to emphasize critical reading have numerous selections to choose from. Those who wish to assign a research paper will find three different assignments in the chapters on research skills, problem solving, and argumentative research. Instructors who wish to use collaborative learning will find that each chapter offers that option for assignments. Finally, while the text contains material sufficient for a two-quarter or two-semester English or philosophy course, instructors can tailor the material to fit the requirements of a one-quarter or one-semester course.

Of all those who contributed to this new edition as it grew during 1993 to 1996, I wish primarily to thank my students at Vista College, the College of Marin, Golden Gate University, and the National Center for Teaching Thinking. My special thanks go to two colleagues: Eugenie Yaryan, of the College of Marin, who met with me weekly in the fall of 1995 to suggest and toss around ideas, and Walter C. Frey, of Contra Costa College, for assistance with the deduction chapter. This book continues to be a collaboration. It is dedicated to my students whose questions always led me.

APPROACH AND COVERAGE

1. This text teaches both critical thinking and composition by emphasizing awareness of the personal thinking process. From the training of personal awareness, it moves to the more advanced stages of analyzing the thinking of others.

2. This book begins on a more fundamental level than most other critical thinking books, yet proceeds to a more advanced level than most, requiring students to develop and demonstrate highly sophisticated analytical skills.

3. The first half of the text works extensively with critical thinking in *nonverbal* problems, using photographs, cartoons, descriptive assignments, and report assignments. The second half moves into the more traditional application of critical thinking to *verbal* problems, analyses, and arguments.

4. The text provokes its readers constantly to think in order to work their way through the materials. Its problem and writing assignments force confrontation with the common ways thinking can go astray. Some of these include reliance upon overused phrases, stereotypes, long-held opinions; missing instructions; the substitution of evaluations and imagination for facts; the use of unexamined assumptions; and the acceptance of false authority.

5. In its style and pedagogy, the text shows consistent concern for the interaction of the cognitive and affective domains of learning. It also addresses directly the problems of distinguishing between feelings that clarify thinking and those that hinder it.

6. The text uses practical, everyday examples, connecting the concepts learned about thinking to life's problems. Direct quotations taken from the media concerning political and social issues are used extensively to illustrate the ubiquity and influence of arguments in our lives as well as the need for standards by which to judge them.

7. The text builds self-confidence by working from what students already know so that they discover key principles for themselves. No more theory is introduced into this book than that which students can bridge from their discoveries and no more information is offered than that which they can apply right away to thinking, discussion, and writing.

SPECIAL FEATURES
AND FURTHER REVISIONS

1. Each chapter begins with *Discovery Exercises*, which provide opportunities for students to uncover principles about thinking for themselves. The exercises also engage and motivate students by asking them to draw on their own experiences and the things that interest them.

2. A study of the table of contents shows that Parts I and II cover basic material not usually presented in such depth in critical thinking texts, whereas Part III offers extensive treatment of the more traditional topics of critical thinking, such as argument, fallacies, inductive reasoning, and deductive reasoning. Part IV, Creating with Critical Thinking, again is unusual in that it includes a research skills and problem-solving chapter.

3. Multiple tools for evaluating student progress appear in this fourth edition. Each chapter ends with a summary and true-false chapter quiz. These quizzes can be used to provoke further learning through oral review as well as for written exams. New to this edition are Objectives Reviews at the end of each major section and the scoring boxes for peer scoring of Core Discovery Writing Applications. The Instructor's Manual contains tests for Parts I and II; content questions and essay questions for each chapter; tests on dictionary skills; additional tests on fallacies, reasons, and conclusions; a model research take-home final; and additional in-class final exams.

4. The writing applications are another special feature. *Two* types of writing applications appear in the text, and this edition seeks to make that distinction clearer. The Composition Writing Applications follow a progression of rhetorical complexity from description and narration through

the longer research papers. The Core Discovery Writing Applications offer experiential understanding of the concepts and skills taught through the text. Each core application is designed to mirror thinking through the writing process, heighten self-awareness, and bring skill deficiencies to the surface. Instructors using this text for an English course can choose from the composition assignments as well as use the core discovery applications, whereas those using this text for a critical thinking course may want to use only the core discovery applications.

5. Multicultural viewpoints and themes predominate in this edition in essays, short stories, and the boxed series on argument.

6. The chapter on research skills and the chapter on problem solving are designed for optional use; they may be taken up in whole or in part at any time during the course, according to course requirements and the instructor's discretion. Instructors who require their students to finish a term paper by the end of the quarter might assign either chapter by the end of the first month.

7. The chapter on argument has been moved from the end to the beginning of Part III in this edition. Argument building and analysis is the most complex skill taught in the text, and it needs to be reinforced in increments. The reorganization is designed to give students an opportunity to integrate what they have learned from Parts I and II as well as to clarify what they still must learn in preparation for a final in-class exam or research exam.

8. I revised several chapters for this edition. I added exercises to the chapter on assumptions to better clarify the difference between hidden assumptions and value assumptions. The chapter on deduction has been expanded to better teach the concepts of validity and the purposes of the syllogism. In this edition, the formal fallacies have been removed with regret because they lacked the depth of treatment they require and that can only be met in a semester-long logic course. The purpose of this chapter is simply to clarify the meaning of deduction, its standards, and how it operates in the mind. New additions to the deduction chapter include a chart that compares induction and deduction as well as a discussion of how these different forms of reasoning alternate in our minds.

9. The presentation of fallacies in this edition has been reorganized for faster comprehension, memory, and assimilation. A new chapter, "The Fallacies of Trickery," introduces more than half of the twenty-two fallacies taught in the book. The remainder of the fallacies appear at the end of the chapter on induction, where they clearly supplement that chapter. Classroom feedback has also led to the fuller explanation of some fallacies and to new names for some that were confusing.

ACKNOWLEDGMENTS

The sixteen years I have spent writing these four editions have brought me many devoted helpers and illuminating advisors. First, I would like to thank the reviewers of the first three editions, who let me know what could best serve their students. They include Gary Christensen, Macomb County Community College; Robert Dees, Orange Coast College; Yvonne Frye, Community College of Denver; Helen Gordon, Bakersfield College; Patricia Grignon, Saddleback College; Elizabeth Hanson-Smith, California State University, Sacramento; Ralph Jenkins, Temple University; Shelby Kipplen, Michael J. Owens Technical College; Eileen Lundy, University of Texas, San Antonio; Daniel Lynch, La Guardia Community College; L. J. McDoniel, St. Louis Community College, Meramec; Paul Olubas, Southern Ohio College; Sue Sixberry, Mesabi Community College; Patricia Smittle, Santa Fe Community College; Fran Bahr, North Idaho College; Charlene Doyon, University of Lowell; Carol Enns, College of the Sequoias; Jon Ford, College of Alameda; Nancy Glock, California Community Colleges; James Haule, University of Texas, Pan American; Jerry Herman, Laney College; Becky Patterson, University of Alaska; Suzette Schlapkohl, Scottsdale Community College; Pamela Spoto, Shasta College; and Mark Weinstein, Montclair State College.

Reviewers I wish to thank for this fourth edition include C. George Fry, Lutheran College of Health Professions; Adrienne Gosselin, Cleveland State University; Marilyn Hill, American River College; Susan A. Injejikian, Glendale Community College; Henry Nardone, King's College; Ronn Talbot Pelley, City University; and Edith Wollin, North Seattle Community College.

Finally, I want to thank those Wadsworth staff members who have given me ongoing support in the creation of this fourth edition. They include Gary Carlson, vice president; Royden Tonomura, editorial assistant; Karen Garrison, production editor; Robert Kauser, permissions editor; Sylvia Haskwitz, my assistant; and Michelle Filippini, who assisted me in preparing the Instructor's Manual.

Introduction to Critical Thinking

"How do people plead insanity? Who's gonna believe a crazy person?"

Used with permission of Richard Guindon.

This is a book about thinking that will constantly require you to think. Usually you will not be told ahead of time what to expect, nor will you be given the "right" answers afterward. Instead, you will be asked to think out problems *for yourself* before they are discussed either in the text or in class. In addition, you will always be asked *to observe the way you think* as you go.

Each chapter in this text starts with Discovery Exercises for you to think about alone before participating in a class discussion. The purpose of these Discovery Exercises is to engage you in some experiences that will demonstrate *how* you think. They will also give you an opportunity to discover some principles about thinking for yourself.

To illustrate what Discovery Exercises are, this introduction will begin with one. After you have completed the discussion and writing that follow, you can continue to read more in this introduction about the attitudes required to develop critical thinking skills, this particular text's definition of critical thinking, and the habits of a critical thinker.

1

Discovery Exercise

Learning How We Think

This is an exercise to be done in class. Look at the photograph on page 3. Based on what you see there, rate each of the following statements as either *true, false,* or *can't answer.* Write your answers without discussing either the questions or your replies with anyone else.

_____ 1. This is graduation day for the Thomas family.

_____ 2. The father is proud of his son.

_____ 3. The sister looks up to her brother.

_____ 4. This is a prosperous family.

_____ 5. The son has just graduated from law school.

   When you have finished this quiz, wait, without talking to anyone else about your choices, until the instructor calls you for discussion. At this point you will be asked to give your answers to each statement and to justify each choice.

After the Discussion

Review the following questions. Were many of these covered in class? Now consider those that were not covered, either through continuing the discussion or by pausing to write out your answers, depending on your instructor's directions.

1. What are your definitions of the following terms?

    True   False   Can't Answer

2. Can a statement be rated *true* if it contains an assumption?

3. Is it possible to determine whether a written statement is *true* if it contains ambiguous words or phrases?

4. Should a statement be rated *true* if it is highly probable?

5. What makes a statement true or false?

6. Did you find yourself reluctant to choose the option of *can't answer*? Why or why not?

7. How can we know whether or not something is true?

8. What did this exercise teach you?

Photo by Rick Fanthorpe-White. Used with permission of the photographer.

LEARNING FROM SHARING HOW WE THINK

Your work on this last assignment took you from isolated thinking to sharing the results with others. In the course of the discussion, you may have been surprised to discover the divisions that occurred in the class on the basis of different perceptions and judgments. Perhaps you even decided to change your original decisions during the discussion.

If doubts and shifts of viewpoint left you feeling confused or unsettled, consider that feeling as something beginning to grow in you that could lead to new perspectives and understanding. The work throughout this book should involve many cycles of clarity surrounded by confusion (or even embarrassment), which is what true learning entails. This assignment was meant to remind you of what it means to learn first from your own *experience*, rather than from what others have told you, and to involve you directly in thinking for yourself.

In the process of developing critical thinking skills, the only essential attitude is to be willing to *learn*—which also means being willing to say "I am confused," or "I am wrong," or even "I don't know." Many of us associate "I don't know" with irresponsibility or ignorance. But it can also mean a greater commitment to honesty and, with that, an allowance of a creative space for something new to develop. Critical thinking, then, does not mean having all the answers but simply being willing to be surprised, to discover, and to learn. And sometimes this requires humility—from instructors as well as students.

The method of learning that you followed in the first Discovery Exercise is what is called the inductive method, or that of deriving principles from experience. In this case, what you learned was not about the people in the photograph but something about the way you think and how your way is similar to, or different from, the ways of others. You also observed your thinking without disguising or altering it to fit any principles offered in advance by the text.

If critical thinking is best developed by observing your own thinking process, sharing your thoughts with others, discovering principles for yourself, and maintaining an open, learning attitude, then what exactly *is* critical thinking?

WHAT IS CRITICAL THINKING?

Dictionaries tell us that we use the word *thinking* to mean more than nineteen different mental operations. These range from reasoning to solving problems, to conceiving and discovering ideas, to remembering, to daydreaming. Some of these forms are conscious, focused, and directed, while others are automatic and undirected. In this book, we will be using the word *thinking* in the sense of conscious purposeful mental activity.

Most of us associate the word *critical* with being negative or finding fault. Although that is one way to use the word, a critical view can also be one of appreciation. The original meaning of the word comes from the root form *skeri*, which means to cut, separate, or sift; thus the original idea conveyed by the word was to take something apart or to analyze it. Here in its core idea is not negativity but a procedure for analyzing knowledge and then evaluating it. Moreover, critical is also related to the Greek word *kri-*

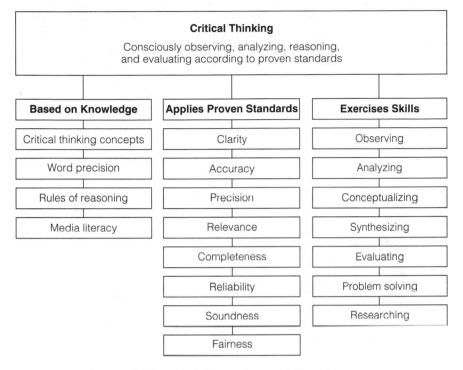

Figure I.1 The Standards and Abilities of Critical Thinking

terion, which means a standard for judging. Putting together these two original ideas, we see that the word *critical* means analyzing on the basis of a standard.

Today there are as many definitions of critical thinking as there are writers on the subject. But all would agree that critical thinking is a purposeful form of mental activity; many would agree that it involves learning conscious awareness of the thinking process itself. Finally, all agree that it is one guided by standards.

Now what are the standards of critical thinking? Critical thinking is based on the same standards that have guided science and scholarship for centuries, standards that have proven usefulness in evaluating reasoning and knowledge (see Figure I.1). They include clarity, accuracy, precision, consistency, relevance, reliability, soundness, completeness, and fairness. All these standards help us to aim for truth or to come as close to truth as we can.

To develop critical thinking abilities we also need knowledge, knowledge such as is taught in this book about critical thinking concepts, word precision, the rules of reasoning, and media literacy. Finally, we need to

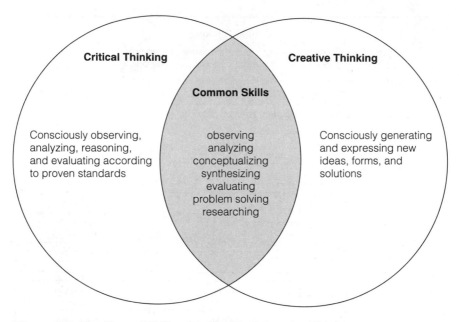

Figure I.2 The Shared Skills of Critical and Creative Thinking

understand and practice the skills of critical thinking: observing, analyzing, reasoning, conceptualizing, synthesizing, evaluating, communicating, researching, and problem solving.

Putting this information together, the definition of critical thinking that will guide this text is as follows:

Critical thinking is consciously observing, analyzing, reasoning, and evaluating according to proven standards.

Creative thinking differs from critical thinking in that it generates and expresses *new* ideas, forms, and solutions. Nevertheless, the analytical and evaluative work of critical thinking enters into many phases of the creative process. Like critical thinking, creative thinking is conscious purposeful mental activity summoned to focus on a problem. But creative thinking can work in a playful spirit while dreaming, fantasizing, or letting an idea percolate during a walk. Creative thinking also gives more attention to aesthetics; it seeks solutions that are not just adequate but elegant. However, some writers feel that it is arbitrary to separate critical from creative thinking; they claim that both are interwoven inextricably. And they point to Einstein's descriptions of how he worked with his own mind.

Unfortunately, it is beyond the scope of this book to fully explore their interconnections since there are considerable differences in the knowledge each requires and the standards applied. However, we can review the skills they commonly share: observing, analyzing, conceptualizing, synthesizing, evaluating, researching, and problem solving (see Figure I.2). And the final chapters of this book on research and problem solving will challenge you to generate new ideas or solutions. Moreover, you need not wait until the end of the term to study these two chapters; they contain exercises that may be applied at any time.

WHY LEARN CRITICAL THINKING?

We already know how to do many complex kinds of thinking, for many purposes. All of us have developed our own way of solving problems, using street smarts and common sense or even trial and error. Yet what we already know can be substantially strengthened by conscious attention, just as those who already know how to walk or fight can greatly improve their abilities by studying dance or karate. This improvement comes from paying closer attention to what we already do, finding the right labels, and finding ways to do it better.

Critical thinking isn't the only form of clear thinking, nor is it always appropriate. If you are just hanging out, swapping stories, sharing feelings, speculating, the killjoy who demands that every term be defined, every fact be supported, every speculation be qualified is completely out of place. You don't use an electric saw to slice a roast, but when you do need an electric saw, it is invaluable.

Critical thinking skills are powerful skills. They can empower those who use them—more so than anything else you can learn in college. They can't be picked up on the run; they require careful, disciplined, systematic study. But such study will also pay off not only in the short run by improving performance in every other single course, and in the long run by (1) providing protection from other people's manipulation; (2) lessening the likelihood of making serious mistakes in important decisions; (3) contributing in groups to better decision and consensus making, whether with family, friends, committees, action groups, co-workers, or even with bosses.

Thus although the study of critical thinking leads to mental independence, it is also a path to more productive work with others. It helps people to openly share the workings of their minds: to recognize and direct inner processes for understanding issues, to express ideas and beliefs, to make decisions and analyze and solve problems. Critical thinking allows us to welcome life's problems as challenges to be solved. And it gives us the confidence that we can make sense and harmony out of a confusing world.

THE HABITS OF CRITICAL THINKING

The kinds of habits you will be cultivating as you work your way through this book are listed below. By the time you finish this text you will have had considerable practice engaging in each of these activities, and they should have become habits that you want to keep throughout your life.

1. Observes self in the process of thinking.
2. Suspends judgments when gathering information.
3. Maintains the concentration and persistence necessary to ask questions, understand communications, and complete problems.
4. Separates facts from inferences, opinions, and evaluations.
5. Notes the presence or lack of evidence.
6. Recognizes assumptions in arguments and situations.
7. Separates the relevant from the irrelevant, the inconsistencies from the consistencies.
8. Recognizes viewpoints and their limitations.
9. Seeks to offer convincing evidence and valid reasoning to support arguments.
10. Has sensitivity to word connotation, to slant, definition, ambiguity, and disguise.
11. Recognizes logical fallacies, unfair persuasion, and propaganda.
12. Seeks truth before rightness; willing to admit mistakes and concede to a better argument.

Many of these habits may already be part of your life; others may be unfamiliar to you. Some will be seen with freshness and clarity as you learn to monitor and direct your own thinking habits. Once you have finished studying this book, return to the habits listed here to see how far you have come. The goal is clear, and the time has come to start down the path toward it.

PART I

Basics of
Critical Thinking

CHAPTER 1

Observation Skills:
What's Out There?

Used with permission of Chronicle Features, San Francisco.

O bservation skills keep us alive, but we can't acquire them from
mottoes—only from staying in spontaneous interaction with life.
Perhaps this is what the Boy Scouts and their master depicted in
the chapter opening cartoon realized too late. The attitude of being prepared cannot be learned from signs or books—only from a willingness to
stay awake, to be curious, and to be able to confront whatever happens. A
wise saying tells us, "You don't have to stay awake at night to get ahead. All
you have to do is stay awake in the daytime." But this does not imply that
having observation skills means being tense and grim. They can also provide us with a lot of fun.

Because developing observation skills is an essential foundation for
critical thinking, this chapter consists mainly of exercises that require you
to observe. The opening Discovery Exercises are meant to show you how
you observe and how that may be different from how others observe. As
you work your way through these exercises, you will begin to discover your
own rules about how to observe better, and in this manner you will begin
to guide your own progress.

Writing is used in this chapter to make your observation skills more visible and conscious. Although the Writing Applications will put your focus on observing *things*, you will also be observing *yourself* at the same time. To put it another way, you will be *observing how you observe* from the reflection of your writing.

This chapter also discusses the mental processes involved in observation tasks: sensing, perceiving, and thinking. It considers qualities and attitudes that you can cultivate to improve your observation skills. And it includes readings to stimulate thought about the observation process.

Discovery Exercises

Comparing Our Perceptions

In class, write a one-paragraph description of the photograph on page 12. Try to describe what you see in such a way that your readers will be able to visualize it even without the picture before them. Do not discuss your work with anyone else in class while you observe and write.

When you have finished, form groups of three or four and read your descriptions aloud to one another. As you listen, notice in what details your descriptions are similar or different. When your group has finished, signal to the instructor that you are ready for a full class discussion of the following questions.

1. How can our differences be explained?
2. How can we know what is correct and what is not?

In completing this exercise, you may have discovered the following principles:

1. What we see is what is familiar.
2. What is not familiar is hard to see.
3. Sometimes we distort unfamiliar situations to make them familiar.
4. When we perceive, we must decide what is relevant and what is irrelevant. This in turn also affects what we see.

What Does Observing Feel Like?

The word *observe* comes from the Latin prefix *ob*, which means in front of, together with the root word *servare*, meaning to keep or hold, to watch, to pay attention. When we observe, therefore, we hold something in front of us. The word *watch*, a synonym for *observe*, comes from the Old English word *waeccan*, which means to stay awake and is derived from the Indo-European root *weg*, which means to be strong. When we watch, therefore, we stay *strong* and *awake*.

Photo by John Pearson. Used with permission of the photographer.

In this exercise, look at Figure 1.1. Observe the cube by watching it, looking at it intently, and staying "strong and awake" in your concentration. Then answer these questions for yourself:

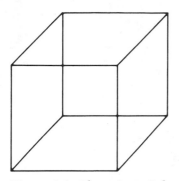

Figure 1.1 Observing a Cube

1. What happens to the cube as you observe it?
2. Can you describe what observing feels like when you do it?

Observation and Insight

Study the cartoons on pages 14–15 carefully. Notice and write down (1) how you decode its meaning, (2) what happens when you cannot yet understand its meaning, (3) how you feel when you experience an insight or revelation.

USING OBSERVATION SKILLS
TO DEVELOP NEW KNOWLEDGE

> The beginning of science is the ability to be amazed by apparently simple things. (Noam Chomsky)

You have learned how careful observation can help you see details that you might otherwise have missed, details that can help you unlock problems or arrive at insights. Careful observation can also enable us to make discoveries and learn new things. The reading that follows illustrates this process. It is the story of a kind of trial a student went through that tested his capacity to do graduate research in science. Samuel H. Scudder (1837–1911) was an American naturalist who attended Lawrence Scientific School at Harvard, where he studied under the great biologist (then called a naturalist) professor Jean Louis R. Agassiz. Pay close attention to the story because after you have finished reading it, you will be asked some questions

"Have you seen a Frisbee?"
Used with permission of Richard Guindon.

"Now I know we're being followed!"
From *I Paint What I See*. Copyright © 1971 by Gahan Wilson. Used with permission of Simon & Schuster, Inc.

From *Totally U.S.* by Simon Bond. Copyright © 1988 by Polycarp Ltd. Used with permission of HarperCollins Publishers, Inc.

about it. Then you will be asked to undertake a similar investigation of familiar objects.

Reading

LOOK AT YOUR FISH

Samuel H. Scudder

It was more than fifteen years ago that I entered the laboratory of Professor Agassiz,   1
and told him I had enrolled my name in the Scientific School as a student of natural

history. He asked me a few questions about my object in coming, my antecedents generally, the mode in which I afterwards proposed to use the knowledge I might acquire, and, finally, whether I wished to study any special branch. To the latter I replied that, while I wished to be well grounded in all departments of zoology, I purposed to devote myself specially to insects.

"When do you wish to begin?" he asked.   2

"Now," I replied.   3

This seemed to please him, and with an energetic "Very well!" he reached   4
from a shelf a huge jar of specimens in yellow alcohol. "Take this fish," he said, "and look at it; we call it a haemulon; by and by I will ask what you have seen."

With that he left me, but in a moment returned with explicit instructions as to   5
the care of the object entrusted to me.

"No man is fit to be a naturalist," he said, "who does not know how to take   6
care of specimens."

I was to keep the fish before me in a tin tray, and occasionally moisten the   7
surface with alcohol from the jar, always taking care to replace the stopper tightly. These were not the days of ground-glass stoppers and elegantly shaped exhibition jars; all the old students will recall the huge neckless glass bottles with their leaky, wax-besmeared corks, half eaten by insects, and begrimed with cellar dust. Entomology was a cleaner science than ichthyology, but the example of the Professor, who had unhesitatingly plunged to the bottom of the jar to produce the fish, was infectious, and though this alcohol had a "very ancient and fishlike smell," I really dared not to show any aversion within these sacred precincts, and treated the alcohol as though it were pure water. Still I was conscious of a passing feeling of disappointment, for gazing at a fish did not commend itself to an ardent entomologist. My friends at home, too, were annoyed when they discovered that no amount of eau-de-Cologne would drown the perfume which haunted me like a shadow.

In ten minutes I had seen all that could be seen in that fish, and started in   8
search of the Professor—who had, however, left the Museum; and when I returned, after lingering over some of the odd animals stored in the upper apartment, my specimen was dry all over. I dashed the fluid over the fish as if to resuscitate the beast from a fainting fit, and looked with anxiety for a return of the normal sloppy appearance. This little excitement over, nothing was to be done but to return to a steadfast gaze at my mute companion. Half an hour passed—an hour—another hour; the fish began to look loathsome. I turned it over and around; looked it in the face—ghastly; from behind, beneath, above, sideways, at a three-quarters' view— just as ghastly. I was in despair; at an early hour I concluded that lunch was necessary; so, with infinite relief, the fish was carefully replaced in the jar, and for an hour I was free.

On my return, I learned that Professor Agassiz had been at the Museum, but   9
had gone, and would not return for several hours. My fellow students were too busy to be disturbed by continued conversation. Slowly I drew forth that hideous fish, and with a feeling of desperation again looked at it. I might not use a magni-

fying glass; instruments of all kinds were interdicted. My two hands, my two eyes, and the fish: it seemed a most limited field. I pushed my finger down its throat to feel how sharp the teeth were. I began to count the scales in the different rows, until I was convinced that that was nonsense. At last a happy thought struck me—I would draw the fish; and now with surprise I began to discover new features in the creature. Just then the Professor returned.

"That is right," said he; "a pencil is one of the best of eyes. I am glad to notice, 10 too, that you keep your specimen wet, and your bottle corked."

With these encouraging words, he added: 11

"Well, what is it like?" 12

He listened attentively to my brief rehearsal of the structure of parts whose 13 names were still unknown to me; the fringed gill-arches and movable operculum; the pores of the head, fleshy lips and lidless eyes; the lateral line, the spinous fins and forked tail; the compressed and arched body. When I finished, he waited as if expecting more, and then, with an air of disappointment:

"You have not looked very carefully; why," he continued more earnestly, "you 14 haven't even seen one of the most conspicuous features of the animal, which is as plainly before your eyes as the fish itself; look again, look again!" and he left me to my misery.

I was piqued; I was mortified. Still more of that wretched fish! But now I set 15 myself to my task with a will, and discovered one new thing after another, until I saw how just the Professor's criticism had been. The afternoon passed quickly; and when, toward its close, the Professor inquired:

"Do you see it yet?" 16

"No," I replied, "I am certain I do not, but I see how little I saw before." 17

"That is next best," said he, earnestly, "but I won't hear you now; put away 18 your fish and go home; perhaps you will be ready with a better answer in the morning. I will examine you before you look at the fish."

This was disconcerting. Not only must I think of my fish all night, studying, 19 without the object before me, what this unknown but most visible feature might be; but also, without reviewing my discoveries, I must give an exact account of them the next day. I had a bad memory; so I walked home by the Charles River in a distracted state, with my two perplexities.

The cordial greeting from the Professor the next morning was reassuring; here 20 was a man who seemed to be quite as anxious as I that I should see for myself what he saw.

"Do you perhaps mean," I asked, "that the fish has symmetrical sides with 21 paired organs?"

His thoroughly pleased "Of course! of course!" repaid the wakeful hours of the 22 previous night. After he had discoursed most happily and enthusiastically—as he always did—upon the importance of this point, I ventured to ask what I should do next.

"Oh, look at your fish!" he said, and left me again to my own devices. In a little 23 more than an hour he returned, and heard my new catalogue.

"That is good, that is good" he repeated; "but that is not all; go on"; and so **24** for three long days he placed that fish before my eyes, forbidding me to look at anything else, or to use any artificial aid. "Look, look, look," was his repeated injunction.

This was the best entomological lesson I ever had—a lesson whose influence **25** has extended to the details of every subsequent study; a legacy the Professor had left to me, as he has left it to many others, of inestimable value, which we could not buy, with which we cannot part.

A year afterward, some of us were amusing ourselves with chalking outlandish **26** beasts on the Museum blackboard. We drew prancing starfishes; frogs in mortal combat; hydra-headed worms; stately crawfishes, standing on their tails, bearing aloft umbrellas; and grotesque fishes with gaping mouths and staring eyes. The Professor came in shortly after, and was as amused as any at our experiments. He looked at the fishes.

"Haemulons, every one of them," he said; "Mr. —— drew them." **27**

True; and to this day, if I attempt a fish, I can draw nothing but haemulons. **28**

The fourth day, a second fish of the same group was placed beside the first, **29** and I was bidden to point out the resemblances and differences between the two; another and another followed, until the entire family lay before me, and a whole legion of jars covered the table and surrounding shelves; the odor had become a pleasant perfume; and even now, the sight of an old, six-inch, worm-eaten cork brings fragrant memories.

The whole group of haemulons was thus brought in review; and whether **30** engaged upon the dissection of the internal organs, the preparation and examination of the bony framework, or the description of the various parts, Agassiz's training in the method of observing facts and their orderly arrangement was ever accompanied by the urgent exhortation not to be content with them.

"Facts are stupid things," he would say, "until brought into connection with **31** some general law."

At the end of eight months, it was almost with reluctance that I left these **32** friends and turned to insects; but what I had gained by this outside experience has been of greater value than years of later investigation in my favorite groups.

Study Questions

1. Why did Agassiz keep saying "Look at your fish!"? What was he trying to teach Scudder?

2. How would you describe the stages in Scudder's process of looking? What happened at each stage?

3. How did Scudder change personally in the course of his "trial"?

4. Do you think Agassiz's method of teaching was effective or wasteful?

Observing the Familiar: Vegetables and Fruit

1. This exercise may be done either at home alone or in class. First of all, prepare a report sheet of two columns with these headings:

Physical Details of the Fruit or Vegetable (what I observe and discover about the object)	Details of My Inner Process (what I observe and discover happening within myself as I work: my moods, reactions, associations, thoughts)

2. Bring to class one vegetable or fruit of any kind in a brown paper bag. It does not have to be of any exotic variety—an ordinary orange or potato will do. (If you are working at home alone, ask a family member or a roommate to give you a fruit when you are seated at a table with your eyes closed.)

3. If you are at school when you begin this exercise, give your sack to someone who does not know what is inside. The first part of the exercise involves exploring and describing the object without seeing it. Place the sack in your lap under the desk; then, still with your eyes closed, take the object out and hold it. (Since this exercise is done in silence, the sack should be discarded because its rattling will be annoying.) Open your eyes. With your other hand, take notes in the left-hand column about your investigation of the object while jotting down in the second column notes about your personal process as you become aware of it.

    Explore this unknown object for twenty minutes, using all senses except sight. This will mean really slowing down sufficiently to experience your senses of touch, smell, temperature, and even, if you dare, taste. Record your findings carefully.

4. At the end of twenty minutes, the instructor will call the time and you can look at your object. But remain quiet. Carefully note your reaction, and write that down and continue to work silently, completing your visual description. If you are at school, you can take your object home to dissect and describe every detail you see inside. Strive to make an exhaustive study of your fruit or vegetable with the attitude of a child or scientist. Make drawings if you wish.

5. If you are working at home, prepare to spend an hour with this fact-gathering aspect of the exercise.

6. Finally, taking your notes, write up a two-page typed paper describing your fruit or vegetable. Include at least one paragraph about your inner process. Did you become bored? angry? stuck? Record your awareness of your self just as Scudder did.

Student Writing Example

This example is not offered as a model for you to imitate like a recipe. Rather, it is meant to demonstrate how one student became absorbed in her work and solved the problem of staying sensitive to her subject and herself at the same time. Read it as a reminder of what the assignment is asking you to do, then forget it, and create your own paper by being true to your own experience.

KIWI

Yvette Padilla

The girl in the row behind me just gave me a bag with some unknown fruit or vegetable inside. I reached inside with my eyes closed and touched a fuzzy and prickly surface. I clasped my fingers and palm against it and drew out of the bag a shape almost like a Wilson tennis ball. As I held it on my lap, I tried to guess what type of fruit it was. By its shape and weight, I knew it could not have been an apple, orange, or banana. My first guess was that it was a potato. It made me feel anxious to not be sure. I had to explore more in order to know. My attention went back to the fuzz. There were hairs, each about 1/8 inch long. They felt like the stubby nubs of fine hair on a man's beard. There was also a gritty feel, almost like the sensation of grit on an unwashed leaf of spinach. It was then I realized it must be a kiwi fruit.

Its temperature was cool, like the weather on a crisp spring day. I explored the whole surface, still with my eyes closed. There were no warm spots; the cool temperature was consistent. I reasoned that this even coolness must mean that it was not handled much by the person who gave it to me. Its gritty feel gave me a sudden urge to wash my hands. I brought my attention back to its shape. I wondered how it could feel so like a tennis ball, although I knew it must not be a perfect sphere. I stroked its hairs some more; it reminded me of the peach fuzz that grows down the nape of your neck.

Now it was time to look at my kiwi. I was expecting an intense green color. But that was only the stereotype in my mind. I realized the color, as usual with kiwis, was more light brown or ashen, like the color of coffee with cream. Underneath the coffee color was only a hint of green in the shade of oak tree leaves. Then I noticed the surface shed brown flakes resembling the splinters from a piece of cherry wood with a size no greater than flea dander off a cat. I began to hold it up to view its shape from different angles. If I would lie it flat in my hand, it looked perfectly round. But if I held it upright and looked down at it, I could see an oval shape with scablike structures protruding from both ends. If I were to measure its size, I would say it was about two inches in diameter with a circumference of four inches. Holding it in my hand again, I noticed how firm it was to the touch yet how easy it would be to squash it with a pressured grip.

After class I took the kiwi home for a dissection. I placed it on a board on the kitchen table and sat down with my notepad. I took a knife and proceeded to cut it slowly into two perfectly even halves. The skin was tougher than I had expected and required more force than I had imagined necessary. As it opened, two individual pieces showed the faces of their inner beauty. Each center contained a wreath of ten or more black specks the size of poppy seeds on green flesh, the color of green-color crayons. Pastel green threads were visible through the darkened green shades; they appeared to be almost woven into the fruit. From its fine layer of outer skin to the direct center of the kiwi half, there was a spiral configuration. It looked to me as though someone had taken the fruit's insides, mashed it flat, then rolled it into a ball, then sliced it down the center. Its pattern was very intriguing to me. The black specks seemed now more like blotches of black ink. As I moved my face closer to see it, its fragrance suddenly burst into my awareness; it was phenomenal: a fruity scent like a fresh piece of tropical-flavored bubble gum. I peeled off its skin, which was like taking off its winter coat. I put one half of the naked green fruit into my mouth. The taste was, as I had imagined, sour-sweet like a lime-flavored Life Saver candy. The texture was soft and moist. I could crush out its juice by pressing my tongue against my palate. What a pleasant tasting experience! Then I quickly ate the second piece. And then I wished I had more.

Used with permission of Yvette Padilla.

EVALUATING YOUR WORK BY USING THE SCORING BOXES

All the Core Discovery Writing Application assignments in this book are followed by a scoring box like the one below. Instructors who decide to incorporate them might use them in a number of ways. First, they can serve as assessment guides to determine the strengths and weaknesses of your first draft. Second, they can be used in class so you and your classmates, working in pairs or small groups, can rate one another's work to decide whether you need yet another revision. In addition to serving as a guide for revision, the scoring boxes have the following purposes:

1. To accent the instruction's essential skill-building components so that you cannot overlook them.

2.   To clarify assessment priorities and criteria.

3.   To offer standards for critical thinking about your own writing as well as that of your peers.

4.   To enable you to turn in your best work for a grade.

Scoring for Description of Fruit or Vegetable

1.   Two full pages. 20 points

2.   All senses used. 24 points (3 points each)

   Touch/texture
   Taste
   Smell
   Temperature
   Sound
   Color
   Shape
   Changes that occur during description

3.   Physical description at least ⅔ of paper. 10 points

4.   Language accuracy. 10 points

5.   Crucial aspects not omitted. (skin, seeds, interior aspects and design) 10 points

6.   Inner process described. 10 points

7.   No distracting errors of spelling, punctuation, sentence structure. 16 points

---

THE OBSERVATION PROCESS: SENSING, PERCEIVING, THINKING

When you worked with your fruit or vegetable, you went through a process of collecting data without preconceptions, arranging them in some kind of order, and drawing some conclusions about their patterns and meaning. As you learned in the Introduction, this is the process called inductive reasoning. If we observe our own mental processes as they are involved in tasks of reasoning, we can learn to recognize different parts of the process. This helps us make finer discriminations in tracking their appearance and disappearance, as well as in understanding their potential.

So what are the parts of this reasoning process? When we take in data without preconceptions we are *sensing*; when we are arranging them into some kind of order, we are *perceiving*; and when we are drawing conclusions about their patterns and meaning, we are *thinking*. *Sensing* and *perceiving* are sometimes confused in popular usage; both are used to refer to a process of experiencing new information through the senses from the world outside or inside ourselves. To use computer language, both *perceiving* and *sensing* are used to refer to means of receiving data input. But to fully understand our observation processes, we need to make a distinction between the terms.

PERCEIVING PERCEPTION

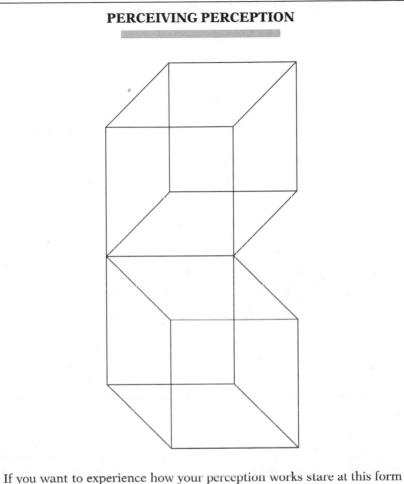

If you want to experience how your perception works stare at this form for a few minutes. What happens to the shape as you look? When do you begin to see some patterns you can identify? When do you make comparisons or give names to what you see?

Sensing occurs through sense organs such as the eyes and skin. When these organs become activated by stimuli—such as by a bright, warm light—they send this information through the nervous system to the brain. When we sense something, we *feel* it; we feel the presence of something and have a certainty about that presence. When we sense, we do not yet have the words to identify or explain what is happening to us, because in order to find words, we have to think. *And when we start to think, we may cut ourselves off from our sensations*. It is difficult to both sense and think at the same time. If someone asks you to go outside and see how warm the

---

MISSING PERCEPTION

When surgeons discovered how to perform safe cataract operations, their first patients were people who had been blind since birth. Those doctors who tested their patients' sense perceptions both before and after the operations discovered that the majority could not perceive space, form, or distance. Postoperative patients had no idea of size. One woman, when asked how big her mother was, set her two index fingers a few inches apart. The world of postoperative patients was a confusion of color-patches. They could not distinguish objects in their field of vision, and indeed, would often find themselves bumping into one of these patches. When one newly sighted girl saw photographs and paintings, she asked her mother, "Why do they put those dark marks all over them?" Her mother explained that these were not dark marks but shadows, and that without shadows things would look flat. Her daughter then replied, "Well, that's how things do look. Everything looks flat, with dark patches."

From Marius von Senden, *Space and Sight*. London: Methuen, 1960.

---

day is, you have to stop talking and thinking to consciously feel the air temperature on your face and skin. To take a good reading, you need to keep an internal silence.

Perceive comes from the root words *percipere*, meaning to receive—*per*, meaning thoroughly, and *capere*, meaning to catch, seize, or hold. Perceiving is both a receptive and an active process. When we perceive something, we catch and hold it in consciousness until we grasp forms, shapes, patterns, or meaning. Sensing comes before perceiving. Sensations have to be held in consciousness long enough to be interpreted by perception. This makes perceiving closer to thinking than to feeling. And as we perceive, we use memory to synthesize all our information in preparation for giving it a name.

For example, consider the process we go through when we taste an unfamiliar food, such as Swedish sweet rolls. When we take a first bite, our tastebuds *sense* the new food and then relay to our brain the message "unfamiliar taste." And so we pause to give this new taste another round of sensation, giving it more attention this time. Our nose also may relay "pleasant but unfamiliar fragrance." Now we begin to *perceive*, or to hold these sensations together in awareness in order to interpret (explain) them. The word *spice* may come to mind; we consult our spice memory file, catalogued according to spice characteristics. This taste and smell may be similar to—but yet different from—those of cinnamon and cloves. Should we ask a friend "What spice is in this food?" the reply will be "It's *cardamom*."

We can then put a new experience into our spice memory file under its name for future reference.

Thinking follows perceiving. So what is thinking? Philosopher Alan Watts once said that the word *think* comes from the European word *tong*, which is related to the word *thing*. When we think we *thing-a-fy*: we make "things" of nature and of events with our perceptions. We name, classify, manipulate, and order what we see. Psychologist Jean Piaget defined thinking as "an active process whereby people organize their perceptions of the world."

These definitions are only two of many that have been offered. As you learned in the definition of critical thinking in the Introduction, dictionaries describe more than nineteen different mental operations for the word *thinking*. In this text, our main concern is with conscious purposeful thinking. Thinking might be understood as the programming and operation in the computer that is our brain. The question remains as to who is the programmer or operator, best described perhaps as our conscious selves. From these definitions, the observation process you have gone through in this chapter's exercises might arbitrarily be divided into the following stages:

1. We take in our data from sensing.
2. We perceive in our data the patterns of similarities, differences, and identities that suggest categories of order. We decide *what* belongs with *what*.
3. We draw comparisons in our data and from our memories about what we see and sense.
4. We apply logical reasoning and standards to the material.
5. We imagine explanations and meanings concerning the data.
6. We assess what is missing and not known and devise strategies for obtaining more data or explanations if needed.
7. We formulate ideas and words to communicate our discoveries to others.
8. We check for errors in our information, our language, and our form of communication.

BARRIERS TO OBSERVATION

Understanding the stages in the observation process can help us recognize conditions that threaten to hinder the process. For instance, in reading "Look at Your Fish" or in the process of describing your shoes, you may have felt that careful observation *seems to take so much time*. Our inward experience can move through predictable stages—ranging from interest, to discovery, to communication, to boredom, followed by a clear determination to stop. However, as we have seen, more persistence and concentration can awaken a new cycle of interest, with more discoveries, followed by boredom and restlessness again. Yet, each time the cycle is renewed, deeper and deeper levels of understanding can be achieved. Experiencing—even suffering through—such a process can teach us that we have a far greater capacity to discover than we knew; it can show us that we do not need to depend on outside sources as much as we had assumed and that we *can* become our own most reliable source of information.

So to begin the process of observing, we have to maintain a willingness to spend time and to persist through boredom, restlessness, uncertainty, and discomfort. We also have to cultivate a willingness to listen. We know, from our discussion of the observation process, that sensing requires first listening in silence, then dialogue with our information and thoughts. Here is how Alan Watts explains, in his film *Buddhism, Man, and Nature*, the importance of suspending thinking while we are sensing:

> If you were to hear what anyone else has to say, you sometimes have to stop talking. And thinking is just talking inside your head. So if you are going to have anything to think about, you sometimes have to stop thinking. Just as if you would have anything to talk about, you have to sometimes stop talking and listen. The secret of the Buddhist view of life is to spend some time every day in which you don't think, but just watch. In which you don't form any ideas about life, but look at it. Listen to it. Smell it. Feel it.

It can take a lot of willpower to hold back thoughts when learning how to observe with the attitude of listening. Remember Samuel Scudder who concluded he had learned *everything* possible about his fish after the first ten minutes. To become a scientist, he had to learn how to stop making premature judgments and go back to his observing. Persistence in observing may even reveal that we are seeing something totally *new* for which we have no established pigeonhole in our mental filing system. To give a historical example, what we now call quasars (an acronym for quasi-stellar radio sources) were originally categorized as stars within our own galaxy. However, further spectroscopic observations showed them to be immense distances away from the earth, far out of our galaxy but with such vast outpourings of energy that they are visible to us. They had been incorrectly categorized as stars, misplaced under a familiar category. Thus a new name had to be invented to reflect their nature (which still remains ambiguous to us).

Discovering new information through observation may lead to discomfort, so we may resist recognizing new information. In ordinary life, when new information suggests that we may have to exert ourselves to study the situation more deeply, our first reaction may be one of inertia. We try first to see whether this new data can be assimilated into old categories of experience: "I haven't been able to get a decent job since I left high school; maybe I just need more luck."

If a problem persists, we are forced to review the situation. We have to ask whether this problem really does fit into our existing mental scheme of categories, explanations, and solutions. In this case, the young man who wants a decent job may have to waive wishing for better luck and consider more training or college. When such problems become insistent enough to interrupt our lives, we are forced to rearrange or erase what we already know, to accommodate new data into new frames of reference.

Let's look again at Jean Piaget's definition of thinking as "an active process whereby people organize their perceptions of the world." At one point, he described this process as involving both *assimilation* (or the simple addition of new information to old) and *accommodation* (when we must change our intellectual organization in order to adjust to a new idea). When our mental scheme of things cannot grasp or easily categorize some new data, we undergo a mental sense of disequilibrium or confusion. This is an extremely uncomfortable feeling that we may not recognize as coming from the learning problem itself. Indeed, we may look for someone or something else to blame for our discomfort. We are only aware of a strong desire to get rid of this awful, uncomfortable feeling. But if we persist and succeed in concentrating on the actual problem, we will find an accommodation of understanding that will restore our equilibrium. And this restoration will not occur if we run away from the problem but only when we return to actually confront it. Seen from another perspective, the mental discomfort of disequilibrium can actually help us persist in our efforts to find truth, for the reward of having arrived at truth is a sense of equilibrium (see Figure 1.2).

The process of gathering and organizing new information also requires the discovery of the right words with which to communicate what we have learned. We may even have to invent new words, as in the case of quasars. We may have to spend considerable time with dictionaries, the encyclopedia, even in questioning other people. And, again, this will require will and persistence so that we don't succumb to the temptation to conclude, "That's not really what I mean, but I'll just put down any old thing and get it over with."

Clearly, all stages of the observation process find their major barriers *within ourselves*. Overcoming such barriers can only be managed with a thorough and conscious awareness of their existence exactly as they appear. When we are *aware* of our own forms of apathy or resistance and when we *acknowledge* such feelings, they tend to lose their power over us. But when we ignore or fight our resistances, they can become more powerful than ever. Only the rewards of achievement can sometimes pull us through all the temptations to get off course.

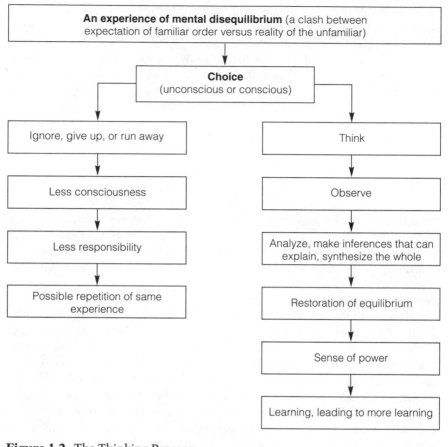

Figure 1.2 The Thinking Process

THE REWARDS OF SKILLED OBSERVATION

Sensitive, accurate observing requires an alertness to inner processes and a carefully built foundation of self-understanding. Anyone who does creative work—whether in writing, in the sciences, in the arts, or in the ordinary tasks of work and living—possesses these skills.

The following reading, "The Innocent Eye," is taken from a book on art design. It suggests what you may have discovered for yourself through the writing exercises you completed in this chapter: that although observing may require self-control and patience, it is nevertheless a process that can lead us to rapture, power, and wonder (see Figure 1.3).

Figure 1.3 Can you see in this design the interaction between positive and negative space described in "The Innocent Eye"? Is either less important than the other?

Reading

THE INNOCENT EYE

Dorr Bothwell

Creative observation of our surroundings revives in us a sense of the wonder of life. 1
Much of this discovery involves the recovery of something that we all once had in childhood. When we were very young we were all artists. We all came into this world with the doors of perception wide open. Everything was a delightful surprise. Everything, at first, required the slow, loving touch of our tongues and our hands. Long before we could speak we knew the comfort of our mother's warm body, the delightful feel of a furry toy. Smooth and rough surfaces, things cold and hot surprised and enchanted us. Touch by touch we built up our store of tactile impressions, keenly sensed in minute detail.

Later on, this tactile sensing was transferred to our eyes, and we were able to 2
"feel" through the sense of vision things beyond the grasp of our hands. This kind of seeing was not the rapid sophisticated eye sweep of the well-informed. This kind

of seeing was a slow, uncritical examination in depth. The more we looked the more lovely and surprising things appeared, until we were pervaded by that wordless thrill which is the sense of wonder.

None of us has lost our store of tactile memories. Nor have we lost our sense 3 of wonder. All that has happened is that we have substituted identifying and labeling, which can be done very rapidly, for the tactile sort of feel-seeing which requires much more time and concentration. For example, if you were asked to look at the edge of your desk and estimate its length, it would only take you a few seconds to flick your eyes back and forth and say it is so many inches long. But suppose you were asked to run the tip of your finger along the edge of the desk and count every tiny nick? You would press your finger along the edge and move it very, very slowly, and your eye would move no faster than your finger. This slow, concentrated way of feeling and seeing is the first step towards regaining our sense of wonder.

There was a time when man moved no faster than his feet or the feet of some 4 animal that could carry him. During that period the artistic or creative spirit seemed to have free expression. Today, in order to be creative and yet move smoothly and efficiently through our fast-paced world, we must be able to function on two different speed levels. The mistake we have made, often with tragic results, is to try to do *all* our living at the speed our machines have imposed upon us.

In order to live at this speed we must scan the surface of things, pick out salient 5 aspects, disregard secondary features; and there is certainly nothing wrong in this if we are driving on a busy freeway. But when we allow this pressure to invade every aspect of our life, we begin to "lose touch," to have a feeling that we are missing something, and we are hungry for we don't know what. When that happens, we have begun to suffer from aesthetic malnutrition. Fortunately, the cure for this condition is very pleasant, and although it takes a little self-discipline at the beginning, the results are worth the effort.

When we see as design artists, we become especially aware of the interaction 6 between positive and negative space. In architecture we are suddenly aware of the spaces between the windows, at the ballet we notice how the spaces between the dancers open and close, and in music we realize that rhythm is made by the shapes of silence between the notes.

Everywhere we look we see this principle in action. Trees are not silhouetted 7 against blank air, but hold blue spangles between their leaves while branches frame living shapes of sky. Space seems to be pulled between the leaves of a fern. We delight in the openings between the petals of a flower or the spokes of a wheel. This endless exchange between form and space excites us. Once more we feel in touch with our world; our aesthetic sense is being fed and we are comforted. . . .

We may have been taught that butterflies are lovely and toads are ugly, so we 8 admire the butterfly and shrink away from the toad without really examining it to find out if what we had been taught is true. Or we are taught that flowers are good and weeds are bad, so we pull up the latter without a glance. To the artist's eye there is no good or bad. There is just the inappropriate. In the garden, weeds are

BUILDING ARGUMENTS

OBSERVATION SKILLS

This is the first of a series running through the text explaining the structure of arguments through readings and exercises.

By definition, an argument consists of a *principal claim* (also called a *conclusion*) supported or justified by *reasons. Reasons* consist of further claims or evidence. We can use observation skills to give us one form of evidence. (Other forms can be records, testimony, or statistics.) When we observe, we not only collect data but form tentative conclusions or *hypotheses* about the data's meaning. Notice how Christopher Columbus bases his argument on his observations.

They came swimming to the ships' boats, where we were, and brought us parrots and cotton thread in balls, and spears and many other things. They all go naked as their mothers bore them . . . they were very well built, with very handsome bodies and very good faces. Their hair is coarse almost like the hairs of a horse's tail and short; they wear their hair down over their eyebrows, except for a few strands behind, which they wear long and never cut. Some of them are painted black, and they are the colour of the people of the Canaries, neither black nor white, and some of them are painted white and some red and some in any colour they can find. . . . They do not bear arms or know them, for I showed to them swords and they took them by the blade and cut themselves through ignorance. (So far all these sentences are claims presented as evidence gained from observation.) *They should be good servants and of quick intelligence, since I see that they very soon say all that is said to them, and I believe that they would easily be made Christians, for it appeared to me that they had no creed.* (Hypothesis, conclusion, or principal claim drawn from evidence.)

Exercise

1. State a conclusion you drew from inspecting a situation firsthand.
2. Describe the evidence that led you to this conclusion.

From the journal of Christopher Columbus, October 12, 1492.

not appropriate, but in the vacant lot they offer a world of enchantment. And after we have learned to see the beauty in weeds, even though we have to pull them out of the garden, we can first admire their design.

When no preconceived ideas keep us from looking and we take all the time we need to really "feel" what we see—when we are able to do that—the universe opens up and we catch our breath in awe at the incredible complexity of design in the humblest things. It is only when this happens that we regain our sense of wonder.

From Dorr Bothwell and Marlys Mayfield, *Notan: The Dark Light Principle of Design*. New York: Dover, 1991. Used with permission of Dorr Bothwell.

Study Questions

1. What do you think of the statement, "When we were very young we were all artists"?

2. Do you understand what the author is talking about when she speaks of the "aesthetic malnutrition" that comes from the high-speed living that makes us "lose touch"?

3. Describe what is meant by the "interaction of positive and negative space."

4. Explain what is meant by the statement, "To the artist's eye, there is no good or bad. There is just the inappropriate." Did you ever find, in the course of writing your descriptions, that you were so turned off by your judgments of an object that you had trouble contacting the object fully? Did you find any change in your attitude as you continued to work for a long period with the same object? Have you ever experienced this with people, moving from prejudice at the start to appreciation through sustained contact?

CHAPTER SUMMARY

1. If we want to develop more conscious thinking habits, we have to first observe our own thinking process so we can recognize our strengths and weaknesses.

2. Careful observation can help us see details that contain the key to unlocking problems or arriving at insights. It can also help us discover new knowledge.

3. Observation is a process of sensing, perceiving, and thinking. Sensing is collecting data through the sense organs. Perceiving is holding sense data in consciousness until we grasp the data's meaning. Thinking organizes our perceptions; it names, classifies, and manipulates our data.

4. Careful observation requires us to stay conscious, take our time, give full attention, suspend thinking in an attitude of listening, both assimilate and accommodate new knowledge, become aware of emerging

insights, and persist in spite of boredom or discomfort. It requires us to face our own barriers and resistances.

5. The rewards of cultivating observation skills are self-understanding, creativity, rapture, power, and wonder.

CHAPTER QUIZ

Rate each of the following statements as *true* or *false*. Justify your answer with an example or explanation to prove and illustrate your understanding. *Do not omit this part of the test. True/false* answers can be guessed. But when you defend your answer by example or explanation, you demonstrate not only your memory and understanding but also a higher order thinking skill of applying what you have learned to life. The first question is answered for you.

FALSE 1. Observation skills are learned mainly through book learning.

> *Support for Answer.* On the contrary, observation is learned from participation, which is more active and spontaneous than reading. Samuel Scudder learned observing through the active coaching of his teacher Agassiz, as well as from his own efforts, curiosity, and persistence in studying his fish.

_____ 2. The standard academic study of all the physical sciences requires observation skills, whether in the field or laboratory.

_____ 3. In thinking, the correctness of our conclusions usually depends on the clarity of our perceptions.

_____ 4. Observation skills can be developed by observing how you observe.

_____ 5. An insight is an experience of understanding that can occur spontaneously after we observe something intently for a while. One illustration of this experience is the story of Archimedes, who, while in his bath, discovered the means of measuring the volume of an irregular solid by the displacement of water.

_____ 6. Agassiz was simply too busy to give his student all the assistance he needed.

_____ 7. *Perception* and *sensation* are synonyms.

_____ 8. It is difficult to feel sensation and to think at the same time. If we want to feel whether a pair of new shoes fits properly, we have to pay attention.

_____ 9. Scientific observation can bring us new knowledge that does not fit our expectations or our familiar categories.

_____ 10. *Assimilation*, according to Piaget, is an experience of easily understanding something that readily fits into our preexisting schemes or world view.

_____ 11. The word *thinking*, according to the dictionary, has only one meaning.

Composition Writing Application

Descriptive Narrative: Re-Observing a Past Experience

First Option: Survival Through Observing

Describe an experience in which your safety, welfare, or survival depended upon your ability to observe a situation or problem clearly. This could involve a danger in city life, in camping, or in sports, or perhaps a life decision *where observation skills were crucial*. Write from three to five pages, telling your story as a narrative. (See F. Bruce Lamb's story on pages 35–37 as a model.) Remember, the theme that should tie your story together is the theme of observation. Be sure to note and emphasize in your story where you observed and where you did not and what the consequences were.

Second Option: A Travel Story

Making use of memory and any written or photo journals you might have, write a travel story as a narrative in three to five typed pages. Emphasize how this experience affected your senses. Strive to make your audience see and feel as you did. If you wish, adopt the point of view of a travel advisor by recommending what a traveler might do or avoid doing when traveling the same route.

Review of Assignment Guidelines

1. *Form*: A story or narrative
2. *Theme*:
   (a) How observation skills helped you survive
   (b) A travel account conveying sensory information
3. *Length*: Three to five typed pages or until you feel the story is complete.

Reading

WIZARD OF THE UPPER AMAZON: THE STORY OF MANUEL CORDOVA-RIOS
F. Bruce Lamb

First published in 1971, this book was written by an American forest engineer who, while working in South America, met the narrator of this story, Manuel Cordova-Rios, then a famous Peruvian healer. Manuel's story begins in 1907, when at the age of 15, he was captured by a tribe of Amazon Indians and taken into a remote jungle area. During the course of the 7 years he lived with them, he gradually began to recognize that he was undergoing a long apprenticeship. In this reading excerpt, he begins to learn what he needs to know in order to survive as a hunter. Note as you read what he has to learn.

1   First we chose a location between four small trees where a palm-leaf roof could be built on a vine-and-pole framework. Material for this we gathered from the forest around us. By the time the scouts had returned at dusk, the shelter was ready with space for six small hammocks and a fire burning in the middle under a meat-smoking platform of interwoven green sticks.

2   Each of the scouts had brought back game: two partridges, a small forest deer and a pair of monkeys. These were cleaned and the choicest tidbits put low over the fire for fast roasting for our first camp meal. The rest were prepared for slow-roasting and smoking on the platform.

3   That night, lying in our hammocks, we heard the minutest details of the hunt in addition to a review of hunting conditions that had been observed in the area. . . .

4   After this recital of the hunting stories was finished, the men listened to the sounds of the night jungle and explained them to me. Their hearing was much more acute than mine. Much of what they described I could not hear. This was true also of my sense of smell. Gradually we drifted off to sleep, all except the one assigned to tend the smoking fire and the turning of the meat on the smoke rack. Sleep was never continuous in a hunting camp—men were up and down and the fire watch changed several times.

5   The man on guard, I learned, was also expected continually to be aware of the sights, sounds, smells of the surrounding jungle as the guard changed during the night hours. Animal activity at night is often more intense than during daylight hours in the tropical forest.

6   As I was settling down to sleep I went over in my mind everything that had happened on the hunting expedition so far. I realized that I had learned more about the forest in these few days out with the Indians than during all my previous experience. I was also well aware that by comparison my knowledge was extremely

limited and the acuity of my senses far below that of my companions. This I was determined to change.

The next day Nixi and I went off with Txaxo Anika to look for his band of wild   7
pigs. One man was left in camp and the other two were to go to the tree with ripening fruit. There they would build covered hunting platforms up in the tree crown. These would make it easy to take the large birds and monkeys that came to eat the fruit.

Single file we went through the forest undergrowth, with me in the middle.   8
Immediately my bodily coordination and sense perceptions were taxed to the utmost to keep up with the pace set and remain alert to the jungle signs I was learning to recognize. We came to the place where Txaxo had observed the trail of the wild pigs and we stopped briefly for consultation to decide what to do next. Before we moved off opposite to the direction the band of pigs had taken I was given additional hunting information.

They explained that in hunting a large band of pigs the timing of approach   9
and an understanding of the animal signals were the major factors in the success of bagging these animals. The two principal signals of this species were imitated and explained to me. At a certain type of grunt from the leader, the band would break into a wild run and scatter in all directions. At a loud clicking of the teeth and a high-pitched squeal, the whole band would immediately bristle and attack any moving object that was not part of the band. To protect oneself in the hunt and obtain meat it was necessary to anticipate and recognize these signals.

We went off again at a killing pace that required all my attention. It seemed we   10
went at this fast speed for a long time and exhaustion was beginning to show on me, when we came to fresh tracks and stopped to look, sniff the air and discuss the signs. The odor I now associated with wild pig was strong here. Tracks and disturbance of the earth gave my companion considerable information—the approximate size of the band, what they were eating, how fast they were traveling and in what direction.

This time we set off at an angle to what appeared to me to be the traveling   11
direction of the pigs. After going up over a hill and down into a small valley with no sign of game, my companions came abreast and strung their bows with arrows. I did the same without sensing any reason why. Suddenly with a loud grunt there were wild pigs all around us, running and squealing in utter confusion. I managed to shoot one arrow and get strung up for another shot when I realized that as suddenly as the pigs had appeared they had gone without a sound. I looked around and my hunting companions were gone also.

My quarry was nearby, gasping his last breath and kicking feebly with my   12
arrow in his side. Soon Txaxo and Nixi came back, each with two pigs and each with a daub of blood on both cheeks. This was another good-luck charm for future hunts, and they insisted that I daub blood on my own cheeks from the animal I had killed and that I also rub some on my new bow.

My first kill with a bow and arrow gave me a feeling of satisfaction. Nixi and   13
Txaxo both showed their pleasure at my accomplishment. We immediately made

vine slings and started back to camp with loads on our backs. On the way the animals were gutted, but only one at a stop in order to leave the least evidence at any one location in case a possible enemy might wander by. . . .

From these discussions and from my own daily experience in the village I   14 became aware of how closely these Indians were molded to their environment. Their muscular coordination and visual sense of their surroundings in the forest made it possible for them to move quickly and with ease through the most tangled undergrowth. They could anticipate the hazards and difficulties and avoid most of them. They reacted to the faintest signals of sound and smell, intuitively relating them to all other conditions of the environment and then interpreting them to achieve the greatest possible capture of game. Development of the other senses compensated for the limited visibility found in the forest. Often on the ground in the forest, visibility is no more than fifteen feet or so. Looking upward into the canopy, one may see one hundred feet but seldom any farther. Most of the jungle animals have protective coloring or camouflage that make them difficult to see even close at hand.

The Indians had great patience when it was required and they used it, together   15 with knowledge and intuition, to capture game with the least possible expenditure of energy. Many of the best hunters seemed to know by some special extra sense just where to find the game they sought, or they had developed some special method of drawing game to them. Knowing how to imitate and to use the signals the animals made to communicate between their kind in various situations helped in locating game and drawing it within sighting range of an astute hunter. It took skill, keen development of all the senses, patience and experience to enable a hunter to provide, constantly, sufficient game to feed a family.

Study Questions

1. How did the Indians train their ability to observe in order to survive?
2. Given the limited visibility of the jungle, how did the hunters learn to compensate in order to succeed?
3. What skills enabled them to kill the pigs?
4. What habits, attitudes, and traits of character did the Indians seem to have developed in order to survive?
5. How does this reading help you better understand why today large numbers of Amazon Indians are committing suicide as they lose their lands and hunting grounds to encroaching miners and ranchers?

For Further Reading

Ackerman, Diane. *A Natural History of the Senses*. New York: Vintage Books, 1991.

Castaneda, Carlos. *A Separate Reality: Further Conversations with Don Juan*. New York: Simon & Schuster, 1971.

————. *The Teachings of Don Juan: A Yaqui Way of Knowledge*. Berkeley: University of California Press, 1968.

Darwin, Charles. *The Voyage of the Beagle*. New York: New American Library, 1972.

Dillard, Annie. *Pilgrim at Tinker Creek*. New York: Harper & Row, 1974.

Hayward, Jeremy. *Perceiving Ordinary Magic*. Berkeley: New Science Library, 1984.

Least-Heat Moon, William. *Blue Highways: A Journey into America*. Boston: Little, Brown, 1984.

Mowat, Farley. *Never Cry Wolf*. New York: Bantam, 1963.

Ornstein, Robert. *Evolution of Consciousness. The Origins of the Way We Think*. New York: Simon & Schuster, 1991.

Schneider, Meir. *Self-Healing: My Life and Vision*. New York and London: Routledge & Kegan Paul, 1987.

Shah, Idries. *Tales of the Dervishes*. New York: Dutton, 1970.

Suzuki, Shunryu. *Zen Mind, Beginner's Mind*. New York: Weatherhill, 1980.

CHAPTER 2

Word Precision:
How Do I Describe It?

*"I liked it because you can read it with
both the TV and the radio on."*

Used with permission of Richard Guindon.

When we discover something, we usually want to tell others about it. To do this, we need to find the right words: search memory, dictionary, or thesaurus, and mentally calibrate between experience and word choice. This chapter takes a close look at the process that brings observation, words, and thinking together. However, the chapter does not attempt to cover everything a college student needs to know about words. The guiding principle of this book is to reinforce only what you might first have learned on your own and to introduce only what can be applied. Now you are being asked to bring the perceiving and word-thinking process together—and to do so with the conscious awareness that you will be exercising your learning throughout this book. When you have finished this chapter, you should know more about how well you work with words, how word confusion and word clarity affect your thinking, and how word precision can satisfy the spirit.

Discovery Exercise

Words Matching Senses

This exercise may be done independently at home or in class with four other people. If you are working with others, take turns reading this selection aloud. Then answer the study questions in writing or in discussion with your group.

Reading

THE HOT SPRING

Barry Lopez

This reading is the second chapter of *Desert Notes*, a short book of lyric prose that is the first of a trilogy followed by *River Notes* and *Field Notes*. Barry Lopez is best known for his book *Arctic Dreams* (1986) for which he received the National Book Award.

I.

1   The man would set off late in the spring, after the dogwood had bloomed, in the blue '58 Chevy pickup with the broken taillight and the cracked Expando mirrors. He would take a thin green sleeping bag and a blue tarpaulin, a few dishes and a one-burner stove. He would take his spoon and only cereal to eat and tea to drink. He would take no books, no piece of paper to write on.

2   He would stop only for gas and would pick up no hitchhikers. He would drive straight through on the two-lane, blacktop roads, cracked and broken with the freeze of last winter, without turning the radio on. He would lift his damp buttocks from the hot naugahyde seat and let the wind, coming in through the window that was stuck halfway down, cool him.

3   It would take seven hours to drive the 278 miles. First, over the mountains, past the great lava flows at the ridge, past the slopes of black obsidian glass, down into the sweet swamp of thick air in the ponderosa forest.

4   He would drive out then into the great basin over arroyos and across sage flats dotted with juniper and rabbit brush, past the fenced squares marked Experimental Station where the government was trying to grow crested wheat grass, trying to turn the high desert into grassy fields for bony Herefords with vacant eyes. He would see few cows. He would see, on a long stretch of road, a golden eagle sitting on a fence post.

There would be more space between the towns and more until there were no   5
towns at all, only empty shacks, their roof ridges bowed, their doors and windows
gone.

He would come around the base of another range of mountains, slip down on   6
the southeastern side and drive on a one-lane dirt road along the edge of the
alkaline desert for twenty miles until he came to the hot spring. There he would
stop. He would stop the truck, but he would leave the motor running to keep the
engine cool. He would always arrive by one in the afternoon.

II.

He inhaled the tart, sulphurous fumes rising up from the green reeds, the only bit   7
of green for miles. He watched the spiders spinning webs in the wire grass and the
water bugs riding the clots of yellow bubbles. He stared at the bullet-riddled walls
of tin that surrounded the sandy basin where the water collected.

When he had seen these things, that they had weathered the winter, the man   8
put the truck in gear and rolled down over the sagebrush and onto the desert floor.
He drove out over the dry, bleached soil for a mile before he put the truck in neutral
and let it coast to a stop. He was careful with the silence. He could hear his fingers
slide over the plastic steering wheel. He could feel the curve of his lips tightening in
the dryness.

He took off his clothes, all of them, and put them in a zippered airlines bag on   9
the floor of the truck. Then he put his sneakers back on and went naked across the
desert back to the hot spring with a pair of linen socks in his hand. The cool breeze
from the mountains raised his flesh into a lattice of pin-pricked hills.

He removed his shoes. He lay on his back in the hot water, his toes grazing the   10
shallow, sandy bottom of the pool. He could hear the water lapping at the entrance
to his ears, the weight of water pulling on his hair; he could feel the particles of dust
falling off his flesh, floating down, settling on the bottom of the pool; he could feel
the water prying at the layers of dried sweat. He concentrated and tried to hear the
dirt and sweat breaking away from his body. The tips of his fingers wrinkled, and
he stared at the water pooling in the cavity of his chest and falling away as he
breathed.

He wanted to stay until the sun set but he couldn't: he could feel himself   11
sinking. He climbed out of the pool and walked out of the roofless tin shelter onto
the floor of the desert. The wind began to evaporate the water and his pores closed
like frightened mussels and trapped the warmth beneath his skin.

When his feet were dry he put on only the linen socks and left. He could feel   12
the wind eddying up around him like a cloak and his feet barely touched the
ground. His eyes felt smoother in their sockets and he could tell, without looking,
how his fingers were curled; he could see the muscles of his legs tied beneath his
kneecaps, feel the patella gliding over the knot. He felt the muscles anchored on
the broad, flat plate of his hipbones and the wind soft deep in the roots of his hair.
He felt the pressure of his parting the air as he walked.

When he got back to the truck he poured a cup of water and placed a handful   13
of cereal into an earthen bowl. He ate and looked out across the desert and imagined that he had come to life again.

From Barry Lopez, *Desert Notes: Reflections in the Eye of a Raven*. New York: Avon Books, 1976.
Copyright 1976 by Barry Holstun Lopez. Reprinted with permission of Andrews and McMeel and
Barry Lopez.

Study Questions

1. What is simple about this writing? What is complex about it?

2. How does this reading affect your body and feelings? Do you identify
    with the protagonist? If so, how did the author manage to get you to
    feel you were inside the man?

3. Read paragraphs 7, 8, and 9 and notice how the verbs, nouns, and
    adjectives convey sensory information. Make a list of these sense-
    conveying words under columns headed *verbs, nouns,* and *adjectives*.

4. Notice the use of the verb *would* in the first paragraphs conveying a
    habitual action. Why do you think this man would regularly take such
    a long drive to a desert location?

5. Explain his last statement: "He ate and looked out across the desert
    and imagined that he had come to life again."

6. Do you think the author chose a boring subject? What makes a subject
    boring?

7. Working on your own or with a partner, choose any *two paragraphs* of
    "The Hot Spring" to analyze. Make column headings for word catego-
    ries that convey different kinds of sensory information. Use the format
    given in the example that follows, which covers the first two sentences.
    Put parentheses around sensations that are associative or implied.

Images	Texture	Kinesthetic	Color	Time	Size	Sound
dogwood	(soft)	bloomed	blue	late	thin	cracked
Chevy pickup	(slick, dirty)	broken	green	spring		
taillight	(shiny)					
mirrors	(reflecting)					
sleeping bag	(soft)					
tarpaulin	(rough)					
dishes	(smooth)					

    Create other word categories to match sensations as you find them.

ON FINDING THE RIGHT WORD

You have just analyzed the writing of a skilled professional author, who, like you, began with conscious observations. Looking back at your descriptive writing in the last chapter, you may explain putting this experience into words in stages. When you were immersed in observing your fruit or vegetable, your first stage was one of silent absorption. If words came to you at that time, you might have had to struggle to keep them from interfering prematurely with your sensing process. Nevertheless, once this stage was finished—when you were ready to write down your experiences—you may have been surprised to find yourself at a loss for words. You knew what you had seen or touched or felt, but you also realized that any word choices would only result in *translations* into another medium that would never fully duplicate your silent experience. And it took a lot of thinking to try to convey that experience in translation.

If you were describing an orange, you might have found that although you have held hundreds of oranges, it still took a lot of reflection to describe its color, texture, smell, and taste. For instance, if you wrote down, "It tastes like an orange," you knew already that the word *orange* was too general to convey exactly how it tasted to you. To erase this and write down "citrus flavor" would have been still more abstract, including the taste of lemons, grapefruit, and tangerines. If you persisted, you might have picked up the orange again to taste, this time with more studied awareness. This conscious savoring could have summoned up such words as *sticky-sweet, tangy-flesh, spicy-warm*. If you still were not satisfied, you could have gone to *Random House Word Menu* or *Roget's International Thesaurus* and looked under the lists of words for *sweetness* and *sourness*, finding choices like *pungent, acidic,* and *fermented*. Here you would have also discovered more words to describe the colors in the orange's rind: reddish-yellow, ocher, pumpkin, gold, apricot, carrot, yellow-orange, gilt, canary, beige, saffron, topaz-yellow, green, emerald, olive, chartreuse, or nut-brown, fawn, rusty, bronze, and chestnut.

Keeping an experience in mind as a constant, while searching both through word memory and thesaurus to find appropriate word correspondences, is a complex mental operation. Writing challenges you to stretch your abilities to use the words you know and to find new ones. Through this process you will move in time toward greater word mastery. To learn the words for things, you have to pay more attention to them. And once you recognize by name a Washington navel orange and a Valencia orange, you also perceive more of their details: the navels' shapes, the rinds' different textures, the subtleties of their shades of color. When someone offers you an orange, you enjoy appreciating its characteristics and talking about them, for your perception, together with your vocabulary, has enabled you to make finer differentiations. *The advantage of experience combined with a precise vocabulary is that you can learn and experience even more.*

Discovery Exercise

Sorting Out Confusion About Dictionaries

Rate each of the following statements as *true* or *false*. Be prepared to defend your answers in writing or in a class discussion.

_____ 1. Dictionaries are like phone books; basically, they all offer the same information.

_____ 2. If a dictionary is named Webster's, that means it is one of the best.

_____ 3. Dictionaries are written by experts who decide how we should speak English.

_____ 4. Small pocket dictionaries are the best kind to use for an in-depth study of words, because they eliminate unnecessary, confusing information and make understanding easier.

_____ 5. Since a dictionary can confuse us with so many definitions for any single word, it is better to try to figure out a word's meaning from its context or ask someone else.

_____ 6. Dictionaries are like cookbooks; a family needs to buy only one for the family's lifetime.

_____ 7. Dictionaries give us information about spelling and definitions, but that is about all they offer.

_____ 8. Dictionaries list word definitions in the order of most frequent use. Therefore, it is usually best to choose the first definition given.

Here is a discussion of the correct answers. Read this only *after* you've completed the quiz.

1. False. A comparative study of several dictionaries—for instance, *The American Heritage Dictionary, Webster's Collegiate Dictionary,* and *Webster's New World Dictionary*—will make this apparent.

2. False. Noah Webster was a nineteenth-century American lexicographer. The rights to his book were purchased by the Merriam Company, which has continued, under the name Merriam-Webster, to publish and revise the large *Webster's New International Dictionary*. However, since the name Webster's is not protected by a copyright, many other

companies have used it to put out both excellent and inferior products. The most prestigious and scientifically researched dictionary is the *Oxford English Dictionary*, bound in versions that range from two to twenty volumes.

3. False. Dictionaries serve as authoritative reference sources; however, they are not authoritative in the sense of being infallible but in the sense of offering reliable historical information about words and their use. In the case of *The American Heritage Dictionary*, this information is based on the opinions of a panel of lexicographers, linguists, writers, and scientists. Dictionaries are not written to dictate dogma but only to reflect agreements and standards about how people use their language, both in popular speech and formal writing.

4. False. Pocket dictionaries may be more convenient to carry and use for understanding simpler words or spellings, but they are too condensed for use in the more serious study of word ideas, concepts, and usage. Moreover, their definitions can sometimes be oversimplified to the point of being misleading. Finally, and more obviously, a pocket dictionary containing 30,000 words cannot offer you as much as an unabridged dictionary with 600,000 words or a college desk-sized one with 60,000 words.

5. False. Although most study skills texts suggest this, and most English composition-reading texts select the vocabulary for you, a guess based on your view of the context may be mistaken, and your friend may be even more confused than you. The result may be having to "unlearn" a misunderstood word later. If you are skilled in dictionary use, it is not a chore to confirm a guess or a friend's definition by consulting the dictionary. Furthermore, certainty about a word's meaning can enable you to cement it more confidently into your memory.

6. False. If your dictionary is more than fifteen years old, it is time to buy a new one. The English language acquires or invents thousands of new words each year, and our customs about word usage change also.

7. False. It's worth spending a little time just browsing through your dictionary to find out all it has to offer. You'll find a concise history of the English language, for one thing.

8. False. This is true of *The American Heritage Dictionary* but not of *Webster's Collegiate Dictionary*, *Webster's New World Dictionary*, or the *Oxford English Dictionary*. These dictionaries begin with the oldest meaning of the word, which, in some cases, has already become obsolete. Thus, if you choose the first definition regardless of the type of dictionary you are using, you might not be able to make yourself understood. It is important, therefore, to make sure you know which system is being used in your dictionary.

HOW SKILLFULLY DO YOU USE YOUR DICTIONARY?

Bring to class a college desk-sized dictionary. If you need to buy one, the following are recommended:

The American Heritage College Dictionary, third edition (Houghton Mifflin, 1994).

Webster's New World College Dictionary, third edition (Macmillan, 1996).

Working with a partner, take turns finding three random entries to discuss. Explain to your partner, who will be writing all this down, every piece of information that you find there, including every symbol and every abbreviation. If you do not understand something, take the time to look it up. (If, for instance, you do not understand what is meant by the abbreviation *OF*, find out where your dictionary explains its abbreviations.) Work together to understand *all* the information given, and do not let one another off the hook until you sense everything interpreted is fully understood.

Using the same sheet of paper upon which your partner wrote your explanations of the three entries, answer the following questions:

1. State the name of the dictionary you own and its date of publication. How many pages does it have? How many entries? Is it a desk-sized dictionary?

2. Do you feel you have had sufficient instruction in school to know how to make use of an unabridged or a desk-sized dictionary?

3. Test your knowledge of the history of the English language by explaining what your dictionary means when it refers to a word as *Anglo-Saxon* or *Middle English, Late Latin*, and *Indo-European*.

4. Look up *Pago Pago*. Write down how it is pronounced. Pronounce it to your partner. Was this easy or difficult for you?

5. Have you ever discovered that you had misunderstood a familiar word and were misusing it? Give an example and explain how you found out.

6. How does the word *plan* differ from the words *design, project*, and *scheme*? The *Webster's New World Dictionary* will explain how they differ in connotation. What are word connotations, and why are they important to consider when you make your selection?

7. Describe the mental signals that show you, in dictionary study, that you have fully understood a new word. Do you usually persist in word study until you have these signals?

8. If you can't find a word or clear definition of a word in one dictionary, do you usually think to consult another dictionary? Explain why or why not.

9. When do you use a thesaurus? How is it helpful when you do not know the word for something?

CLEAR THINKING DEPENDS
ON CLEAR WORD DEFINITIONS

If we want to think and communicate well, we have to fully understand the words we hear and use. Yet, as obvious as this may seem, it is not necessarily a common practice. It means continuous striving for word precision. And it means that when we recognize word confusion, we have to stop, identify the word, and clarify our understanding through discussion or dictionary study. The recognition of word confusion is essential. It leads us to examine our uncertainty, not only about the meaning of unfamiliar words but familiar ones as well. We need to recognize the "blank" felt on hearing the word *libertarian* for the first time as well as to acknowledge a long-term perplexity about a word heard as often as *liberal*.

Words that describe the thinking process fall in this latter category of being familiar but nevertheless not always clearly understood and defined. Such words are given special attention in this text, as you have seen in the previous chapter's discussion of perceiving, sensing, and thinking. And just as you can see more of an orange when you can name its different parts, knowing the names and definitions of the elements of thinking enables you to make closer observations of them as they occur.

Although dictionaries can give readers the power of fully understanding words, few of us are in the habit of using them as automatically as we would use a napkin at a meal. This is understandable because, when we are engrossed, it can be annoying to interrupt our reading to look up a word. Or, in conversation, we can even feel embarrassed. Yet word confusion can create the same kind of mental discomfort or disequilibrium that an unsolved problem does. If you come across a word that you do not understand, you might tell yourself that if you keep going, you might understand it from the context. Indeed, textbooks on reading often advise that. However, if you do not get the meaning from the context, you will actually find yourself *losing consciousness*, better known as becoming drowsy or falling asleep. The knack here is to recognize the early inner signs of word confusion before drowsiness takes over and to exert sufficient willpower to clear up misunderstanding through dictionary study. It can take a special effort to reach for the dictionary sometimes, but once the meaning is clarified, the perceptible sense of relief makes it worthwhile. Moreover, you will find yourself more alert, with a renewed energy for continuing your work. But this may take referring to more than one dictionary, diagramming the word, and using it in sentences.

The word definitions of concepts offered in every chapter of this text are designed to lay the foundation for the development of better word-understanding habits. However, you will also find many words that are unfamiliar to you while reading this textbook. *It will remain your responsibility to use the dictionary to understand any unfamiliar words that you may find while reading this textbook and thus to reinforce this important critical thinking habit.*

WHAT MAKES A DEFINITION?

The etymology, or history, of the word *definition* shows us something interesting; it comes from the Latin roots *de*, meaning off or away from, and *finis*, meaning end or boundary; the Latin word *definire* means to set bounds to. So when we *define* something, we discover or establish its boundaries. When we learn a new word, the definition shows us what boundaries separate it from every other word. For example, the definition of the word *framboise* establishes four distinct boundaries (see also Figure 2.1):

Framboise: a French raspberry brandy; an alcoholic drink

Brandy: alcoholic liquor distilled from fermented fruit juice

Raspberry: edible berry of the plant *Rubus* (called *framboise* in French)

French: pertaining to France, a republic of western Europe

In a definition, the word to be defined is called a *term*. Every term can be included in a *class*, or the largest family to which it is related within this particular boundary. Thus the term *framboise* belongs in the class of alcoholic drinks whose boundaries exclude all nonalcoholic drinks. A characteristic they all share is alcoholic content, even though the boundaries include beer, wine, whiskey, and brandy. Nevertheless, *framboise* is still different from all these drinks in that it has the characteristics of being a brandy that is French and distilled from raspberries. Each of these characteristics brings us into smaller and smaller boundaries that gradually single out its uniqueness. Thus, when we define a thing, we methodically set it

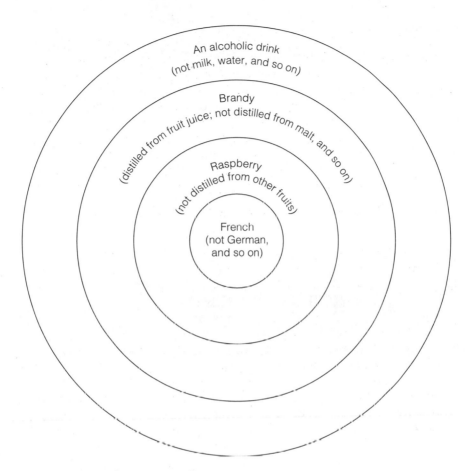

An alcoholic drink
(not milk, water, and so on)

Brandy
(distilled from fruit juice; not distilled from malt, and so on)

Raspberry
(not distilled from other fruits)

French
(not German,
and so on)

Figure 2.1 Definition Boundaries

apart from everything else. And when we have made all the necessary differentiations, we have the certainty to think more clearly about that word and to communicate our understanding about it to others as well.

Exercise

Word Boundaries

Set up a piece of paper with three columns headed *Term, Class,* and *Characteristics*. For each of the words below, list the class and characteristics, and diagram the boundaries as we did for *framboise*.

Example

Term	Class	Characteristics
Scissors	are a cutting tool	with two blades, each with a loop handle joined by a swivel pin

1. mailbag
2. moppet
3. November
4. pneumonia
5. cat

KINDS OF DEFINITIONS

When you looked up the word *cat*, you probably found it described as a mammal of the family felidae, or of the genus and species *Felis catus*. This taxonomic description indicates the boundaries that differentiate cats from all other animals. The cat family includes lions and tigers as well as house cats, while a particular breed name distinguishes a Siamese from a Persian cat. The rules that govern this system of classification are based on a science called *taxonomy*. This science, established by an international commission, enables us to know what *agreements* have been made to identify all plants and animals so that no two can be confused. Just as taxonomy helps us distinguish one living thing from another, *dictionary* (or *logical*) definitions describe terms according to the boundaries established by shared and separate characteristics. Both taxonomy and dictionary definitions owe their value to agreements that everyone can refer to.

This is especially important for *scientific* definitions, which remain more fixed than other kinds of definitions because they are specific and technical. Nurses or medical students learning and communicating about the heart have to define a number of words in their minds such as *aorta, artery, atrium, diastole, endocardium*. And, indeed, a large part of scientific training is word training in a vocabulary handed down from one decade or century to the next.

At the other extreme are *stipulative* definitions based on individual or group agreements. The term *middle-class* no longer has any commonly agreed-upon meaning in the United States. Most Americans call themselves middle class whether they live in a mansion or a trailer. When considering a tax cut in 1995, the Democrats made a *stipulative* definition of the middle class as making up to $75,000 a year, while the Republicans set that amount at $200,000. Other commentators suggested that middle class could be better defined in terms of financial stability, rather than income, and the debate continues. Other areas in which stipulative definitions are based on agreements have to do with *functional illiteracy, disability,* and *sexual harassment.* In all these cases, definitions need to be reached for reasons such as law, research, or policy implementation. In these instances, dictionary definitions are not of much use.

Writers will also sometimes spell out stipulative definitions when they want to bestow a special meaning on a word within their particular context. They might do this for the sake of clarity and consistency or to convey a specific theory. Notice what the following author does with the word *information* (which is defined in the *Webster's New World Dictionary* as "knowledge acquired in any manner"):

> In this monograph, *information* is data about the world which is a result of interactions between persons and persons and persons and events. (Charles K. West, *The Social and Psychological Distortion of Information,* p. 7)

Definitions can be *inventive,* expressing new categories or concepts that have not yet been recognized. This might be said for the words *hippie, yuppie,* and *punk,* words that gave names to groups that previously had no names, words that confirmed their existence and identity. Consider this inventive definition:

> What is the difference between bad and BAD? Bad is something like dog-do on the sidewalk, or a failing grade, or a case of scarlet fever—something no one ever said was good. BAD is different. It is something phony, clumsy, witless, untalented, vacant, or boring that many Americans can be persuaded is genuine, graceful, bright, or fascinating. Lawrence Welk is a low example, George Bush a high. (Paul Fussell, "What Is Bad?" *BAD or the Dumbing of America.* New York: Simon & Schuster, 1991)

People can also take familiar concepts and give them *personal* definitions. In an essay called "A Few Fine Words for Envy," the author describes his boyhood experiences of envy, then has this to say:

> Envy is apparently more easily felt than defined. . . . Envy and jealousy, envy and emulation, envy and invidiousness, envy and ambition, envy and desire, the distinctions, the connections, the shades of meaning. . . . The standard dictionaries, I fear, are not very helpful on this troublesome word either. I have, therefore, decided to supply my own definition: envy, I say is desiring what someone else has—a desire usually heightened by the knowledge that one is unlikely to attain it. (Joseph Epstein, *A Line Out for a Walk*)

Definitions may also be *poetic* and *whimsical,* like "Happiness is a commute before the rush hour," or *philosophical,* like "Death is the invisible companion of life." Below this level are eccentric definitions that disregard the kind of agreements that make communication possible. A classic dialogue illustrating the eccentric definition takes place between Alice and Humpty Dumpty (from Lewis Carroll's *Through the Looking Glass*).

Another category of definitions might be called *persuasive* definitions. These are definitions formulated for the purpose of praising or condemning something. Examples of these would be such statements as the following:

"A state lottery is a form of voluntary taxation."

"A state lottery is a disease in the body politic."

"To be anti-abortion is to be pro-life."

"To be for abortions is to be pro-choice."

All these personal equations are expressed as given truths in order to win others over to the same view. Obviously, they should not be confused with dictionary definitions.

THE CONNOTATIONS OF WORDS

An important aspect of definitions is the *connotations* of words or the *associations* that they suggest to us. These associations can evoke reactions, images, emotions, or thoughts. For instance, let's take the word *snake*. The *denotation* of this word, or its literal meaning, is a reptile without legs. There it is: simply a "thing," nothing to get excited about. But for most people the word *snake* carries many negative *connotations*, such as being slimy, treacherous, poisonous, or evil. These common reactions can nevertheless be overcome through conscious familiarity with snakes.

Do dictionaries provide connotations? Not so in the case of the snake, where such connotations are universally understood. But in some cases, dictionaries can help. Imagine you are a Cambodian student who wonders why your American friend John got so upset when you said he was *lying*. You consult the *Oxford English Dictionary* to find ". . . in modern use, the word *lie* is normally a violent expression of moral reprobation, which in polite conversation is to be avoided. . . ." You wonder, what word should I have used? You find some help in the *Webster's New World Dictionary of the American Language*, second edition, which offers synonym and antonym discussions for most items. Here a paragraph explains the connotative differences among *lie, prevaricate, equivocate,* and *fib*.

Feeling enlightened, you look for John and find him in the cafeteria. You say to him, "Excuse me, I only meant you were *fibbing*!" And that word magically turns him into your friend again. The denotation was the same—

"I don't know what you mean by 'glory,'" Alice said.

Humpty Dumpty smiled contemptuously. "Of course you don't—till I tell you. I meant 'there's a nice knock-down argument for you!'"

"But 'glory' doesn't mean 'a nice knock-down argument,'" Alice objected.

"When *I* use a word," Humpty Dumpty said in rather a scornful tone, "it means just what I choose it to mean—neither more nor less."

"The question is," said Alice, "whether you *can* make words mean so many different things."

"The question is," said Humpty Dumpty, "which is to be master—that's all."

his past action remained the same—but you used a word with a more acceptable connotation.

Class Discussion

1. Explain the meaning and connotative differences among *disinformation*, *misspeaking*, and *falsifying*.

2. Make a list of the synonyms for *cheating*, and rank their connotations as either negative, positive, neutral, or phony neutral (a euphemism that hides a true negative meaning).

3. Repeat the procedure for the word *stealing*.

In later chapters of this book we will look at how connotations show our judgments of things and how they can be used to manipulate others to accept the same evaluations. But for now simply consider connotations in your word choices and reading by asking questions or by dictionary study.

THE LADDER OF ABSTRACTION

> Do not perambulate the corridors in the hours of repose in the boots of ascension. (sign in Austrian ski resort)

The above statement was written by an Austrian who used an English dictionary to translate what he was thinking in German. His sign seems ludicrous to those fluent in English because the author was not able to choose appropriate words. He could not recognize that *perambulate, repose, ascension* connote more formality and abstraction than suited his meaning.

When we are working with words, we can choose between synonyms that are more abstract (sometimes also more formal) and words that are more concrete (or sometimes more colloquial). Many words that we reserve for more abstraction are of Latin or Greek origin. In the list given below, which of the words do you consider to be more concrete and which more abstract?

felicitations	nodding and handshaking
vehicle	car
pet	dog
sexy	libidinous
red-in-the-face	wrathful
yellow	mustard
bird	oriole
dog	greyhound
computer	my Powerbook laptop

To communicate well, we need to learn sensitivity to the measure of a word's abstraction. If we describe a person by the expression "a wrathful man," meaning to us a man who is red in the face and holding his fists tight, our listeners could mentally construct a dozen different pictures to fit the idea. One might see a samurai with a sword, another a pirate knocking people overboard, another a Rambo cop. On the basis of the words "wrathful man" alone, there would be no way for listeners to know exactly the picture we have in mind. Words too far abstracted from specific description cannot adequately convey intended meaning.

On the other hand, conveying precision sometimes can be accomplished only through more abstract words. You cannot get very far in talking about economic assets by repeating "my car and house and furniture and stocks, etc." That would be like trying to do math when you can count only to ten. It can also be frustrating to try to understand someone who

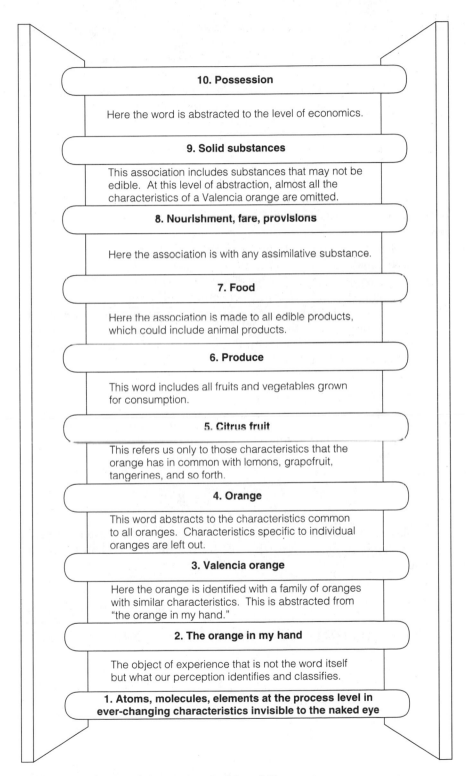

Figure 2.2 The Word *Orange* in a Ladder of Abstraction

lacks the specificity of a technical vocabulary. A child who says, "My tummy hurts" will need a lot of questions and probing from parent or doctor to determine whether the problem is gastric, intestinal, or appendicitis.

We have to find the right correlation between what we perceive and word choice on the ladder of abstraction. If we don't perceive and think but only choose words, the correlation may be too far apart.

> You always write it's bombing, bombing, bombing. It's *not* bombing! It's air support! (Col. David Opfer, U.S. air attaché in Cambodia, in talking to reporters)

Here the colonel seems to think that by persuading the reporters to use the more acceptable abstraction of "air support," he can make the effects of the bombings abstract as well. Thus "air support" suggests military defense tactics rather than the horrors of bloody mangled bodies. And the colonel may have convinced himself that by thinking in abstractions he is magically remaking such events into abstractions. His thinking moves from the words to the events rather than the other way around.

The relationship of words to perception and thought can best be explained through the "Ladder of Abstraction" first developed by the semanticist Alfred Korzybski. In this diagram, the word *orange* is used to illustrate the range of abstraction possible for any word that describes an object or living thing (Figure 2.2).

We can see how wide the boundaries may become for anything that exists; although abstractions are valuable for categorizing and conceptualizing, they can take us very far away from the concrete and specific that we can touch, observe, and verify. We need to develop word sensitivity so that we can make word choices align to our purposes, our perception, and our thinking. But to do this we have to begin with a clear awareness of our thoughts and perceptions.

Exercise

Try making some abstraction ladders of your own. Suggested subjects: (a) from atoms to horse to wealth; (b) from atoms to woman to welfare dependent.

THE IMPORTANCE OF DEFINING KEY IDEAS

The French philosopher Voltaire once said, "If you would argue with me, first define your terms." What he was talking about was not arguing in the sense of quarreling but in the sense of persuasive reasoning. He did not say *how* terms should be defined but that one should be very clear about what one has decided that key ideas mean. For example, if you wanted to argue in defense of the unregulated use of drugs, you should first define what you mean by *drugs*. Do you mean aspirin, or heroin, or both? How you define the term affects not only what you include within your boundaries to consider but also what remains outside to ignore. Undefined words have to be confronted sooner or later, and that is better done by you than by your opponent, because an argument based on undefined words will simply crumble when challenged.

Clear definitions are an essential part of all fields of learning. For example, in law, definitions help juries decide the difference between crimes and misdemeanors, between sanity and insanity. In public affairs, definitions often lead to considerable debate, as, for instance, was the case with the meaning of the expression "family values." So formulating and understanding definitions comprise a large part of any subject of learning. If you want to study thinking, you have to spend some time just studying the word *thinking*. If you study political science, you have to begin by asking what the word *political* really means. Serious study of any subject calls for learning a lot of new words. It seems obvious that one would need to spend time learning an unfamiliar technical term like *alkynes*, but it is just as essential to take a fresh look at familiar words such as *thinking* and *political*.

The skill of readily understanding a word from its dictionary definitions is not always learned in school. When the word is still not understood after several readings, often only some one-on-one coaching is needed to pinpoint the difficulty. Does it lie in the need for more decoding knowledge or is the problem due to the dictionary's limitations? A comparison of several dictionaries will sometimes show that a word is more easily understandable in one reference source than in another. On the other hand, reading a definition in a pocket dictionary can sometimes make us feel we have grasped a word when we actually haven't because its meaning has been oversimplified for the sake of brevity. So it is desirable to have some knowledge about what kinds of dictionaries there are as well as the curiosity to explore them.

WORD CONCEPTS

To understand critical thinking, we have to understand a lot of concepts. Each chapter of this book takes up a new concept. The word *concept* comes from the Latin *conceptus*, a thing conceived, suggesting a mental creation. Concepts convey abstractions of experience from the past like *pluralism,*

DEFINING REALITY

Reality comes from the Latin word *res*, which means thing, property, possession. Related to *res* is *reri*, which means to reason and from which we derive the words *reason, ratio, realize*. The past participle of *reri* is *ratus*, which means fixed by calculation, established, for certain. The ideas etymologically involved in the word *reality* are therefore:

1. That which is thought of
2. That which belongs to the thing itself
3. That which belongs to you
4. Something ascertained by thoughtful consideration
5. Something established as certain

Here is what other noted thinkers have said about reality:

Everything flows.
Heraclitus, Greek philosopher

The world was created by the word of God so that what is seen was made out of things which do not appear.
St. Paul

Reality is what we bump against.
William James, American psychologist

Reality is something as it actually is, independent of our thoughts about how it is.
Mortimer J. Adler, American philosopher

Reality is an unknown and undefinable totality of flux that is the ground of all things and of the process of thought itself, as well as the movement of intelligent perception.
David Bohm, philosopher and physicist

aristocracy, hegemony, or they convey new ideas like *cultural diversity, postmodern, ecology, ergonomics,* and *cybernetics.* Fully learning the meaning of concepts so that we can think, discuss, and write with them is an important part of higher education. Learning a new concept can help us align a lot of information that we had observed but not categorized. (This happened with the invention of the words *hippie* and *punk*.) And learning new concepts can open new opportunities for us, as when we learn to distinguish between a *heuristic* and an *algorithm*, thus gaining some new ways of approaching problem solving. In sum, concept learning can give us vocabularies adequate to express our ideas as well as enable us to learn new ideas.

If we want to study and learn concepts, it can be interesting to begin with the word's etymology or history, with its earliest root idea. This idea

Reality is nothing but a collective hunch.
Lily Tomlin

   And about the difficulty of defining reality:

As far as the laws of mathematics refer to reality, they are not certain; and as far as they are certain, they do not refer to reality.
Albert Einstein

The Eastern mystics are well aware of the fact that all verbal descriptions of reality are inaccurate and incomplete. . . . The direct experience of reality transcends the realm of thought and language, and since all mysticism is based on such a direct experience, everything that is said about it can only be partially true.
Fritjof Capra, physicist

Reality is process. . . . Not only is everything changing, but all is flux. That is to say, what is is the process of becoming itself, while all objects, events, entities, conditions, structures, etc., are forms that can be abstracted from this process.
David Bohm

There is no reality until that reality is perceived. Our perceptions of reality will, consequently, appear somewhat contradictory, dualistic, and paradoxical. The instantaneous experience of the reality of Now will not appear paradoxical at all. It is only when we observers attempt to construct a history of our perceptions that reality seems paradoxical.
Fred Alan Wolf, physicist

can give us a concrete sense of the word's logic that helps us better remember the word and recognize its relationship to other words with the same roots. Dictionaries are not, however, always our best guides for understanding concepts sufficiently to think, write, and discuss with them. To learn the concepts that make up the language of ideas, we need other kinds of books or teachers.

> The language of ideas and the language of ordinary discourse are not the same. The language of ideas is not learned informally through casual conversation. Nor is it learned from listening to the media. . . . As soon as one gets to college, however, knowledge of the language of ideas is assumed. Few professors spell out the key concepts and ideas that are presupposed for understanding their fields, and many freshmen get lost in a sea of strange words during their first few months of college. Some never get their linguistic and conceptual bearings

DEFINING TRUTH

The word *true* comes from the Old English form of *troewe*, which means loyal, trustworthy, which in turn comes from the Indo-European base *deru*, meaning firm, solid, steadfast. Related to the base word *deru* is *dru*, meaning firm as a tree, hard as wood. This etymology suggests that *truth* is something as hard and firm and as steadfast as a tree or its wood.

Here are some definitions and descriptions of truth:

Truth suggests conformity with the facts or with reality, either as an idealized abstraction ("What is truth?" said jesting Pilate) or in actual application to statements, ideas, acts, etc. ("There is no truth in that rumor").
The American Heritage Dictionary

Truth is a correspondence or agreement between our minds and reality.
Mortimer J. Adler

The ordinary mode of language is very unsuitable for discussing questions of truth and falsity, because it tends to treat each truth as a separate fragment that is essentially fixed and static in its nature. . . . However, truth and falsity have to be seen from moment to moment, in an act of perception of a very high order.
David Bohm

Truth is said to lie at the bottom of a well, for the very reason, perhaps, that whoever looks down in search of her sees his own image at the bottom.
J. R. Lowell

and fake it throughout their college careers and beyond. They use words they hear their professors using, but without a clear sense of the nuances of meaning and the correctness of usage that are needed to speak and write well . . . without ever developing the fluent use of complex ideas and concepts that can lead to clear and sensitive thinking. (Herbert Kohl, *From Archetype to Zeitgeist*)

Traditional aids for concept study are encyclopedias, textbooks, and books written by leading thinkers in their special fields of knowledge. Yet, even scholars cannot always agree on the definition of a term. *Critical thinking,* for instance, has as many definitions as people who write on the subject or teach it. Yet each definition provides insights concerning the boundaries that this new field of study might include or exclude.

Defining terms is a dynamic process in any field of learning. And there are some words that challenge each new generation. Two of these words, *truth* and *reality*, appear in the insert boxes on these pages. They are both ordinary but profound words; they both remain elusive, yet they are the standards for measuring our ways of knowing and proceeding in the world and for thinking critically about the world.

WHAT IS CRITICAL READING?

When we read a detective story, we like to get lost in the experience; when we read a motor vehicle department's driver's manual, we follow and memorize. In both cases, we do not need to question what we read. It is more like boarding a train: we get on and then we get off. However, if we were to apply this attitude to newspaper reading, we might believe either everything or nothing. Critical reading requires a different attitude that is both skeptical and informed; such a reader knows standards for determining the reliability of information and reasoning. A critical reader can read six arguments for and against a proposition in a voter's pamphlet and quickly decide which is the soundest. As a television viewer, a critical reader is immune to commercial and political propaganda. A critical reader interacts with information.

Learning critical reading involves learning how to exercise two different mental attitudes in two different stages. The first is closer to what we use in reading the driver's manual or an anatomy text: it is a modality of receptivity—maintaining an openness—that can ensure *accurate comprehension*. Challenging or questioning comes later; first the reader must make an accurate mental reconstruction of the information. Indeed, in this first stage, judgments interfere with the concentration needed to correctly decipher words and meaning. And sometimes this process of accurately comprehending takes many rereadings to achieve.

Although it is beyond the scope of this text to teach reading comprehension skills, much can be self-taught by cultivating the habit of *mental receptivity* in the first stage of reading. When we do not remain open (as we learned in the chapter on observation skills), we tend to alter or distort whatever appears before us. *Receptive reading* does not distort the message by substituting different words or ideas but faithfully and accurately records what is said, regardless of whether it agrees with the reader's personal values, experiences, or expectations or not.

In reading this book, you may not feel receptive to all of its arguments. When an argument goes against our values, it can be painful to hear it out. We tend to look for reasons to support the views we already hold rather than consider alternative views. *Both effort and discipline are needed to maintain neutrality, even with what we favor.*

USING WORDS

"Is your name Caspar?" asked the Queen.

"No."

"Is your name Hans?"

"No. Now or never, woman! I've been patient long enough! If you don't guess my name right—I'll give you just one more time—then your baby is mine!"

"I wonder . . . I wonder . . . Could your name be . . . Could it be . . . *Rumplestiltskin?*"

"The Devil told you that! The Devil told you that!" shrieked the ugly little man.

And in a fury, he flew out the window on his cooking spoon.

And he was never heard from again.

Questions

1. Have you ever been disturbed by a feeling, symptom, or sense that you could not put into words?
2. If and when you found you could name it, how did you feel?
3. Have you ever argued with someone over a word?
4. How did you solve the problem?

And although neutrality or objectivity can never be perfectly achieved, it can be understood as the practice of holding off personal reactions. Objectivity does not mean that you have changed what you feel, but it does mean that your reactions have been consciously taken into account and weighed for bias.

Once the material is understood, the critical reading phase can begin with analyzing and evaluating. This is a stage that cannot be hurried; it is a slow and careful process accompanied by many questions. The definition of *critical* given earlier traces the original ideas of this term back to the words *sift* and *separate*. When one reads critically, one sifts out words and ideas, separates content from structure, questions, and reflects. Yet, critical reading must begin with an accurate reproduction of the message. We cannot be skeptical and receptive at the same time. When we are critical too soon, we lose the focus needed to make an accurate reading of the material. And a criticism of information or argument based on an inaccurate reading is a waste of time.

BUILDING ARGUMENTS

WORD CHOICES

When we make a claim, each word appearing in the claim needs careful thought and definition. (*"If you would argue with me, first define your terms."* Voltaire) Word choices vary according to the values and purposes of the speaker. Notice how this author uses his definition of *Indians* to sway others to accept his beliefs.

Mr. Baily:

With the narrative enclosed, I subjoin some observations with regard to the animals, vulgarly called Indians. (definition of key term)

In the United States Magazine in the year 1777, I published a dissertation denying them to have a right in the soil. (principal claim, conclusion, or thesis)

The whole of this earth was given to man, and all descendants of Adam have a right to share it equally. There is no right of primogeniture in the laws of nature and of nations. (moral reasoning made through further claims to back principal claim)

What use do these ringed, streaked, spotted and speckled cattle make of the soil? Do they till it? Revelation said to man, "Thou shalt till the ground" . . . *I would as soon admit a right in the buffalo to grant lands, as in Kill-buck, the Big Cat, the Big Dog, or any of the ragged wretches that are called chiefs. What would you think of going to a big lick or place where the beasts collect to lick saline nitrous earth and water, and addressing yourself to a great buffalo to grant you land?* (analogy used to support principal claim)

(H. H. Brackenridge, 1782)

Exercise

1. The *issue* here is whether Indians should have the right to their land. What is the author's claim on this issue?
2. How does the author use his definition of Indians to help his argument?
3. What reasoning does he offer to prove Indians are not human?
4. What is *primogeniture*?
5. What is unfair about this argument?
6. Write a one-paragraph argument in which you make a claim about anything. Make either a neutral or controversial definition of your key term or subject. Then offer two reasons to support your definition.

Above all, a critical thinker knows what questions to ask. Throughout this text you will be learning new questions to ask. In this chapter, you have been considering three questions:

Is this the most accurate word choice?

What is the connotation of this word?

Does this word need defining?

The reading selections in this text are followed by study questions intended to stimulate critical thinking. You are encouraged to read each selection at least twice—once for comprehension and once for critical interaction. If it is helpful, think of your first reading as a sponge reading and your second as a sifting. Consult your dictionary regularly as you read, and write down questions you need to ask to clarify or challenge what is said. Make your reading an active thinking endeavor.

CHAPTER SUMMARY

1. Words help us think better. They give forms to our thoughts so that we can make use of them. Words enable us to communicate with ourselves and others. Knowing the words for things and experiences helps us see and perceive more.

2. Writing helps us learn more about words and how to use them. When we struggle to select words that will describe our experiences, we realize that words are only *translations* of experience and not the experience itself.

3. Clear thinking depends on a clear understanding of the words we use. Word confusion leads to less consciousness, or disequilibrium, which can only be restored through word clarification.

4. We need to understand what dictionaries can and cannot offer us and how to use them skillfully and frequently.

5. The thesaurus helps us when we are writing and translating nonverbal experiences and ideas into words; the dictionary helps us when we are reading and interpreting the words of others.

6. Definitions set boundaries for word ideas and show us their specific and general characteristics and how they are related to or distinguished from one another.

7. Dictionary definitions show us the agreements that society has made about a word's meaning. But we may also compose our own personal or stipulative definitions of experiences or compose persuasive defini-

tions to sway the opinions of others. In critical thinking it is important not to confuse these different kinds of definitions, or to believe that personal, persuasive, or stipulative definitions carry the same agreements as those to be found in a dictionary.

8. The test of our understanding of a word is our ability to define it. This ability is particularly important for words representing key ideas that we wish to explain or defend. Taking the time to define the words we use is an essential preliminary to genuine communication.

9. A study of a word's etymology can help us trace a word back to its earliest root idea and can give us an image that conveys a more concrete sense of the word's logic. Learning a word's etymology can also help us recognize its relationship to other words with the same root meanings.

10. The connotations of a word are its associative meanings, which can be positive, negative, or neutral. These associations can take the form of feelings, ideas, images, or thoughts. Thus, although politicians would never admit to *lying* or being *confused*, it is quite acceptable for them to admit they *misspoke*.

11. The first stage of critical reading is objective receptivity to the material; this means having the technical ability as well as the willingness to accurately reproduce its content without alterations or distortions. If we question and interact with material that we have not accurately interpreted, our criticisms will not be fair or worthwhile.

12. To communicate well we need to understand the difference between concrete and abstract words and to choose appropriately from either category. The ladder of abstraction shows us how one word for a thing can range from a specific perceived directly to a concept that is part of a much larger collective.

CHAPTER QUIZ

Rate each of the following statements as *true* or *false*. To answer some of these questions, you will need to consult your dictionary.

_____ 1. Abstract words convey a word's meaning better than concrete words.

_____ 2. Words can be used to do a better or worse job of describing experiences but can never be more than translations of the experiences themselves.

_____ 3. A dictionary can help us think better when we use it to clear up word confusion.

_____   4. Definitions of a word show the word's boundaries.

_____   5. Knowing the words for things helps us see them better.

_____   6. We do not fully understand a word unless we can define it.

_____   7. When people debate a topic, understanding is greatly helped by their taking the time to define the key terms.

_____   8. Etymology gives us word histories.

_____   9. Pocket dictionaries are sufficient guides for a critical study of word meanings.

_____ 10. The word *ohm* comes from the Sanskrit language and means the sound of creation.

_____ 11. According to most dictionaries, there is more than one acceptable spelling of the word *cooperate*.

_____ 12. The term *French leave* means to say goodbye with a big kiss.

_____ 13. The prefix *in* in the words *insignificant* and *inflammable* means *not* in Latin.

_____ 14. The following words all contain the sound called a schwa: *mass, polite, placement, bogus, visible*.

_____ 15. The word *nausea* can be pronounced at least three different ways.

_____ 16. The word *round* can function as six different parts of speech: adjective, noun, transitive and intransitive verb, adverb, and preposition.

_____ 17. *Egregious* comes from a Latin word meaning standing out from the herd.

_____ 18. The word *nadir* in the phrase "the nadir of politics" means the highest point.

_____ 19. A *cogent* argument is a convincing one.

_____ 20. The word *decimate* means to dice something up into pieces.

Composition Writing Application

A Short Essay of Definition

Write an essay based on an extended definition or full discussion of a word or phrase, with the support of examples. It should also be an essay of exposition, which is a form of writing that explains something. In this case you will want to *explain your definition* as fully as you can through stories, examples, or specific information. The thinking tasks of making definitions followed by explanations play a frequent part in our daily conversations. If you are having a conversation with a friend and say, "She just isn't *mature*," your friend may reply, "What do you mean by *mature*?" Thus, you are challenged to respond with a definition together with an explanation of how you use that term.

The directions for this assignment, and for all the other writing assignments in this book, are designed to make you conscious of the thinking elements involved in solving it as a given problem, much as you would solve a problem in mathematics. In order to solve the problem, however, you must follow the instructions exactly. To help you grasp the details of each assignment, the instructions are set up in terms of parameters.

A parameter is a fixed limit or boundary (*para* = alongside, *meter* = measure); it is also a variable or a fixed constant. In the case of this assignment, you will be asked to observe the four parameters listed below. These parameters are intended to provide you with both *guidelines* for solving the problem and *standards* for evaluating your work. In order to succeed in this assignment, therefore, be careful not to ignore or neglect any of these specified parameters.

1. *Objective*: To give your own definition of a word, and to explain that word's meaning through your own experience.

2. *Form and length*: Write at least one typed page.

3. *Structure*: Begin with a topic sentence and end with a conclusion.

4. *Suggested topics*:

    (a) What is an adult?
    (b) A word that I came to understand through experience
    (c) A word that I misunderstood
    (d) A word that I had trouble understanding
    (e) A word that interests me

Step 1   Suppose you choose the first topic—defining *adult*. Think of what the word has come to mean to you in your own life. Think about how you have heard others use this word. Look up its definition in several dictionaries. Now turn back to the diagram of the word *framboise*. Draw and define the boundaries for the word *adult* using dictionary definitions or whatever you can add in terms of your own experience.

Step 2   Now try *clustering* with the word *adult*. Clustering (or mapping) is a warm-up exercise that invites both hemispheres of the brain to work with an idea. It can be a magical way to quickly release all the ideas, memories, and associations you have on a particular subject.

Step 3   Next, take the information you discovered from your cluster, and begin to write a good paragraph about the various meanings and boundaries of the word *adult*. Contrast what you feel to be the true meaning of the word with some false meanings. Bring together your findings into one sentence that announces all you want to say about the definitions

CLUSTERING

To begin clustering, place an oval in the center of a page and write your key word inside that oval. Focus on that word. As thoughts, symbols, memories, or new word associations come, draw lines to new ovals that contain these words. As words stimulate new associations, draw lines to these. In time you will have a number of new clusters, all radiating from the key word. Notice how this is done with the word *family*.

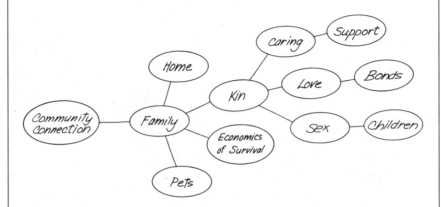

Clustering cuts through the frustration of thinking linearly (left brain) and allows us to think more naturally. When we list or outline thoughts, we force our thinking into a sequence without yet knowing all of what we think. In clustering, we invite input from the right brain as well as the left and achieve a visual sense of the whole picture. Clustering is a free-association method that is best done without censorship, allowing discoveries and surprises at the results. (If you wish to learn more about this subject, see the books by Tony Buzan and Gabriele Rico listed at the end of this chapter.)

and boundaries of *adult*. This is a *topic sentence*, which generalizes your findings into a kind of conclusion. The rest of the sentences in the paragraph should support, or provide examples that support, the topic sentence. In this paragraph you can see how well you think about words while also working on the college level in expository writing.

Peer Review

In class read your essays of definition to one another in small groups. For each paper, write a critique that answers these questions:

1.   Was each of the parameters observed?

2. Did you understand all that was said? Did anything need to be explained more?
3. Did you honestly find the writing interesting?

Student Writing Example

MUSIC

Gary Aguirre

The word *music*, from the Greek word *mousike*, meaning "art of the muses," is defined in *Webster's New World Dictionary* as, "1. the art of combining tones to form expressive compositions 2. such compositions 3. any rhythmic sequence of pleasing sounds." This literal explanation understates the importance of music in my life. To me music is the axle around which all human spiritual experience revolves. It is the common thread linking all religions and cultural expressions. From Spanish *cante hondo*, or deep song, to Balinese *gamelan*, to American jazz, musicians use song to define their heritage and their interpretation of the human experience. Music is a tangible representation of what I consider to be the unexplainable central creative force in the world that some call God.

The word *music*'s deeper meaning becomes clearer when you find that some synonyms given in *Roget's Thesaurus* are *order* and *universe*. Music is an improvised creative expression, or melody, skillfully woven over a tapestry of mathematically juxtaposed rhythms and harmonies. It mimics the relationship of an individual's life experience against the solid background of history and culture. For instance, when American jazz great John Coltrane plays the standard "My Favorite Things," he begins with the familiar melody that accompanies the words "raindrops on roses and whiskers on kittens." The audience is drawn in because they have experienced this "place" before; in other words, they recognize the tune. From this starting point Coltrane soars into a whirl of spontaneous improvisation, while the drums, piano, and bass continue to pound out the original background collage of sound and rhythm. When he sees fit, Coltrane returns to the original melody, completing a cycle not unlike that of birth and death. The musician, in his expertise, provides a higher *order* to a world of sound that can, at times, seem completely chaotic. Songs begin, travel through time and space, and then end. They live and die, like everything in the universe, serving no practical purpose. But like Coltrane's "My Favorite Things," the universe began, and may eventually end, also serving no practical purpose but to host those of us who were lucky enough to be here.

To me music is not just "the art of combining tones to form expressive compositions" but a universe within itself that we humans can use to define our place in the infinite. Growing up in a nonreligious family, music was my sole (or soul) connection with spirituality. The painstaking hours of teaching myself to play have afforded me the opportunity to worship in the only way I know how. As a song composer, I can offer my little bit to that which was here long before me and will continue long after I'm gone. Making music to me *is* prayer. Life and music are not separate entities; neither reflects the other, nor could either continue without the other. They are two parts of the greater whole, the everything.

Used with permission of Gary Aquirre.

Readings

ADDICTION

Anne Wilson Schaef

In this book, Anne Wilson Schaef, a therapist, begins with an original definition of addiction. Notice as you read how her definition gives her an advantage over authors who assume that everyone already knows what addiction is.

An addiction is any process over which we are powerless. It takes control of us, 1 causing us to do and think things that are inconsistent with our personal values and leading us to become progressively more compulsive and obsessive. A sure sign of an addiction is the sudden need to deceive ourselves and others—to lie, deny, and cover up. An addiction is anything we feel *tempted* to lie about. An addiction is anything we are not *willing* to give up (we may not *have* to give it up *and* we must be *willing to* do so to be free of addiction).

Like any serious disease, an addiction is progressive, and it will lead to death 2 unless we actively recover from it. I shall give some examples of how addiction affects individuals and also what it does at a cultural level.

An addiction keeps us unaware of what is going on inside us. We do not have 3 to deal with our anger, pain, depression, confusion, or even our joy and love, because we do not feel them, or we feel them only vaguely. We stop relying on our knowledge and our senses and start relying on our confused perceptions to tell us what we know and sense. In time, this lack of internal awareness deadens our internal processes, which in turn allows us to remain addicted. At some point we must choose to recover—to arrest the progress of the addiction—or we will die. This dying process does not happen only at a personal level: it is also systemic to our culture.

As we lose contact with ourselves, we also lose contact with other people and 4 the world around us. An addiction dulls and distorts our sensory input. We do not receive information clearly; we do not process it accurately; and we do not feed it back or respond to it with precision. Since we are not in touch with ourselves, we present a distorted self to the world—in AA terms, we "con" people—and eventually lose the ability to become intimate with others, even those we are closest to and love the most.

We are aware that something is very wrong, but the addictive thinking tells us   5 that it could not possibly be our fault. This kind of thinking also tells us that we cannot make things right, that someone else will have to do it for us.

When they cannot (of course), we blame them for what is happening. (On a   6 system level, we believe we are not causing the unrest in the world. If others would only behave, we would not *have to* retaliate.) An addiction absolves us from having to take responsibility for our lives. We assume that someone—or something—outside ourselves will swoop down to make things better or help us to deal with what we are going through. Since addicts tend to be dependent and to feel increasingly powerless and bad about themselves, the notion that they can take responsibility for their lives is inconceivable to them.

The longer we wait to be rescued, the worse our addiction becomes. Regard-   7 less of what we are addicted to, it takes more and more to create the desired effect, and no amount is ever enough.

Addictions can be divided into two major categories: substance addictions and   8 process addictions. Both function in essentially the same way and produce essentially the same results. Although I shall describe each separately, it is important to remember that addictions are quite common in our culture and that most addicts have multiple addictions. Although not all addictions are of equal severity, all eventually exhibit similar behavioral dynamics and processes and lead to death.*

*At this point the author includes under substance addictions alcohol, drugs, nicotine, caffeine, and food; under process addictions she lists money accumulation, gambling, sex, work, religion, and worry.

SAVED

Malcolm X

Interest in the life and achievements of Malcolm X has recently been revived, in large part because of the successful film by Spike Lee. In this selection, now a classic, Malcolm X describes how he managed through self-education to pull himself out of a life of street hustling and prison into literacy and power.

It was because of my letters that I happened to stumble upon starting to acquire   1 some kind of a homemade education.

I became increasingly frustrated at not being able to express what I wanted to   2
convey in letters that I wrote, especially those to Mr. Elijah Muhammad. In the
street, I had been the most articulate hustler out there—I had commanded attention when I said something. But now, trying to write simple English, I not only
wasn't articulate, I wasn't even functional. How would I sound writing in slang, the
way I would *say* it, something such as, "Look, daddy, let me pull your coat about a
cat, Elijah Muhammad—"

Many who today hear me somewhere in person, or on television, or those who   3
read something I've said, will think I went to school far beyond the eighth grade.
This impression is due entirely to my prison studies.

It had really begun back in the Charlestown Prison, when Bimbi first made me   4
feel envy of his stock of knowledge. Bimbi had always taken charge of any conversation he was in, and I had tried to emulate him. But every book I picked up had
few sentences which didn't contain anywhere from one to nearly all of the words
that might as well have been in Chinese. When I just skipped those words, of
course, I really ended up with little idea of what the book said. So I had come to
the Norfolk Prison Colony still going through only book-reading motions. Pretty
soon, I would have quit even these motions, unless I had received the motivation
that I did.

I saw that the best thing I could do was get hold of a dictionary—to study, to   5
learn some words. I was lucky enough to reason also that I should try to improve
my penmanship. It was sad. I couldn't even write in a straight line. It was both ideas
together that moved me to request a dictionary along with some tablets and pen-
cils from the Norfolk Prison Colony school.

I spent two days just riffling [sic] uncertainly through the dictionary's pages.   6
I'd never realized so many words existed! I didn't know *which* words I needed to
learn. Finally, just to start some kind of action, I began copying.

In my slow, painstaking, ragged handwriting, I copied into my tablet every-   7
thing printed on that first page, down to the punctuation marks.

I believe it took me a day. Then, aloud, I read back, to myself, everything I'd   8
written on the tablet. Over and over, aloud, to myself, I read my own handwriting.

I woke up the next morning, thinking about those words—immensely proud   9
to realize that not only had I written so much at one time, but I'd written words
that I never knew were in the world. Moreover, with a little effort, I also could
remember what many of these words meant. I reviewed the words whose meanings I didn't remember. Funny thing, from the dictionary first page right now, that
"aardvark" springs to my mind. The dictionary had a picture of it, a long-tailed,
long-eared, burrowing African mammal, which lives off termites caught by sticking
out its tongue as an anteater does for ants.

I was so fascinated that I went on—I copied the dictionary's next page. And   10
the same experience came when I studied that. With every succeeding page, I also
learned of people and places and events from history. Actually the dictionary is
like a miniature encyclopedia. Finally the dictionary's A section had filled a whole
tablet—and I went on into the B's. That was the way I started copying what
eventually became the entire dictionary. It went a lot faster after so much practice

helped me to pick up handwriting speed. Between what I wrote in my tablet, and writing letters, during the rest of my time in prison I would guess I wrote a million words.

I suppose it was inevitable that as my word-base broadened, I could for the 11 first time pick up a book and read and now begin to understand what the book was saying. Anyone who has read a great deal can imagine the new world that opened. Let me tell you something: from then until I left that prison, in every free moment I had, if I was not reading in the library, I was reading on my bunk. You couldn't have gotten me out of books with a wedge. Between Mr. Muhammad's teachings, my correspondence, my visitors—usually Ella and Reginald—and my reading of books, months passed without my even thinking about being imprisoned. In fact, up to then, I never had been so truly free in my life.

The Norfolk Prison Colony's library was in the school building. A variety of 12 classes was taught there by instructors who came from such places as Harvard and Boston universities. The weekly debates between inmate teams were also held in the school building. You would be astonished to know how worked up convict debaters and audiences would get over subjects like "Should Babies Be Fed Milk?"

Available on the prison library's shelves were books on just about every general 13 subject. Much of the big private collection that Parkhurst had willed to the prison was still in crates and boxes in the back of the library—thousands of old books. Some of them looked ancient: covers faded, old-time parchment-looking binding. Parkhurst, I've mentioned, seemed to have been principally interested in history and religion. He had the money and the special interest to have a lot of books that you wouldn't have in general circulation. Any college library would have been lucky to get that collection.

As you can imagine, especially in a prison where there was heavy emphasis on 14 rehabilitation, an inmate was smiled upon if he demonstrated an unusually intense interest in books. There was a sizable number of well-read inmates, especially the popular debaters. Some were said by many to be practically walking encyclopedias. They were almost celebrities. No university would ask any student to devour literature as I did when this new world opened to me, of being able to read and *understand*.

I read more in my room than in the library itself. An inmate who was known to 15 read a lot could check out more than the permitted maximum number of books. I preferred reading in the total isolation of my own room.

When I had progressed to really serious reading, every night at about ten P.M. 16 I would be outraged with the "lights out." It always seemed to catch me right in the middle of something engrossing.

Fortunately, right outside my door was a corridor light that cast a glow into 17 my room. The glow was enough to read by, once my eyes adjusted to it. So when "lights out" came, I would sit on the floor where I could continue reading in that glow.

At one-hour intervals the night guards paced past every room. Each time I 18 heard the approaching footsteps, I jumped into bed and feigned sleep. And as soon as the guard passed, I got back out of bed onto the floor area of that light-glow, where I would read for another fifty-eight minutes—until the guard approached again. That went on until three or four every morning. Three or four hours of sleep a night was enough for me. Often in the years in the streets I had slept less than that.

For Further Reading

Buzan, Tony. *Use Both Sides of Your Brain*. New York: Dutton, 1983.

Epstein, Joseph. "A Few Words for Envy," *A Line Out for a Walk Familiar Essays*. New York: Norton, 1991.

Friere, Paulo, and Donaldo Macedo. "The Importance of the Act of Reading," *Literacy: Reading the Word and the World*. New York: Bergin & Garvey, 1987.

Fussell, Paul. "What Is Bad?" *BAD or the Dumbing of America*. New York: A Touchstone Book, Simon & Schuster, 1991.

Galeano, Eduardo. *Walking Words*. New York: Norton, 1993.

Kohl, Herbert. *From Archetype to Zeitgeist*. Boston: Little, Brown, 1992.

McPhee, John. *Oranges*. New York: Noonday Press, Farrar, Strauss & Giroux, 1967.

Rico, Gabriele Lusser. *Writing the Natural Way*. Los Angeles: J. P. Tarcher, Inc., 1983.

CHAPTER 3

Facts: What's Real?

© Jared Lee 1985. Reprinted with permission of Jared Lee.

Why is it funny to find fresh milk confirmed as fact through observation? Is it because we are embarrassed by cows' udders? Or does it remind us that the fresh milk claims we usually accept may not be factual?

This is an easy problem compared to some of the difficulties we run into when trying to establish facts. Because facts are judged on the basis of "truth" and "reality," establishing them can be a tricky business. But we *can* learn to recognize pitfalls and to apply standards in gathering them. These are the skills that this chapter aims to teach.

We begin by considering what a fact is and proceed to unravel some common confusion about the relationship of facts to reality. We then practice discovering and describing facts accurately, which should bring more clarity to both our thinking about and communication of facts.

Discovery Exercises

The following three Discovery Exercises can be done on an individual or collaborative basis; they can be done outside class in preparation for discussion or in class itself.

Beginning with the Word *Fact*

After consulting at least two dictionaries, write down your own definitions of the following words:

1. know   4. existence
2. certain   5. real
3. verified   6. fact

Then read your definitions of *fact* aloud in class. Which definitions seem to cover all kinds of facts?

Does your definition of *fact* contain the following elements?

1. *Fact* comes from the Latin *factum*, meaning a deed, something done.
2. A fact is something known with certainty through experience, observation, or measurement.
3. A fact is something that can be objectively demonstrated and verified.
4. A fact becomes a fact when we can get another source or person to *agree* that it corresponds to a reality.

Learning to Recognize Facts

Answer the following questions in writing, in preparation for a class discussion.

1. List five facts about the room you are in right now. Do not just name objects or events (such as window, door, breeze), but make statements describing exactly what you see in a full context. For instance, do not say "Four windows" but "There are four open windows without blinds or curtains in this room."
2. Write an example of how each of the five senses gives us factual information; for instance, "An ear hears the sound of a telephone ringing."
3. Why do you think the chapter on observation skills preceded this one on facts?
4. Which of the following are statements of fact?

    (a) Water freezes at 0 degrees Celsius and 32 degrees Fahrenheit at sea level or under standard pressure.

  (b) The major religion in Mexico is Roman Catholicism.
  (c) The food is awful in the cafeteria.
  (d) No volcanoes are located in North America.
  (e) Everybody should jog every day.
  (f) She must have forgotten her lunch; it is still on the table.
  (g) Advertisement: "Johnson's Music offers you the best buys in records and tapes."

5. Explain why items 4c through 4g are not facts.

Verifying Facts

One characteristic of facts is that they can be objectively verified—that is, proven to be true through the testimony of witnesses, through agreed-upon observations, or through records or documentation. Read the facts listed below. Select three to study. How would you go about verifying that each is indeed a fact?

1. Jan Vermeer was a Dutch painter who lived from 1632 to 1675.

2. Captain James Cook arrived in Hawaii in 1778.

3. The average number of Harlequin romance novels sold in Hungary each day in 1989 was 17,800.

4. One hundred percent of Japanese graduating high-school seniors have taken at least six years of English-language classes.

5. The mean height and weight for children between one and three years old in the United States are 35 inches and 29 pounds.

6. Tallahassee is the capital of Florida.

7. It takes 90 minutes to hard-boil an ostrich egg.

8. William and Mary College is located in Williamsburg, Virginia.

9. Gravity is a force that tends to draw all bodies in the earth's sphere toward the center of the earth.

10. Water is wet.

11. The word *bible* comes from the Greek word *biblia*, meaning a collection of writings.

FACTS AND REALITY

Although a search for facts can raise many questions, the basic question is the correspondence between facts and reality. In the history of human thought, some have considered *reality* to be relative and others have viewed it as absolute. That is, some say the observer determines what reality is, and others say that reality is what it is regardless of what people may think about it. Yet, no matter what our theory, we must be reminded of reality's elusiveness when we see our most sacred "facts" changing. In the nineteenth century, doctors determined that 98.6 Fahrenheit represented normal body temperature. This "fact" was fully accepted as law; it was never questioned until 1992, when research concluded that 98.6 wasn't normal at all; indeed, it was downright unusual. A study concluded that healthy people thrive between 96.0 and 99.9, depending on the individual, time of day, sex, and race.

To cite another medical example, more than twenty years ago Linus Pauling advocated taking large doses of vitamin C to prevent colds and other diseases. Although he was a Nobel Prize winner in chemistry, the medical establishment dismissed Pauling's theory and in effect told him to mind his own business. Nevertheless, some researchers became curious enough to conduct studies that now suggest that vitamin C, at least when consumed through fruits and vegetables, can curtail the length of colds; additionally, it can protect against stomach cancer and heart disease. Science moved forward in both the body temperature case and the vitamin C case because accepted facts were reexamined. Such questioning was led by the understanding that facts are not necessarily truths but, at best, only our decisions about what seems to be most real.

DISCERNING FACTS FROM FICTION

In the Introduction to this book you met the Thomas family. The majority of people who take the quiz in that Discovery Exercise never realize that they are making not one but two assumptions when they accept the statement "This is graduation day for the Thomas family." In their preoccupation with whether the photo really depicts a graduation day for one or all family members, they overlook assumptions made about the actuality of family name and family status. Yet, if they go along with the assumption that this is a family with the name "Thomas," they fall into believing that most of the following statements are true as well. The photo is actually an advertisement designed to sell Amway products. The "family" consists of paid models taken to the Stanford University campus to have their picture taken. (Actually, three of the older adults were related; the little girl was borrowed from a family next door.) This was a *contrived* situation, not a real one, yet had the photo appeared contrived, it would not have succeeded in its purpose of convincing magazine readers that selling Amway products would make them feel as successful and happy as this family.

Commercial advertising uses a lot of sophisticated knowledge about how to get consumers to accept fakery. Actors in television commercials have to convince us that they are not actors: they should look "real"—like one of us. They have to persuade us that it is natural for two homemakers doing aerobics together to share advice on laundry detergents or that a celebrity is sincere in making a product testimonial.

The blurring of fact and fiction extends beyond commercials, sometimes with little concern for the distinctions. We watch documentaries that alternate between actual news footage and reenactments. We watch adventure stories that use news footage with pseudo-newsreels. Consider the following instances of fact mixed with fiction.

1. Ronald Reagan was known for his "presidency by photo ops." When he went to the demilitarized zone in Korea, his video managers wanted to get footage of Reagan at the most exposed American bunker, Guardpost Collier, which overlooked North Korea. However, the Secret Service vetoed the idea for fear of sharpshooters or infiltrators. After several days of negotiation, the problem of protection was solved by erecting posts strong enough to hold 30 thousand yards of camouflage netting in front of the bunker. Then, to get the most dramatic shots, the army built camera platforms on the hill beyond the guardpost so Reagan could be snapped standing there at the front. In the final shot, he was to be seen surrounded by sandbags, peering with his binoculars toward North Korea, evoking the memory of General Douglas MacArthur (from "The Storybook Presidency," *Power Game: How Washington Works*, by Hedrick Smith, 1988).

2. In a newspaper cartoon a father is changing a flat tire in the rain while his two children complain from the car window. The father says, "Don't you understand? This is *life*, this is what is happening. We *can't* switch to another channel."

3. Some TV stations regularly reenact true local crime events for the news, using actors to play the parts on the exact locations. They claim this is done as a public service.

4. A film star who regularly played the surgeon Colonel Potter on the TV series "M*A*S*H" appeared, wearing a doctor's white coat, in an aspirin commercial to endorse the product.

5. In the summer of 1985 the House Democratic Task Force on Agriculture brought in three Academy Award–winning actresses—Jessica Lange, star of the movie *Country*, Sissy Spacek, who portrayed a farm wife in *The River*, and Jane Fonda, who played the part of a rural woman in the movie *The Dollmaker*—to testify about the problems facing American agriculture.

6. In 1990 both the Mexican government and some U.S. Drug Enforcement Administration agents protested gross factual inaccuracies in the

Photo by John Pearson. Used with permission of the photographer.

NBC miniseries *Drug Wars: The Camarena Story*. In defense, a DEA spokesperson said, "We're not going to go through it all with a fine-tooth comb. In our view, it captures the spirit of events."

For all of us, *discerning the distinction between fiction and fact* requires more and more alertness, although at times we can be deluded into thinking the difference doesn't really matter.

FEELINGS CAN BE FACTS

Is it as important to separate feelings from facts as it is to separate facts from fiction? It is often said that we should be objective and not subjective to determine facts. Some interpret this to mean that to be subjective is to be swayed by feelings and prejudices that must be suspect and irrational. From such reasoning we can say that to be objective, we must deny or suppress any feelings that would keep us from being coolly rational or observant. Such thinking certainly expresses an ideal. But, without faking, can it be achieved?

In some situations feelings are inappropriate or irrelevant to one's purpose. A lawyer accepts her job of defending the rights of a felon, even if she personally finds the crime appalling. An ambulance attendant may flinch but nevertheless do all he can to help the victim of a freeway accident. Neither would consider their personal reactions as reasons for not doing their duty. They could harden themselves or suppress their feelings, or they could choose how to simply recognize and respect these feelings while continuing to do their jobs.

Let's look now at some circumstances in which our feelings do provide relevant information for us to communicate. Look at the picture opposite. Suppose the photo gives you a summer laid-back feeling. If you described it to someone else without mentioning this feeling, wouldn't that be omitting relevant information? And if you showed the photograph to other people and found they felt the same way, that reaction could become an agreed-upon fact for all of you. Or even if they disagreed, you could still say these feelings were a fact for you.

So when are feelings appropriate as data and under what conditions? When we are studying art, a conscious awareness of subjective reactions provides important clues for understanding a work's meaning. An artist does not state purpose directly but manipulates the viewer to experience the work, and through that experience, to understand it. An artist, like the photographers whose pictures appear in this book, may want to evoke reactions of puzzlement or distaste. Indeed, you cannot decipher these photos unless you can identify your feeling reactions as facts. In music a joyful waltz entices us to dance. The joy we feel and the desire to express that joy in movement are facts and quite appropriate, not irrelevant, reactions. To disregard that fact because it is a feeling is to miss the whole purpose of art.

In the arts, a feeling response is a reality that can be shared by many people, and its stimulation and transmission are the communication. All of us have experienced this while in movie theaters with a group of strangers all laughing or crying together. In this context, feeling is not irrational or irrelevant. When we learn through experiencing, the issue is not the polarity between objectivity and subjectivity but whether we can be *objective about feelings*. When you can clearly experience your feelings while observing them at the same time, you have a useful skill for recording, evaluating, and learning. To be subjective about feelings, on the other hand, is to be unaware of their influence on your thoughts and decisions.

FACTS ARE NOT ABSOLUTES

Facts that are most useful to us are those that have received verification from many sources and from repeated tests over time. On this planet, we don't worry about whether we'll see the sun in the east in the mornings and in the west in the evenings, and when we drop a book, we can expect it to fall to the floor. But, nevertheless, the most we can say about any fact is that it has a higher or lower probability of being certain. We feel better when we have certainties because they help us survive. The problem is that it is not always easy for us to determine what is real and true. And all this causes us a lot of confusion.

The sciences have their own way of coming to terms with this dilemma. Many statements that most people would call facts are considered *probability* statements by the sciences. If a thermometer says the temperature is 65 degrees, a scientist would say that there is a 99 percent chance that the temperature is between 62.5 and 67.5 degrees. This would take into account any inaccuracies of the instrument. *Certainty* in science usually means probability that approaches certainty.

Why are facts probabilities and not absolute certainties? For one thing, facts describe a physical universe that is eternally changing— from the invisible-to-the-eye subatomic level to obvious levels of wrinkles in our skin, the courses of rivers, the growth of children, and the motion of the sun and stars. Furthermore, facts are based on social agreements that can and do change as human knowledge evolves. For centuries the earth was considered to be the center of the universe. This belief came to be sanctioned by both scholars and clergy. As the case of Galileo shows, anyone who openly questioned this "fact" could get in serious trouble. History provides many other examples of ideas long accepted as truths (such as the notion that women and some races are inferior) that were later seen as strangely mistaken. And the future will determine that many of our most accepted ideas are mistaken as well.

All this happens because facts are human made. Facts are based on human senses and perceptions that are limited and fallible. Facts are based only on how people *interpret* the way things are.

Disagreements about facts are ongoing—not only in an advancing scientific community but also in the discourse of a healthy society. Such a society preserves the freedom to debate, the right to investigate, the license to disagree with one another's claims about "realities." Indeed, this is the only kind of society in which critical thinking can flourish. A government seeking absolute power over its citizens would suppress every stimulus to critical thinking. It would buy out the media, censor a dissident press, discourage public protests, close down schools, kill those who dissent. Critical thinking is a fragile product of civilizations that value the freedom to search for truth. For the advancement of human knowledge and welfare, we need to value the right and the kind of thinking necessary to continue to reexamine the equations made between reality and the "facts."

FACTS AND SOCIAL PRESSURE

Our senses and our perceptions are what we use to determine the correspondence between facts and reality. To test the accuracy of our perceptions, we need confirmation from other sources. For instance, if we feel warm and dizzy, we might ask a friend to put a hand on our forehead and tell us if our forehead feels feverish. If we have a thermometer, we can verify our temperature more certainly by a reading over 100 degrees. Often verifications cannot be done with the objectivity of instruments, yet we need them for psychological certainty or for what might be called social agreements. In the following exchanges consider how confirmations of perceptions are requested and needed to establish something's factuality.

1. JOHN: "Tell me, am I asleep or awake?"
   MARY: "You are awake."
2. BILL: "Did that woman make a pass at me or did I imagine it?"
   JANE: "She made a pass, alright."
3. EMILY: "I think this suit is too large for me. What do you think?"
   MAY: "Much too large."
4. VERNA: "My checking account balances."
   NORMA: "My figures show you are correct."
5. JOSE: "I was hurt by what you said."
   WANDA: "I can see that on your face."

In each of these examples, a personal examination of senses and perceptions was not enough to determine what was real. To test their accuracy, confirmation was needed from other sources.

To understand how the principle works, ask yourself how you feel after someone verifies your experience. And how do you feel when they do not?

6. JOSE: "I didn't have too much to drink last night."
   WANDA: "Yes, you did! You were drunk!"
7. CHILD: "I don't want to eat my carrots. They taste icky."
   PARENT: "Yes, you do want to eat them. You are just imagining things. They taste good."

As these examples illustrate, a perception becomes a fact when we can get another person to agree with our perception. And receiving this confirmation makes us feel good, while not receiving it can make us angry, uncomfortable, self-doubting, even crazy. Disagreements about perception can be settled by various arbiters: an umpire in a game, a speedometer in a car, or a thermometer on the wall. But in matters where there are no such instruments, our need for confirmation can make us vulnerable to manip- ulation. This was demonstrated by American psychologist Solomon Asch, who conducted some simple experiments to test how a group could affect the perceptions of an individual. He found that in a small group, people are willing to deny the evidence of their own senses if the other members of the group interpret reality differently.

In one experiment, Asch assembled groups of seven to nine college students in what was described as a test of visual judgment. In each group, only one of the students was actually a subject in the experiment; the others were the researcher's secret accomplices. The researcher informed the stu- dents that they would be comparing the lengths of lines. He showed them two white cards. On the first was a single vertical black line—the standard whose length was to be matched. On the second white card were vertical lines of various lengths. The subjects were to choose the one line of the same length as the standard line (see Figure 3.1).

A series of eighteen trials was conducted. When the first pair of cards was presented, the group gave a unanimous judgment. The same thing happened on the second trial. In twelve of the remaining sixteen trials, however, all of Asch's accomplices agreed on what was clearly an incorrect answer. The real subject of the experiment was left to react.

In about a third of the cases, the subject yielded to the majority and conformed to its decision. In separate experiments with a control group consisting of only genuine subjects, Asch found that people made mistakes less than 1 percent of the time. Subsequent interviews with those who yielded to the majority revealed that only a few of them had actually be- lieved that the majority choice was correct. They admitted that they thought they had judged the length of the lines correctly but did not want to "rock the boat" or "spoil the results" by giving the right answer. And then there were those who had doubted their own perceptions and had con- cluded that they had better hide this from the others. The test made a significant demonstration of the power of consensus to bring about con- formity and to make a person invalidate his or her own perception.*

Class Discussion

1. Why did a third of the subjects in Asch's experiments conform to the incorrect majority even when their perceptions told them they were correct?

*Figure and text adapted from Solomon Asch, "Effects of Group Pressure upon Modification and Distortion of Judgments," in H. Proshansky and B. Seidenberg (eds.), *Basic Studies in Social Psychology* (New York: Holt, Rinehart & Winston, 1965), pp. 393–401. Used with permission of CBS College Publishing.

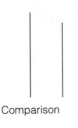

Figure 3.1 Standard and Comparison Lines in the Asch Experiment

2. Did these subjects have any other means of judging the correctness of their perceptions than from the others in the group?

3. If group pressure can affect us this much in such a simple problem as determining the relative length of a line, what do you think are the implications in more complex problems such as public opinion on controversial issues?

4. If you are familiar with the story "The Emperor's New Clothes," what parallels do you see between its theme and Asch's experiment?

FACTS AND OUR LIMITED SENSES

We have seen how consensus and conformity influence perception and thus limit our ability to know the facts. But even aside from the influence of social pressure, we are limited in our ability to know the facts because our human senses are limited. We now know that dogs can hear levels of pitch that we cannot and that butterflies can see colors invisible to us. If we look at a chart of the electromagnetic spectrum, the portion visible to us is only a tiny slit in the whole band. We have to use instruments—X rays, radar, the seismograph, smoke detectors—to compensate for our sense limitations.

But aside from all this, our senses are affected by many other variables such as mental preoccupations, distractions, or our varying degrees of alertness in different circumstances. How much do you actually see on your commute route? How much attention do you pay to background sounds when you live in the city? Has a friend ever complained you didn't notice when he shaved off his beard?

Another human failing is that we interpret what we perceive on the basis of our experience. And this experience may be too narrow and limited to embrace what lies before us. The Buddha once succinctly illustrated this point and more in the following short parable.

Reading

THE BLIND MEN AND THE ELEPHANT

Once upon a time a king gathered some blind men about an elephant and asked them to tell him what an elephant was like. The first man felt a tusk and said an elephant was like a giant carrot; another happened to touch an ear and said it was like a big fan; another touched its trunk and said it was like a pestle; still another, who happened to feel its leg, said it was like a mortar; and another, who grasped its tail, said it was like a rope. Not one of them was able to tell the king the elephant's real form.

Study Questions

1. What do you think the elephant represents?
2. Why did each of the blind men think in terms of comparisons?
3. What was wrong with their comparisons?
4. Can you think of examples in your life where you could not experience something new because you were comparing it to something familiar?

STATEMENTS OF FACT

As the preceding sections have demonstrated, some facts are not easily determined. And what makes a fact can also depend upon the language used to state it. There is a considerable difference between saying, "There is a male football player in this photograph" and "I see the rear of an individual dressed in a football uniform in this photograph." The first statement makes assumptions about sex and sport activity that are probable but not necessarily factual. The second statement uses language that reflects the limitations of certainty.

When we make statements of fact, our language needs to be quite specific and on guard against assumptions. This does not mean we must use tentative language all the time. But if we are stating facts, our language makes a difference.

Study the photograph on page 87. Then read the following statements, and notice how those in italics differ from those in regular type.

1. *This is a lone football player.*

    Prominent in the center of this black-and-white photograph is a rear view of an individual wearing smooth white knee-length pants and a

Photo by John Pearson. Used with permission of the photographer.

dark jersey. The texture of bare skin can be seen below the elbows and calves. A white mop-like covering hides the back of the head; its spaghetti strands hang down over the person's shoulders and back. A light-colored padding, suggestive of leather because of its smoothness and solidity, lies beneath these strands. The padding extends over the scapula and into flaps over the shoulders. From midback to the waist appears a single white vertical line on a horizontal base that suggests the letters *T* or *I*. This is the dress usually worn as a football uniform. From this view it is not possible to guess whether this person is male or female, but I will assume male.

2. *He is acting like a clown on roller skates.*

He is wearing high white socks and high-top shoes with small wheel shapes visible beneath each. The left leg extends back, raised at an angle. The right leg is bent forward at the knee, and the foot is parallel to the surface. In the whole body, no bulge of fat or muscle is visible. The left arm is swinging outward, and a dark triangular shape extended from the hand resembles a swimming flipper. The right elbow appears to be close to the torso; extending from the fist is a dark rod connected to an oval gray canopy that resembles an umbrella.

3. *He is trying to catch up with the school bus.*

On the far right of the photo, parallel with the man's head and torso, is a large white-domed square. Below it are dark perpendicular curves suggesting tires. Across the white shape's upper part extends a dark rectangle interrupted by two white vertical lines. The black material has the reflective translucent quality of windows. The whole shape is reminiscent of a school bus.

4. *He is in a parade in New York City.*

The central figure is perpendicular to a plane of gray diagonals with one thin white diagonal between them. This surface also contains a random arrangement of larger white squares and tiny white rectangles that resemble pieces of paper and confetti. To his left and in front of the figure, extending through the top of the picture, horizontal and vertical lines are suggestive of office building floors and windows. To the left of the skater at the lower perimeter of one dark rectangular building are white blobs and vertical lines, suggesting the heads, chests, arms, and legs of four standing individuals. Three of these blobs appear beneath a prominent white number, 7000.

As you probably have guessed, the statements in regular type are statements of fact, while the italicized sentences are interpretations of these facts, or inferences. Given the information available, they may or may not be reliable. From looking at this photograph alone we cannot tell if the figure is male, lone, or a football player, whether he is acting like a clown, trying to catch up with the bus, or in New York City.

The factual statements in regular type, on the other hand, have the following characteristics:

1. Factual statements show an awareness of the limitations of the data under consideration. If a photo is being described, the writer does not forget this is not a life situation where one can see all angles or ask questions.

   "From this view it is not possible to guess whether this person is male or female, but I will assume male."

2. Factual statements use appropriate qualifiers to indicate uncertainties, such as the words and phrases *probably, generally, may, might, possibly, suggest, likely, it seems to be, there's a chance that, it could be*.

   "white blobs and vertical lines, suggesting the heads, chests, arms, and legs of three standing individuals."

3. Factual statements state the obvious.

   "black-and-white photograph"

4. Factual statements show a disciplined effort to describe what is present and restrain the impulse to jump to conclusions.

   "a dark triangular shape . . . resembles a swimming flipper."

5. Factual statements are not inappropriately cautious, such as to say

   "This individual *appears* to have arms and legs."

6. Factual statements do not make guesses expressed as though they were certainties.

   "He is in a parade in New York City."

7. Factual statements provide specific details that others can verify.

   "The central figure is perpendicular to a plane of gray diagonals"

8. Factual statements are willing to be dull in the name of accuracy rather than exciting in the name of possibility.

   "the foot is parallel to the surface"

9. Factual statements do not confuse inferences with facts.

   "He is trying to catch up with the school bus."

Class Discussion

1. Do the detailed statements resemble police reports? Why are police taught to write like this?

2. If you were on a jury, how could it be useful to know the difference between factual statements and claims that are interpretations of data?

3. Why would it be important to know the difference if you were an attorney or judge, a witness, a defendant?

4. Why would a reporter be concerned with the difference between facts and interpretations?

5. Why would the difference matter to (a) a doctor, (b) a car mechanic, (c) a biologist, (d) a pharmacist?

CORE DISCOVERY WRITING APPLICATION

Using a List of Facts to Describe a Photograph

This is an exercise that challenges your mental and verbal awareness. Its task seems simple: to describe a photograph by making a list of at least ten factual statements about it. This exercise is best done by the whole class first, working together on one photograph. Then small groups can work with other photographs.

1. Choose one photograph from this book for your group to study that has not already been described by the author. Each person should work quietly alone, then discuss his or her effort when everyone is finished. Spend some time absorbing the photograph, then take notes. Imagine that you are writing for someone who cannot see the photograph. Be as specific and detailed as you can, even about the picture's most obvious aspects. Be on guard against jumping to conclusions. Stay with your evidence. Arrange your list in some kind of logical order. (Don't jump around from the background to a person's clothes to another's hair.)

2. Write out your list of ten or more factual statements. Then compare your list with others in your group who worked on the same picture. How do you agree or differ about the facts you found? Star the facts you can agree upon.

Scoring for Using a List of Facts to Describe a Photograph

1. Obvious details not ignored.	20 points
2. Things are described, not just labeled. (To say "bus" is not to describe the evidence of the clues you actually see; besides, this label could be a mistaken inference.)	20 points
3. Facts are stated in at least 10 sentences.	10 points
4. Inferences are not stated.	30 points

5. Systematic presentation of data.   10 points

6. No distracting errors of spelling,   10 points
   punctuation, sentence structure.

STANDARDS WE USE
TO DETERMINE FACTS

A fundamental task of critical thinking is determining the facts in a given situation. Such a situation may involve practical problems like proving you have paid a bill, or it may involve intricate forms of investigation in a field like business, science, or politics. In the course of time, standards have been developed to help us determine the facts and how reliable they might be. When we think critically, we know and use these traditional standards, many of which have already been mentioned in this chapter. In review, let's look at four of them: verifiability, reliability, plausibility, and probability.

Verifiability means the data can be confirmed by another source. This source can be a reference source (like a dictionary), a record (like a marriage license), or a standard (like Greenwich mean time). Another source could be the testimony of a witness or of an expert. Data can be verified by the senses, by agreements, by measurements, or by documentation.

A second standard for determining facts is *reliability*. When we obtain agreements or disagreements about facts, we have to consider their degree of dependability. To do this we have to ask some critical questions. Is the witness biased? Do we need a larger survey? Were the senses used carefully and consciously? Were they adequate to the task? Were the measurements accurate? Were the documents genuine?

Another standard used to determine reliability is the test of time and repetition (probability). If the weather pattern in one region alters radically over a period of several years, this phenomenon of change becomes a fact. If things always drop when they fall on this planet, gravity remains a fact. Still another standard test for reliability is to consider whether a given fact confirms or contradicts other known facts (plausibility). If a person claims to be over twenty-one, whereas his ID and birth certificate show he is now eighteen, this contradiction calls into question his statement. The same can be said of a senator who claims to support a particular issue but whose voting record demonstrates no support at all.

PROBLEM SOLVING

FACTS

Norman Cousins had what his doctors called an incurable illness; he decided to apply to himself the old saying "Laughter is the best medicine." He rented some old Charlie Chaplin movies and found that ten minutes of solid belly laughter could give him two hours of sleep free of pain from severe spine and joint inflammation.

  In 1976, after he was healed, he wrote a book about his experience called *Anatomy of an Illness*. In 1989 Cousins was informed by the American Medical Association that his discovery that laughter helps combat serious illness was indeed a fact. Intervening research has confirmed his findings. Laughter therapy is now used in cancer wards in Houston, Texas, and Durham, North Carolina.

Questions

1. What was Cousins's problem?
2. How did he solve his problem?
3. How did his solution help others?

From "Proving the Power of Laughter," *Psychology Today*, October 1989.

  The standards of *plausibility* and *probability* are familiar ones that we all use but may not always recognize as standards. It does not seem plausible or probable that a person is actually twenty-one if he offers up an ID that says he is eighteen. For facts to be accepted, they have to make sense to us or seem to be the most likely possibility.

CHAPTER SUMMARY

1. By definition, a fact is something known with certainty through experience, observation, or measurement. A fact can be objectively demonstrated and verified. A fact depends on other sources to agree that it corresponds to reality.

2. It is not easy for us to determine whether facts correspond to reality. This can only be determined over time with repeated feedback and testing.

3. We need to be alert to discern facts from fiction.

BUILDING ARGUMENTS

USING FACTS

One powerful form of argument is to let the facts speak for themselves in support of a principal claim or purpose. Notice how this is done in the words of a Blackfoot woman who explains in 1835 why she left her husband to live with a white trapper.

I was the wife of a Blackfoot warrior, and I served him faithfully. (principal claim) *I brought wood in the morning, and placed water always at hand. I watched for his coming; and he found his food cooked and waiting. If he rose to go forth there was nothing to delay him. I searched the thought that was in his heart, to save him the trouble of speaking. When I went abroad on errands for him, the chiefs and warriors smiled upon me, the braves spoke soft things, in secret; but my feet were in the straight path, and my eyes could see nothing but him.*

When he went out to hunt, or to war, who aided to equip him but I? When he returned I met him at the door; I took his gun; and he entered without further thought. When he sat and smoked, I unloaded his horses; tied them to stakes, brought in their loads, and was quickly at his feet. If his moccasins were wet I took them off and put on others which were warm and dry. I dressed all the skins that were taken in the chase. . . . I served him faithfully; and what was my reward? A cloud was always on his brow, and sharp lightning on his tongue. I was his dog; and not his wife. Who was it scarred and bruised me? It was he.

Exercise

1. Put into words the principal claim the Blackfoot woman suggests but does not articulate. (This is called an implicit conclusion.) What factual claims does she use to support it?
2. Compose an argument in which you state two paragraphs of facts that speak compellingly to support a conclusion.

4. Feelings can be facts. Feelings about art can offer us clues to the artist's intentions.

5. Facts are not absolutes but statements of probability.

6. Because we are dependent on confirmation from others in our search for facts, we are susceptible to distorting our perceptions as a result of social pressure.

7. Our senses are limited both in range and capacity and are affected by many factors, such as selective focus and mental preoccupations.

8. Facts must be expressed in carefully formulated statements that have the following characteristics:
    (a) They define their own limitations.
    (b) They are objectively stated.
    (c) They use appropriate qualifiers.
    (d) They state the obvious.
    (e) They are not inappropriately cautious.
    (f) They do not include guesses or inferences.
    (g) They are specific and offer their evidence for others to verify.

9. The standards traditionally used to determine facts are verifiability, reliability, plausibility, and probability. Facts have to undergo the test of time and repetition and not contradict other known facts.

CHAPTER QUIZ

Rate each of the following statements as *true* or *false*. In class discussion or in writing, give an example to substantiate your answer in each case.

_____ 1. Some facts can be determined by measurements.

_____ 2. Some facts can be confirmed by the senses, others by records.

_____ 3. The most reliable facts are those that have been repeatedly confirmed by tests over time.

_____ 4. Facts often consist of obvious details that are seen but not consciously recognized.

_____ 5. Sometimes what we claim to be facts are untrue because the human perceptions used to determine them are limited and fallible.

_____ 6. A person educated in critical thinking qualifies statements to reflect probabilities and uncertainties using provisional phrases such as "it appears that . . ."

_____ 7. Often it is hard to make a decision because we do not have enough facts.

_____ 8. The study of many subjects consists of memorizing facts, because they are the nearest thing we have to certainties.

_____ 9. All newspapers can be depended upon as reliable sources of facts about world events.

_____ 10. An atmosphere that permits disagreements about widely accepted perceptions and beliefs helps critical thinking to flourish.

Composition Writing Application

Writing a Short Fact-Finding Report

First Option

Select a topic—such as choosing a college or choosing a car—for a fact-finding report. Imagine that you have narrowed your choice to two candidates. Make a list of the most essential needs you have to consider. Then make a list of the facts you have, or what verified information you have, about each candidate. For instance:

Needs	Facts: Ravenwood	Facts: Greenspan
a college in my hometown	in town	in suburbs
low tuition	free	free
evening classes	yes	yes
accreditation	don't know (need to see catalogue)	yes

Put all this information into a composition of one coherent paragraph (*coherent* means clear, logically connected, and consistent in a manner that is easy for the reader to follow). Begin with a sentence that sums up the decision you made (or didn't make). This is known as your topic sentence. Everything that follows in your paragraph should support that statement with the information you discovered through your research and your comparisons. Your last sentence or sentences in this paragraph should make a summary statement that brings all this information together.

Here is a summary of the parameters:

1. *Objective*: To write a simple report about using facts to make a personal decision involving at least two choices.
2. *Form and length*: The equivalent of one typed page.
3. *Structure*: Begin with a topic sentence and end with a summary statement. On another sheet of paper, attach your list of essential needs and your list of facts regarding each candidate for your choice.
4. *Suggested topics*:
    (a) Choosing a college
    (b) Choosing a car
    (c) Choosing a friend
    (d) Choosing a computer

   (e) Choosing a job
   (f) Choosing a career

Student Writing Example

CHOOSING A HAMBURGER

Russell Matulich

Needs:	Facts: McDonald's	Facts: Burger King	Facts: Wendy's
Cheeseburger	yes	yes	yes
Fresh taste	not always	yes	yes
Nearby	yes	yes	yes
Lettuce & tomato	no	yes	yes
Stomachache afterward	yes	no	no
Greasy tasting	yes	no	yes
Onion rings available	no	yes	no
Chocolate shake	yes	yes	yes
Crisp fries	yes	yes	no
Too much salt	yes	yes	yes
Cost	$4.15	$4.34*	$4.06

*Burger King cost includes onion rings, while the others include medium fries since no onion rings were available.

I am in search of a good-quality burger meal tonight. The top three suspects are out there—McDonald's, Burger King, and Wendy's—and they are all within a few minutes' drive. While they all have decent-tasting delicacies, the McDee's burger brings a slight shudder to my stomach. Now I remember the gross contortions my stomach makes almost exactly 30 minutes after the McDee's burger is consumed. Not only that, but there are no onion rings to complement my burger enjoyment—McDonald's is out!

   Now Burger King's (BK's) Whopper with cheese is substantial. It's quite tasty and the vegetables are always fresh as far as I can remember. BK also has onion rings to complement the burger experience. Not only that but BK makes a decent shake; it's nothing to write home about, mind you, but it can wash those wandering onion rings down the esophagus. But Wendy's does make a good burger, too. While this is true, it has happened more than once that their burgers were a tad on the greasy side. Besides that the fries are too large and uncrisp. But while it is true they do have the best shake out of the three competitors, I am focusing on the food itself.

So since a good quality burger with onion rings is what I am after, I must choose Burger King. One can't deny the facts!

Used with permission of Russell Matulich.

Second Option

Think of a problem that was solved through an investigation and verification of the facts. This could be a case of injustice, a mysterious illness affecting a community, an unexpected business loss, a miscommunication between people or nations, or an investment decision. Find a problem that interests you for the writing of a simple report on the subject.

1. Describe the problem.
2. Describe each stage of the investigation and verification of the facts involved. Describe where you got your facts.
3. Describe the final outcome—how an ascertainment or application of the facts helped solve the problem.
4. Follow the parameters for form, length, and structure listed under First Option.

Student Writing Example

A PROBLEM SOLVED BY FACTS

Anthony Choy

I am an auto mechanic; a large part of my job requires skills in observing, investigating, and determining facts. Often people bring in cars with problems they can't identify, much less repair. In such cases, they hire me to get the facts. And the final test of whether or not I got the facts right is a car that runs right. Let me illustrate this with a story.

One day a customer brought in a 1977 Ford Pinto. His complaint was about the awful noise in his V-6 engine, which was louder when it revved high and quieter when it revved low. I began my inspection by locating the noise at the front of the engine area. I checked the alternator, water pump, valve adjustment, cam gears. Nothing was out of the ordinary. I was stumped.

I then removed the timing chain cover. I noticed there was a gear-to-gear system that is known to make a racket, but nothing comparable to the sound this engine was producing. Again the gears checked out okay. I was stumped again.

Then I started looking at the obvious. I retraced my diagnosing steps to study the engine some more. I noticed an excessive amount of silicone on the oil pan gasket where the bottom of the timing chain cover meets the oil pan. I noticed some broken gears inside the oil pan. I wondered: "Why didn't the last mechanic take care of this?"

I examined the gears again and noticed how hard it was to remove the crank gear. The only way to remove that gear would be to remove the oil pan by lifting the engine off its mounts first. I realized then that the last mechanic who replaced the cam and crank gears did not do the job correctly: if the mechanic had removed the gears, there would not have been an excessive amount of silicone on the oil pan gasket. The gasket had not been replaced, otherwise the broken pieces in the oil pan would have been cleaned out. Why did the mechanic omit doing this? I realized it was probably because he or she could not figure out how to remove the oil pan.

Well, I replaced the parts and proceeded to repair the vehicle the way I was taught. I started up the engine, checked for leaks, and there were none. Then I revved the engine high for a moment and left it at idle, and the noise was completely gone. It purred like a kitten. I felt good to have corrected the problem. When my customer returned, he shook my hand and gave me a bonus.

Used with permission of Anthony Choy.

Readings

THE ACCIDENT AND AFTERMATH

Hayden Herrera

"I made two terrible mistakes in my life: the one was a bus accident and the other was Diego Rivera." Thus did Frida Kahlo, a Mexican artist of great charismatic beauty, sum up her life. Her writing and paintings had a lot to say about these two events: the first was a disaster suffered at age eighteen that left her crippled, and the second was her stormy marriage to Diego Rivera, the most famous Mexican muralist of this century. This reading selection describes her first "mistake"—the bus accident. Although the trauma would seem to have been so terrible as to be unconfrontable, through its telling and retelling, Kahlo achieved a measure of transcendence over its impact. In the years that followed, she managed to lead a highly creative life. Her own healing seemed to have begun with simply confronting the reality of the facts.

It was one of those accidents that make a person, even one separated by years from   1
the actual fact, wince with horror. It involved a trolley car that plowed into a flimsy
wooden bus, and it transformed Frida Kahlo's life.

Far from being a unique piece of bad luck, such accidents were common   2
enough in those days in Mexico City to be depicted in numerous *retablos*. (Small
votive paintings offering thanks to a holy being, usually the Virgin, for misfortunes
escaped.) Buses were relatively new to the city, and because of their novelty they
were jammed with people while trolley cars went empty. Then, as now, they were
driven with toreador bravado, as if the image of the Virgin of Guadalupe dangling
near the front window made the driver invincible. The bus in which Frida was riding
was new, and its fresh coat of paint made it look especially jaunty.

The accident occurred late in the afternoon on September 17, 1925, the day   3
after Mexico had celebrated the anniversary of its independence from Spain. A light
rain had just stopped; the grand gray government buildings that border the Zócalo
looked even grayer and more severe than usual. The bus to Coyoacán was nearly
full, but Alejandro [Frida's boyfriend] and Frida found seats together in the back.
When they reached the corner of Cuahutemotzín and 5 de Mayo and were about
to turn onto Calzada de Tlalpan, a trolley from Xochimilco approached. It was
moving slowly but kept coming as if it had no brakes, as if it were purposely aiming
at a crash. Frida remembered:

> A little while after we got on the bus the collision began. Before that we had taken
> another bus, but since I had lost a little parasol, we got off to look for it and that
> was how we happened to get on the bus that destroyed me. The accident took
> place on a corner in front of the San Juan market, exactly in front. The streetcar
> went slowly, but our bus driver was a very nervous young man. When the trolley
> car went around the corner the bus was pushed against the wall.
>
> I was an intelligent young girl, but impractical, in spite of all the freedom I had
> won. Perhaps for this reason, I did not assess the situation nor did I guess the kind of
> wounds I had. The first thing I thought of was a *balero* [Mexican toy] with pretty
> colors that I had bought that day and that I was carrying with me. I tried to look for
> it, thinking that what had happened would not have major consequences.
>
> It is a lie that one is aware of the crash, a lie that one cries. In me there were no
> tears. The crash bounced us forward and a handrail pierced me the way a sword
> pierces a bull. A man saw me having a tremendous hemorrhage. He carried me and
> put me on a billiard table until the Red Cross came for me.

When Alejandro Gómez Arias describes the accident, his voice constricts to an   4
almost inaudible monotone, as if he could avoid reliving the memory by speaking
of it quietly:

"The electric train with two cars approached the bus slowly. It hit the bus in   5
the middle. Slowly the train pushed the bus. The bus had a strange elasticity. It
bent more and more, but for a time it did not break. It was a bus with long benches
on either side. I remember that at one moment my knees touched the knees of the
person sitting opposite me, I was sitting next to Frida. When the bus reached its
maximal flexibility it burst into a thousand pieces, and the train kept moving. It ran
over many people.

"I remained under the train. Not Frida. But among the iron rods of the train, 6 the handrail broke and went through Frida from one side to the other at the level of the pelvis. When I was able to stand up I got out from under the train. I had no lesions, only contusions. Naturally the first thing that I did was to look for Frida.

"Something strange had happened. Frida was totally nude. The collision had 7 unfastened her clothes. Someone in the bus, probably a house painter, had been carrying a packet of powdered gold. This package broke, and the gold fell all over the bleeding body of Frida. When people saw her they cried, '*La bailarina, la bailarina!*' With the gold on her red, bloody body, they thought she was a dancer.

"I picked her up—in those days I was a strong boy—and then I noticed with 8 horror that Frida had a piece of iron in her body. A man said, 'We have to take it out!' He put his knee on Frida's body, and said, 'Let's take it out.' When he pulled it out, Frida screamed so loud that when the ambulance from the Red Cross arrived, her screaming was louder than the siren. Before the ambulance came, I picked up Frida and put her in the display window of a billiard room. I took off my coat and put it over her. I thought she was going to die. Two or three people did die at the scene of the accident, others died later.

"The ambulance came and took her to the Red Cross Hospital, which in those 9 days was on San Jeronimo Street, a few blocks from where the accident took place. Frida's condition was so grave that the doctors did not think they could save her. They thought she would die on the operating table.

"Frida was operated on for the first time. During the first month it was not 10 certain that she would live."

The girl whose wild dash through school corridors resembled a bird's flight, 11 who jumped on and off streetcars and buses, preferably when they were moving, was now immobilized and enclosed in a series of plaster casts and other contraptions. "It was a strange collision," Frida said. "It was not violent but rather silent, slow, and it harmed everybody. And me most of all."

Her spinal column was broken in three places in the lumbar region. Her collar- 12 bone was broken, and her third and fourth ribs. Her right leg had eleven fractures and her right foot was dislocated and crushed. Her left shoulder was out of joint, her pelvis broken in three places. The steel handrail had literally skewered her body at the level of the abdomen; entering on the left side, it had come out through the vagina. "I lost my virginity," she said.

From Hayden Herrera, *Frida: A Biography of Frida Kahlo*. New York: Harper & Row, 1983. Copyright © 1983 by Hayden Herrera. Reprinted with permission of HarperCollins Publishers, Inc.

Study Question

1. This excerpt gives two observers' accounts of the bus accident—its impact and aftermath. Compare and contrast the details given from the two viewpoints. How do you account for their different assessment of the most important facts?

SHADOWS ON THE WALL

Donna Woolfolk Cross

This reading is taken from the last chapter in a book about the way television affects our minds. Donna Woolfolk Cross has been a professor of English in upstate New York.*

> *I see no virtue in having a public that cannot distinguish fact from fantasy. When you start thinking fantasy is reality you have a serious problem. People can be stampeded into all kinds of fanaticism, folly and warfare.*
>
> –Isaac Asimov
>
> *Why sometimes I've believed as many as six impossible things before breakfast.*
>
> –Queen to Alice in Lewis Carroll's *Through the Looking Glass*

In Book Four of *The Republic*, Plato tells a story about four prisoners who since birth 1 have been chained inside a cave, totally isolated from the world outside. They face a wall on which shadows flicker, cast by the light of the fire. The flickering shadows are the only reality they know. Finally, one of the prisoners is released and permitted to leave the cave. Once outside, he realizes that the shadows he has watched for so long are only pale, distorted reflections of a much brighter, better world. He returns to tell the others about the world outside the cave. They listen in disbelief, then in anger, for what he says contradicts all they have known. Unable to accept the truth, they cast him out as a heretic.

Today, our picture of the world is formed in great part from television's flicker- 2 ing shadows. Sometimes that picture is a fairly accurate reflection of the real world; sometimes it is not. But either way, we accept it as real and we act upon it as if it were reality itself. "And that's the way it is," Walter Cronkite assured us every evening for over nineteen years, and most of us did not doubt it.

A generation of Americans has grown up so dependent on television that its 3 images appear as real to them as life itself. On a recent trip to a widely advertised amusement park, my husband, daughter, and I rode a "white-water" raft through manufactured "rapids." As we spun and screamed and got thoroughly soaked, I noticed that the two young boys who shared our raft appeared rather glum. When the ride ended, I heard one remark to the other, "It's more fun on television."

As an experiment, Jerzy Kosinski gathered a group of children, aged seven to 4 ten years, into a room to show them some televised film. Before the show began, he announced, "Those who want to stay inside and watch the films are free to remain in the classroom, but there's something fascinating happening in the corridor, and those who want to see it are free to leave the room." Kosinski describes what happened next:

---

*Notes to the original reading have not been included here.

No more than 10 percent of the children left. I repeated, "You know, what's outside is really fantastic. You have never seen it before. Why don't you just step out and take a look?"

And they always said, "No, no, no, we prefer to stay here and watch the film." I'd say, "But you don't know what's outside." "Well, what is it?" they'd ask. "You have to go find out." And they'd say, "Why don't we just sit here and see the film first?" . . . They were already too corrupted to take a chance on the outside.

In another experiment, Kosinski brought a group of children into a room with two giant video screens mounted on the side walls. He stood in the front of the room and began to tell them a story. Suddenly, as part of a prearranged plan, a man entered and pretended to attack Kosinski, yelling at him and hitting him. The entire episode was shown on the two video screens as it happened. The children did not respond, but merely watched the episode unfold on the video screens. They rarely glanced at the two men struggling in the front of the room. Later, in an interview with Kosinski, they explained that the video screens captured the event much more satisfactorily, providing close-ups of the participants, their expressions, and such details as the attacker's hand on Kosinski's face.

Some children can become so preoccupied with television that they are oblivious to the real world around them. UPI filed a report on a burglar who broke into a home and killed the father of three children, aged nine, eleven, and twelve. The crime went unnoticed until ten hours later, when police entered the apartment after being called by neighbors and found the three children watching television just a few feet away from the bloody corpse of their father.

Shortly after this report was released, the University of Nebraska conducted a national survey in which children were asked which they would keep if they had to choose—their fathers or their television sets. *Over half* chose the television sets!

Evidence of this confusion between reality and illusion grows daily. Trial lawyers, for example, complain that juries have become conditioned to the formulas of televised courtroom dramas.

Former Bronx District Attorney Mario Merola says, "All they want is drama, suspense—a confession. Never in all my years as a prosecutor have I seen someone cry from the witness stand, 'I did it! I did it—I confess!' But that's what happens on prime-time TV—and that's what the jurors think the court system is all about." He adds, "Such misconceptions make the work of a district attorney's office much harder than it needs to be." Robert Daley describes one actual courtroom scene in which the defendant was subjected to harsh and unrelenting cross-examination: "I watched the jury," he says. "It seemed to me that I had seen this scene before, and indeed I had dozens of times—on television. On television the murderer always cracks eventually and says something like 'I can't take it any more.' He suddenly breaks down blubbering and admits his guilt. But this defendant did not break down, he did not admit his guilt. He did not blubber. It seemed to me I could see the jury conclude before my eyes: ergo, he cannot be guilty—and indeed the trial ended in a hung jury. . . . Later I lay in bed in the dark and brooded about the trial. . . . If [television courtroom dramas] had never existed, would the jury have found the defendant guilty even though he did not crack?"

Study Questions

1. This reading begins with an analogy. What is it?
2. What does the author seek to prove in the examples describing the behavior of the children, in Kosinski's experiments as well as in the two other reports?
3. How do the customary expectations about jury trials derived from watching television dramas seem to affect actual jurors?

For Further Reading

Ash, Russell. *The Top 10 of Everything 1996*. New York: Dorling Kindersley, 1995.

Berman, Sanford I. *Why Do We Jump to Conclusions?* San Francisco: International Society for General Semantics, 1969.

Milgram, Stanley. *Obedience to Authority*. New York: Harper Torchbooks, 1974.

Mitroff, Ian I., and Warren Bennis. *The Unreality Industry*. New York: Oxford University Press, 1989.

Ornstein, Robert, and Paul Ehrlich. *New World, New Mind*. New York: Touchstone, 1989.

CHAPTER 4

Inferences: What Follows?

"Dump all my shares of Peabody and Fenner!"

From *I Paint What I See*. Copyright © 1971 by Gahan
Wilson. Used with permission of Simon & Schuster, Inc.

Maybe the man on the phone in this cartoon is right in inferring
that news of financial ruin is causing everyone at Peabody and
Fenner to jump out of the windows. And maybe his second inference is also correct, that he had better dump all his stock there. But what if
it's a fire?

We can be excellent observers, we can have a set of facts plainly before
us, and we can still err in our judgment about a situation if we're not careful
about our inferences. For inferences are shakier ground than facts when it
comes to building a solid structure of critical thinking. Still, inferences can
be useful tools in the thinking process if we learn to wield them skillfully.
This chapter is dedicated to helping you do just that.

We begin by learning to distinguish inferences from facts and then consider how inferences can be used skillfully. We then practice drawing inferences from facts. We conclude by learning to combine facts, inferences, and
generalizations to create an effective piece of descriptive writing.

Discovery Exercises

Recognizing Inferential Thinking

Study the cartoons on pages 106–107. What kind of thinking is going on in the cartoons? How does the humor relate to this kind of thinking? What kind of thinking did you have to do in order to understand the cartoons?

Defining *Infer*

After consulting at least two dictionaries, write down your own definitions of the following words:

1. reasoning
2. conclusion
3. guess
4. explanation
5. imagine
6. infer
7. inference
8. interpret

UNDERSTANDING THE WORDS
INFER AND *INFERENCE*

Did your study of *infer* reveal that it comes from the Latin root *inferre*, meaning to bring in or to carry? When we infer, we bring in our imagination or reasoning power to explain something. When we infer, we make a guess; we seek explanations to bridge what we know with what we don't know.

When we make an inference, we draw conclusions from *evidence* or premises. A statement that reasons from evidence would be: "It was easy to infer the child was happy because she was jumping up and down." An inference can also be a conclusion drawn from premises or from a logical progression of statements that leads to a conclusion: "All children who jump up and down are happy. This child is jumping up and down. Therefore she is happy."

We can also use the word *infer* as a synonym for the word *conclude*, as in this example: "After he had dozed off at the wheel once, he inferred he shouldn't travel any more that day without more sleep." The word *infer* is

From *I Paint What I See*. Copyright © 1971 by Gahan Wilson. Used with permission of Simon & Schuster, Inc.

also used as a synonym for *guess, speculate, surmise*: "I inferred he liked me when he asked me to dance."

Sometimes the word *infer* is used incorrectly to mean imply, hint, or suggest: "He inferred that I didn't have to wait in line if I wanted to tip him."

"If I'm right in my guess that this is the Atlantic, then we're the biggest fish in the world."
Used with permission of Richard Guindon.

This use of *infer* for *imply* is what linguists call a *solecism*, or a use of the word that is nonstandard. In this text the word *infer* is *never* used in the sense of imply, hint, or suggest.

Discovery Exercises

Drawing Inferences from Evidence

Read the following scenarios and think of three inferences you could make to explain each situation:

1. Your neighbors have regular habits and spend a lot of time at home. One day you notice that no lights have been on in their house in the evenings for at least a week.

2. In an airport waiting room, you sit down next to a nun wearing a dark blue dress, starched white collar, and starched white headdress. You notice she is reading *Playboy* magazine.

3. Your child, age four, who usually has a good appetite, says no this morning when you offer her a dish of applesauce.

4. You are on a Greyhound bus. A man gets on and sits beside you. He is carrying an expensive briefcase although he is shabbily dressed,

unshaven, and perspiring heavily. When you suggest he place his briefcase on the rack overhead, he refuses, saying he doesn't mind holding it in his lap.

5. You are looking in your wife's closet for your missing shoe, and you notice a new and expensive man's sports jacket hanging there.

6. After a class you go to see your professor about an error in addition on your test score. You explain to him respectfully that 100 minus 18 is 82, not 79. He tells you to get the hell out of his office.

7. You are driving through a valley on a spring morning in a heavy rainstorm. You are on a two-lane highway, and you notice that only about half the cars that pass you head-on have their lights on.

Drawing Inferences from Facts

When we interpret the meaning of facts, we draw inferences about them. How many inferences can you draw from the following facts?

Most Highly Populated Countries in the World*

1. China
2. India
3. United States
4. Indonesia
5. Brazil

Top Five Albums of All Time, Worldwide*

1.	Michael Jackson	*Thriller*
2.	Sound track	*The Body Guard*
3.	Sound track	*Saturday Night Fever*
4.	Beatles	*Sgt. Pepper's Lonely Heart's Club Band*
5.	Carole King	*Tapestry*

Five Richest Self-Made Businessmen in the United States in 1995†

		Worth in billions
1.	Bill Gates (Microsoft)	$15.0
2.	Warren Buffett (investments)	$12.0
3.	John Kluge (Metromedia)	$6.7
4.	Paul Allen (Microsoft)	$6.1
5.	Sumner Redstone (Viacom)	$4.8

*Source: *Top 10 of Everything, 1996.* Russell Ash, editor. New York: Dorling Kindersley, 1995.

Five Richest Self-Made Businessmen in 1982†

		Worth in billions
1.	Daniel Ludwig (shipping)	$3.0
2.	Philip Anschutz (oil)	$1.5
3.	Forest Mars (candy)	$1.5
4.	David Packard (Hewlett-Packard)	$1.5
5.	Marvin Davis (oil, real estate)	$1.5

Do you know how it feels when you are making an inference now? Can you describe how this is done mentally?

DISTINGUISHING INFERENCES FROM FACTS

Inferences are very often confused with facts, as you may well have discovered from taking the quiz on the mythical Thomas family in the Introduction.

1. This is graduation day for the Thomas family.
2. The father is proud of his son.
3. The sister looks up to her brother.
4. This is a prosperous family.
5. The son has just graduated from law school.

If you said *true* to any of these assertions, you were confusing inferences with facts. And if you had recognized this, you would have realized that you had no facts but were basing your answers on a guess about missing details. The only right response in each case is *can't answer* because all five statements are inferences.

As you learned when you described a photograph in the last chapter, the work of identifying the facts by stating details instead of substituting inferences made *about* these details is the primary challenge of descriptive writing. Usually, specific details are the most conspicuous and obvious information we see; indeed, they can be so obvious that we do not even realize that we are seeing them. One of the most difficult things about learning how to write descriptive reports is to remember to give the details and let them speak for themselves as much as possible instead of substituting our inferences or interpretations of what they mean.

†Source: *New York Times,* 19 November 1995. Data taken from *Forbes* magazine's list of 400 richest people in America.

CONTRASTING OBSERVING WITH INTERPRETING

Observing	Interpreting
senses, investigates	reasons
aware concentration on subject	focus on thought
establishes and verifies facts	infers, imagines, hypothesizes
describes evidence in specifics of concrete neutral language	labels, interprets, categorizes
open, present-centered, exploratory attitude	tends to connect with past associations, experience, rules
arrives at spontaneous insights as well as reasoned conclusions	usually arrives at only reasoned conclusions
seeks to establish certainty	establishes probability

To review the difference between statements of fact and inferences, suppose for example that a number of individuals were asked to describe what they saw when they looked at a photograph of a man wearing overalls, lying with eyes closed under a tree. One person might say, "This is a picture of a man who is dead drunk"; another might say, "This is a farmer resting during his lunch hour"; or another: "This is a picture of a man who just had a car wreck." Such statements are inferences or *interpretations*; though they all may be plausible, they cannot all be factual. The only statements of fact that can be made describe the basis for these interpretations. So in order to describe accurately, *we have to state the obvious*.

The practice of stating the obvious also helps the writer think through what can be said. When we articulate the details that led to our inferences, we often discover that our interpretations were hasty. Thus, descriptive writing is a process that cannot be rushed; it takes time to find the right words to describe details and to distinguish facts from inferences. Nevertheless, the results are worth it, for a responsible statement is also an *interesting* statement. When we observe carefully and clearly describe what we observe, our work always becomes more alive and interesting to ourselves and to others.

You may have the impression now that you should avoid inferences or not use them at all in your writing. You might feel you should take on the personality of a police detective who says, "Just give me the facts, please!" Although to restrict yourself in this way might be appropriate for writing some kinds of objective reports, it is *not* appropriate for descriptive writing. If you are describing a hospital ward and you mention only that you see men and women in beds, you might leave the reader with a misleading impression of the circumstances. To withhold a reasonable inference that seems to tie all the facts together is an unnecessary restraint, as well as a denial to the reader of useful information.

USING INFERENCES SKILLFULLY

We do not need to make inferences when we have all the facts about a situation or a satisfactory explanation of its meaning. We make inferences when some important facts and a fully satisfying explanation are missing. Some questions exist that may take years or a lifetime or many generations to answer. In our generation, these might include how to cure AIDS, how to safely and reliably prevent unwanted pregnancy, or how to communicate about conflicts in a way that makes war obsolete. Yet, in order to solve these problems, all we can do is to continue asking questions, gathering facts, making inferences from them, and then letting these inferences suggest strategies for finding new facts, which in turn lead to new inferences, until the objective is reached. When we use inferences consciously and imaginatively, they help us reach the certainties we need to solve life's problems.

Therefore, inferences are not something to be avoided, either in thinking or in writing—they are *essential* mental operations in the search for knowledge. The important thing to remember is that inferences are imaginative constructs and should not be confused with facts or acted upon as though they were facts. When we use inferences with conscious skill, they lead us to knowledge. When we use them without conscious awareness, they lead us to confusion and illusion.

Let us consider examples of both skillful and careless use of inferences. For an example of the former, we turn to that master of inference, Sherlock Holmes. Holmes gained fame for his ability to examine facts and make the best inferences from them.

Reading

A STUDY IN SCARLET

Sir Arthur Conan Doyle

"I wonder what that fellow is looking for?" I asked, pointing to a stalwart, plainly   1
dressed individual who was walking slowly down the other side of the street, looking anxiously at the numbers. He had a large blue envelope in his hand, and was evidently the bearer of a message.

"You mean the retired sergeant of Marines," said Sherlock Holmes.   2

"Brag and bounce!" thought I to myself. "He knows that I cannot verify his   3
guess."

The thought had hardly passed through my mind when the man whom we   4
were watching caught sight of the number of our door, and ran rapidly across the
roadway. We heard a loud knock, a deep voice below, and heavy steps ascending
the stair.

"For Mr. Sherlock Holmes," he said, stepping into the room and handing my   5
friend the letter.

Here was an opportunity of taking the conceit out of him. He little thought of   6
this when he made that random shot. "May I ask, my lad," I said in the blandest
voice, "what your trade may be?"

"Commissionaire, sir," he said, gruffly. "Uniform away for repairs."   7

"And you were?" I asked, with a slightly malicious glance at my companion.   8

"A sergeant, sir, Royal Marine Light Infantry, sir. No answer? Right, sir."   9

He clicked his heels together, raised his hand in salute, and was gone. . . .   10

"How in the world did you deduce that?" I asked.   11

"Deduce what?" said he, petulantly.   12

"Why, that he was a retired sergeant of Marines."   13

"It was easier to know it than to explain why I know it. If you were asked to   14
prove that two and two made four, you might find some difficulty, and yet you are
quite sure of the fact. Even across the street I could see a great blue anchor tattooed
on the back of the fellow's hand. That smacked of the sea. He had a military carriage, however, and regulation side whiskers. There we have the marine. He was a
man with some amount of self-importance and a certain air of command. You must
have observed the way in which he held his head and swung his cane. A steady,
respectable, middle-aged man, too, on the face of him—all facts which led me to
believe he had been a sergeant."

"Wonderful!"   15

From Sir Arthur Conan Doyle, *A Study in Scarlet*. New York: Penguin Books, 1982. (Originally published in 1887.)

Study Questions

1. Where in the story does Sherlock Holmes make an inference about the
   profession of the man seen walking down the street?

2. On what observations does he base this inference?

3. Describe a situation in which one of the following individuals would
   be required to make skillful inferences:

   (a) A physician
   (b) A salesperson
   (c) A car mechanic
   (d) A cook

MORE ON USING INFERENCES SKILLFULLY

In contrast to Holmes, many people fall into the trap of building inference on top of inference without ever stopping to check inferences against facts. Inferences, as you may have discovered in your writing and thinking, are not isolated explanations or conclusions. One inference can lead to another and another and another, with each new inference built on the one suggested by those that came before. This can lead different people to entirely different conclusions based on the same set of facts. In this situation, the conscious person is alert to check each inference against available evidence, while the less aware person sinks deeper into illusion at each step. Let's look at an example of two different chains of inference drawn by two different neighbors from the same set of facts.

Neighbor #1

FACTS:

1. I see my neighbor sitting on the front steps of his house.

2. It is Monday morning. He usually is at work at this time.

CHAIN OF INFERENCES:

1. He must be taking the day off.

2. He probably called work to say he was sick.

3. If he were really sick, he'd be in bed.

CONCLUSION:

He's pretending to be sick.

CHAIN OF INFERENCES:

4. If he's pretending, he's a loafer.

CONCLUSION:

He is a loafer.

CHAIN OF INFERENCES:

5. If this keeps up, he'll lose his job.

6. If he's unemployed, his property will deteriorate and that will affect the value of my property.

7. Maybe he's unemployed already.

CONCLUSION:

I had better sell my house now.

Neighbor #2

FACTS:

1. I see my neighbor sitting on the front steps of his house.

2. It is Monday morning. He usually is at work at this time.

CHAIN OF INFERENCES:

1. Either he is sick or on vacation or he has lost his job.

2. In any case, I don't think he'd mind talking to me.

CONCLUSION:

I'll go over and ask him what's up.

Photo by Arthur Rothstein, "Mrs. Thaxton's Daughters," from *The Depression Years*, Dover Publications, 1978. Courtesy Library of Congress.

Class Discussion

1. Why do the inferences drawn by Neighbor #1 and Neighbor #2 go in such different directions?

2. What is the difference between the way Neighbor #1 and Neighbor #2 work with their facts and inferences?

3. Is it all right to build inferences on inferences?

4. Read the following story, which describes the photo above. What happens here in terms of inferences, and at what point does this description begin to go wrong?

   It is a special day for the little girls since they are wearing their best dresses and holding new dolls. They don't like their gifts, since they are frowning. They are also unhappy because they are orphans. Their parents have just died. The little sisters are having their last picture taken before they leave their home for an orphanage. Their neighbors brought them the dolls to cheer them up on their trip, but they did not succeed. The girls would prefer to have their parents and their home back again the way it used to be.

5.   Write your own example of a story in which the inferences take off, leading someone astray.

DRAWING INFERENCES
FROM CAREFUL OBSERVATION

Though we may not have all the facts about a photograph, we can learn a lot from it by observing carefully and drawing inferences skillfully. It's easier to show than describe how this is done, so we'll examine how one person used observation and inference to describe the photo on page 116. As you read this description of the reading woman, notice these features:

1.   The facts appear first, followed by the inferences that can reasonably be drawn from them.

2.   More than one inference can be drawn from each set of facts.

3.   The factual information groups together the details of one segment or feature of the photograph at a time. (For instance, it does not describe the person's hair, then the background, then her posture.)

4.   The conclusion draws together the facts and the possible inferences into a plausible explanation of the message, purpose, and meaning of the photograph.

Facts

My attention is drawn first to the human figure seated flat on a plane with her legs straight out in front, forming a right angle on the central right side of this black-and-white photograph. Most prominent is the body covering that forms a dress pattern of bold gray-and-white stripes. Emerging from the dress are the pale flesh shades of her neck and face, one bent arm, and both legs; the latter are in a darker shade capped by black ovals. Most striking are the values of white, the lightest coming from a stack of straight-edged shapes on her lap, then from a spot at her wrist, then from some specks of white over her ear, and finally from a flash of white in a straight line from the top of her ear to her eye speck where it meets a perpendicular curved line. Another curved line appears in front of the other eye. Her shoulders are rounded, and her head is bent forward toward her lap where the stack of white shapes rests.

Photo by John Pearson. Used with permission of the photographer.

Inferences

1. This is a woman with gray hair and glasses who is wearing a dress, low-heeled shoes, and stockings while seated on a floor reading. She wears a wristwatch and glasses and is bent over a stack of three hard-back books that she holds on her lap.
2. Although she is seated on the floor, she does not seem to mind since she is absorbed in her reading.

Facts

Her dress forms a pattern of horizontal stripes that intersect at the wide lapels and ripple across her lap. This wide-banded, striped pattern with short sleeves was a conservative summer dress style in the 1950s. Her hair style forms shapes close to her head that curve like curly waves, ending at the nape of her neck.

Inferences

1. She is middle aged. Her sensible dress, hairstyle, shoes, and stockings suggest middle-class values of neatness, conservatism, practicality, and modesty.
2. She could be stereotyped as a schoolteacher, nun, or homemaker.
3. Although her appearance is conservative, her behavior is nonconformist. She is an eccentric scholar.

Facts

Only one angle of gray, an eye, appears at the edge of her glasses. Her lips are one tight line. Her visible left arm rests on her upper thigh, and her hand rests, fingers hidden, at the bottom of a curved dark line that appears to be a half-open page.

Inferences

1. She finds her reading so interesting that she does not care how awkward this bent position must feel to her body; she does not even notice that the floor may be dirty and cold. She reads rapidly and can hardly wait to turn the next page.
2. She is resting from standing and reading in the store.
3. She cannot sit in a cross-legged position because she is wearing a skirt.

Facts

Above her on her right is a tall shelf with seven full rows of paperback-sized books. The covers of a few of the books face forward, revealing the name of one mystery author, Agatha Christie. Above her feet, a display stand offers popular magazines such as *People* and *Harper's*.

Inferences

1. This is a public place but not a library. It is a magazine and newspaper store that also carries books or a bookstore that also sells magazines.
2. The store offers no chairs so that its patrons keep moving.
3. She is a mystery fan.
4. She is reading the books so that she will not have to pay for them.
5. She wants to buy one of these books but has to do some reading in order to make her selection.
6. She doesn't care what people think.

Facts

The floor upon which the woman is seated shows the lines of tile squares decorated with a speckled paint pattern and spattered with some larger dark spots and streaks. About three feet away from the woman's feet lies a dark shell-shaped crumpled object of two contrasting textures and shades of color. No other people are visible in this scene.

Inferences

1. It is a linoleum floor and dirty. Perhaps it is just before cleaning time; or perhaps the store has such constant traffic that it does not attempt to keep the floor spotless.
2. The crumpled object is her coat; she was so excited to get on with her reading that she forgot that she had dropped it there.
3. On the other hand, she appears to be too tidy a person to have scattered her belongings in public; perhaps it belongs to a second reader out of the camera's view.
4. If other people are in the store, this woman is not inhibited by what they may think or whether she is taking up too much space and blocking other customers from the shelves. She is lost in her books.

Conclusion

This photograph plays with some incongruities of public and private, formality and informality. Here a conventionally dressed woman is behaving unconventionally in a public bookstore. Although one would expect her to seek to remain clean and inconspicuous, here she is sitting legs stretched out on a dirty floor, blocking access to at least part of the store. Moreover, although one might expect her to browse standing up, later taking her books home to read, she seems to be absorbed by a stack of books that she may not even pay for. The photographer makes us uncomfortable by poking fun at some of our social rules.

CORE DISCOVERY WRITING APPLICATION

A COLLABORATIVE LEARNING OPPORTUNITY

Using Facts and Inferences to Describe a Photograph

1. This is a mental exercise that uses writing. Choose a photograph in this book not described by the author. (Do not use the photos on pages 86 and 116.) For your notes, make yourself a page with columns like this:

Photo by John Pearson. Used with permission of the photographer.

Facts About the Photograph	Inferences I Make About This Fact
My description of a detail: a form, texture, shade, relationship, configuration that I see.	What I imagine this detail represents or what I interpret it to mean.

2. Survey the photograph in a systematic way, beginning with what is central, then moving to relationships of the parts and the background.

3. Write out your list using the columns in step 1 to match each statement of fact with an inference. (Actually, in your thinking, the

Photo by John Pearson. Used with permission of the photographer.

inference will probably come to mind first. If so, write it down, then restudy the photo to discover and describe the evidence upon which this inference was based.)

4. Write a conclusion that draws your list of facts and inferences together into an explanation of the photograph. (See the example on page 118.) This summary should not introduce new information or provide a story that your evidence cannot support.

5. Now write your description in the paragraph form illustrated for you in the preceding exercise on pages 115–118. Remember to end with a summary.

6. The length should be about two typed pages.

Scoring Using Facts and Inferences to Describe a Photograph

1. Obvious details not ignored.	10 points
2. Statements of fact described rather than just named or interpreted.	10 points
3. Facts not confused with inferences.	20 points
4. Systematic organization of data: systematic sectioning of photo; small groupings of related facts, shown with inferences clearly drawn from each grouping.	20 points
5. Some imaginative use of inferences beyond the obvious.	10 points
6. Conclusion brings given facts and inferences together in a logical interpretation (not introducing new facts or a fantasy).	10 points
7. No distracting errors of spelling, punctuation, sentence structure.	10 points
8. Minimum length 2 typed pages.	10 points

GENERALIZING FROM
FACTS AND INFERENCES

Samuel Scudder, whose encounter with a fish was described in Chapter 1, stated that "Agassiz's training in the method of observing facts and their orderly arrangement was ever accompanied by the urgent exhortation not to be content with them. 'Facts are stupid things,' he would say, 'until brought into connection with some general law.'" We can apply this statement to our concerns about thinking and writing: it is not enough to collect and state facts and inferences alone; we need to look for patterns in them and see how we can make generalizations to describe their organizing principles or "laws."

> "Do you perhaps mean," I asked, "that the fish has symmetrical sides with paired organs?"
> His thoroughly pleased "Of course! Of course!" repaid the wakeful hours of the previous night.

In science, laws are generalizations that are based on observations and that deal with recurrence, order, and relationships. Generalizations, in turn, relate individual members of a class or category to a whole. To arrive at laws or generalizations, we must look for information, then look for patterns or configurations, analyze them, and finally draw conclusions about the relationships, recurrences, and order of the gathered data. These were the mental actions you followed when drawing conclusions in the last exercise.

It takes experience to know when you have gathered enough information to make accurate generalizations. Beginners, like Scudder, may decide they have seen everything after 10 minutes or, at the other extreme, refrain from drawing conclusions for too long. A good scientist, like a good writer, recognizes how much evidence is needed to support reliable generalizations.

When you first listed facts about the photograph you chose for the exercise, you may have experienced the sense of the "stupidity" of facts that Agassiz referred to. Perhaps you had a sense of not knowing where to stop or how to separate the relevant details from the irrelevant. However, this first stage of simpleminded observing and collecting is important.

In the second stage of writing and of thinking, we begin to separate, compare, categorize, and organize our information. In photograph description we may be led by a feeling, an idea, or an intuition that seems to put everything together. Eventually, we are able to formulate all this into a generalization that is a summary statement. In paragraph writing, this statement becomes our topic sentence. This (usually first) sentence states in a general way the main idea to be proven or explained. What then follows is the evidence—the facts and inferences that support the main idea. So we present our topic sentence, which is actually our conclusion, *first* in our writing, although we arrived at it *last* in our thinking. This is exactly what you did in the exercise where you first wrote down your facts and inferences in columns and then drew a conclusion at the end that summarized all your information.

The topic sentence becomes a kind of commitment as well as a guide, aiding us in sorting out our facts for their significance or insignificance as supportive evidence. Some may turn out to be entirely irrelevant. Some may even contradict the topic sentence. This discovery could lead us to reexamine our facts, or search for new ones. A topic sentence can serve as a magnet to pick up supporting details, leaving all the rest behind. It also *tests* our facts and our inferences about them. We may even discover that we really can't support our topic sentence very well at all. In such cases, we can simply discard it and begin again.

The willingness to loop back and forth between the evidence and the generalization takes persistence fueled by a resolve to arrive at truth as best we can. Such a process must be familiar to you from your own writing experience, although you may never have looked at what you were doing in this conscious way before. The final exercise is designed to have you write with this conscious awareness in mind.

Composition Writing Application

Writing a Paragraph from Facts, Inferences, and Generalizations

Choose a photograph from this chapter that you have not described before. Working alone, observe your photograph for a while, noticing what is plainly visible. Make notes by listing your facts and seeing what inferences you can draw from them.

Putting this information together, draw a conclusion about the photograph as a whole. What message, what statement about life do you think is being conveyed by the photographer here? What does the photographer say to you through the work? Write this conclusion at the top of your page. Use this sentence as a *topic sentence* for a paragraph to follow that makes a general statement or conclusion about your evidence.

Now write the rest of the paragraph in sentences. Describe the photograph using all the facts you can to support your topic sentence. Link these facts to your inferences appropriately throughout. At the end, bring everything together into a second conclusion or a summary of what you have demonstrated.

Doonesbury © 1985, G. B. Trudeau. Reprinted with permission of Universal Press Syndicate. All rights reserved.

Questions

1. What is the professor trying to teach his students?
2. What inferences does he expect them to make?
3. What inferences do they make?
4. What clues led you to your own conclusions about this cartoon?
5. How would you describe the professor's teaching style?

Read your paragraph aloud to one to three other students who selected the same photo. Do you find that you supported your topic sentence adequately?

Analyzing the Use of Facts and Inferences in a Newspaper Article

1. Work with the article of page 126 called "Tougher Grading Better for Students" or with another article assigned to you by the instructor. Read the article carefully. Then make yourself a chart with four headings in columns. After you read each sentence, choose the column that seems appropriate for entering quotes or comments. The example below should explain the analysis format.

Data claimed to be factual	Inferences made	Pertinent missing information	My own inferences as I read
This article was reprinted with the permission of the *San Francisco Chronicle*.	"Tougher Grading Better for Students."	Who wrote the article? Who drew this conclusion?	This may be an authoritative study.

2. To save time, you can make a photocopy of the article and cut and paste some sentences into the appropriate columns. When working with quotations, note that although the public statement may be a fact, its content could be an inference. In such cases, put the quote in the first column and in the second note that it expresses an inference.

3. Line for line, as you proceed through the article, notice if you find any information missing. Consider what you or an ordinary reader would need to have in order to understand and believe its claims. Is enough information given about the source of the facts so that they could be verified? Are there enough facts, enough inferences, sufficient explanations? As you read, notice the times you feel puzzled, curious, confused, or suspicious. Then consider if these reactions could be due to pertinent missing information.

4. In the last column, record your thinking about each recorded fact and/or inference. Write down your conclusions, questions, comments, and reactions.

5. When you have finished going through the whole article systematically, prepare your chart in final form by typing and/or by cutting and pasting.

6. On a final sheet of paper, sum up in one paragraph what you learned through your analysis. Did you conclude that the article offers reliable information? Did your final impressions differ from your first?

Reading

TOUGHER GRADING BETTER FOR STUDENTS

1 America's high school students may not be getting much smarter, but their teachers are getting more generous—at least when it comes to grading.

2 A national survey released this month showed that a record 28 percent of incoming college freshmen had A averages, up from only 12.5 percent in 1969. During much of that period, ironically, student scores on standardized tests actually declined.

3 Higher grades and lower test scores may be related, according to new research by economists Julian Betts and Stefan Boedeker at the University of California, San Diego. They find a strong relationship between school grading standards and student achievement: The tougher a school grades, the harder its students work and the more they learn.

4 Their finding is enormously significant. "For thirty years, social scientists have been trying to decide why some schools are good and some are bad," said Betts. "They looked at class size, teacher education and per pupil spending, none of which seem to matter much. So I decided to look at standards set in the schools."

5 If Betts and Boedeker are right, spending more money on schools may help a lot less than simply changing the incentives facing students. If they are allowed to slack off and still earn good grades, most will take it easy. But holding them to higher standards costs nothing and can motivate them to achieve more.

6 Betts and Boedeker studied the math and science performance of roughly 6,000 middle- and high-school students nationwide over five years, starting in 1987. Students were tested each year to measure how much they were learning. The researchers also had information on grading standards, amount of homework assigned and other factors.

7 The two scholars found large differences in grading standards between schools and a strong relationship between those standards and how much students learned each year. Over five years, otherwise similar students at tough schools scored about 6 points more than students at easy schools on standardized tests with 100 as the top score. A 6-point difference is huge, Betts said.

8 Stronger students seem to benefit the most from tougher standards, suggesting that other policies must also be sought to "help the weaker students match the gains in achievement of their (better) prepared counterparts."

One solution to uneven grading standards would be to hold standardized state 9 or national graduation exams to test high school achievement and thus give students more incentive to take their studies seriously. Such exams are routine in Europe and Japan, where graduating students are much further advanced than their American counterparts.

Bishop tested this theory by comparing the math performance of 13-year-olds 10 (measured by an international test administered in 1991) in Canadian provinces that have standardized graduation exams and in those that don't.

His findings were striking. In Canadian provinces with testing, students learned 11 about two-thirds of a grade level more than those in provinces without.

"One of the most cost-effective methods of improving achievement in Ameri- 12 can schools would be to create curriculum-based exams for each state," Bishop said.

Reprinted with permission. © 1995 *San Francisco Chronicle*.

Scoring for Analyzing Facts and Inferences in a Newspaper Article

1. Correct identification of all facts and inferences appearing in the article. — 30 points

2. Does not confuse own inferences with those made in article. — 10 points

3. Shows an understanding that although a quotation may be presented as fact, its content may express an inference. — 10 points

4. Shows understanding that estimates, predictions, and opinions are inferences. — 10 points

5. Missing information column shows thoughtful reflection on *pertinent* missing data. — 10 points

6. Own inferences are drawn systematically, item for item, and show careful reflection on the data. — 10 points

7. Format is systematic, methodical, and easy to read. — 10 points

8. Final conclusion assesses how the information is presented in the article. — 10 points

---

BUILDING ARGUMENTS

INFERENCES

No reasonable man can for one moment believe that such a Beautiful country (America) was intended by its Author (God) to be forever in the possession and occupancy of serpents, wild fowls, wild beasts and savages who derive little benefit from it. (Caleb Atwater, 1850)

Exercise

1. Above is a claim based on an inference. Put the claim into your own words. Explain how its reasoning is an inference.
2. What conclusion is implied by this statement?
3. Is any evidence offered in support of the claim?
4. Explain how the claim justifies the author's values.
5. Make a claim that is based on an inference.

CHAPTER SUMMARY

1. The word *infer* means (a) to derive by reasoning; (b) to conclude; (c) to guess. When we infer, we use imagination or reasoning to provide explanations for situations where all the facts are either not available or not yet determined.

2. Responsible report writing or descriptive writing lets the facts speak for themselves as much as possible. This often means taking the time to find the right words to describe the obvious and abandoning inferences drawn too hastily that cannot be supported.

3. Writing that offers specific detailed support for its conclusions makes interesting writing. When we perceive and think clearly, we interest both ourselves and others.

4. Reasonable inferences can be used in descriptive writing to tie facts together. Care must be taken to distinguish facts from inferences, though.

5. In solving problems, inferences can be used as a strategy in planning and choosing alternatives. When we think well, we assess all facts, derive as many inferences as we can, and devise strategies for confirming or obtaining more information.

USING INFERENCES

Archimedes, a Greek mathematician, was a friend of King Hieron of Syracuse. The king had a problem: he had his doubts about the purity of the gold in his crown. He had given his goldsmith a cube of pure gold with which to make the crown, but now he was wondering if the goldsmith could have substituted some silver or copper alloy and kept the rest of the gold for himself.

The king asked Archimedes to solve the problem for him. Archimedes knew that if he could figure out the volume of the crown and compare that to the original volume of the golden cube, they would have to be the same. While thinking over how it would be possible to measure the volume of an irregular shape like a crown, he went down to the public baths. As he stepped into his tub, he noticed something he had seen countless times before: how the water ran over the top. Then he shouted "Eureka!"

Archimedes had realized that the volume of the water overflow was equal to the bulk of his body under water. When Archimedes measured the volume of the water displaced by the king's crown, he found it to be far greater than that of the original cube of gold, which was due to the substitution of alloys. Subsequently Archimedes was rewarded, but the poor goldsmith was executed.

Question

1. Describe a problem you solved by making inferences that led to facts.

From Royston M. Roberts, *Serendipity: Accidental Discoveries in Science*. New York: John Wiley, 1989.

6. Detectives and consultants of all kinds are valued for their ability to examine facts and make the best inferences from them.

7. Inferences can build on inferences in chains of association. Unless each inference is tested for its support of evidence, a series of inferences can mislead us into flights of imagination, away from reliable knowledge.

8. Facts and inferences are linked together through generalizations. Facts have little significance in themselves until generalizations or laws can be derived from them. Generalizing too soon, before we have gathered a sufficient number of facts, is hazardous; this does not mean that we should not generalize at all. It simply means that we should learn how to draw generalizations that can be supported.

9. The topic sentence of a paragraph is a generalization that summarizes the main idea to be demonstrated in that paragraph. When we think, we usually arrive at this generalization last, after we have examined all our facts and inferences; nevertheless, we state it first, at the beginning of the paragraph. The topic sentence is a kind of conclusion, which is repeated again in another form at the end of the paragraph.

10. By the time you have finished this chapter, you should understand more about the thinking operations involved in the construction of a paragraph or descriptive writing: how it requires observation to determine facts, imagination and reasoning to link the facts with explanations, and how a generalization ties all this information together into a meaningful whole.

CHAPTER QUIZ

Write two inferences to explain each of the following events:

1. An elderly woman is being pushed down Main Street in a large baby carriage by a little girl.

2. Your best friend leaves you a note saying she has joined the marines.

3. You have received no mail for the past two weeks.

4. A recent study found that men between fifty and seventy-nine years old married to women one to twenty-four years younger tended to live longer or had a mortality rate 13 percent below the norm.

5. The same study found that men married to older women died sooner or had a death rate that was 20 percent higher than the norm.

Rate each of the following statements as *true* or *false*. Explain your choice in each case or give an example to defend your choice.

_____ 6. To state that "the total U.S. sales of VCRs in 1984 were more than 8 million—just about double the number of VCRs sold in 1983" is to make a generalization without facts.

_____ 7. To state the obvious is to state the sensory details of what is actually seen, as opposed to what is *thought* or interpreted about what is seen.

_____ 8. Good thinking does not continue to build inferences on top of inferences but stops whenever possible to check these inferences against the original facts or to find new ones.

——— 9. One should always avoid making inferences in every kind of writing.

——— 10. Strategies help us check out our inferences.

Readings

THE THREE PERCEPTIVES

Idries Shah

This is an old teaching story of the Sufis, a mystic Muslim sect that claims to be far older than Islam. Their stories are parables told to help people understand the nature of the mind and how to use it to gain wisdom. The term *perceptives* might also be translated as wise men. This reading was translated by Idries Shah, one of the leading interpreters of Sufi philosophy in the West. As you read it, take note of how accurately the three men connect their inferences to their observation skills and their past experiences.

There were once three Sufis, so observant and experienced in life that they were known as The Three Perceptives. 1

One day during their travels they encountered a camelman, who said, "Have you seen my camel? I have lost it." 2

"Was it blind in one eye?" asked the first Perceptive. 3

"Yes," said the cameldriver. 4

"Has it one tooth missing in front?" asked the second Perceptive. 5

"Yes, yes," said the cameldriver. 6

"Is it lame in one foot?" asked the third Perceptive. 7

"Yes, yes, yes," said the cameldriver. 8

The three Perceptives then told the man to go back along the way they had come, and that he might hope to find it. Thinking that they had seen it, the man hurried on his way. 9

But the man did not find his camel, and he hastened to catch up with the Perceptives, hoping that they would tell him what to do. 10

He found them that evening, at a resting-place. 11

"Has your camel honey on one side and a load of corn on the other?" asked the first Perceptive. 12

"Yes," said the man. 13

"Is there a pregnant woman mounted upon it?" asked the second Perceptive. 14

"Yes, yes," said the man. 15

"We do not know where it is," said the third Perceptive. 16

The cameldriver was now convinced that the Perceptives had stolen his camel,   17
passenger and all, and he took them to the judge, accusing them of the theft.

The judge thought that he had made out a case, and detained the three men   18
in custody on suspicion of theft.

A little later, the man found his camel wandering in some fields, and returning   19
to the court, arranged for the Perceptives to be released.

The judge, who had not given them a chance to explain themselves before,   20
asked how it was that they knew so much about the camel, since they had apparently not even seen it.

"We saw the footprints of a camel on the road," said the first Perceptive.   21

"One of the tracks was faint; it must have been lame," said the second   22
Perceptive.

"It had stripped the bushes at only one side of the road, so it must have been   23
blind in one eye," said the third Perceptive.

"The leaves were shredded, which indicated the loss of a tooth," continued   24
the first Perceptive.

"Bees and ants, on different sides of the road, were swarming over something   25
deposited; we saw that this was honey and corn," said the second Perceptive.

"We found long human hair where someone had stopped and dismounted, it   26
was a woman's," said the third Perceptive.

"Where the person had sat down there were palm-prints, we thought from the   27
use of the hands that the woman was probably very pregnant and had to stand up
in that way," said the first Perceptive.

"Why did you not apply for your side of the case to be heard so that you could   28
explain yourselves?" asked the judge.

"Because we reckoned that the cameldriver would continue looking for his   29
camel and might find it soon," said the first Perceptive.

"He would feel generous in releasing us through his discovery," said the sec-   30
ond Perceptive.

"The curiosity of the judge would prompt an enquiry," said the third   31
Perceptive.

"Discovering the truth by his own enquiries would be better for all than for us   32
to claim that we had been impatiently handled," said the first Perceptive.

"It is our experience that it is generally better for people to arrive at truth   33
through what they take to be their own volition," said the second Perceptive.

"It is time for us to move on, for there is work to be done," said the third   34
Perceptive.

And the Sufi thinkers went on their way. They are still to be found at work on   35
the highways of the earth.

From Idries Shah, *The Caravan of Dreams*. New York: Penguin Books, 1972. Author and date of origin of "The Three Perceptives" unknown. Reprinted with permission of The Octagon Press Ltd., London.

Study Questions

1. Make a list with two columns. On one side state the inferences made by the three men. On the other side show the facts to which they related these inferences.

2. Why were the men so restrained in defending themselves?

3. What do you think of their statement: "It is our experience that it is generally better for people to arrive at truth through what they take to be their own volition"? Can you apply this to learning and teaching?

4. What would you say is the most important value of the three men?

THE STONE BOY

Gina Berriault

This story was first published in *Mademoiselle* magazine; it was then scripted by Berriault into a Hollywood film—with a happy ending—in 1984. The author has received many awards and has served on the faculty of San Francisco State University. In your first reading of this story, look at (1) how the plot of this story revolves around the inference making of its characters, and (2) how your own inference making enables you to "participate" in the story, thus achieving a deeper understanding of it.

Arnold drew his overalls and raveling gray sweater over his naked body. In the other 1 narrow bed his brother Eugene went on sleeping, undisturbed by the alarm clock's rusty ring. Arnold, watching his brother sleeping, felt a peculiar dismay; he was nine, six years younger than Eugie, and in their waking hours it was he who was subordinate. To dispel emphatically his uneasy advantage over his sleeping brother, he threw himself on the hump of Eugie's body.

"Get up! Get up!" he cried. 2

Arnold felt his brother twist away and saw the blankets lifted in a great wing, 3 and, all in an instant, he was lying on his back under the covers with only his face showing, like a baby, and Eugie was sprawled on top of him.

"Whassa matter with you?" asked Eugie in sleepy anger, his face hanging close. 4

"Get up," Arnold repeated. "You said you'd pick peas with me." 5

Stupidly, Eugie gazed around the room as if to see if morning had come 6 into it yet. Arnold began to laugh derisively, making soft, snorting noises, and was thrown off the bed. He got up from the floor and went down the stairs, the laughter continuing, like hiccups, against his will. But when he opened the staircase door and entered the parlor, he hunched up his shoulders and was quiet because his parents slept in the bedroom downstairs.

Arnold lifted his .22-caliber rifle from the rack on the kitchen wall. It was an old 7
lever-action Winchester that his father had given him because nobody else used it
any more. On their way down to the garden he and Eugie would go by the lake,
and if there were any ducks on it he'd take a shot at them. Standing on the stool
before the cupboard, he searched on the top shelf in the confusion of medicines
and ointments for man and beast and found a small yellow box of .22 cartridges.
Then he sat down on the stool and began to load his gun.

It was cold in the kitchen so early, but later in the day, when his mother canned 8
the peas, the heat from the wood stove would be almost unbearable. Yesterday she
had finished preserving the huckleberries that the family had picked along the
mountain, and before that she had canned all the cherries his father had brought
from the warehouse in Corinth. Sometimes, on these summer days, Arnold would
deliberately come out from the shade where he was playing and make himself as
uncomfortable as his mother was in the kitchen by standing in the sun until the
sweat ran down his body.

Eugie came clomping down the stairs and into the kitchen, his head drooping 9
with sleepiness. From his perch on the stool, Arnold watched Eugie slip on his green
knit cap. Eugie didn't really need a cap; he hadn't had a haircut in a long time and
his brown curls grew thick and matted, close around his ears and down his neck,
tapering there to a small whorl. Eugie passed his left hand through his hair before
he set his cap down with his right. The very way he slipped his cap on was an
announcement of his status; almost everything he did was a reminder that he was
eldest—first he, then Nora, then Arnold—and called attention to how tall he was
(almost as tall as his father), how long his legs were, how small he was in the hips,
and what a neat dip above his buttocks his thick-soled logger's boots gave him.
Arnold never tired of watching Eugie offer silent praise unto himself. He wondered,
as he sat enthralled, if when he got to be Eugie's age he would still be undersized
and his hair still straight.

Eugie eyed the gun. "Don't you know this ain't duck-season?" he asked gruffly, 10
as if he were the sheriff.

"No, I don't know," Arnold said with a snigger. 11

Eugie picked up the tin washtub for the peas, unbolted the door with his free 12
hand and kicked it open. Then, lifting the tub to his head, he went clomping down
the back steps. Arnold followed, closing the door behind him.

The sky was faintly gray, almost white. The mountains behind the farm made 13
the sun climb a long way to show itself. Several miles to the south, where the range
opened up, hung an orange mist, but the valley in which the farm lay was still cold
and colorless.

Eugie opened the gate to the yard and the boys passed between the barn and 14
the row of chicken houses, their feet stirring up the carpet of brown feathers
dropped by the molting chickens. They paused before going down the slope to the
lake. A fluky morning wind ran among the shocks of wheat that covered the slope.
It sent a shimmer northward across the lake, gently moving the rushes that formed
an island in the center. Killdeer, their white markings flashing, skimmed the water,

crying their shrill, sweet cry. And there at the south end of the lake were four wild ducks, swimming out from the willows into open water.

Arnold followed Eugie down the slope, stealing, as his brother did, from one 15 shock of wheat to another. Eugie paused before climbing through the wire fence that divided the wheatfield from the marshy pasture around the lake. They were screened from the ducks by the willows along the lake's edge.

"If you hit your duck, you want me to go in after it?" Eugie said. 16

"If you want," Arnold said. 17

Eugie lowered his eyelids, leaving slits of mocking blue. "You'd drown 'fore 18 you got to it, them legs of yours are so puny," he said.

He shoved the tub under the fence and, pressing down the center wire, 19 climbed through into the pasture.

Arnold pressed down the bottom wire, thrust a leg through and leaned for- 20 ward to bring the other leg after. His rifle caught on the wire and he jerked at it. The air was rocked by the sound of the shot. Feeling foolish, he lifted his face, baring it to an expected shower of derision from his brother. But Eugie did not turn around. Instead, from his crouching position, he fell to his knees and then pitched forward onto his face. The ducks rose up crying from the lake, cleared the mountain background and beat away northward across the pale sky.

Arnold squatted beside his brother. Eugie seemed to be climbing the earth, as 21 if the earth ran up and down, and when he found he couldn't scale it he lay still.

"Eugie?" 22

Then Arnold saw it, under the tendril of hair at the nape of the neck— 23 a slow rising of bright blood. It had an obnoxious movement, like that of a parasite.

"Hey, Eugie," he said again. He was feeling the same discomfort he had felt 24 when he had watched Eugie sleeping; his brother didn't know that he was lying face down in the pasture.

Again he said, "Hey, Eugie," an anxious nudge in his voice. But Eugie was as 25 still as the morning about them.

Arnold set his rifle on the ground and stood up. He picked up the tub and, 26 dragging it behind him, walked along by the willows to the garden fence and climbed through. He went down on his knees among the tangled vines. The pods were cold with the night, but his hands were strange to him, and not until some time had passed did he realize that the pods were numbing his fingers. He picked from the top of the vine first, then lifted the vine to look underneath for pods and then moved on to the next.

It was a warmth on his back, like a large hand laid firmly there, that made him 27 raise his head. Way up the slope the gray farmhouse was struck by the sun. While his head had been bent the land had grown bright around him.

When he got up his legs were so stiff that he had to go down on his knees 28 again to ease the pain. Then, walking sideways, he dragged the tub, half full of peas, up the slope.

The kitchen was warm now; a fire was roaring in the stove with a closed-up, rushing   29
sound. His mother was spooning eggs from a pot of boiling water and putting
them into a bowl. Her short brown hair was uncombed and fell forward across her
eyes as she bent her head. Nora was lifting a frying pan full of trout from the stove,
holding the handle with a dish towel. His father had just come in from bringing the
cows from the north pasture to the barn, and was sitting on the stool, unbuttoning
his red plaid Mackinaw.

"Did you boys fill the tub?" his mother asked.   30

"They ought of by now," his father said. "They went out of the house an hour   31
ago. Eugie woke me up comin' downstairs. I heard you shootin'—did you get a
duck?"

"No," Arnold said. They would want to know why Eugie wasn't coming in for   32
breakfast, he thought. "Eugie's dead," he told them.

They stared at him. The pitch cracked in the stove.   33

"You kids playin' a joke?" his father asked.   34

"Where's Eugene?" his mother asked scoldingly. She wanted, Arnold knew,   35
to see his eyes, and when he had glanced at her she put the bowl and spoon down
on the stove and walked past him. His father stood up and went out the door after
her. Nora followed them with little skipping steps, as if afraid to be left alone.

Arnold went into the barn, down along the foddering passage past the cows   36
waiting to be milked, and climbed into the loft. After a few minutes he heard a
terrifying sound coming toward the house. His parents and Nora were returning
from the willows, and sounds sharp as knives were rising from his mother's breast
and carrying over the sloping fields. In a short while he heard his father go down
the back steps, slam the car door and drive away.

Arnold lay still as a fugitive, listening to the cows eating close by. If his parents   37
never called him, he thought, he would stay up in the loft forever, out of the way.
In the night he would sneak down for a drink of water from the faucet over the
trough and for whatever food they left for him by the barn.

The rattle of his father's car as it turned down the lane recalled him to the   38
present. He heard voices of his Uncle Andy and Aunt Alice as they and his father
went past the barn to the lake. He could feel the morning growing heavier with
sun. Someone, probably Nora, had let the chickens out of their coops and they
were cackling in the yard.

After a while another car turned down the road off the highway. The car drew   39
to a stop and he heard the voices of strange men. The men also went past the barn
and down to the lake. The undertakers, whom his father must have phoned from
Uncle Andy's house, had arrived from Corinth. Then he heard everybody come
back and heard the car turn around and leave.

"Arnold!" It was his father calling him from the yard.   40

He climbed down the ladder and went out into the sun, picking wisps of hay   41
from his overalls.

Corinth, nine miles away, was the county seat. Arnold sat in the front seat of the   42
old Ford between his father, who was driving, and Uncle Andy; no one spoke. Uncle

Andy was his mother's brother, and he had been fond of Eugie because Eugie had resembled him. Andy had taken Eugie hunting and had given him a knife and a lot of things, and now Andy, his eyes narrowed, sat tall and stiff beside Arnold.

Arnold's father parked the car before the courthouse. It was a two-story brick   43
building with a lamp on each side of the bottom step. They went up the wide stone steps, Arnold and his father going first, and entered the darkly paneled hallway. The shirt-sleeved man in the sheriff's office said that the sheriff was at Carlson's Parlor examining the Curwing boy.

Andy went off to get the sheriff while Arnold and his father waited on a bench   44
in the corridor. Arnold felt his father watching him, and he lifted his eyes with painful casualness to the announcement, on the opposite wall, of the Corinth County Annual Rodeo, and then to the clock with its loudly clucking pendulum. After he had come down from the loft his father and Uncle Andy had stood in the yard with him and asked him to tell them everything, and he had explained to them how the gun had caught on the wire. But when they had asked him why he hadn't run back to the house to tell his parents, he had had no answer— all he could say was that he had gone down into the garden to pick the peas. His father had stared at him in a pale, puzzled way, and it was then that he had felt his father and the others set their cold, turbulent silence against him. Arnold shifted on the bench, his only feeling a small one of compunction imposed by his father's eyes.

At a quarter past nine, Andy and the sheriff came in. They all went into the   45
sheriff's private office, and Arnold was sent forward to sit in the chair by the sheriff's desk; his father and Andy sat down on the bench against the wall.

The sheriff lumped down into his swivel chair and swung toward Arnold. He   46
was an old man with white hair like wheat stubble. His restless green eyes made him seem not to be in his office but to be hurrying and bobbing around somewhere else.

"What did you say your name was?" the sheriff asked.   47

"Arnold," he replied; but he could not remember telling the sheriff his name   48
before.

"Curwing?"   49

"Yes."   50

"What were you doing with a .22, Arnold?"   51

"It's mine," he said.   52

"Okay. What were you going to shoot?"   53

"Some ducks," he replied.   54

"Out of season?"   55

He nodded.   56

"That's bad," said the sheriff. "Were you and your brother good friends?"   57

What did he mean—good friends? Eugie was his brother. That was different   58
from a friend, Arnold thought. A best friend was your own age, but Eugie was almost a man. Eugie had had a way of looking at him, slyly and mockingly and yet confidentially, that had summed up how they both felt about being brothers. Arnold had wanted to be with Eugie more than with anybody else but he couldn't say they had been good friends.

"Did they ever quarrel?" the sheriff asked his father.   59

"Not that I know," his father replied. "It seemed to me that Arnold cared a lot   60
for Eugie."

"Did you?" the sheriff asked Arnold.   61

If it seemed so to his father, then it was so. Arnold nodded.   62

"Were you mad at him this morning?"   63

"No."   64

"How did you happen to shoot him?"   65

"We was crawlin' through the fence."   66

"Yes?"   67

"An' the gun got caught on the wire."   68

"Seems the hammer must of caught," his father put in.   69

"All right, that's what happened," said the sheriff. "But what I want you to tell   70
me is this. Why didn't you go back to the house and tell your father right away?
Why did you go and pick peas for an hour?"

Arnold gazed over his shoulder at his father, expecting his father to have an   71
answer for this also. But his father's eyes, larger and even lighter blue than usual,
were fixed upon him curiously. Arnold picked at a callus in his right palm. It
seemed odd now that he had not run back to the house and wakened his father,
but he could not remember why he had not. They were all waiting for him to
answer.

"I come down to pick peas," he said.   72

"Didn't you think," asked the sheriff, stepping carefully from word to word,   73
"that it was more important for you to go tell your parents what had happened?"

"The sun was gonna come up," Arnold said.   74

"What's that got to do with it?"   75

"It's better to pick peas while they're cool."   76

The sheriff swung away from him, laid both hands flat on his desk. "Well, all I   77
can say is," he said across to Arnold's father and Uncle Andy, "he's either a moron
or he's so reasonable that he's way ahead of us." He gave a challenging snort. "It's
come to my notice that the most reasonable guys are mean ones. They don't feel
nothing."

For a moment the three men sat still. Then the sheriff lifted his hand like a man   78
taking an oath. "Take him home," he said.

Andy uncrossed his legs. "You don't want him?"   79

"Not now," replied the sheriff. "Maybe in a few years."   80

Arnold's father stood up. He held his hat against his chest. "The gun ain't his   81
no more," he said wanly.

Arnold went first through the hallway, hearing behind him the heels of his   82
father and Uncle Andy striking the floor boards. He went down the steps ahead of
them and climbed into the back seat of the car. Andy paused as he was getting into
the front seat and gazed back at Arnold, and Arnold saw that his uncle's eyes had
absorbed the knowingness from the sheriff's eyes. Andy and his father and the
sheriff had discovered what made him go down into the garden. It was because he

was cruel, the sheriff had said, and didn't care about his brother. Was that the reason? Arnold lowered his eyelids meekly against his uncle's stare.

The rest of the day he did his tasks around the farm, keeping apart from the 83 family. At evening, when he saw his father stomp tiredly into the house, Arnold did not put down his hammer and leave the chicken coop he was repairing. He was afraid that they did not want him to eat supper with them. But in a few minutes another fear that they would go to the trouble of calling him and that he would be made conspicuous by his tardiness made him follow his father into the house. As he went through the kitchen he saw the jars of peas standing in rows on the workbench, a reproach to him.

No one spoke at supper, and his mother, who sat next to him, leaned her head in 84 her hand all through the meal, curving her fingers over her eyes so as not to see him. They were finishing their small, silent supper when the visitors began to arrive, knocking hard on the back door. The men were coming from their farms now that it was growing dark and they could not work any more.

Old Man Matthews, gray and stocky, came first, with his two sons, Orion, the 85 elder, and Clint, who was Eugie's age. As the callers entered the parlor, where the family ate, Arnold sat down in a rocking chair. Even as he had been undecided before supper whether to remain outside or take his place at the table, he now thought that he should go upstairs, and yet he stayed to avoid being conspicuous by his absence. If he stayed, he thought, as he always stayed and listened when visitors came, they would see that he was only Arnold and not the person the sheriff thought he was. He sat with his arms crossed and his hands tucked into his armpits and did not lift his eyes.

The Matthews men had hardly settled down around the table, after Arnold's 86 mother and Nora had cleared away the dishes, when another car rattled down the road and someone else rapped on the back door. This time it was Sullivan, a spare and sandy man, so nimble of gesture and expression that Arnold had never been able to catch more than a few of his meanings. Sullivan, in dusty jeans, sat down in the other rocker, shot out his skinny legs and began to talk in his fast way, recalling everything that Eugene had ever said to him. The other men interrupted to tell of occasions they remembered, and after a time Clint's young voice, hoarse like Eugene's had been, broke in to tell about the time Eugene had beat him in a wrestling match.

Out in the kitchen the voices of Orion's wife and of Mrs. Sullivan mingled with 87 Nora's voice but not, Arnold noticed, his mother's. Then dry little Mr. Cram came, leaving large Mrs. Cram in the kitchen, and there was no chair left for Mr. Cram to sit in. No one asked Arnold to get up and he was unable to rise. He knew that the story had got around to them during the day about how he had gone and picked peas after he had shot his brother, and he knew that although they were talking only about Eugie they were thinking about him and if he got up, if he moved even his foot, they would all be alerted. Then Uncle Andy arrived and leaned his tall, lanky body against the doorjamb and there were two men standing.

Presently Arnold was aware that the talk had stopped. He knew without look-　88
ing up that the men were watching him.

"Not a tear in his eye," said Andy, and Arnold knew that it was his uncle who　89
had gestured the men to attention.

"He don't give a hoot, is that how it goes?" asked Sullivan, trippingly.　90

"He's a reasonable fellow," Andy explained. "That's what the sheriff said. It's　91
us who ain't reasonable. If we'd of shot our brother, we'd of come runnin' back to
the house, cryin' like a baby. Well, we'd of been unreasonable. What would of been
the use of actin' like that? If your brother is shot dead, he's shot dead. What's the
use of gettin' emotional about it? The thing to do is go down to the garden and
pick peas. Am I right?"

The men around the room shifted their heavy, satisfying weight of un-　92
reasonableness.

Matthews' son Orion said: "If I'd of done what he done, Pa would've hung my　93
pelt by the side of that big coyote's in the barn."

Arnold sat in the rocker until the last man had filed out. While his family was　94
out in the kitchen bidding the callers good night and the cars were driving away
down the dirt lane to the highway, he picked up one of the kerosene lamps and
slipped quickly up the stairs. In his room he undressed by lamplight, although he
and Eugie had always undressed in the dark, and not until he was lying in his bed
did he blow out the flame. He felt nothing, not any grief. There was only the same
immense silence and crawling inside of him; it was the way the house and fields felt
under a merciless sun.

He awoke suddenly. He knew that his father was out in the yard, closing the doors　95
of the chicken houses so that the chickens could not roam out too early and fall
prey to the coyotes that came down from the mountains at daybreak. The sound
that had wakened him was the step of his father as he got up from the rocker and
went down the back steps. And he knew that his mother was awake in her bed.

Throwing off the covers, he rose swiftly, went down the stairs and across the　96
dark parlor to his parents' room. He rapped on the door.

"Mother?"　97

From the closed room her voice rose to him, a seeking and retreating voice.　98
"Yes?"

"Mother?" he asked insistently. He had expected her to realize that he wanted　99
to go down on his knees by her bed and tell her that Eugie was dead. She did not
know it yet, nobody knew it, and yet she was sitting up in bed, waiting to be told,
waiting for him to confirm her dread. He had expected her to tell him to come in,
to allow him to dig his head into her blankets and tell her about the terror he had
felt when he had knelt beside Eugie. He had come to clasp her in his arms and, in
his terror, to pommel her breasts with his head. He put his hand upon the knob.

"Go back to bed, Arnold," she called sharply.　100
But he waited.　101
"Go back! Is night when you get afraid?"　102

At first he did not understand. Then, silently, he left the door and for a stricken   103
moment stood by the rocker. Outside everything was still. The fences, the shocks
of wheat seen through the window before him were so still it was as if they moved
and breathed in the daytime and had fallen silent with the lateness of the hour. It
was a silence that seemed to observe his father, a figure moving alone around the
yard, his lantern casting a circle of light by his feet. In a few minutes his father
would enter the dark house, the lantern still lighting his way.

Arnold was suddenly aware that he was naked. He had thrown off his blankets   104
and come down the stairs to tell his mother how he felt about Eugie, but she had
refused to listen to him and his nakedness had become unpardonable. At once he
went back up the stairs, fleeing from his father's lantern.

At breakfast he kept his eyelids lowered as if to deny the humiliating night.   105
Nora, sitting at his left, did not pass the pitcher of milk to him and he did not ask
for it. He would never again, he vowed, ask them for anything, and he ate his fried
eggs and potatoes only because everybody ate meals—the cattle ate, and the cats;
it was customary for everybody to eat.

"Nora, you gonna keep that pitcher for yourself?" his father asked.   106

Nora lowered her head unsurely.   107

"Pass it on to Arnold," his father said.   108

Nora put her hands in her lap.   109

His father picked up the metal pitcher and set it down at Arnold's plate.   110

Arnold, pretending to be deaf to the discord, did not glance up but relief   111
rained over his shoulders at the thought that his parents recognized him again.
They must have lain awake after his father had come in from the yard: had they
realized together why he had come down the stairs and knocked at their door?

"Bessie's missin' this morning," his father called out to his mother, who had   112
gone into the kitchen. "She went up the mountain last night and had her calf, most
likely. Somebody's got to go up and find her 'fore the coyotes get the calf."

That had been Eugie's job, Arnold thought. Eugie would climb the cattle trails   113
in search of a newborn calf and come down the mountain carrying the calf across
his back, with the cow running down along behind him, mooing in alarm.

Arnold ate the few more forkfuls of his breakfast, put his hands on the edge of   114
the table and pushed back his chair. If he went for the calf he'd be away from the
farm all morning. He could switch the cow down the mountain slowly, and the calf
would run along at its mother's side.

When he passed through the kitchen his mother was setting a kettle of water   115
on the stove. "Where you going?" she asked awkwardly.

"Up to get the calf," he replied, averting his face.   116

"Arnold?"   117

At the door he paused reluctantly, his back to her, knowing that she was seek-   118
ing him out, as his father was doing, and he called upon his pride to protect him
from them.

"Was you knocking at my door last night?"   119

He looked over his shoulder at her, his eyes narrow and dry.   120

"What'd you want?" she asked humbly.   121

"I didn't want nothing," he said flatly.   122

Then he went out the door and down the back steps, his legs trembling from   123
the fright his answer gave him.

From Gina Berriault, "The Stone Boy," *Mademoiselle*, 1957. Copyright © 1957 by The Condé Nast Publications, Inc. Reprinted courtesy *Mademoiselle*.

Study Questions

1. What inferences do you make, before the tragic incident, about the relationship between Arnold and Eugie? What evidence do you base your inferences on?

2. What does Arnold do immediately after the shooting? What inferences do you make about that?

3. What inferences do his parents and the sheriff and the family's friends make about Arnold's behavior?

4. What information does the author give you about how well Arnold understands his own feelings and behavior?

5. What inferences do you make by the end of the story about Arnold's needs? Explain your evidence.

6. What inferences do you make by the end of the story about Arnold's future?

OBJECTIVES REVIEW OF PART I

When you have finished Part I, you will understand

- The following concepts on an experiential basis: observing, labeling, describing, interpreting, facts, inferences, sensing, perceiving, thinking.
- That it is possible to maintain awareness of one's own thinking-feeling-perceiving process.
- How clear thinking depends on "staying awake" to what is.

And you will have practice in developing these skills:

- Suspending thinking in order to freshly sense and gather data.
- Describing the obvious evidence without substituting labels and interpretations.
- Recognizing when you and others are formulating facts and when you are formulating inferences.
- Recognizing how facts and inferences can become confused.

PART II
Problems of Critical Thinking

CHAPTER 5

Assumptions: What's Taken for Granted?

"Only a minute or so more and man will have his first view of the other side of the moon!"

From *I Paint What I See*. Copyright © 1971 by Gahan Wilson. Used with permission of Simon & Schuster, Inc.

I t's always a shock, and not necessarily a funny one, to discover that we have made a basic wrong assumption. Perhaps these astronauts might have been less astonished to find the moon to be a hunk of cheese. Yet, learning that assumptions and reality don't match is an everyday occurrence. In this chapter, we will study types of assumptions and how they operate in our thinking. We will take what we now know about inferences and use them to consider assumptions as unrecognized inferences. And we will connect what we have learned about aware observing to not only detecting assumptions but also to creating with them. In short, we will continue to build the fundamental skills of critical thinking.

Discovery Exercises

A COLLABORATIVE LEARNING OPPORTUNITY

The following three exercises can be done with a partner or alone, depending on your instructor's directions.

144

What Is an Assumption?

Using at least two dictionaries, write your own definition of *assumption*.

Finding Assumptions in Cartoons

For the cartoons on page 146 decide what assumption was made—either by a character in the cartoon or by you—that resulted in a humorous situation.

Finding Assumptions in Stories

As you read the stories recounted in each of the paragraphs below, think how each depends on an assumption. Write your answers to the questions that follow each paragraph, in preparation for a class discussion.

1. You are a guard at Alcatraz. One day a prisoner was found to be missing. When you inspected his cell, you found a hole dug through the concrete under his bed. All that was next to the hole was a bent metal spoon. What assumptions of the guards did the prisoner exploit in order to escape?

2. You are a guard at a station on the border of the country of Mesamania. Your duty is to inspect for smuggled goods. Every day some notorious smugglers pass through carrying heavy loads of goods on donkeys. You always examine their loads carefully for contraband but never find anything. What are the smugglers smuggling?

3. You have a dinner guest from a foreign country who belches loudly all through the meal. You find him disgusting and want to get rid of him. But he insists that he be allowed to return your hospitality. So you go to his house for dinner. There everyone but you belches loudly all through the meal. Before you leave, your host says, "I am sorry you did not like my dinner, but you didn't have to be so rude about it." What was the assumption of the foreign guest?

4. George Bernard Shaw was once approached by a woman who proposed marriage. "Imagine a child," she said, "with my body and your brains." "Yes," he said, "but what if the child has my body and your brains?" What was his assumption?

5. In his struggles to receive backing for the voyage of his ships to the Far East by sailing west, Christopher Columbus once spent some hours trying to persuade a nobleman to lend his support. The nobleman maintained that he was trying to do the impossible, like making an egg stand on end. Then the nobleman called for an egg and handed it to Columbus, who was sitting across from him at a table. Taking up the challenge, Columbus tried wobbling the egg on one end and then the other, while the nobleman laughed in derision. Then, picking up the

Used with permission of Richard Guindon.

BIZARRO By DAN PIRARO

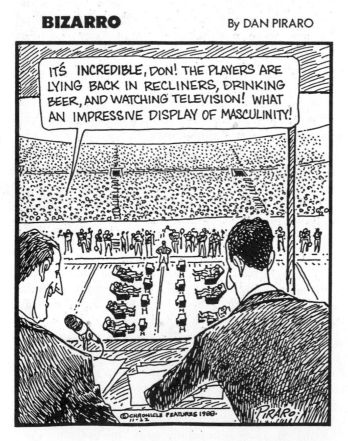

Reprinted with permission of Chronicle Features, San Francisco.

egg, Columbus gently smashed its end on the table, allowing it to stand firmly in position, while its contents oozed out. What assumption about the problem did the nobleman make that Columbus did not?

6. In California, a bank holdup was staged by a man wearing a Levi's jacket and pants, a beard, and hair in a "dreadlock" style. He waved a hand grenade and pointed to some sticks of "dynamite" strapped to his waist, which were actually road flares. After leaving the bank he ran into a warehouse next door where he shed his wig, beard, the flares, and clothing and changed into a blue, pin-striped suit. Stopped by a police officer outside, he insisted, "I'm not the one!" And because he didn't look the same as the robber, the police officer let him go. What assumptions did the robber count on in his strategy?

UNDERSTANDING ASSUMPTIONS

The etymology of the word *assume* shows us something interesting. *Assume* comes from the Latin *assumere*—to take, adopt, accept. To assume is to take and accept something. In time, this word came to mean accepting something without checking it out carefully.

Our study of inferences in Chapter 4 prepares us to understand assumptions better. Assumptions don't cause us problems when they turn out to be correct inferences. If we take for granted that we will need a rain jacket on a hike and it does not rain, we can be glad for that. *Usually, we speak of assumptions as inferences made without awareness.* Assumptions usually are recognized only after their negative consequences have become clear. For example, most tourists visiting San Francisco in foggy July shiver on the streets in light summer clothing. Of course, since most of the United States is warm in July, and because California has a reputation for sunny weather, their expectation of a warm climate is reasonable. Only the facts of the northern coast's foggy summer season brings their assumption to light.

Awareness of the thinking process can help us avoid some, but not all, faulty assumptions, although we cannot avoid them altogether. The factors of probability and randomness affect us all. Moreover, we have to prioritize what we can take for granted. We don't call the bus company every morning to see whether the 8 A.M. bus is running on time. But if we need that bus to connect us to an international flight, we might be more cautious.

Whenever our assumptions bring us unpleasant surprises, we usually resolve to think things through more carefully next time, which means being more aware of our inference-making process. Sometimes these disappointments are minor, like shivering in the fog, or missing a bus that came early. But they can also be traumatic, like discovering deceit from someone you trusted, or fatal, like being hit by a car in a crosswalk. To survive more easily, we would all prefer to avoid the unpleasant consequences of mistaken assumptions.

There are many types of assumptions to consider, and not all types cause problems. Some, when consciously held, guide the scientific method and allow discoveries, inventions, and creative problem solving. We will begin to consider the different types of assumptions by looking at the difference between conscious and unconscious assumptions and between warranted and unwarranted ones.

TYPES OF ASSUMPTIONS

Making assumptions can be a pitfall in the thinking process, but it can also be a tool—it all depends on the type of assumption you are making. Assumptions can be conscious or unconscious, warranted or unwarranted.

If you take something for granted, you have an *unconscious assumption*. If you sit at the counter of a restaurant that promises home cooking and your food is dished out of a saucepan by a motherly figure dressed in a housecoat and hair curlers, you might realize that you had taken for granted that home cooking would not be so informal. Unconscious assumptions are beliefs, values, or ideas that are not consciously recognized or expressed.

A *conscious assumption*, on the other hand, can be defined as a kind of creative strategy. Sometimes we can make a conscious assumption and use it to guide us to new information. This is also known as a working assumption. Imagine a person looking for a house in an isolated rural area. He comes to a fork in the road and does not know which way to go. He decides to *assume* for the time being that the house is to the left and to proceed for 2 miles. If at the end of that distance he still has not found the house, he will return to the fork and proceed to the right. He has not *believed* in his assumption—he has only borrowed it. When assumptions are used consciously, they can be helpful as temporary guides to action. When assumptions are unconscious, choices based on them may lead to surprising and undesirable consequences.

As another example, suppose your family has to make an investment decision. Finally, your family decides to invest in real estate, *assuming* that property values will continue to rise in the years to come. In this case, the assumption is made consciously; nothing is taken for granted. To make a decision, the family makes a conscious assumption to work with the best possible interpretation of the unknown factors. The assumption may turn out to be incorrect, but as a conscious assumption it will not lead to the shock or surprise of discovering the wrongness of an unconscious one.

In mathematics, conscious assumptions are essential. For example, 2 + 2 = 4 is not a fact but a conclusion or theorem based on axioms that are *assumed* to be fundamental. An *axiom* is defined as a statement assumed as a basis for the development of a subject. Usually, axioms are very acceptable assumptions—not outlandish ones—that can be applied to the real world. Sometimes, as in this case, they are said to be self-evident, but basically they are labeled "assumptions." We will return in Chapter 11 to the topic of creating working assumptions—or hypotheses.

A distinction can also be made between warranted and unwarranted assumptions, or those that are reasonable to make and those that are not. If you buy a carton of milk at your neighborhood grocery dated for use within a week, you can make a *warranted assumption* that it will not be sour when you open it. The same can be said of assumptions that the city buses will arrive and leave on schedule, that the post office will be open on weekdays but not holidays, and that gas and electricity will be available at the flick of a switch. Routine matters like these offer us convenience because they are based on an agreed-upon code of warranted assumptions.

Unwarranted assumptions are those based on ignorance of or lack of awareness of unwritten codes or agreements. If a friend offers you a ride to school one day, or even two days in a row, it would be an *unwarranted assumption* to expect her to provide the same service for you regularly. If a friend breaks a promise, you discover that your assumption that this person was dependable was unwarranted.

Critical thinking helps us recognize unconscious and unwarranted assumptions that lead to faulty reasoning and poor decisions, as we shall see.

IDENTIFYING HIDDEN ASSUMPTIONS IN REASONING

When unconscious assumptions form the basis for reasoning that leads to a particular conclusion, we call them hidden assumptions. The ability to identify hidden assumptions is an important critical thinking skill. Critical thinking articulates hidden assumptions to expose the fundamental but unexamined thoughts that form the basis for reasoning. It exposes what was taken for granted that should not have been and thus what made the reasoning unsound. We can learn to identify hidden assumptions in reasoning through practice and through awareness of some of the common forms of hidden assumptions.

Stereotypes are one form of hidden assumption that crops up often in reasoning. Stereotypes might be described as automatic mental filing systems for classifying new data in old and familiar categories. For instance, consider the statement "All cocker spaniels are friendly dogs; this dog looks mean; therefore it's not a cocker spaniel." The obvious hidden assumption here is that all cocker spaniels fit into one category of friendly dogs. Consider the stereotypes behind the reasoning offered in these sentences:

1. Don't you have a girlfriend to sew on that button?
2. If your friend is Japanese, he must be moody.
3. He must be intelligent if he has a college degree.

Some hidden assumptions are based on belief in the superiority of a particular race, nationality, religion, gender, or individual viewpoint. For instance, someone who says, "Indians do not eat cows because they are superstitious" is judging Indians according to Western beliefs. The speaker shows an ignorance of the philosophy, logic, and culture of the Hindu tradition. Such a viewpoint is both ethnocentric and religiocentric. Belief in the superiority of males is called *androcentrism;* of humankind over other living things—*anthropocentrism;* and of one's individual viewpoint—*egocentrism.* We will examine these *isms* in more detail in Chapter 8, "Viewpoints." For now, it's important to recognize when any of these beliefs takes the form of a hidden assumption in reasoning.

Still another kind of hidden assumption, related to the others we've mentioned, is based on value judgments. These are called value assumptions. For instance, the statement "Anyone with a million dollars would be happy" is based on the hidden assumption that happiness depends on money, perhaps beginning with a $1 million minimum. Moreover, an additional assumption is that this is a commonly shared value.

Any of these forms of hidden assumptions lead to faulty reasoning. We need to learn to recognize when hidden assumptions creep into our reasoning or someone else's.

Class Discussion

Identify and express the hidden assumptions behind each of the following statements:

1. What's a nice girl like you doing in a place like this?
2. I couldn't visit a Buddhist temple because they worship idols there.

3. How can that marriage counselor help people if he himself is divorced?

4. Interviewer to couple on TV show: "What would your parents say if they knew you both belonged to a swingers' club?"

5. You shouldn't be critical of corporations. Aren't you in favor of free enterprise?

6. I can't understand why I haven't met my soulmate this year. My astrologer said I would.

7. Native Americans need to learn the importance of competition for success.

8. People in the Fiji Islands live in poverty and hardship, lacking running water, baths, and toilets in their homes.

9. In a cartoon two men are sitting on the edge of a river polluted with floating oil cans, syringes, industrial wastes, and dead fish. Smoke billows over them from a factory smokestack and diesel trucks in the background. One man says to the other, "Can you imagine what would happen if some irresponsible nut got hold of chemical weapons?"

10. In a television program about earthquake preparedness, an expert demonstrated his gas-driven generator. "In the event of a major disaster," he said, "this generator would run our children's television set so that they would have something to do."

HIDDEN ASSUMPTIONS IN ARGUMENTS

Arguments, as defined in critical thinking, are claims supported by reasoning and evidence that are used to defend an idea or persuade others to accept an idea. Therefore, a successful argument is one built from a carefully considered structure of reasoning. A poor argument lacks the kind of careful construction that requires a questioning of all underlying assumptions. Thus, in writing an argument, you need to stop from time to time to ask whether you have taken for granted anything that might affect your reasoning. The same holds true for reading an argument. This is a fundamental critical thinking habit that you can acquire over a short time with practice.

Exercise

Articulating Hidden Assumptions Underlying Arguments

Write down the hidden assumptions you find in the following quotations, to share in a later class discussion:

1. "The $280 million special revenue bond earmarked for construction of new county jails is a misguided, expensive attempt to solve a very real problem: overcrowded, inhumane conditions in our jails.

   "But that very problem is rooted in our current criminal justice system and the existence of oppressive laws which create a whole category of victimless 'crimes.'

   "Over 50 percent of those arrested in California are victimized by the existence of these laws—which regulate drug use, voluntary sexual activities, gambling, and other aspects of personal life. Most of those convicted and serving time are sent to our county jails. While violent criminals roam our streets, our extensive county jail system is filled to overflowing with people who have injured no one else." (*California Voters' Pamphlet* [Libertarian party view], November 1982)

2. "The federal government is doing a great many things for which there is no warrant in the Constitution. Among these are collecting taxes for Social Security, providing Medicare and Medicaid, imposing a *graduated* income tax, prohibiting child labor, and granting low-cost loans to students." (*Your Heritage News* [a far-right publication], November 1983)

3. "In 1921, Mongolia was just being liberated [by the Communists]. Centuries of feudalism and Lamaist [Buddhist] theocracy had put a stranglehold on the land. Out of a population of 650,000, almost a third of the able-bodied males were lamas [monks] in the Buddhist monasteries, living a life of idleness." (*World Magazine* [a communist publication], March 19, 1983)

4. "I'm nothing," he said. "You understand that, nothing. I earn $250,000 a year, but it's nothing, and I'm nobody. My expenses range from maintaining an apartment on Park Avenue for $20,400 a year to $30,000 a year for private schools for my children. My total expenses come to over $300,000 a year, leaving nothing left over for dinner parties, paintings, furniture, a mistress, psychiatrists, or even a week in Europe." (from Lewis Lapham, "The Gilded Cage," *Money and Class in America*. New York: Random House, 1988)

5. A federal judge ruled that schools violate the Constitution by requiring fundamentalist Christian children to use textbooks that offend their religious beliefs. He ordered the Hawkins County Tennessee public schools to excuse fundamentalist children from reading class to avoid books that their parents say promote feminism, pacifism, and other themes that they regard as anti-Christian.

VALUE ASSUMPTIONS

Value assumptions are our unquestioned beliefs. They are so familiar and fundamental to our thinking that we take them for granted as much as we take gravity for granted. It usually takes something like a startling experience to bring them to the surface for reexamination. An example from the life of the author Jean Liedloff can serve as an illustration.

She spent two-and-a-half years living with a Stone Age tribe, the Yequana Indians of the rain forests of Brazil. One thing that puzzled her was that the tribe did not have a word for *work*, nor did members distinguish work from other ways of spending time. She observed the women thoroughly enjoying the task of going down to a stream for water several times a day, even though they had to descend a steep bank with gourds on their heads and babies on their backs. Gradually the author came to realize that the idea that work is unpleasant and leisure is pleasant is only a Western value assumption. She had to consider that this idea was not necessarily a truth about life, but a cultural attitude. This insight led her to reexamine other Western beliefs, such as the idea that progress is good and that a child belongs to its parents.

Another account of a woman's discovery of some Western value assumptions appears in *Mutant Message Down Under* by Marlo Morgan. In the first chapter of this novel, the storyteller finds herself in a jeep being driven across the desert to meet a tribe of Australian Aborigines gathered for a ceremony in her honor. Although the weather is hot, she is wearing stockings, a suit with a pink silk blouse, and carrying those necessities of a tape recorder, 35mm camera, and a purse with credit cards. She is dressed in expectation of a ceremony and banquet. The jeep comes to a stop at a small corrugated tin shed where the tribe waits for her outside beside a fire. They greet her warmly, then ask her to cleanse herself of all her garments and possessions. They give her one wrap-around rag to wear. Next, to her amazement, they throw all of her possessions into the fire—camera, credit cards and all—then offer her their greatest token of trust: an invitation to join them on a barefoot walkabout across Australia. She accepts their gift and begins an adventure. On this journey with one of the oldest peoples on earth, she gradually discovers many Western value assumptions.

Value assumptions lie deep within all of us. We live by their guidance—sometimes well, sometimes poorly. The cartoon on page 154 depicts some values. Their effect can be startling when we recognize that these values are what our great grandparents called the seven deadly sins. (This cartoon omits lust.) It awakens us to the possibility that, without awareness, we have transformed what once were sins into virtues and virtues (such as thrift, sobriety, generosity, and modesty) into sins. They have

THE 6 VIRTUES OF CONSUMER CULTURE

Used with permission of Kirk Anderson.

become new value assumptions. Thus, value assumptions differ not only from culture to culture but can even reverse themselves over time within a society. Bringing these assumptions to conscious awareness allows us to choose whether we want to continue to live by them.

ASSUMPTION LAYERS IN ARGUMENTS

Once we understand the meaning of hidden assumptions and value assumptions, we have the opportunity to discover how they can appear in layers, with a fundamental value assumption lying beneath a pyramid of reasoning assumptions. Consider this example, taken from a statement made by a politician upon hearing that twelve million Americans were unemployed: *"If you women would stay at home, maybe we could solve America's unemployment problem."*

First, we have to unravel all the assumptions inherent in such a statement. Some of them are as follows:

1.   All women could have men to support them.

2. Women are taking jobs away from men.
3. Women do not really need jobs since they can stay at home.
4. Men want and will take women's jobs (and pay).
5. Work for all women is a kind of indulgence.

Then the question remains: what value assumption would lead a person to make a statement that contains all these assumptions? One is certainly the idea that a woman's place is in the home.

Class Discussion

Consider the following statements and list any hidden assumptions. Then see if you can discover at least one underlying value assumption. (Ask yourself what a person would have to believe in order to create this argument.)

1. Schools should teach children to believe in the Bible.
2. Hospitals shun the poor and suffering. John Andrews, who was severely beaten, was brought to a private hospital by a friend. He was suffering from a collapsed lung, concussion, and broken rib. Because he couldn't prove he had insurance, he was turned away and dumped on a county hospital.
3. "The cruelest thing you could say to a woman who is pregnant, poor, alone, and afraid is that she has the right to terminate her child." (Vatican representative at U.N. Women's Conference in Beijing, 1995)
4. "The first thing you do is sit down with your wife and say something like this: 'Honey, I've made a terrible mistake. I've given you my role. I gave up leading this family.' I'm not suggesting that you ask for your role back, I'm urging you to take it back. . . . Be sensitive. Listen. Treat the lady gently and lovingly. But lead!" (Tony Evans, *Seven Promises of a Promise Keeper*)
5. "The government has painted all their helicopters black. These helicopters are monitoring patriotic Americans and are prepared to take their arms away, round them up, and put them in internment camps." (member of a militia group)
6. "The anti-environmental forces in Congress are escalating their all-out war on America's environment. If they succeed, they will rob us of our national heritage, pollute our air and water, cut down our forests, close some of our beloved national parks, and threaten the health and quality of life of thousands of Americans." (Sierra Club newsletter, 1995)
7. *Radio Interviewer*: "The U.S. government released figures yesterday to show that rural highways that had increased their speed limits from 55 to 65 mph also had an increase of 20,000 more fatalities per year. What do you, as a representative of the Society for Sane Speed Limits, think of this?"

Spokesperson: "Well, first of all, it has not been proven that the increase in the speed limit was the cause of the increase of fatalities. However, even if it were, our organization feels this statistic is within acceptable limits as needed for speed, accessibility, and for our greater economic growth and welfare." (interview on National Public Radio, Washington, D.C., October 1989)

ASSUMPTIONS, INCONGRUITIES, AND THINKING

When we see a picture of a mannequin in a bathing suit in a church tower window, it challenges our assumptions of how a church is supposed to be: concerned with spiritual, not commercial matters. An image that is so *incongruous* (from the Latin *in* = not, *congruere* = meet together) does not *meet together with* our memories and assumptions; it makes us uncomfortable. Yet, despite this discomfort, it is good for us to have our assumptions challenged, because this is the way we learn and grow.

Recall from Chapter 1 that according to Jean Piaget, we are required to think, or reorganize what we know, when we have experiences that we cannot easily assimilate. This process, which Piaget calls accommodation, is provoked by an inner sense of disequilibrium between ourselves and our environment. This is what happens when our assumptions are challenged by something we observe. For instance, seeing a woman in a hardhat pounding nails at a construction site may challenge our assumptions about what women can do. Only when we successfully accomplish a reorganization of our mental categories to accommodate this new experience do we restore our sense of equilibrium.

While describing many of the photographs in this book so far, you may have felt especially uncomfortable. This is because all of them, whether you realized it while viewing them or not, are *based on incongruities*. In studying the photographs, you have had the choice of either suppressing or avoiding the disequilibrium they aroused, or of staying with the task long enough to reach equilibrium by finding a satisfactory explanation for their incongruities.

To return to the picture of the mannequin in the church window, you might find your explanation by inferring (1) the church has a liberal pastor concerned with fund raising; (2) the church has been sold and turned into a boutique; or (3) an architect designed a commercial building with a bell tower. To find a satisfactory explanation that *reconciles* all our facts sometimes means tolerating a period of doubt and confusion; we have to

Photo by John Pearson. Used with permission of the photographer.

AVOIDING ASSUMPTIONS

	Start-Up Costs	Average Yearly Expenses	Average Yearly Income	Expected Value
San Antonio	$100,000	$125,000	$270,000	$45,000
Houston	$140,000	$140,000	$375,000	$95,000
Dallas	$130,000	$120,000	$350,000	$100,000

A Vietnamese family living in San Antonio, Texas, decided to open up their own restaurant. They learned from a bank what the start-up costs would be in three cities. They learned that it would cost less in San Antonio than in Houston or Dallas. However, their eldest son, who was a business major at Trinity University, suggested that they get more information before making their final decision and analyze their options through a decision tree. He explained to his parents that to use this method, it would be necessary to take the average annual income and subtract the average yearly expenses and start-up costs to find the expected value. After obtaining more figures from the chambers of commerce involved, he was able to make the diagram above.

Questions

1. What choice do you think they made?
2. What assumptions did the decision tree keep them from making?
3. Describe a problem you prevented by discovering an assumption.

Used with permission of Mark Frey.

experience and mentally contain incongruity until we can bring our information into another pattern of order. And although we may never be able to confirm the final truth of our explanation, we at least have the satisfaction of having reconciled all the available information. Persistence in this process of moving from disequilibrium to equilibrium is what Piaget says develops our thinking skills.

Thinking comes about in life through provocation: when we meet situations that do not fit a familiar pattern, that do not fall into familiar stereotypes, that do not meet expectations. In such cases, we have the personal choice to deny or ignore—or to think, to learn, and to grow. When we were toddlers, if we touched a hot stove, the experience of being burned was an unpleasant encounter with reality. And yet, even then, if we had not stopped to analyze even in a simple way what caused the pain, we would

> ## BUILDING ARGUMENTS
>
> ### ASSUMPTIONS
>
> Some of our chiefs make the claim that the land belongs to us. It is not what the Great Spirit told me. He told me that the lands belong to Him, that no people owns the land; that I was not to forget to tell this to the white people when I met them in council. (Kannekuk, Kickapoo prophet, 1827)
>
> *Exercise*
>
> 1. What claim is being refuted here?
> 2. What assumption lies in the claim?
> 3. What counterclaim is being made?
> 4. State a claim that you feel contains an assumption. State why you believe it is an assumption. Formulate your own counterclaim.

have had to suffer the same pain over and over again. Even if we decided to always depend on someone else to think for us and protect us, we would eventually have found such a solution to be impractical. We survive best when we can think for ourselves. And the more we think, the more willing, open, and able we are to accept life's challenges of our assumptions.

Class Discussion

1. Give an example of an incongruity that you have experienced that has challenged one of your assumptions.
2. Can you describe the disequilibrium you felt when you saw this incongruity?
3. How did you restore your equilibrium?
4. Have you experienced disequilibrium at times while studying this textbook? How was your equilibrium restored?

CHAPTER SUMMARY

1. An assumption is something we take for granted, something we buy before checking it out carefully. Often, we do not recognize that we have made an assumption until it causes a problem for us.

2. Assumptions can be conscious or unconscious, warranted or unwarranted. Unconscious and unwarranted assumptions can lead to faulty reasoning, whereas conscious and warranted assumptions can be useful tools for problem solving. We need to recognize the difference.

3. Hidden assumptions are unconscious assumptions that form the basis for reasoning that leads to a particular conclusion. Common forms of hidden assumptions are stereotypes, where we file new experiences in old categories; belief in the superiority of a particular race, nationality, religion, gender, or individual viewpoint; and assumptions based on value judgments, known as value assumptions.

4. Arguments are the use of reasoning to defend an idea or to persuade someone else to believe in the idea. Arguments that contain assumptions are easily demolished, so it is important to make an argument as conscious a mental construction as possible.

5. Incongruities are things we observe that do not meet our expectations or assumptions. When our assumptions are challenged by incongruities, we can choose to reexamine our assumptions and adjust them to regain our equilibrium. This is the process of growth and learning.

6. Someone who brings a fresh perspective to a problem that has stumped others is often able to find a solution because he or she does not buy the assumptions that restrain others. As a conscious tool, we can look for assumptions when we are confronted with a problem to solve.

CHAPTER QUIZ

Rate each of the following statements as *true* or *false*. Justify your answer with an example or explanation.

_____ 1. When we articulate hidden assumptions, we simply read what we find in print before us.

_____ 2. A good argument invariably contains a few hidden assumptions.

_____ 3. To make a value assumption is to offer a line of reasoning based on a value or belief assumed to be shared by everyone.

_____ 4. "Can you believe it? She is twenty-three years old and not even thinking of getting married." This statement, made by a Puerto Rican, contains no value assumption.

_____ 5. Assumptions are often recognized only in retrospect because of the problems they cause.

_____ 6. In mathematics, conscious assumptions are called *axioms*.

_____ 7. A *conscious* assumption can be used as a strategy to lead us to new information. If a child does not come home from school at the usual time, we might first decide to call the homes of the child's friends; if that turns up no information, we might call the police.

_____ 8. Stereotypes contain no assumptions.

_____ 9. To be uncomfortable is to be in disequilibrium. Thinking through a problem restores the comfort of our mental equilibrium.

_____ 10. Incongruities can provoke us into thinking in order to resolve their conflict with our assumptions and expectations.

Composition Writing Application

Expository Essay: Solving a Problem by Uncovering Assumptions

Think of a major problem from your own life (or someone else's) that was solved by the discovery of one or more hidden assumptions. If you prefer to use historical examples from the lives of explorers, artists, or scientists, do some research on the kinds of problems they succeeded in solving. (Besides using ordinary encyclopedias, you might also look for some special science encyclopedias in the library.)

Write in sketch form your basic findings, searching for the following elements to develop and emphasize:

1. What particular problem concerned your subject?

2. What assumptions were embedded in the problem?

3. How were these assumptions discovered?

4. What restraints did these assumptions impose?

5. What, if any, wrong assumptions were made?

Prepare a working outline for an essay of about three typewritten pages. Then begin your essay with a thesis statement that explains what you concluded from your research and analysis.

The *thesis statement*, also called the *thesis*, has some similarity to the topic sentence in that it states a generalization. However, it may be introduced and stated through several sentences instead of one, and it proposes an idea that will be developed, explained, and illustrated over many pages and many paragraphs. By definition, the thesis is the idea that the essay intends to prove. Again, in the process of thinking, the thesis, like the topic sentence, may come only after some study of the subject. However, in the academic essay, it is stated in the first paragraph. A thesis is also called the *controlling idea* because everything written in the essay is based on the dictates of its objective. We can visualize the thesis as a frame, like a picture frame: everything that will appear in that picture—the essay—is contained in and limited by the thesis.

The act of stating the thesis also assists us in organizing our thoughts around one main purpose; it enables us to decide what information would be relevant to this subject and what would not be. If we are writing about assumptions, for instance, we do not need to cover opinions as well. Every statement and every fact appearing in the essay should either support or develop the thesis.

Let's look at the anatomy of a thesis. Suppose you decided to write an expository essay to explain a problem you solved at work through the discovery of a hidden assumption. Your thesis might begin like this:

> (1) All of us have heard fables about villages that suffered long and hard from a particular problem, like a famine or a wayward dragon. (2) Then one day a stranger appeared and solved the problem simply, quickly, and miraculously. (3) In such stories, what seemed to be a miracle to the villagers was only a matter of a newcomer's bringing a fresh perspective, unbiased by any past assumptions. (4) My own life had a parallel situation several years ago when I went to work for the municipal utilities district. (5) And although I did not arrive on a horse or in a suit of armor, I did bring a fresh perspective that solved an "insoluble problem."

These five sentences comprise the thesis statement. The first two introduce the topic and invite interest. The third states a principle and a limitation of focus. The fourth makes the transition to a personal incident that will illustrate this principle. And the fifth sentence states the actual thesis that the narrative will prove.

Here is a summary of the parameters for this assignment:

1. *Topic*: How one creative individual challenged the restraints of some mistaken assumptions in solving a problem.

2. *Objective*: To isolate a component in the creative thinking process of an individual and to explain how its manifestations, whether conscious or unconscious, correct or incorrect, affected the outcome.

3. *Form*: Essay using personal or researched information for illustration and exposition to support the thesis statement.

4. *Length*: Three to four typed pages.

Submit your working outline with your paper if your instructor requests that you do so. To follow up in class, read your essays to one another in pairs or small groups. Check over one another's work to see whether the parameters were followed. Critique each essay with these questions in mind:

1. Does the writer state the thesis clearly and develop it well?

2. Does the essay really stay with the topic of illustrating how an individual solved one major problem through working with some mistaken assumptions?

Student Writing Example

A MISPLACED ASSUMPTION

Terry Ruscoe

All of us have heard fables about villages that suffered long and hard from a particular problem, like a famine or a wayward dragon. Then one day a stranger appeared and solved the problem simply, quickly, and miraculously. In such stories, what seemed to be a miracle to the villagers was only a matter of a newcomer's bringing a fresh perspective, unbiased by any past assumptions. My own life had a parallel situation several years ago when I went to work for the municipal utilities district. And although I did not arrive on a horse or in a suit of armor, I did bring a fresh perspective that solved an "insoluble problem."

My work as a storekeeper was to receive and distribute merchandise, such as plumbing supplies, to our work crews. Here was the problem: after our trucks rolled out of the yard to make deliveries, we would often get calls asking for a modification in the order. But, we had no way of getting in touch with the trucks once they left. This could mean even more frustration for the frantic caller who needed just one more of those special pipeline fittings to complete the job and get traffic moving again.

"Radios, that's what we need," said the foreman as he burst into the office. He had just been chewed out by the supervisor of maintenance for a work delay of two hours because of some missing material. "The only problem is the budget. How can we afford $800 right away to put a radio in each of the trucks?" Carl, the receiving clerk, who was instructing me on the proper manner of keeping stock records, looked up and quipped, "Yeah, not only is that too much money, but say the driver is out of his truck unloading . . . he may not even hear the thing."

Later that day at lunch, several of us were in the break room. We began tossing the problem around. One of the guys came up with a good idea, suggesting that we augment the radios with an attachment to automatically sound the horn of the truck when it was called. But this would be even more expensive and still be useless if the driver was out of range or was out in a pool vehicle.

Another problem that arose was the lack of firsthand communication; every message would have to be channeled through the base station operator unless we bought our own base station transmitter, which would cost even more money. And then there was the question of privacy: what if we wanted the driver to stop on the way back to pick up some doughnuts? We didn't need the whole district to know about it. "It's the same old problem," moaned one driver. "Face it, we're just going to have to pop for the whole deal, base station and all, and be done with it. Consider it a long-term investment into our sanity."

I had been listening, just listening, for about twenty minutes when I realized that what we had here were two misplaced assumptions: the first was that we had to reach the *truck*; and the second was that we had only *one* way of communicating. It's the driver we need to reach, I reasoned. And what else was there besides radios? Telephones? He couldn't carry a phone around with him but . . . what about a beeper? That way, when he got our message, he could go to any nearby phone and call us. (Remember that this was back in the times when only doctors carried beepers.) "Okay," I said, "why not supply each driver with a remote-controlled beeper, so that when he gets our message he can go directly to a phone and call us. As they say, 'phoning is the next best thing to being there.'" And guess what? It worked. If we wanted to contact a driver we simply beeped him. It was far less expensive, and we were able to rent the beepers immediately. Above all, the troops could now get what they wanted without any of those old-fashioned glazed-or-chocolate mix-ups.

Used with permission of Terry Ruscoe.

Readings

LATERAL AND VERTICAL THINKING
Edward de Bono

Edward de Bono has been a professor at Cambridge, Oxford, and Harvard and has written many innovative books about thinking, maintaining it is a learnable and teachable skill. He was the first to develop the term *lateral thinking*, which is particularly useful for creative problem solving. Lateral thinking allows a person to overcome binding assumptions and see a problem in an entirely different way, thus allowing novel solutions. In the illustrative story presented here, Edward de Bono explains the differences between lateral and vertical thinking.

Many years ago when a person who owed money could be thrown into jail, a merchant in London had the misfortune to owe a huge sum to a money-lender. The money-lender, who was old and ugly, fancied the merchant's beautiful teenage 1 daughter. He proposed a bargain. He said he would cancel the merchant's debt if he could have the girl instead.

Both the merchant and his daughter were horrified at the proposal. So the cunning money-lender proposed that they let Providence decide the matter. He told them that he would put a black pebble and a white pebble into an empty money-bag and then the girl would have to pick out one of the pebbles. If she chose the black pebble she would become his wife and her father's debt would be cancelled. If she chose the white pebble she would stay with her father and the debt would be cancelled. But if she refused to pick out a pebble her father would be thrown into jail and she would starve.

Reluctantly the merchant agreed. They were standing on a pebble-strewn path in the merchant's garden as they talked and the money-lender stooped down to pick up the two pebbles. As he picked up the pebbles the girl, sharp-eyed with fright, noticed that he picked up two black pebbles and put them into the money-bag. He then asked the girl to pick out the pebble that was to decide her fate and that of her father.

Imagine that you are standing on that path in the merchant's garden. What would you have done if you had been the unfortunate girl? If you had had to advise her what would you have advised her to do?

What type of thinking would you use to solve the problem? You may believe that careful logical analysis must solve the problem if there is a solution. This type of thinking is straight-forward vertical thinking. The other type of thinking is lateral thinking.

Vertical thinkers are not usually of much help to a girl in this situation. The way they analyze it, there are three possibilities:

1. The girl should refuse to take a pebble.
2. The girl should show that there are two black pebbles in the bag and expose the money-lender as a cheat.
3. The girl should take a black pebble and sacrifice herself in order to save her father from prison.

None of these suggestions is very helpful, for if the girl does not take a pebble her father goes to prison, and if she does take a pebble, then she has to marry the money-lender.

The story shows the difference between vertical thinking and lateral thinking. Vertical thinkers are concerned with the fact that the girl has to take a pebble. Lateral thinkers become concerned with the pebble that is left behind. Vertical thinkers take the most reasonable view of a situation and then proceed logically and carefully to work it out. Lateral thinkers tend to explore all the different ways of looking at something, rather than accepting the most promising and proceeding from that.

The girl in the pebble story put her hand into the money-bag and drew out a pebble. Without looking at it she fumbled and let it fall to the path where it was immediately lost among all the others.

"Oh, how clumsy of me," she said, "but never mind—if you look into the   10
bag you will be able to tell which pebble I took by the colour of the one that
is left."

Since the remaining pebble is of course black, it must be assumed that she has   11
taken the white pebble, since the money-lender dare not admit his dishonesty. In
this way, by using lateral thinking, the girl changes what seems an impossible
situation into an extremely advantageous one. The girl is actually better off than if
the money-lender had been honest and had put one black and one white pebble
into the bag, for then she would have had only an even chance of being saved. As
it is, she is sure of remaining with her father and at the same time having his debt
cancelled.

Vertical thinking has always been the only respectable type of thinking. In its   12
ultimate form as logic it is the recommended ideal towards which all minds are
urged to strive, no matter how far short they fall. Computers are perhaps the best
example. The problem is defined by the programmer, who also indicates the path
along which the problem is to be explored. The computer then proceeds with its
incomparable logic and efficiency to work out the problem. The smooth progression of vertical thinking from one solid step to another solid step is quite different
from lateral thinking.

If you were to take a set of toy blocks and build them upwards, each block   13
resting firmly and squarely on the block below it, you would have an illustration of
vertical thinking. With lateral thinking the blocks are scattered around. They may
be connected to each other loosely or not at all. But the pattern that may eventually
emerge can be as useful as the vertical structure.

Study Questions

1.   What role do assumptions play in vertical thinking?

2.   How does lateral thinking work with assumptions?

3.   "Vertical thinkers take the most reasonable view of a situation and then
     proceed logically and carefully to work it out. Lateral thinkers tend to
     explore all the different ways of looking at something, rather than ac-
     cepting the most promising and proceeding from that." Look again at
     the story of Columbus and the egg cited in the Discovery Exercises at
     the beginning of this chapter. Was Columbus a vertical or lateral
     thinker?

4.   Is the author saying that vertical thinking is wrong?

5.   Can lateral and vertical thinking be used creatively together to solve a
     problem? Give an example.

6.   In the state-operated health care program offered in China, village phy-
     sicians are paid not for their services to the sick but for the number of

their assigned patients who stay well. How does this represent a lateral thinking solution? What do you think are its advantages and disadvantages? What is just interesting about this idea?

7. A persistent U.S. problem is illegal drug use. One unsuccessful solution has been the "war on drugs." Do you think this was a vertical or lateral solution? If you feel it is vertical, suggest some lateral solutions. If you claim it is lateral, then describe some vertical solutions.

WINTERBLOSSOM GARDEN

David Low

The following is an excerpt from an autobiographical short story. Born in 1952 in Queens, New York, David Low now lives in the East Village of New York City. This story may be viewed from many dimensions, including as a study of the frustrations of a mother and son separated by their different value assumptions. The short story "Winterblossom Garden" appeared in an anthology, *Under Western Eyes* (New York: Doubleday, 1995), edited by Garrett Hongo.

My mother pours two cups of tea from the porcelain teapot that has always been 1 in its wicker basket on the kitchen table. On the sides of the teapot, a maiden dressed in a jade-green gown visits a bearded emperor at his palace near the sky. The maiden waves a vermilion fan.

"I bet you still don't know how to cook," my mother says. She places a plate 2 of steamed roast pork buns before me.

"Mom, I'm not hungry." 3

"If you don't eat more, you will get sick." 4

I take a bun from the plate, but it is too hot. My mother hands me a napkin so 5 I can put the bun down. Then she peels a banana in front of me.

"I'm not obsessed with food like you," I say. 6

"What's wrong with eating?" 7

She looks at me as she takes a big bite of the banana. 8

"I'm going to have a photography show at the end of the summer." 9

"Are you still taking pictures of old buildings falling down? How ugly! Why 10 don't you take happier pictures?"

"I thought you would want to come," I answer. "It's not easy to get a gallery." 11

"If you were married," she says, her voice becoming unusually soft, "you 12 would take better pictures. You would be happy."

"I don't know what you mean. Why do you think getting married will make 13 me happy?"

My mother looks at me as if I have spoken in Serbo-Croatian. She always gives 14 me this look when I say something she does not want to hear. She finishes the banana; then she puts the plate of food away. Soon she stands at the sink, turns on the hot water and washes dishes. My mother learned long ago that silence has a power of its own.

She takes out a blue cookie tin from the dining-room cabinet. Inside this tin, my 15 mother keeps her favorite photographs. Whenever I am ready to leave, my mother brings it to the living room and opens it on the coffee table. She knows I cannot resist looking at these pictures again; I will sit down next to her on the sofa for at least another hour. Besides the portraits of the family, my mother has images of people I have never met: her father, who owned a poultry store on Pell Street and didn't get a chance to return to China before he died; my father's younger sister, who still runs a pharmacy in Rio de Janeiro (she sends the family an annual supply of cough drops); my mother's cousin Kay, who died at thirty, a year after she came to New York from Hong Kong. Although my mother has a story to tell for each photograph, she refuses to speak about Kay, as if the mere mention of her name will bring back her ghost to haunt us all.

My mother always manages to find a picture I have not seen before; suddenly 16 I discover I have a relative who is a mortician in Vancouver. I pick up a portrait of Uncle Lao-Hu, a silver-haired man with a goatee who owned a curio shop on Mott Street until he retired last year and moved to Hawaii. In a color print, he stands in the doorway of his store, holding a bamboo Moon Man in front of him, as if it were a bowling trophy. The statue, which is actually two feet tall, has a staff in its left hand, while its right palm balances a peach, a sign of long life. The top of the Moon Man's head protrudes in the shape of an eggplant; my mother believes that such a head contains an endless wealth of wisdom.

"Your Uncle Lao-Hu is a wise man, too," my mother says, "except when he's 17 in love. When he still owned the store, he fell in love with his women customers all the time. He was always losing money because he gave away his merchandise to any woman who smiled at him."

I see my uncle's generous arms full of gifts: a silver Buddha, an ivory dragon, a 18 pair of emerald chopsticks.

"These women confused him," she adds. "That's what happens when a Chi- 19 nese man doesn't get married."

My mother shakes her head and sighs. 20

"In his last letter, Lao-Hu invited me to visit him in Honolulu. Your father refuses 21 to leave the store."

"Why don't you go anyway?" 22

"I can't leave your father alone." She stares at the pictures scattered on the 23 coffee table.

"Mom, why don't you do something for yourself? I thought you were going 24 to start taking English lessons."

"Your father thinks it would be a waste of time." 25

While my mother puts the cookie tin away, I stand up to stretch my legs. I gaze 26 at a photograph that hangs on the wall above the sofa: my parents' wedding picture. My mother was matched to my father; she claims that if her own father had been able to repay the money that Dad spent to bring her to America, she might never have married him at all. In the wedding picture she wears a stunned expression. She is dressed in a luminous gown of ruffles and lace; the train spirals at her feet. As she clutches a bouquet tightly against her stomach, she might be asking, "What am I doing? Who is this man?" My father's face is thinner than it is now. His tuxedo is too small for him; the flower in his lapel droops. He hides his hand with the crooked pinky behind his back.

I have never been sure if my parents really love each other. I have only seen   27
them kiss at their children's weddings. They never touch each other in public. When I was little, I often thought they went to sleep in the clothes they wore to work.

Study Questions

1. Working individually or in small groups, take a piece of paper and draw a vertical line down the center in order to make two columns. Write the words *Mother* at the top of one column and *Son* at the top of the other. Then reread the story carefully, this time taking particular note of the value assumptions that underlie their thinking. As you read, compose statements that express these assumptions (they will usually take the form of "shoulds," like "People should like to eat.") In the first list, write out the assumptions the mother holds about what her young Chinese-American son should do, how he should live, what he should understand. In the second column, write down the assumptions held by the son about what she should do, how she should live, and what she should understand.

2. When you have finished, compare and discuss your lists.

3. Do you find that one is more aware than the other of these assumptions? How does this awareness level affect their relationship?

For Further Reading

Brookfield, Stephen D. *Developing Critical Thinkers: Challenging Adults to Explore Alternative Ways of Thinking and Acting*. Chapter 6, "Helping Others Examine the Assumptions Underlying Their Thoughts and Actions." San Francisco: Jossey-Bass, 1991.

de Bono, Edward. *Serious Creativity: Using the Power of Lateral Thinking to Create New Ideas*. New York: HarperBusiness, 1992.

Liedloff, Jean. *The Continuum Concept*. Menlo Park, Calif.: Addison-Wesley, 1977.

Morgan, Marlo. *Mutant Message Down Under*. New York: HarperPerennial, 1995.

Quinn, Daniel. *Ishmael*. New York: Bantam, 1992.

Thompson, Charles. *What a Great Idea: Key Steps Creative People Take*. New York: HarperPerennial, 1992.

Weatherford, Jack. *Indian Givers: How the Indians of the Americas Transformed the World*. New York: Fawcett Columbine, 1988.

CHAPTER 6

Opinions: What's Believed?

"ARE THERE ANY OTHER WRONG OPINIONS SOMEONE ELSE WOULD CARE TO EXPRESS ?"

Used with permission of Ted Goff.

We can hold contradictory attitudes about opinions. We might fondly repeat the cliché "Everyone is entitled to an opinion," but that does not mean we agree to listen. Thus, when a cartoon character asks for opinion without disguising the intolerance in the request, the incongruity of such honesty can be funny.

This chapter explores that familiar word *opinion* and how it affects our ability to think critically. Opinions might be defined as inferences about life. We draw them from our experiences or collect them from others and keep them on mental record. On occasion, we draw them from our memory files to repeat to ourselves and others. They may be based on a careful study of evidence, or they may not. They also cause us problems, especially when we confuse them with facts. In this chapter, we will take a lighter look at the characteristics of and problems with opinions.

Discovery Exercises

The three discovery exercises that follow can be done either alone or with a partner in preparation for class discussion of this chapter.

Comparing a Sample of Opinions

Study the following statements of opinion:

1. "It's a proven fact that capital punishment is a known detergent [sic] to crime." (Archie Bunker, in the TV series *All in the Family*)

2. "Those who indulge in sex for sheer excitement and physical pleasure get exactly what they bargained for and nothing more. After the fleeting moments of pleasure, they are spent and empty." (*Ann Landers Talks to Teen-Agers About Sex*, Crest Books, 1963)

3. "'I need to meet a new woman. I need to have an affair. I may not look the part, but I'm a man who needs romance. I need softness. I need flirtation. I'm not getting any younger, so before it's too late I want to make love in Venice . . . and exchange coy glances over red wine and candlelight. You see what I am saying?'
    "Dr. Mandel shifted in his chair and said, 'An affair will solve nothing. You're so unrealistic. Your problems run much deeper.'" (Woody Allen, "The Kugelmass Episode," *Woody Allen Side Effects*, Random House, 1980)

4. "Chinese Communists have this view that only after the liberation of the whole world can one liberate oneself. But I believe that if each person would liberate himself first, then the world could liberate itself." (Shen Tong, Chinese student leader at Tiananmen Square)

5. Any person on welfare is a bum.

6. "All this . . . persuades us that the word 'person' as used in the Fourteenth Amendment does not include the unborn. . . . We need not resolve the difficult question of when life begins. When those trained in the respective disciplines of medicine, philosophy, and theology are unable to arrive at any consensus, the judiciary, at this point in the development of man's knowledge, is not in a position to speculate as to the answer." (U.S. Supreme Court, *Roe v. Wade*, 1973)

In writing or class discussion, answer these questions about the statements:

1. What do these opinions have in common?
2. How are they different?
3. Do they all have equal weight and value?

*"I'd say it's your gallbladder, but if you insist on a
second opinion, I'll say kidneys."*
Used with permission of Universal Press Syndicate.

Why Do We Get Confused by the Word *Opinion*?

Find at least three different meanings in a dictionary for the word *opinion*.
(Be sure to look at the word's etymology.) Write down each definition, and
compose a sentence that clearly expresses each meaning. Do you find that
some of these meanings of *opinion* seem to contradict one another? Explain exactly how.

After you have finished, compare your different meanings to those
given here:

1. No one can say if our weather has changed permanently for the worse
    or not, but it's my *opinion* that it has. (a judgment that, though open to
    dispute, seems probable to the speaker)

2. There'll always be an England. (a belief held with confidence but not
    substantiated by proof)

3. This editor is of the *opinion* that the community colleges' enrollment of
    students would not be seriously affected by charging tuition if this esti-
    mate is not based on initial enrollments but final enrollments. A payment

of tuition implies a commitment that may make even more students stay with their courses who might drop out casually otherwise. (a *claim* or statement about what is considered to be true, supported by reasoning)

4. As your doctor of long standing, it is my *opinion* that you should not have surgery at this time. (a judgment formed by an expert)

5. Public opinion supports arms talks. (prevailing sentiment)

6. It is the *opinion* of the court that the defendant is guilty. (a formal statement of a judgment drawn after a legal hearing)

Rating Opinions

Rate the following opinions as:
   A. An opinion I would accept and act on.
   B. Worthy of consideration.
   C. I'd want another opinion.
   D. Forget it!

_____ 1. Your doctor says you need surgery immediately to remove your _____ .

_____ 2. A psychiatrist testifies in court that the defendant is not guilty by reason of insanity.

_____ 3. The weather forecaster says it will rain tomorrow.

_____ 4. Your attorney says you should sue your neighbor for damages.

_____ 5. You want to rent an apartment but the neighbor next door says the landlord is a weirdo.

_____ 6. Your best friend tells you your fiance is tacky.

_____ 7. Your English instructor says you don't know how to think and should see a psychiatrist.

_____ 8. Your astrologer tells you not to go on any long trips in May.

_____ 9. Your biorhythm advisor tells you to stay home February 13.

_____ 10. The judge says you are guilty of driving under the influence of alcohol.

_____ 11. An engineer says you can prevent your basement from flooding by blasting holes for drainage in your foundation.

_____ 12. Your utility energy advisor says you can conserve energy by having your floors insulated.

_____ 13. Ann Landers says you should see a psychiatrist.

_____ 14. You are an investigator for the FBI getting information about a government employee. His secretary says she thinks he is a security risk because he subscribes to *Mother Jones*.

_____ 15. The general advised that we should invade Iran.

TYPES OF OPINIONS

Let's review what you may have discovered so far by categorizing opinions into types. First, there are what could be called the *judgments*: this is *good*, this is *bad*; this is *right*, this is *wrong*; this *should be*, this *should not be*. Look at the two following examples and provide a third example of your own.

1.   Men and women should not share college dorms.

2.   That car you bought was a lemon.

3.   _____

Judgments are based on personal or collective codes of values. They are conclusions, arrived at through a long chain of reasoning. Judgments can also be simple *evaluations* of good and bad, desirable and undesirable. These are all discussed fully in the next chapter, on evaluations. At root, all forms of judgments are based on values or belief systems not necessarily shared by everyone. However, a person can state a judgment as an opinion without having to offer substantiation.

A second type of opinion could be seen in the *advice* category: *you should do this; you should not do this*. Examples of such opinions are as follows:

1.   I wouldn't advertise for a roommate if I were you.

2.   You need a new car.

3.   _____

As you must have concluded from the earlier rating exercise, whether one chooses to accept advice is an individual matter depending on how one evaluates the circumstances.

A third category of opinions includes simple *generalizations*, typically preceded by the words *all*, *no*, or *some*. In this manner, the opinion is housed in a generalization to suggest that it represents a general truth.

1.   All of today's adolescents are taking longer to grow up.

2.   Nothing comes without a price.

3.   _____

Here again, support for the opinion may be offered or not. Those who take more responsibility for their opinions do offer their reasons and might defer expressing any opinion until all evidence has been considered. A person trained in critical thinking always takes the time to gather and evaluate evidence before generalizing and, in turn, examines all generalizations for their basis in evidence.

A final category of opinions is *personal taste* or *sentiments: I like this; I don't like that*. Such opinions do not need to be defended with evidence or reasons. They are matters of preference that do not need to be justified. Examples of such opinions would be:

1. Movies aren't much fun without popcorn.
2. Backpacking is the best kind of vacation.
3. _____

DISTINGUISHING BETWEEN RESPONSIBLE AND IRRESPONSIBLE OPINIONS

As you have probably gathered by now, it's no wonder the word *opinion* causes confusion since it has many contradictory meanings. The word is used to mean (1) an expert's judgment, *as well as* an unsubstantiated belief or conclusion; (2) a well-reasoned argument presented with an openness to challenge and dispute, *as well as* a final legal judgment; and (3) the prevailing sentiment (feeling) on a topic. When we study critical thinking, we understand the contradictions in a word used for feelings without reasons, on the one hand, and reasoned judgment, on the other; for arguments based on proof, as well as arguments based on no proof; and finally, for final judgments as well as no judgments.

Given the contradictions in the meaning of the word *opinion*, there is even more confusion when it becomes linked with the popular truism "Everyone is entitled to an opinion." To some of us this expression means anything goes: people are entitled to be heard on any subject that they have strong convictions about; the only important thing is that they speak from strong feelings. For others, "Everyone is entitled to an opinion" merely means that all have a right to free speech; however, every opinion is not equal in its significance to every other opinion, nor is strong conviction a criterion for truth.

Reverence for opinion involves many problems when it does not discriminate between those expressed responsibly and those expressed irresponsibly. If you wanted to decide how to vote on a safe drinking water bond issue, whose opinion would you respect the most? that of the League of Women Voters? of your assembly representative? of the Save-Us-from-More-Taxes Association? of your uncle George?

Actually, your uncle George might be the most knowledgeable person in the world on this subject. To determine the value of his contribution, you would need to know how well he had studied the subject, how much inside knowledge he had, what sources he had consulted, to what extent his viewpoint was independent of bias or vested interests, how much evidence he had to offer, how sound his reasoning appeared. We should apply these same standards to any opinion offered to influence us. On the other hand, opinions that merely reflect personal tastes or beliefs are of a different category; they do not require evidence or substantiation. In critical thinking, the essential thing is to make a distinction between the two kinds of opinions: between those for which we should expect responsible support and those that we need not take that seriously.

Yet, the objective study of opinions is not always that easy, especially when an opinion is accompanied by a lot of emotion. Well-supported opinions can also carry conviction that will move us from its basis in feelings that are truly justified. On the other hand, strong emotional expression can camouflage a lack of evidence or logic. This is well illustrated by the old country joke about a preacher who wrote in the margin of his sermon, "Argument weak here, shout like hell!" Therefore, when you find an opinion loaded with emotional language, look carefully for its supporting evidence.

To sum up, well-founded, carefully weighed opinions can be very valuable, and they are necessary when decisions must be made without all the facts available. Expert opinions are—and should be—highly esteemed and well paid for. But to be a specialist or expert in any field means to know exactly which facts are available and which are missing, what the variables are, and how much risk is involved in judging and predicting the odds. The ability to form a useful opinion lies not only in the ability to gather and evaluate data but also in the recognition of the unknowns and uncertainties the opinion must bridge. If we mistake our opinions for truths or facts, we are headed for trouble.

LOOKING AT PUBLIC OPINION POLLS

Some congressional representatives and senators regularly poll their constituents by sending questionnaires with questions like the following:

> Of every dollar now spent by state government, how much do you feel is wasted?
>   1. None
>   2. 0–10 cents
>   3. 10–20 cents
>   4. 20–40 cents

5. 40–50 cents
6. Over 50 cents

On the whole, do you consider the following institutions and people to be trustworthy and credible?

1. Major industry and corporations	Yes	No
2. Small businesses	Yes	No
3. Labor unions	Yes	No
4. Government bureaus and agencies	Yes	No
5. Elected officials	Yes	No
6. Judges	Yes	No
7. Print journalists	Yes	No
8. TV journalists	Yes	No

Here, the constituent is asked to give opinions without the assistance of any facts. Moreover, judgments are requested on the basis of general impressions or feelings. The government representative who formulated this poll appears to have relinquished the expectation that an electorate should give informed consent. And thus the polled constituents might also draw the same conclusion. In tabulating the poll's results, legitimacy and weight will be given equally to conclusions based on vague impressions and to those based on study and knowledge.

Unfortunately, such polling practices are becoming more common in the United States. Indeed, with citizens voting less and less, polls provide at least some kind of feedback for representatives, but nevertheless polls carry none of the legal safeguards of a public vote or election. Poll results can also be influenced by many factors that do not affect voting, such as how the question was phrased, how the sampling was taken, and how the poll was interpreted. Finally, although election results must be released, the release of poll results depends upon the discretion of individuals. Poll results can be published for the calculated purpose of *creating* public opinion. (Remember what Solomon Asch taught us?) Thus, their purpose need not necessarily simply reflect public sentiment. In sum, polls are not equivalent to public elections in terms of legal safeguards, the extent of their representation, or even the measure of responsibility assumed for them by either pollsters or the public.

Class Discussion

1. If the president announced that a recent poll has shown that 3 out of every 5 Americans favor invading Canada, do you think this should give the president a mandate to go ahead?

2. Do you think it is becoming too complex for most Americans to be well informed on public issues and that this is why many tend to fall back on sentiments and feelings?

OPINIONS AS CLAIMS IN ARGUMENTS

> Often what people call "thinking" is merely recycling the opinions of others.
> (Nathaniel Branden)

Arguments begin with opinions. We have to have an opinion that we want to express and defend to motivate us to build an argument.

Yet, a mere statement of opinion is not an argument.

> Americans are overworked.

We make an argument when, with the intent to persuade others to accept our idea, we provide supporting reasons that they should do so:

> Unemployment in Americans is growing while the employed are overworked. [opinion that is a conclusion or principal claim] Employers are hiring fewer workers because they can use their existing workforce for more hours. [supporting claim or reason] In the Detroit area the average workweek is 47.5 hours; Saturn workers have a regular 50-hour week, and in some plants, workers are doing 60 hours a week. The United Auto Workers (UAW) estimates that 59,000 automobile jobs would be created if the plants were on a 40 hour week. [supporting claims offering verifiable statistics] (Juliet Schor, *A Sustainable Economy for the Twenty-first Century,* 1995)

Thus, an argument consists of an idea supported by reasons. The argument is like a table; the tabletop is the principal claim, whereas its legs are supporting claims (Figure 6.1). More simply, an argument is a conclusion supported by reasons.

The principal claim in an essay is called a *thesis*:

> Unemployment in America is growing while the employed are overworked.

In the language of argument, this thesis is also called a *conclusion*. It is not a conclusion in the sense that it is a final summary but in the sense that it is the conclusion of a line of reasoning:

> Employers are hiring fewer workers because they can use their existing workforce for more hours.

The argument's credibility is greatly increased by the support of additional claims offering verifiable statistics about the working hours of autoworkers. This is what is known as *evidence*: data that can be verified as factual. Evidence includes statistics, testimony, personal experience, witnesses, records: information whose accuracy can be examined independently.

In the Composition Writing Application that follows, you are asked to write an essay in which you make a short argument in support of an opinion, express an opinion, or analyze three opinions. Such an exercise can remind you how opinions function as primary claims in an argument and

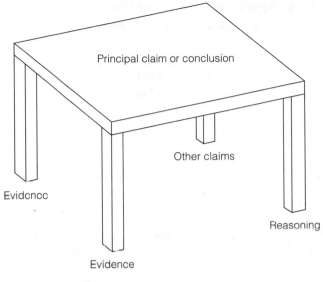

Figure 6.1 Argument Structure

how the support of evidence, other claims, and reasoning gives these opinions credibility and persuasiveness.

Composition Writing Application

First Option: A Short Argument Supporting an Opinion

Write a one- to two-page essay *stating and defending* an opinion you believe in. Follow these steps:

1. *What*: State the opinion or principal claim in one sentence.
2. *Support*:
    (a) Give three or more reasons why you believe this opinion to be true or false.
    (b) Also provide evidence in the form of facts or statistics or specific examples to support your claim.
3. *Persuasion*: Explain why you feel others should accept or reject this opinion.
4. *Conclusion*: Bring your ideas together in a summary or a generalization.

Second Option: A Short Expository Essay About an Opinion

Write a short essay *describing* an opinion of your own. Follow these steps:

1. *What*: State an opinion.
2. *Source*: Was this opinion based on your own experience or something you heard or read? Be specific about the circumstances within which you formulated it.
3. *Reasons*: Why is it a good opinion or a poor one? What tests of life and time has it survived? Have any experiences suggested that you need to alter this opinion?

The length of your essay should be two to three typed pages. It should take the form of an essay with a thesis. The first paragraph should cover step 1. The second or next two paragraphs should cover step 2. The main part of your essay (two to three paragraphs) should offer the support of reasons described in step 3. The final paragraph should sum up the whole.

Third Option: A Short Essay Analyzing Three Opinions

Study your local newspaper's editorial pages to find some editorials and letters to the editor that interest you. Select three to analyze, and photocopy them. For each, paste your photocopy at the top of a page and then analyze the piece of writing by answering these questions:

1. Is the opinion a judgment, advice, an expression of taste or sentiment, a belief, or a generalization? Support your answer in each case, providing an example and explaining it fully in these terms.
2. Is this opinion just a personal expression of taste or sentiment, or is it offered in an attempt to influence others? Explain fully.
3. Does the person giving this opinion show any special expertise regarding the subject or have any special qualifications? Explain what information you have and what is lacking.
4. Is the opinion backed up by evidence and sound reasoning? Show why or why not.
5. Does this opinion appear to be based on an objective study of the facts, or does it seem to be motivated by vested interests or a profit motive? Explain your judgment.
6. Would you call this a responsible opinion? Why or why not?

Peer Review

To follow up in class, form groups of two or more and read your papers aloud. Check one another's work to determine whether all the parameters

---

PROBLEM SOLVING

OPINIONS

In 1992 the pope announced that after considerable study of the question, the Roman Catholic church wished to admit it was wrong in 1642 when it forced Galileo to renounce his claim that the earth was not the center of the universe.

Questions

1. What problem did the church try to solve by pressuring Galileo to renounce his theory?
2. What problem did this opinion subsequently cause the church?
3. Why is it so rare for religious or political groups to reexamine old opinions and admit they were wrong?

---

given were observed. Evaluate the amount and strength of support given for the arguments involved.

CHAPTER SUMMARY

1. Opinions can be well substantiated or not. They can be based either on reasons or solely on whim, feelings, emotions, or prejudice.

2. Critical thinking requires that we recognize the difference between responsible and irresponsible opinion and that we distinguish statements based on evidence from statements based on feelings.

3. People enjoy expressing and reading opinions.

4. Fixed opinions can prevent us from thinking clearly and restrict our growth toward more understanding.

5. Expert opinion is based on an understanding of evidence and risks in a situation and is important and highly valued.

6. Public opinion polls can be used to *determine* public sentiment on social and political issues as well as to *manipulate* public sentiment. This occurs when we forget that sentiment is not the same as informed opinion and that opinion polls are not subject to the same safeguards as public elections.

BUILDING ARGUMENTS

OPINIONS

Indians ought not to buy whiskey. It is hot in his heart for a little while, then it is gone; the Indian is cold, his head is sore, and he does not remember what he did when the poison was in him. Whiskey is hot poison for the Winnebagoes. My head is like the snow with age, I have seen the ruin that it has brought upon our nation, and I advise them to buy no more whiskey. (Decori, Winnebago chief, 1828)

Exercise

1. What is the principal claim made here?
2. What reasons are given to support it?
3. State an opinion of your own with supportive reasons or complete the Composition Writing Application on pages 179–180.

---

7. Although the word *opinion* is a common one, it is just as commonly misunderstood, since the same word covers so many varieties of thought, ranging from expert judgments to expressions of sentiment or personal taste.

8. Opinions should not be confused with facts.

CHAPTER QUIZ

Rate each of the following statements as *true* or *false*. Justify each answer.

_____ 1. Expert opinion calculates the risk involved in spacing the gap between the known and the unknown for a particular situation.

_____ 2. People enjoy expressing their opinions.

_____ 3. The results of public opinion polls are equivalent to votes in elections.

_____ 4. Opinions in the form of judgments state what is right and wrong, bad and good.

_____ 5. Some opinions are based on generalizations, such as stereotypes, as in the statement "All Chinese look alike."

_____ 6. Opinions can be treasured but become obsolete when they are abstracted too far from the original experiences upon which they were based.

_____ 7. Responsible opinions are based on a careful examination of the evidence.

_____ 8. Opinions are the same as facts.

_____ 9. Gossip is a kind of recreation because it permits opinion sharing without any requirement for substantiation.

_____ 10. Everyone is entitled to his or her own opinion because all opinions carry equal value.

Readings

A MODEST PROPOSAL

Jonathan Swift

Long acknowledged as a classic of English literature, this eighteenth-century essay has delighted generations of college students. Swift, who was Irish, was writing about his country at a time when it was suffering from both famine and British rule. As you read, ask yourself what exactly is this author's opinion?

It is a melancholy object to those who walk through this great town or travel in the country, when they see the streets, the roads, and cabin doors, crowded with beggars of the female sex, followed by three, four, or six children, all in rags and importuning every passenger for an alms. These mothers, instead of being able to work for their honest livelihood, are forced to employ all their time strolling to beg sustenance for their helpless infants, who, as they grow up, either turn thieves for want of work, or leave their dear native country to fight for the Pretender in Spain, or sell themselves to the Barbados. 1

I think it is agreed by all parties that this prodigious number of children in the arms, or on the backs, or at the heels of their mothers, and frequently of their fathers, is in the present deplorable state of the kingdom a very great additional grievance; and therefore whoever could find out a fair, cheap, and easy method of making these children sound, useful members of the commonwealth would deserve so well of the public as to have his statue set up for a preserver of the nation. 2

But my intention is very far from being confined to provide only for the children of professed beggars; it is of a much greater extent, and shall take in the whole number of infants at a certain age who are born of parents in effect as little able to support them as those who demand our charity in the streets. 3

As to my own part, having turned my thoughts for many years upon this important subject, and maturely weighed the several schemes of other projectors, 4

I have always found them grossly mistaken in their computation. It is true, a child just dropped from its dam may be supported by her milk for a solar year, with little other nourishment; at most not above the value of two shillings, which the mother may certainly get, or the value in scraps, by her lawful occupation of begging; and it is exactly at one year that I propose to provide for them in such a manner as instead of being a charge upon their parents or the parish, or wanting food and raiment for the rest of their lives, they shall on the contrary contribute to the feeding, and partly to the clothing, of many thousands.

There is likewise another great advantage in my scheme, that it will prevent   5
those voluntary abortions, and that horrid practice of women murdering their bastard children, alas, too frequent among us, sacrificing the poor innocent babes, I doubt, more to avoid the expense than the shame, which would move tears and pity in the most savage and inhuman breast.

The number of souls in this kingdom being usually reckoned one million and a   6
half, of these I calculate there may be about two hundred thousand couples whose wives are breeders; from which number I subtract thirty thousand couples who are able to maintain their own children, although I apprehend there cannot be so many under the present distress of the kingdom; but this being granted, there will remain an hundred and seventy thousand breeders. I again subtract fifty thousand for those women who miscarry, or whose children die by accident or disease within the year. There only remain an hundred and twenty thousand children of poor parents annually born. The question therefore is, how this number shall be reared and provided for, which, as I have already said, under the present situation of affairs, is utterly impossible by all the methods hitherto proposed. For we can neither employ them in handicraft or agriculture; we neither build houses (I mean in the country) nor cultivate land. They can very seldom pick up a livelihood by stealing till they arrive at six years old, except where they are of towardly parts; although I confess they learn the rudiments much earlier, during which time they can however be looked upon only as probationers, as I have been informed by a principal gentleman in the country of Cavan, who protested to me that he never knew above one or two instances under the age of six, even in a part of the kingdom so renowned for the quickest proficiency in that art.

I am assured by our merchants that a boy or a girl before twelve years old is no   7
salable commodity; and even when they come to this age they will not yield above three pounds, or three pounds and half a crown at most on the Exchange; which cannot turn to account either to the parents or the kingdom, the charge of nutriment and rags having been at least four times that value.

I shall now therefore humbly propose my own thoughts, which I hope will not   8
be liable to the least objection.

I have assured by a very knowing American of my acquaintance in London,   9
that a young healthy child well nursed is at a year old a most delicious, nourishing, and wholesome food, whether stewed, roasted, baked, or boiled; and I made no doubt that it will equally serve in a fricassee or a ragout.

I do therefore humbly offer it to public consideration that of the hundred and   10
twenty thousand children, already computed, twenty thousand may be reserved

for breed, whereof only one-fourth part to be males, which is more than we allow to sheep, black cattle, or swine; and my reason is that these children are seldom the fruits of marriage, a circumstance not much regarded by our savages, therefore one male will be sufficient to serve four females. That the remaining hundred thousand may at a year old be offered in sale to the persons of quality and fortune through the kingdom, always advising the mother to let them suck plentifully in the last month, so as to render them plump and fat for a good table. A child will make two dishes at an entertainment for friends; and when the family dines alone, the fore or hind quarter will make a reasonable dish and seasoned with a little pepper or salt will be very good boiled on the fourth day, especially in winter.

11   I have reckoned upon a medium that a child just born will weigh twelve pounds, and in a solar year if tolerably nursed increaseth to twenty-eight pounds.

12   I grant this food will be somewhat dear, and therefore very proper for landlords, who, as they have already devoured most of the parents, seem to have the best title to the children.

13   Infant's flesh will be in season throughout the year, but more plentiful in March, and a little before and after. For we are told by a grave author, an eminent French physician, that fish being a prolific diet, there are more children born in Roman Catholic countries about nine months after Lent than at any other season; therefore, reckoning a year after Lent, the markets will be more glutted than usual, because the number of popish infants is at least three to one in this kingdom; and therefore it will have other collateral advantage, by lessening the number of Papists among us.

14   I have already computed the charge of nursing a beggar's child (in which list I reckon all cottagers, laborers, and four-fifths of the farmers) to be about two shillings per annum, rags included; and I believe no gentleman would repine to give ten shillings for the carcass of a good fat child, which, as I have said, will make four dishes of excellent nutritive meat, when he hath only some particular friend or his own family to dine with him. Thus the squire will learn to be a good landlord, and grow popular among the tenants; the mother will have eight shillings net profit, and be fit for work until she produces another child.

15   Those who are more thrifty (as I must confess the times require) may flay the carcass; the skin of which artificially dressed will make admirable gloves for ladies, and summer boots for fine gentlemen.

16   As to our city of Dublin, shambles may be appointed for this purpose in the most convenient parts of it, and butchers we may be assured will not be wanting; although I rather recommend buying the children alive, and dressing them hot from the knife as we do roasting pigs. . . .

17   I can think of no one objection that will possibly be raised against this proposal, unless it should be urged that the number of people will be thereby much lessened in the kingdom. This I freely own, and it was indeed one principal design in offering it to the world. I desire the reader will observe, that I calculate my remedy for this one individual kingdom of Ireland and for no other that ever was, is, or I think ever can be upon earth. Therefore let no man talk to me of other expedients: of taxing our absentees at five shillings a pound: of using neither clothes nor household

furniture except what is of our own growth and manufacture: of utterly rejecting the materials and instruments that promote foreign luxury: of curing the expensiveness of pride, vanity, idleness, and gaming in our women: of introducing a vein of parsimony, prudence, and temperance: of learning to love our country, in the want of which we differ even from Laplanders and the inhabitants of Topinamboo: of quitting our animosities and factions, nor acting any longer like the Jews, who were murdering one another at the very moment their city was taken: of being a little cautious not to sell our country and conscience for nothing: of teaching landlords to have at least one degree of mercy toward their tenants: lastly, of putting a spirit of honesty, industry, and skill into our shopkeepers; who, if a resolution could now be taken to buy only our native goods, would immediately unite to cheat and exact upon us in the price, the measure, and the goodness, nor could ever yet be brought to make one fair proposal of just dealing, though often and earnestly invited to it.

Therefore I repeat, let no man talk to me of these and the like expedients, till 18 he hath at least some glimpse of hope that there will ever be some hearty and sincere attempt to put them in practice.

But as to myself, having been wearied out for many years with offering vain, 19 idle, visionary thoughts, and at length utterly despairing of success, I fortunately fell upon this proposal, which, as it is wholly new, so it hath something solid and real, of no expense and little trouble, full in our own power, and whereby we can incur no danger in disobliging England. For this kind of commodity will not bear exportation, the flesh being of too tender a consistence to admit a long continuance in salt, although perhaps I could name a country which would be glad to eat up our whole nation without it.

After all, I am not so violently bent upon my own opinion as to reject any offer 20 proposed by wise men, which shall be found equally innocent, cheap, easy, and effectual. But before something of that kind shall be advanced in contradiction to my scheme, and offering a better, I desire the author or authors will be pleased maturely to consider two points. First, as things now stand, how they will be able to find food and raiment for a hundred thousand useless mouths and backs. And secondly, there being a round million of creatures in human figure throughout this kingdom, whose sole subsistence put into a common stock would leave them in debt two millions of pounds sterling, adding those who are beggars by profession to the bulk of farmers, cottagers, and laborers, with their wives and children who are beggars in effect; I desire those politicians who dislike my overture, and may perhaps be so bold to attempt an answer, that they will first ask the parents of these mortals whether they would not at this day think it a great happiness to have been sold for food at a year old in this manner I prescribe, and thereby have avoided such a perpetual scene of misfortunes as they have since gone through by the oppression of landlords, the impossibility of paying rent without money or trade, the want of common sustenance, with neither house nor clothes to cover them from the inclemencies of the weather, and the most inevitable prospect of entailing the like or greater miseries upon their breed forever.

I profess, in the sincerity of my heart, that I have not the least personal interest 21 in endeavoring to promote this necessary work, having no other motive than the public good of my country, by advancing our trade, providing for infants, relieving the poor, and giving some pleasure to the rich. I have no children by which I can propose to get a single penny; the youngest being nine years old, and my wife past childbearing.

From Jonathan Swift, "A Modest Proposal," *The Portable Swift*. New York: Penguin, 1977. Originally published in 1729.

Study Questions

1. Satire is a literary form that uses irony or parody to expose or criticize an idea or custom considered objectionable. At what point in this essay did you realize that Swift was writing satire?

2. In thinking terms, a satirical essay may be defined as one that states one opinion while actually conveying a very different one. Put into your own words Swift's thesis as stated and then the thesis you can read between the lines.

3. One definition of *irony* is an incongruity between what might be expected and what actually occurs. How does Swift's incongruous proposal highlight the existing incongruities in the treatment of the Irish poor?

4. In his essay excerpted at the end of Chapter 5, De Bono describes a lateral thinker as provocative, generative, and unjudging in his or her ideas. What part does lateral thinking play in Swift's style and purpose?

5. Do you think Swift is prejudiced against Catholics (Papists) and Jews, or is he using irony? What about his attitude toward absentee British landlords? (If you need to familiarize yourself with British history during this period, see an encyclopedia for a quick review.)

6. "Let no man talk to me of other expedients." What are the proposals that Swift claims not to be proposing? If taken seriously, do you think they could have improved the situation?

7. Describe any parallels you might see between this situation and that of the poor and the homeless in the United States today.

A NATION OF VICTIMS

Charles J. Sykes

Charles J. Sykes has written several books critical of U.S. higher education. In this excerpt from the first chapter of *A Society of Victims*, he expresses his opinions about "the decay of American character." (Notes to the original reading have not been included here.)

Something extraordinary is happening in American society. Criss-crossed by invisible 1
trip wires of emotional, racial, sexual, and psychological grievance, American life is
increasingly characterized by the plaintive insistence, *I am a victim.*

The victim-ization of America is remarkably egalitarian. From the addicts of the 2
South Bronx to the self-styled emotional road-kills of Manhattan's Upper East Side,
the mantra of the victims is the same: *I am not responsible; it's not my fault.*

Paradoxically, this don't-blame-me permissiveness is applied only to the self, 3
not to others; it is compatible with an ideological puritanism that is notable for its
shrill demands of psychological, political, and linguistic correctness. The ethos of
victimization has an endless capacity not only for exculpating one's self from blame,
washing away responsibility in a torrent of explanation—racism, sexism, rotten
parents, addiction, and illness—but also for projecting guilt onto others.

If previous movements of liberation may have been characterized as Revolu- 4
tions of Rising Expectations, this society is in the grips of a Revolution of Rising
Sensitivities, in which grievance begets grievance. In the society of victims, individuals compete not only for rights or economic advantage but also for points on the
"sensitivity" index, where "feelings" rather than reason are what count. This ethos
is fueled by a hypersensitivity so delicately calibrated that it can detect racism in the
inflection of a voice, discover sexism in a classroom's seating pattern, and uncover
patriarchal oppression in a mascara stick or a Shakespeare sonnet.

The new culture reflects a readiness not merely to feel sorry for oneself but to 5
wield one's resentments as weapons of social advantage and to regard deficiencies
as entitlements to society's deference. Even the privileged have found that being
oppressed has its advantages. On the campuses of elite universities, students
quickly learn the grammar and protocols of power—that the route to moral superiority and premier griping rights can be gained most efficiently through being a
victim—which perhaps explains academia's search for what one critic calls the
"unified field theory of oppression."

Americans, of course, have a long tradition of sympathy for the downtrodden; 6
compassion for the less fortunate has always been a mark of the nation's underlying
decency and morality. But our concern for the genuine victims of misfortune or
injustice is sorely tested as the list of certifiable victims continues to grow; victim
status is now claimed not only by members of minority groups but increasingly by
the middle class, millionaire artists, students at Ivy League colleges, "adult children," the obese, codependents, victims of "lookism" (bias against the unattrac-
tive), "ageism," "toxic parents," and the otherwise psychically scarred—all of
whom are now engaged in an elaborate game of victim one-upmanship. Celebrities
vie with one another in confessing graphic stories of abuse they suffered as children,
while television talk shows feature a parade of victims ranging from overweight
incest victims to handicapped sex addicts. "A Martian would be forgiven for thinking," columnist Barbara Amiel wrote in *McLean's,* "that the primary problem of
North Americans is a population of females totally absorbed with their personal
misery—addictions, abuse experiences and pain. . . . We are suffocating in our own
pain."

Describing the new "politics of dependency" of the poor in the 1990s, 7
Lawrence Mead notes that its practitioners "claim a right to support based on the
injuries of the past, not on anything that they contribute now. Wounds are an asset
today, much as a paycheck was in progressive-era politics. One claims to be a
victim, not a worker."

Everybody wants in on this. 8

But the competition is stiff: If you add up all the groups—women, blacks, 9
youths, Native Americans, the unemployed, the poor, etc.—that consider themselves to be oppressed minorities, Aaron Wildavsky calculates, their number adds
up to 374 percent of the population. The media continue to create new categories
of victimization. A recent CBS report, for example, breathlessly revealed the existence of "the hidden homeless"—people living with their relatives. As a reporter
for *The Washington Post* pointed out, "Once we called these situations '*families.*'"

Study Questions

1. Underline the thesis of the essay.

2. In an outline show how each paragraph contains generalizations that
   develop that thesis.

3. Outline in detail paragraph 6, showing how the author supports the
   claim made in his topic sentences. Name the types of support he
   chooses from the possibilities of illustration, description, listing, specific examples, facts and statistics, testimony, and authoritative corrob-
   orating opinions.

4. What underlying assumptions do you find in his argument? What value
   assumptions?

5. Did he persuade you to agree with his opinion or not?

CHAPTER 7

Evaluations: What's Felt and Judged?

"This is not the mood we're trying to get across out here, Parker!"

From *Gahan Wilson's America*. Copyright © 1985 by Gahan Wilson. Used with permission of Simon & Schuster, Inc.

Why is Parker getting into trouble? *Senseless*, in this instance, is an *evaluative* word. And one evaluative word can change the whole nature of a communication. Evaluations are based on feelings. We like something or we do not; this in turn leads us to judge something as good or bad. Often we seek to influence others to accept the same judgment. Evaluations can be applied consciously, skillfully, and fairly, or they can be used carelessly or dishonestly. This chapter teaches both recognition and detachment from that variety of opinion called *evaluations*.

Discovery Exercises

A COLLABORATIVE LEARNING OPPORTUNITY

Both Discovery Exercises can be studied alone or with a partner in preparation for class discussion of this chapter.

Defining *Evaluate*

First, study the etymology of the word *evaluate*. What do its prefix and root mean?

Then, write out definitions of the following words:

1. judge
2. appraise
3. estimate
4. value
5. evaluate

Based on your work, answer these questions either in writing or in class:

1. What does *evaluate* mean?
2. Is an evaluation an inference?
3. Is an evaluation an opinion?
4. Can an evaluation be based on an assumption?

Recognizing Evaluations

Evaluations can appear in the form of single words as well as ideas that judge something as positive or negative. Circle the words in the following passages that state or suggest evaluations. Note whether any evidence or reasons are given to support the evaluations made.

A reminder about Discovery Exercises: these are not tests in which you are expected to know all the answers; they are meant only to help you acknowledge what you already know and to inspire your curiosity to learn what you do not know.

1. "I think contraception is disgusting—people using each other for pleasure." (director, Pro-Life Action League)
2. "The harsh truth is that sub-Saharan Africa today faces a crisis of unprecedented proportions. The physical environment is deteriorating. Per-capita production of food grains is falling. Population growth rates are the highest in the world and rising. National economies are in disarray. And international assistance in real terms is moving sharply downward." (Robert S. McNamara, 1986)
3. "*The Gods Must Be Crazy*: This peculiar comedy, from South Africa's premier filmmaker, Jamie Uys, is whimsically amusing and probably well-meant—but the racial undertones are bothersome." (review by N.W. in *Express*, November 1, 1985)
4. *Friends are worth Smearoff.* When the friends are close and the mood is right, the party starts in the kitchen. And, of course, Smearoff vodka

is there. Because nothing but Smearoff makes drinks that are as light and friendly as the conversation. Crisp, clean, incomparable Smearoff. *Friends are worth it.*

Discuss the following questions in writing or in class:

1. Look at your circled words. What can you generalize about how they work as evaluations?
2. Did you find differences here between evaluations that were directly stated and those that were suggested or implied?
3. Were any passages more indirect than others in their use of evaluations?
4. Where the evaluations were unsupported, should they have been supported?

ON EVALUATIONS

Evaluate comes from the Latin *ex* = from, and *valere* = to be strong, to be of value. To evaluate, then, is (1) to determine or fix the value or worth of something or (2) to examine and judge, appraise, estimate. To evaluate, appraise, and estimate the value of something according to a standard is a thinking operation that involves comparisons and measurements. These comparisons are made according to ideals that may be either conscious or unconscious, or both. We may value watching football on TV more than any other pastime both for reasons we can explain and for those we cannot.

Without evaluations, we would not be able to make decisions: what car to buy, what school to go to, what friends to spend our time with. To determine the value of something, we have to decide what exchange we would be willing to offer in terms of time, energy, and money. But this exchange value depends on the individual and the situation—not on the items or ideas themselves. Today I might feel a $20,000 car is a bargain in value to me because it gives me prestige and power in my eyes and those of my friends and customers. Five years ago I might have felt that a $2,000 used car was a bargain for me because it gave me a sense of pride in my economy and left my assets free for other priorities. Here needs and standards have to be measured against price—or the exchange of energy, time, and money required.

To evaluate wisely, we first have to observe and compare, as well as clarify our standards. We have to gather information to measure against our needs, priorities, and assets. After this process is completed, we can make our final evaluation or decision.

"Oh hey! I just love these things! . . . Crunchy on the outside and a chewy center!"

Used with permission of Chronicle Features, San Francisco.

THE PROBLEM OF PREMATURE EVALUATIONS

Premature evaluations are evaluations (decisions about "good" or "bad") made before we have taken sufficient time to explore and think about a situation. "I knew before I spoke to him that he was too young for the job."

Premature evaluations may deceive us into thinking that we base them on our accumulated wisdom and experience, but actually they bypass the observing and thinking process, substituting prejudice or vague impressions for immediate study of what is present. Yet, when we recognize premature evaluations as such, we can reexamine them in light of present circumstances, which leads us back into experience and learning.

COREY: "How do you know he is too young for the job?"

ALEX: "OK, I'll interview him and see."

Premature evaluations also allow us to avoid thinking by substituting or simply *reasserting* a judgment as though it were a fact, instead of offering the evidence or considerations that led to that judgment.

ALICE: "He looks like a turkey to me."

RUTH: "What do you mean by a *turkey*?"

ALICE: "You know—a TURKEY!"

The use of evaluations in this manner is also called the *fallacy of circular reasoning*, which means repeating and insisting on a judgment instead of offering evidence or valid argument in its support. (We will discuss this fallacy in Chapter 10.)

At times we make evaluations without thought. These feeling reactions may have their own wisdom, as in sensing that a person or situation is unsafe. The art is knowing the difference between intuitive intelligence and a hasty conclusion. Since we tend to evaluate before we think, we often have to backtrack to our original data and look the situation over again.

An honest examination of our feelings is an important part of the process of making sound evaluations. If the feelings are highly emotional, they are especially important to review for their measure of rationality or irrationality. Feelings can be blind and misguided at times, or they can be carriers of highly intelligent information. We all have to learn the skill of sorting feelings out. This requires development of the kind of sensitivity that is so helpful to artists and scientists.

On the basis of feelings, a choreographer chooses the right dancers and offers the right kind of coaching to get them to execute the movements he or she has in mind. Staying true to that sense of rightness is a matter of calibrating inner feelings in relationship to outer events. Likewise, a scientist has to make many decisions on the basis of feelings: a test may show good results, and, yet, the scientist may have a feeling that something essential has been neglected that needs further pursuit. The soundness of evaluations depends on the clarity of perceptions, including the perception of personal feelings. To evaluate well, we must first observe well.

Class Discussion

Premature evaluations bypass close observing and thinking. What observing and thinking could alter the following evaluations?

1. She drives an old VW van. We'd better not take her in as a housemate.

2. He has bleached blonde hair. Don't go out with him.

3. A couple is driving down a road early one morning when they pass a Cadillac parked on the curb. A man is standing, bent forward, in front of the car with one hand on the hood. He is swaying slightly and violently ill. The woman in the car remarks, "Look at that drunk."

4. You buy a new answering machine and it cuts off your messages. Your brother says, "That machine is no good. You should ask for your money back."

EVALUATIONS ARE NOT FACTS

In making premature evaluations, we sometimes confuse evaluations with facts.

> CONSTANCE: "This sausage pizza I just made is good. That's a fact!"
>
> JOHN: "What do you mean, 'That's a fact'? It is not a fact as far as I am concerned."

If Constance thought some more about her claim, she might reply as follows.

> CONSTANCE: "Well, you're vegetarian! But I like sausage and I like food that tastes fresh. That's a fact. When I took the sausage and cheese out of the refrigerator, they both smelled fresh to me. These are facts."
>
> JOHN: "I agree. These are all facts."
>
> CONSTANCE: "And I added oregano and marjoram—spices I love the smell and taste of and that bring back pleasant memories. That's a fact. So 'This sausage pizza is good' is my *evaluation*, based on facts, my memories, and my standards."
>
> JOHN: "Right on!"

Substitution of evaluations for evidence, or even for objective description, is often based on confusion about the difference between the two. Constance was no doubt convinced that her personal evaluation of the pizza *was* objective factual information. Until John questioned her, she was not consciously aware of what her standards were or that her standards were just personal ones that others might not share.

The same situation occurs when we evaluate others with the self-righteous conviction that we are offering the last word in truth:

"You are just lazy!"

"You're a drip!"

"She's a bitch! And her brother's a wimp!"

Critical thinking teaches us to avoid stating evaluations as if they were facts.

EXPECTATIONS INFLUENCE EVALUATIONS

Premature evaluations are often based on expectations we hold. This is illustrated by the following story, told by psychologist Dr. John Enright. Read it aloud and then, in a class discussion, answer the questions that follow.

Photo by John Pearson. Used with permission of the photographer.

This morning I had a longing for some orange juice. I knew there must be some in the freezer, since my roommate went shopping yesterday. I took an orange-labeled can out of the freezer, and made myself a glass; as I did so, I noticed that it was a little darker than usual, but I concluded that it must just be another variety of orange or a different mix of rind and juice. Then when I tasted it, it was just *awful*. I spit it out in the sink and really made a mess of things, but I was sure it was spoiled, and I didn't want to make myself sick. Then I decided that I might as well take it back to the grocer's and get our money back. I fished the can out of the garbage and looked at the label. To my surprise it said "Tangerine Juice." I couldn't believe it. I tasted some of the juice left in the glass and . . . it was *good tangerine juice*!

Class Discussion

1. Why did the evaluation change?
2. Neither the liquid nor the taste buds of the person changed. How can you explain what happened?
3. What information was missing in the first evaluation?
4. What can you conclude from this story about the effect of expectations on our perceptions and evaluations?
5. Can you think of instances where new information made you backtrack and reconsider an earlier evaluation?

This story demonstrates that expectations and standards can influence perceptions and the evaluations made from them. In this case, when the person's expectations changed from orange to tangerine juice, so did his acceptance of its actual taste. Under the influence of expectations, evaluations of the same stimuli can switch from one extreme to another. All of us might have experienced this on our good days and bad days, when the same situation is seen in a radically contrasting light. One day the supermarket can be a neon nightmare—and on another an opportunity for a feast.

All this suggests that if we want to think critically, we should recognize evaluations for what they are and not accept them as final judgments about the truth of things. This is not meant to imply that we should *never* evaluate or that we are not entitled to evaluations in matters of personal taste and pleasure. It means only that we should remember that evaluations are not facts and that, under different circumstances, they might change.

SKILLED USE OF EVALUATIONS

Once we learn to avoid making premature evaluations, confusing evaluations with facts, and having our evaluations distorted by expectations, we're well on the way to using evaluations skillfully. And when we can use

Used with permission of the Universal Press Syndicate.

them skillfully, we can begin to evaluate others' evaluations. We can discern the difference between evaluations that are used responsibly and openly and those that seek covertly to slant or persuade.

In the writing or study of argumentation, it is important to consider how evaluations are used to sway opinion, whether fairly, expertly, or clumsily. When we evaluate according to critical thinking standards of objectivity and fairness, we are *direct* about what we are doing, and we *state our evidence*. This is what we look for when we evaluate others' evaluations. And we are careful to distinguish between forms of writing that are *not* expected to evaluate, such as news reports, and those that *are*, such as reviews. Indeed, film, theater, book, and music reviews are prized for their evaluations, which entertain the reader at the same time that they offer recommendations.

Experts in any field can function as skilled evaluators, and, indeed, this is often why they are highly paid. Those who evaluate well provide important services for others. Offered here are two examples of skillful evaluations. One is written by a professional film reviewer, the second by a famous paleoanthropologist.

Readings

THE MALTESE FALCON

Humphrey Bogart at his most cynical, director John Huston at his nastiest, and the detective genre at its most hard-boiled and case-hardened (faithfully adapted from Dashiell Hammett's novel). Bogart's Sam Spade is the original Looking Out for Number One carrying on an affair with his partner's wife, shedding not a tear when his partner is murdered, and selling his private eye skills to the highest bidder in the search for the jewel-studded Maltese Falcon. Everything Bogart does in this film is galvanizing—from the casual way he wraps the priceless bird in newspaper and deposits it with an old man in a checkroom, to the magnificent rage he throws for Sydney Greenstreet (archvillain) and Peter Lorre, a rage which evaporates the instant he slams the door on them and steps into the corridor with a self-satisfied grin on his face, the satisfaction of a job well-done, a rage well-acted. With Mary Astor as the love interest Bogart sends to Death Row (1941).—M.C.

From *Express*, September 7, 1984, p. 2. Used with permission of the publisher.

DISCARDING THE CONCEPT
OF MAN AS "KILLER APE"

Richard Leakey

Richard Leakey is a world-renowned paleoanthropologist. He has made major contributions to the study of human evolution.

"Evidence for Aggression Does Not Exist"

I am concerned about the widespread belief that humans are innately aggressive.   1
Many people think that there is good anthropological evidence for this. But when you actually look at the past, the evidence for aggression and violence does not exist.

The only evidence of what people did in that primitive period is what they left   2
behind, and no weapons of death and destruction—no clubs—have been found. The archeological record tells us what people used to eat and to gather things, but there is no evidence of their behavior. Behavior doesn't fossilize. So where does the view of violent and aggressive man come from? It's obviously created to explain present-day problems.

The popularity of the concept of man as "killer ape" and macho male was   3
needed to explain the terrible atrocities that occurred in World War II. Even before
that, there was a feeling in Western culture that Neanderthal man was primitive
and brutish. Many people grew up with images drawn from comics of the cave
man as the hairy brute with a club who used to beat fellow brutes on the head in
the course of stealing women and dragging away victims.

These developments have created psychological acceptance of violence and   4
aggression rooted in a primitive past. It's a dangerous perspective that leads to the
conclusion that such behavior is inevitable. But I would argue very strongly that
violence and its acceptance are purely cultural.

Today, given what we know about the working of the mind and about tech-   5
niques of education, we could take an infant from any family anywhere in the world
and by involvement in a particular cultural environment make the child *this* or *that*.
The child's attitudes are not innate; they are learned. We could just as easily insist
that everybody be taught from childhood that everyone is beautiful and that everybody should love everyone else as that people should hate each other.

I'm not necessarily taking a moral position on these matters. I'm simply saying   6
that what happens to this world is within our power to determine.

Study Questions

1.   In his article Leakey is correcting a mistaken evaluation. How does he
     say it came about? How has it affected us?

2.   For what different purpose are evaluations used in the review of *The
     Maltese Falcon?*

RECOGNIZING EVALUATIONS
CONVEYED BY CONNOTATIVE WORDS

Some evaluations we read or hear present us with evidence or state
straightforwardly that they are opinions. These are the kind that stimulate
our own thinking. Others seek to manipulate our feelings and thoughts
without our being aware of what's going on and thus seek to discourage
independent thought. Arguments of the latter type often use connotative
words for this purpose.

In Chapter 2, "Word Precision," we looked at definitions and examples
of word connotations. At that time we were considering how to select

words with connotations that accurately convey our intentions. At this point we are concerned with how connotations can carry *evaluations* that may be used to convey or influence opinions.

Evaluations may be made directly or covertly. If we say about a woman, "I don't like her sexual behavior," we are clearly recognizing our feelings and separating them from the woman herself. If we say instead, "She is a tramp," we show our disapproval indirectly through the use of a word with a negative connotation. With the choice of this word, however, we move one step away from openly stating our feelings about a person's behavior, to making an assertion about her identity. All of this will become even more complicated should we begin to mistake labels for reality.

Class Discussion

Show how the connotations of each of the following words differ by writing a plus or minus beside each word that carries either a positive or a negative connotation. Then share your evaluations in class.

1. girl	doll	lady
2. undependable person	flake	carefree spirit
3. to cheat	ripoff	defraud
4. drinker	wino	alcoholic
5. soldier	terrorist	military advisor

You may have found some differences in your evaluations of these words, even for those that most people would consider to be neutral. What is a neutral word for one person may be highly charged for another. Our concern in critical thinking is with calculated choices of words with connotations that are not easily detected yet that are powerful enough to arouse the feelings of most people toward a bias. It is one thing to state judgments directly and openly and another to cloak them in words that seek to persuade through hidden emotional appeals. Such appeals seek to covertly *transfuse* evaluations rather than to invite *choice* through thinking.

Exercise

Recognizing Evaluative Words' Persuasive Powers

Underline the words in the following passages that carry feeling connotations. How do they persuade either for or against an issue? Do any make a charged issue seem more neutral?

1. "I listen to the feminists and all these radical gals—most of them are failures. They've blown it. Some of them have been married, but they

married some Caspar Milquetoast who asked permission to go to the bathroom. These women just need a man in the house. That's all they need. Most of these feminists need a man to tell them what time of day it is and to lead them home. And they blew it and they're mad at men. Feminists hate men. They're sexist. They hate men—that's their problem." (Rev. Jerry Falwell)

2. "We saved these helpless pets from being butchered for 'gourmet' food in South Korea. You can help us save thousands more from the cruel 'Cages of Despair.'" (International Fund for Animal Welfare)

3. (Photograph of a happy white middle-class family walking into the arms of a grandfatherly figure) *"All these years we've been protecting you.* When you walk into our insurance office, you'll learn how we can protect the lives of a husband and wife. Your children. Or even the lives of your business associates."

HOW PROPAGANDA USES
HIDDEN EVALUATIONS

Usually, the word *propaganda* bears a negative connotation, meaning the manipulation of public opinion for purposes not necessarily in the public's best interest. The benefit of the propaganda goes to the propagandist.

There are many tools of propaganda. One is the use of hidden evaluations that bypass the reader's awareness to embed reactions. The use of propaganda in this manner is not as distant as a World War II airplane dropping pamphlets on the enemy but as close as the checkout stand in your neighborhood supermarket. During that boring wait for your turn in line, you can soak up hidden evaluations through such popular magazines as *Time* and the *National Enquirer*. Evaluations can spice things up for the reader, and journalists and advertising copywriters know well how to exploit their appeal. On social and political issues, writers and editors of many publications are quite willing to do all the thinking for you; with the pretense of offering objective news reports, they serve up their own conclusions for your digestion with all the convenience of fast-food service.

Advertisers also find it advantageous to do the thinking for you, through a calculated and generous offering of the evaluations they want you to absorb about their products. This technique has the additional advantage of not requiring evidence. It is only necessary to get "good, good, good" identified with their product in the time it takes to turn a page or glance at a TV commercial.

> These are times when only the BEST will do! Fine Distinction Whiskey is the BEST. Fine Distinction Whiskey—"The BEST in the House."

To discern objective reports demands painstaking attention from readers. For those whose only reading time is while commuting or when the children are in bed, careful attention is not always easy to muster. A person considering purchasing some expensive equipment might be willing to do careful research and thus might appreciate wordy ads, such as those for computers, but generally speaking, ads are most effective when they are both simple and entertaining. The approach most frequently used is to offer some images surrounded by a few repeated words or phrases. The additional advantage of this formula is that it can imprint itself directly on the unconscious memory before the viewer or reader is aware that it has happened. Thus, resistance as well as a thinking choice can be warded off. Before they know it, consumers find themselves reaching automatically for the advertised products on the shelves—never fully aware that a mental imprint of images and evaluative phrases is instructing them to do so. Simple messages filed under the category of "good" make a purchasing decision easy.

Evaluations are especially powerful if they are transmitted while the viewer or reader is in a form of trance. Trance reception, also called hypnotism, is a routine event, if *hypnotism* is defined as altering a person's state of consciousness and making the person prone to suggestion. Hypnotism is not, as commonly believed, something performed only by a magician on stage or by a psychiatrist. Receptivity to hypnotism can be accomplished through personal contact by establishing rapport with someone, through imitation of his or her breathing patterns, and through subtle imitation of gestures.

Television, according to the book *The Plug-In Drug* (by Marie Winn, Bantam, 1978), induces an immediate trance state in viewers, regardless of the subject matter. The induction into an altered state is achieved by the television projection itself, by the manner in which it affects our eyes and consciousness. Perhaps you have become aware of this phenomenon yourself when you have found it requires an extreme effort to get up out of your chair and turn the television off. And if that were not enough, commercials themselves use all the techniques standardly associated with hypnotic induction: an object waved in front of the eyes and a pleasant, comforting, slow-speaking voice repeating evaluations over and over again. "Reach for aspirin for relief, aspirin for relief, for relief. Reach for aspirin for relief whenever you have those awful headaches, those awful headaches again. Aspirin."

Thinking critically requires that we simply *wake up*. It means watching television and studying magazine and billboard advertisements from the perspective of their method as well as their content. It means maintaining an attitude of analysis rather than passively absorbing those ads that encourage consumption of addictive products such as sugar, liquor, caffeine, and cigarettes. It means observing, instead of soaking up, the appeals made to our less conscious needs for status, recognition, sex appeal, potency, or escape. Staying awake also means taking an interest in the contradictions: the cigarette ads that promise you beauty with an athletic, strong, sexy body; the beer ads that assure you beer will make you into a cowboy or

PROBLEM SOLVING

USING AN EVALUATION

There's part of me that I didn't even know I had until recently—instinct, intuition, whatever. It helps me and protects me. It's perceptive and astute. I just listen to the inside of me and I know what to do. (Inez, thirty-year-old mother of three)

Questions

1. Describe a problem in your life caused by not knowing what to trust.
2. How was the problem resolved?

From Mary Belenky, Blythe Clinchy, Nancy Goldberger, and Jill Tarule, "Women's Ways of Knowing," *The Development of Self, Voice, and Mind*. New York: Basic Books, 1986.

football athlete. Advertisers use extremely sophisticated psychology to make you associate desirable qualities with their products. And it is only when you remain alert to their strategies that you can retain the power of making your own choices. In short, all of us have to continuously reclaim the right to think for ourselves.

Class Discussion

Read the following advertisements and notice how much actual information they offer you about products.

1. Ask for the cigarette with the *smooth* taste.
2. First class. For you, first class is a way of life. For you, there is CADMON's finest ... "THE MONTE CARLO." Elegant. Dependable. Distinctive. Supremely comfortable. Superbly engineered. A car for those who seek the better things in life. Drive CADMON'S finest ... an American model of luxury.
3. ORAL GRAT COOKIES. When you gotta have one, you gotta have two!

CHAPTER SUMMARY

1. Making evaluations is a complex thinking task that requires making judgments according to standards that are both conscious and unconscious.

BUILDING ARGUMENTS

EVALUATIONS

Yet, while there were whites who preferred to live like Indians, there are few, if any, Indians who regarded a completely civilized form of living as superior to their own way of life. This is true even of Indian children who were educated in the schools of the white colonists and who were later permitted to return to their own people. With the opportunity of choosing between the two ways of life, they rarely cast their lot with civilization.

The reason for this decision was because the Indian was convinced that the white man's style of life, with its lack of freedom; innumerable laws and taxes; extremes of wealth and poverty; snobbish class divisions; hypocritical customs; private ownership of land; pent-up communities; uncomfortable clothing; many diseases; slavery to money and other false standards, could not possibly bring as much real happiness as their own ways of doing things. . . .

. . . the great mass of white people and the great mass of Indians realized that their two ways of life were directly opposed. Each race looked upon the other as inferior; neither felt inclined to adopt the ways of the other; and that is why the Indians and the whites could not get along together. (Alexander Henry, American trader, 1764)

Exercise

1. What is the principal claim made in the first paragraph?
2. What behavior is cited to support this claim?
3. What characteristics of the white man did the Indians find objectionable? What do these evaluations tell us about the values of the Indians?
4. Write an argument that expresses and supports an evaluation.

2. Premature evaluations are prejudicial and bypass observing and thinking.

3. Evaluations appear sometimes as instinctive reactions that can help us survive. The problem is to distinguish sound instinct from hasty conclusion. The feelings invoked in evaluations have to be sorted out carefully.

4. Evaluations are not facts. Factual reports keep the distinction between facts and evaluations clear.

5. Expectations affect our perceptions and evaluations. We need to guard against making premature evaluations based on expectations.

6. We need not completely avoid making evaluations. Evaluations make descriptive writing interesting and colorful. Used skillfully by experts, evaluations provide a service for us.

7. Connotative words convey evaluations that can be used to sway us toward a bias. When we think critically, we recognize their hidden emotional appeals.

8. Evaluations are used in advertising and journalism to persuade us, sometimes hypnotically, to make positive associations with products.

9. Critical thinking requires that we stay alert to manipulative advertising techniques, which are most effective when we are not alert—or when we are in a trance state.

10. Propaganda is an art with many sophisticated techniques for manipulation that may or may not be ethical. One of these is the use of hidden evaluations. A critical thinker detects propaganda and evaluates its true objectives.

CHAPTER QUIZ

Rate the following statements as *true* or *false*. Give an example to substantiate your answer in each case.

_____ 1. Evaluations are not facts but judgments based on conscious as well as unconscious standards.

_____ 2. Premature evaluations bypass observing and thinking.

_____ 3. The use of highly connotative words to influence opinion can be a form of hidden evaluation.

_____ 4. Evaluations should never be used in writing reviews, such as of films and books.

_____ 5. Repeating evaluations, as is done in advertising, is a way of hypnotizing and swaying opinion.

_____ 6. A critical thinking skill is the ability to detect when evaluations are substituted for evidence in an argument.

_____ 7. Prior expectations influence perceptions and our evaluation of these perceptions.

_____ 8. Our first reactions, when we evaluate experiences before we have the facts, are usually the best.

_____ 9. To evaluate wisely, we first have to observe and then compare, and then be clear about our standards.

_____ 10. Words that carry a lot of feelings or connotations for us need not be universally considered negative or positive. If you were once trampled on by a cow, for you the word *cow* might always have a negative connotation.

Composition Writing Application

First Option: Observing and Analyzing Evaluations in Advertisements

Select two printed advertisements of the same product or type of product and circle all the evaluative words used. Photocopy them to hand in with your paper, or save the originals to hand in. Write at least a one-page analysis of each advertisement; then compare the ads to one another in a final page. Write a summation at the end that states your thesis. Try to decide which ad uses evaluations less responsibly, with distortions or confusing language that might mislead or trick the reader. Which ad is the more honest? Which is the more *effective* as an advertisement?

In your one-page analysis of each, go over every major evaluative word you have circled and thoroughly discuss both its literal and connotative (associative) meanings. Notice what appeals they carry to make you want to buy the product. Do the words make a pattern of evaluation that conveys a subliminal message? Is one key or primary evaluation repeated a lot, reinforced by secondary or lesser evaluations?

In review, the parameters are:

1. *Topic*: Comparison of the use of evaluative language in two advertisements of the same or related products.
2. *Method*: Descriptive analysis using exposition, comparison, and evaluation.
3. *Length*: Three typed pages.
4. Summation at the end can state your thesis.

Second Option: Writing a Critical Review

Write a review that evaluates a film, music album, or concert. Be conscious of your standards for evaluation. Try working with just three criteria, such as *exciting, entertaining,* and *instructive*. Be sure to define each. Describe strengths as well as weaknesses. Make this into a one-page paragraph, like the review of *The Maltese Falcon* that you read in this chapter. Let your topic sentence be your recommendation for (or against) consumption.

In review, the parameters are:

1. *Topic*: A review of a film, music album, or concert.
2. *Method*: A summary and evaluation of an event or product on the basis of three criteria. The topic sentence states your recommendation as a reviewer.
3. *Length*: One-page paragraph.

Readings

THE INHERENT NEED TO CREATE NEED

Jerry Mander

Jerry Mander holds degrees in economics and spent fifteen years in the advertising business. His book title, *Four Arguments for the Elimination of Television*, is provocative, and he means it. In this excerpt Mander evaluates the value of products advertised on television.

Advertising exists only to purvey what people don't need. Whatever people do   1
need they will find without advertising if it is available. This is so obvious and simple that it continues to stagger my mind that the ad industry has succeeded in muddying the point.

No single issue gets advertisers screaming louder than this one. They speak   2
about how they are only fulfilling the needs of people by providing an information service about where and how people can achieve satisfaction for their needs. Advertising is only a public service, they insist.

Speaking privately, however, and to corporate clients, advertisers sell their ser-   3
vices on the basis of how well they are able to create needs where there were none before.

I have never met an advertising person who sincerely believes that there is a   4
need connected to, say, 99 percent of the commodities which fill the airwaves and the print media. Nor can I recall a single street demonstration demanding one single product in all of American history. If there were such a demonstration for, let's say, nonreturnable bottles, which were launched through tens of millions of dollars of ads, or chemically processed foods, similarly dependent upon ads, there would surely have been no need to advertise these products. The only need that is expressed by advertising is the need of advertisers to accelerate the process of conversion of raw materials with no intrinsic value into commodities that people will buy.

If we take the word "need" to mean something basic to human survival—   5
food, shelter, clothing—or basic to human contentment—peace, love, safety, companionship, intimacy, a sense of fulfillment—these will be sought and found by people whether or not there is advertising. In fact, advertising intervenes between people and their needs, *separates* them from direct fulfillment and urges them to believe that satisfaction can be obtained only through commodities. It is through this intervention and separation that advertising can create value, thereby justifying its existence.

Consider the list of the top twenty-five advertisers in the United States. They   6
sell the following products: soaps, detergents, cosmetics, drugs, chemicals, processed foods, tobacco, alcohol, cars, and sodas, all of which exist in a realm beyond need. If they were needed, they would not be advertised.

People do need to eat, but the food which is advertised is *processed* food: 7
processed meat, sodas, sugary cereals, candies. A food in its natural state, unpro-
cessed, does not need to be advertised. Hungry people will find the food if it is
available. To persuade people to buy the processed version is another matter because it is more expensive, less naturally appealing, less nourishing, and often
harmful. The need must be created.

Perhaps there is a need for cleanliness. But that is not what advertisers sell. 8
Cleanliness can be obtained with water and a little bit of natural fiber, or solidified
natural fat. Major world civilizations kept clean that way for millennia. What is
advertised is *whiteness*, a value beyond cleanliness; *sterility*, the avoidance of all
germs; *sudsiness*, a cosmetic factor; and *brand*, a surrogate community loyalty.

There is need for tranquility and a sense of contentment. But these are the last 9
qualities drug advertisers would like you to obtain; not on your own anyway.

A drug ad denies your ability to cope with internal processes: feelings, moods, 10
anxieties. It encourages the belief that personal or traditional ways of dealing with
these matters—friends, family, community, or patiently awaiting the next turn in
life's cycle—will not succeed in your case. It suggests that a chemical solution is
better so that you will choose the chemical rather than your own resources. The
result is that you become further separated from yourself and less able to cope.
Your ability dies for lack of practice and faith in its efficacy.

A deodorant ad never speaks about the inherent value of applying imitation- 11
lemon fragrance to your body; it has no inherent value. Mainly the ad wishes to
intervene in any notion you may have that there is something pleasant or positive
in your own human odor. Once the intervention takes place, and self-doubt and
anxiety are created, the situation can be satisfied with artificial smells. Only through
this process of intervention and substitution is there the prospect of value added
and commercial profit.

The goal of all advertising is discontent or, to put it another way, an internal 12
scarcity of contentment. This must be continually created, even at the moment
when one has finally bought something. In that event, advertising has the task of
creating discontent with what has just been bought, since once that act is completed, the purchase has no further benefit to the market system. The newly purchased commodity must be gotten rid of and replaced by the "need" for a new
commodity as soon as possible. The ideal world for advertisers would be one in
which whatever is bought is used only once and then tossed aside. Many new
products have been designed to fit such a world.

From Jerry Mander, *Four Arguments for the Elimination of Television*. New York: William Morrow, 1978.
© 1977, 1978 by Jerry Mander. Used with permission of William Morrow & Company.

Study Questions

1. What is the thesis of this essay and where is it stated?
2. List the examples Mander uses to illustrate his thesis.

3. How does the author define *need*? How does he say advertising separates us from our needs and creates new needs?

4. According to Mander, what do drug ads do?

5. Explain the process of intervention and substitution.

6. Give examples to support the author's statement that "the goal of all advertising is discontent."

7. How does television advertising evaluate for us and thus affect our behavior and values?

8. Go through some magazines and clip out six advertisements. See if Mander's claims apply to each ad. Is it designed to make you feel discontent or to buy something you don't need? Decide whether they support Mander's claims.

Contrasting Evaluations of Multiculturalism: Two Readings

WHOSE AMERICA?

Sam Allis
Jordan Bonfante
Cathy Booth

The following excerpt is taken from an essay on multiculturalism that appeared in *Time* magazine on July 8, 1991. (You may wish to read the entire article, which may be obtained from your library.) Included here are a series of commentaries that appeared beneath some time-line illustrations. Notice how the statements contrast traditional evaluations of key historical events in U.S. history with statements that emphasize multicultural evaluations of the same events. As you read, make notes of the evaluative words used. Do they show a bias that would tend to sway the reader toward one side or another?

- 1492 Columbus Lands in the Americas.   1

Instead of teaching that Columbus discovered the New World, multiculturalists stress that America was already inhabited and ask whether European explorers should be blamed for despoiling a continent.

- 1619 Arrival of Slaves from Africa.   2

Blacks who were treated as property were dehumanized. California's multicultural curriculum urges students to imagine how the victims felt on being sold into bondage.

- 1621 Pilgrims at Plymouth Celebrate Their First Thanksgiving. 3

The bounteous harvest after the European colonists' first harsh winter in New England is celebrated as, among other things, a symbol of the harmony between newcomers and Native Americans. Multiculturalists criticize this as an idealization of the destructive effects of colonial culture upon a variety of nonwhite peoples.

- 1836 Texans Defend the Alamo. 4

The site of the battle is now a shrine to Texan independence and a monument to eventual U.S. statehood. Multicultural critics decry the historical disregard for long-established Hispanic influence.

- 1863 North Versus South in the War Between the States. 5

The war is usually taught as a battle to end slavery. The New York report (a report recommending a multicultural study program for the New York schools) suggests that students now need to see "race" as a cultural, not a physical, description, which would lead to a "better understanding of the stunting effect of racism on U.S. society and its people."

- 1864 Conquering the West. 6

The westward migration of white America was a violent process. Multiculturalists charge that retelling of such expansions downplays the loss of life and native culture comparable to that of the Holocaust.

- 1869 Spanning the Continent with Rails. 7

The link joined at Promontory Point, Utah, was the product of Chinese and other immigrant labor. The New York report argues for teaching history from a perspective in which such people would be known not as minorities but as "part of the world's majorities."

- 1905 European Immigrant Wave. 8

Ellis Island was the focus for the "melting pot." Revisionists say that ethnic groups should "maintain and publicly celebrate their differences."

- 1911 Women Demand the Vote. 9

After seventy-two years of protests, women finally won the vote in 1920. The New York report declares that their contributions are still "marginalized."

- 1957 School Integration. 10

Desegregation of public schools was a civil rights milestone. Afrocentrists now advocate a new form of educational separatism.

MULTICULTURALISM AND ME:
A WHITE MALE'S VIEW

Jay Walljasper

This sympathetic evaluation of multiculturalism, taken from *Utne Reader* magazine, is a rejoinder to the *Time* magazine article that was just excerpted. Write out the author's principal claim and outline its support.

I am fascinated by the brawling debate going on across America about multicultur- 1 alism. The subject touches a raw nerve in many people. The merest hint that the United States is not one big, happy culture seems to jab something hidden but very near the surface in our national psyche. Why else would *Time* magazine, in a special Fourth of July issue, ominously report that "the customs, beliefs, and principles that have unified the United States, however imperfectly, for more than two centuries are being challenged with a ferocity not seen since the Civil War?"

Some of my interest in this topic stems from the fact that I am the product of 2 a multicultural background—you see, my ancestry is *only* seven-eighths German. In the late 1800s, my great-great grandfather Stirling made his way to the woolen mills of Franklin, Iowa, from the woolen mills of his native Scotland.

I mention this only partly as a joke. While no one, not even me, is clamoring 3 for the distinct contributions of Scottish-Americans and German-Americans (with separate categories for Catholics and Lutherans, please!) to be included in the curriculum of every 11th grade history class, I believe it's misleading to lump all citizens of European ancestry into a single cultural category.

One thing that makes the debate on multiculturalism so intense and bitter is 4 that many whites now resent all the sacrifices their ancestors underwent in order to be accepted as "Americans"—they envy other ethnic groups' spirited celebrations of roots. I, for one, have always gotten a little steamed when people mistake my background as just plain WASP. I'm not sure how deep my German roots go, but I remember feeling distinctly at home the first time I stepped into a beer hall in the Black Forest, much more so than I have ever felt in a country club dining room, country-western bar, or airport cocktail lounge. I don't feel that being German, Catholic, or Midwestern defines who I am, but I do admit to finding some pleasure and comfort in knowing where I came from.

Even many people who *do* qualify as WASPs have been robbed of the rich 5 satisfaction of their roots. Throughout New England, the Atlantic states, and the South live white people whose ancestors in the area go back two or three centuries, yet they've been taught to think of themselves not as Yankees or Appalachians but as some abstract entity called Americans.

Why should someone in Maine or Harlem or Skokie or East L.A. feel any more 6 kinship with me than with the people of New Brunswick, Jamaica, Tel Aviv, or Tijuana? Such a question might strike some as unpatriotic. That's because it confronts the carefully maintained myth that America is one culture under the same god, indivisible, with liberty and justice for all. That's clearly not true, as a glance at any day's headlines over the last century will tell. But rather than admit it, enforcers of the patriotic party line in academia, government, and the media have pushed 100 percent Americanism down our throats—to the point where many people now believe we are a homogenous culture like Denmark or Japan. Or at least we could be if only those pesky minorities, immigrants, and troublemakers in the alternative press would shut up.

There are distinct advantages to being a homogenous culture. The European 7
tradition of social democracy, for instance, works in part because taxpayers feel secure that the welfare system they pay for helps people much like themselves—not unfamiliar folks who can easily be dismissed as "lazy."

But there are severe disadvantages in pretending you are a homogenous soci- 8
ety when you are not, starting with racism and continuing through conformity and cultural schizophrenia. Multicultural societies have their own set of strengths, including a vibrant energy sparked by numerous traditions that mingle and bounce off each other. I don't know anyone thrilled by Danish or Japanese pop music, but Amsterdam and Tokyo bustle to the beat of jazz, rock, and other sounds of multiculturalism.

Much of 20th-century American life has been a crusade to convince us that we are 9
not a land of rich ethnic and regional diversity. In the quest to minimize our ethnic and local pride (the very thing now sparking broad political movements all over the world), proponents of 100 percent Americanism had to offer us something in return. One compensation has been a set of ideals about individualism and liberty, enshrined in the Bill of Rights and Declaration of Independence. These are important principles and I am thankful to live under a political system that embraces them, no matter how imperfectly. But ideas alone—even noble ones—are not enough to bind together millions of people of varied backgrounds. What has proved more effective in uniting us is a common enemy. Since the turn of the century we've been pressured to join together in hating the Germans, the Bolsheviks, the Japanese, the communists, and more recently, the Iranians, Qadhafi, Noriega, and Saddam Hussein.

But victory parades cannot keep a culture united indefinitely. This is where the 10
American Dream comes in—everyone's inalienable right to a home, two cars, and a cornucopia of consumer goods. Material wealth, or at least the dream of it, is what has cemented our culture. And through the years it's held together remarkably well, as American prosperity seemed to endlessly expand. But cracks are now appearing as Americans' unrivaled domination of the world economy slips away. The United States is now less capable of delivering the fruits of prosperity to all its citizens. It shouldn't be surprising that those people who are being increasingly left out economically—Indians, blacks, Hispanics, some immigrants, some young people, some women, some gays and lesbians—are also the most ardent advocates of multiculturalism.

For now, most working-class and middle-class whites still believe that the   11
American system looks out for their interests. But if that faith continues to be shaken
by further economic downturns and more giveaways to the wealthy, who knows
what might happen? I'm not expecting the rise of a militant German-American
political movement, but regional loyalty and class awareness might become growing factors in American politics.

Some people view these possibilities with horror. *Time* magazine gravely im-   12
plied that more momentum toward multiculturalism might bring disaster: "There
is no guarantee that the nation's long test of trying to live together will not end in
fragmentation and collapse, with groups gathered around the firelight, waiting for
the attack at dawn." I don't see it that way. I think an America that recognizes and
respects the richness of its many cultures will be a better place to live.

Blind allegiance to the myth that America is a melting pot has brought us mili-   13
tarism and consumerism, as well as a bland, soulless, lowest-common-denominator
culture typified by identical fast food outlets and shopping malls from coast to
coast. But there is another America that endures, embodying the idea that cultures
can coexist side by side and even cross-pollinate. This is the America that has given
us Louis Armstrong, Tennessee Williams, and Lauren Bacall as well as filet gumbo,
flautas, fettucine, and much, much more.

The battle now raging over multiculturalism is a showdown between these   14
two cultures. As a white male, I'm selfishly rooting for the triumph of a multicultural
America, a nation that celebrates diversity along with purple mountains' majesty
and amber waves of grain. Perhaps Americans will be able to move into the 21st
century with more sureness and pride about who we really are—and with genuine
liberty and justice for all.

From *Utne Reader*, Nov./Dec. 1991. Used with permission of *Utne Reader*.

Study Questions

1.   What exactly is the melting pot concept in U.S. history?

2.   What are the advantages of a homogenous culture on the one hand and
     a multicultural one on the other, according to this author?

3.   What do you think of Walljasper's view that 100 percent Americanism
     has been pushed down our throats?

4.   What is your reaction to his statement that the ideals of individualism
     and liberty have not bound Americans together as much as hating com-
     mon enemies?

5.   What has the melting pot myth brought to the United States, according
     to Walljasper?

6.   In the *Time* article from which this excerpt was taken, the claim was
     made that multiculturalism could bring the United States to disaster.

Walljasper, however, claims that multiculturalism will make the United States a better place to live. Whose evaluation do you tend to agree with?

For Further Reading

Bagdikian, Ben H. *The Media Monopoly*. Boston: Beacon Press, 1983. See "Democracy and the Media," pp. 176–194.

Bernstein, Richard. *Dictatorship of Virtue: How the Battle over Multiculturalism Is Reshaping Our Schools, Our Country, Our Lives*. New York: Vintage Books, 1994.

Huxley, Aldous. *Brave New World Revisited*. New York: Harper & Row, 1960. See especially "Propaganda in a Democratic Society," "Propaganda Under Dictatorship," "The Arts of Selling," "Brainwashing," "Subconscious Persuasion."

Keen, Sam. *Faces of the Enemy*. San Francisco: Harper, 1986.

Key, Wilson Bryan. *The Clam-Plate Orgy and Other Subliminal Techniques for Manipulating Your Behavior*. New York: Signet, 1980.

Mander, Jerry. *Four Arguments for the Elimination of Television*. New York: William Morrow, 1978.

Winn, Marie. *The Plug-In Drug*. New York: Bantam, 1978.

CHAPTER 8

Viewpoints: What's the Filter?

"That was incredible. No fur, claws, horns, antlers, or nothin'...
Just soft and pink."

Used with permission of Chronicle Features, San Francisco.

From the point of view of the crocodile, the meal of a human being is certainly a delicacy without any problems, "just soft and pink." The humor in this cartoon results from the shift to an unaccustomed viewpoint, which nevertheless has its own reality and logic.

The ability to step out of one's point of view and to assume another's is an important critical thinking skill. When we are stuck in our own viewpoints, we have difficulty in either understanding or evaluating what others tell us. If we forget that content is shaped by point of view, we tend to confuse information with reality. This also makes us more susceptible to propaganda. A person trained in critical thinking does not passively absorb information but asks, Who said this? Where is this coming from? What do they want of me? This chapter is about how to ask these questions and get some answers.

216

Discovery Exercises

These exercises may be done alone or with a partner in preparation for class discussion of the chapter.

Understanding Point of View

Using at least two dictionaries, formulate your own definition of *point of view*. Then answer these questions either in writing or in a class discussion.

1. Name some different kinds of points of view.
2. What do we call some of the points of view that writers assume in telling stories?
3. If you were a professional writer for *Reader's Digest*, do you think its readers would be interested in your article entitled "Where and How to Pick Up Safe Prostitutes Abroad"? Why or why not?
4. If you were writing for *Esquire*, do you think your article "Living on Social Security Through Farming Communes" would be accepted by its editors? Why or why not?
5. How do we go about assuming another person's point of view?

Studying One Man's Viewpoint

Read the following excerpt and then answer in writing the questions that follow, in preparation for a class discussion.

THIS IS MY LIVING ROOM

Tom McAfee

My Living Room

it ain't big but big enough for me and my family—my wife Rosie setting over there 1
reading recipes in the Birmingham *News* and my two girls Ellen Jean and Martha Kay watching the TV. I am setting here holding *Life* magazine in my lap. I get *Life*, the *News,* and *Christian Living*. I read a lots, the newspaper everyday from cover to cover. I don't just look at the pictures in *Life*. I read what's under them and the stories. I consider myself a smart man and I ain't bragging. A man can learn a lots from just watching the TV, if he knows what to watch for and if he listens close. I do. There ain't many that can say that and be truthful. Maybe nobody else in this whole town, which is Pine Springs.

Yonder in the corner, to the other side of the Coca-Cola calendar, is my 12 **2** gauge. When I go in to bed, I take it with me, set it against the wall, loaded, ready to use, so I can use it if I need to. I've used it before and maybe will again. The only one to protect you is yourself and if you don't you're a fool. I got me a pistol and a .22 locked up in the back room. I could use them too.

Rosie can shoot, I taught her how, but she's afraid. The noise scares her. She **3** said, Don't make me shoot that thing one more time. We was in the forest. The girls was waiting for us in the car. Don't make me shoot that thing again, she said, and started to cry. I slapped her face and told her to shoot the rifle. She did. Then I took it and told her to go back to the car with the girls. She started to cry again, but I stayed a long time—till it was dark—and shot the rifle and pistol and shotgun.

You can't tell what people are going to do in a town like this. They want your **4** money and they're jealous of you. They talk about you in front of the courthouse and plan up schemes. You can't trust the police or sheriff. You got to watch out for yourself.

My Two Girls

are fourteen and sixteen year old. Both of them want to go on dates but I won't let **5** them. I know what the boys will do, what they want to get out of a girl.

Ellen Jean, the oldest, is a right good-looking girl but sassy and you can't hardly **6** do anything with her. She started to paint her face at school, so I took her out. I've got her working at my store.

I seen her passing notes to Elbert. I seen her get out of his car one night. She **7** said she was going to the picture show by herself. She's a born liar and sassy. Like as not he's had her. Like as not she's got a baby starting in her belly right now. She's a sassy bitch-girl and don't take after her ma or me. Sometimes I wonder if she's mine.

Martha Kay is like her ma. She cries all the time, minds good. I let her stay in **8** high school and will keep on letting her as long as she can act right. The first time I see lipstick, out she comes. She can work at the store too. I could use her to dust and sweep up. You can always use somebody to keep things clean.

I ask Martha Kay, Why're you late gettin' in from school? Where you been? Off **9** in the woods with some boy? She starts to cry. She's like her ma.

Martha Kay helps at the store on Saturdays but can't add up figures good. **10**

Ellen Jean is watching that man on TV make a fool of hisself and she's laughing. **11** She'll end up a Birmingham whore. Her sister is laughing too and they look like a bunch of fools.

People

in this town are like they are in any other town on earth. I was in the World War I **12** and seen a good many places. Since then I've stayed here most of the time. What's the good of moving? People are as mean one place as they are another and they're always out to get you. They won't get me because I won't let them.

Take Sam Coates who owed me twenty dollars for that fencing. Sam wouldn't   13
pay. I said to him pay up by first of the month or I'll make you pay. He says how will
I make him. Sue him for twenty dollars? Won't no lawyer in town take it anyway,
he says, because they're all looking out for election. You pay, I told him.

When first of the month come I got in my car and rode out in the country to   14
his front door. Where is your husband? I said to his wife. Milking, she said, and I
went around to the barn with my .22, stuck it in his face, and told him to pay me
or I'd blow the hell out of him. Sam turned as white as that bucket of milk. Him and
his wife counted me out the money.

There ain't one on earth that wouldn't try to cheat you if they could.   15

I use to think that women was worse than men but now I think just the oppo-   16
site. Women are easier to handle. About the worst they can do is talk and what
does that matter?

Niggers are better than anybody because you can handle them. They don't   17
hardly ever give you any trouble. Except that one time with Ezmo. I didn't have no
trouble handling him. . . .

Old Ezmo

was what you'd call a low class of nigger. He'd come into the store and say, Give   18
me a pound of sugar and I'll pay you Saturday evening. I wouldn't do it. I'd say,
You give me the money. I give you the best prices in town. You give me the money.

One time Ellen Jean let him have a loaf of bread on credit. I smacked her for it   19
and told her she was a fool, which she is. On Saturday Ezmo come in and wanted
some side meat for cooking greens. Pay me off, I told him, for that loaf of bread.
What loaf? he wanted to know.

Ellen Jean, didn't you charge this nigger a loaf of bread? She said yes and he   20
said she didn't. You ain't calling my girl a liar, are you? Naw, he said, but he didn't
get no loaf of bread. Somebody's a liar, I told him, and it ain't my girl.

He said he wouldn't pay me. You're a crooked, low-down nigger, I told him,   21
and they ain't nothing much worse than that. You ain't fit for making side meat out
of. I told him if he had any younguns he better watch out. I didn't wants lots of
black bastards like him growing up in my town. You get out of here right now.

That night I was setting in this chair where I am right now—this same chair.   22
The girls was watching TV. Rosie was shelling peas.

I heard somebody outdoors and I knew right off who it was. I got better ears   23
than most people. Any time somebody sets foot in this yard, I know it. Even if I'm
asleep.

That's Ezmo, I said to myself. I got up, picked up my 12 gauge over in the   24
corner and said I was gonna clean it, went through the house without turning any
lights on, then eased out the back door.

There wasn't much moon but I spotted Ezmo right off, standing behind some   25
hedge bushes over by my bedroom window. I got just this side of him without him
hearing. EZMO! I hollered, and up he comes with a knife about eight inches long. I
was ready for him. I triggered my 12 gauge and got him square in the face.

Rosie and the girls come running to the back door. Get me a flashlight, I told 26
them. I never seen such a blowed-up face. The girls started getting sick and Rosie
started crying. I want you to take a good look, I told Rosie, and see what this world
is coming to. You see that knife he had. I held Rosie's arm and made her stand there
till Ellen Jean could get Sheriff Claine.

Rosie

ain't exactly good-looking. She's got to be dried-up but once was on the fat side. 27
She makes a good wife. I've been married to her for going on thirty years. Sometimes I get fed up with her and go to my woman in South Town. I take her a couple
of cans of beans and some hose or a pair of bloomers. There ain't nothing much a
woman won't do for food or clothes.

Rosie knows about her, all about her. I talk about it sometimes when we're in 28
bed. I wouldn't trade Rosie for her but Rosie don't know that.

Tomorrow's Saturday and I got to get some sleep. 29

"Turn off the TV, girls. Get in yonder to bed. Tomorrow's Saturday." 30

I stand in front of Rosie. "Go in yonder and get in bed." She starts to cry and 31
that's all right. It wouldn't be a bit like her if she didn't.

From Tom McAfee, *Poems and Stories*. Used with permission of Jeanie K. McAfee and the Department
of English at the University of Missouri–Columbia on behalf of the Thomas McAfee Memorial Fund.

Study Questions

1. Why is this story entitled "This Is My Living Room"?

2. What kind of mental living room does the storyteller live in? How does
    he see his world and himself in it?

3. How does he justify his sexist and racist behavior?

4. How well does he understand his wife, daughters, and "Old Ezmo"?
    Does he observe or stereotype them?

5. What clichés do you find in his speech? What does this suggest about
    his capacity to perceive life freshly and clearly?

6. Why isn't he capable of compassion or sympathy for others?

ON UNCONSCIOUS VIEWPOINTS

So far in Part II, "Problems of Critical Thinking," we have been careful
to distinguish between the conscious and unconscious uses of assumptions,
opinions, and evaluations. To recognize assumptions, we have to know that

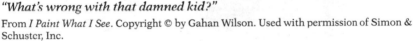
"What's wrong with that damned kid?"

From *I Paint What I See*. Copyright © by Gahan Wilson. Used with permission of Simon & Schuster, Inc.

an assumption can be unconscious. To appreciate well-supported opinions, we need to distinguish them from superficial sentiment or fixed opinions immune to conscious reexamination. To make sound evaluations, we need to guard against jumping to them prematurely. In this chapter, as we work with viewpoints, we also have to consider the distinction between conscious and unconscious use of them.

To return to the example of the story just read, a person can live in a viewpoint as narrow as one room and yet believe this is the world. Another way of describing this level of consciousness is to say that this person is not even aware that *viewpoints are just viewpoints*. He cannot step outside of himself and say, "Well, I have a way of looking at things, but that does not mean that I am always right. Other people also have viewpoints, which I could assume and even learn from." Thus, his viewpoint remains unconscious. He confuses the way he sees things with the way things are, and uses his "thinking" to rationalize feelings that others would identify as selfish, paranoid, racist, and sexist. He is what we call *egocentric*.

Egocentric individuals find it very difficult to put themselves in someone else's shoes. Psychologist Jean Piaget, who studied learning stages in children, theorized that egocentrism is typical for most young children before the age of seven. The ability to grow beyond this cognitive limitation

Used with permission of Mark Stivers.

varies from one individual to another, depending on the measure of intelligence, emotional stability, or cultural and educational factors. As we grow out of egocentrism, we also develop the ability to be *exterior* to our own viewpoint—to see and recognize it from the outside, objectively. We learn how to see the world through the eyes of others. Such a capacity enables us to respect ourselves and others more, to separate who we are as human beings from how we sometimes think and behave. We learn the meaning of the word *compassion* and move from the unconsciousness of egocentrism to the consciousness of objectivity.

Other viewpoints that might be described as less conscious, that share this feature of self-identification, include ethnocentrism and religiocentrism. *Ethnocentrism,* in its milder forms, is an attitude that judges other peoples by one's own cultural practices, values, and standards, as though these were the only reasonable norm. The relativity of ethnocentrism is well illustrated in the Gahan Wilson cartoon about the prehistoric family. To the caveman father, the child is deviant and obstinate, whereas for us, of course, it is the parents who are disgusting. This ethnocentric comedy of judging relative cultural mores in absolutes of right and wrong extends from nation to nation. Americans consider it bizarre that Indians reserve the right hand for eating and the left for toilet details, while Indians are shocked by the immodesty of American women in their shorts and sleeveless dresses. And ethnocentrism can lead to tragedy, as is so clearly depicted in the novel *A Passage to India* by E. M. Forster.

In its most severe forms, ethnocentrism has provided a justification for extreme nationalism, imperialism, racism, and genocide.

> We are the chosen, we are the only true men. Our minds give off the true power of the spirit; the intelligence of the rest of the world is merely instinctive and animal. They can see, but they cannot foresee. . . . Does it not follow that nature herself has predestined us to dominate the whole world? . . .
>
> We shall paint the misdeeds of foreign governments in the most garish colors and create such ill-feeling towards them that the peoples would a thousand times rather bear a slavery which guarantees them peace and order than enjoy their much touted freedom. The peoples will tolerate any servitude we may impose on them, if only to avoid a return to the horrors of wars and insurrection. (Alfred Rosenberg in *The Myth of the Twentieth Century*, Noontide, 1982)

The author of these lines provided some philosophical arguments that were later eagerly adopted by Hitler for the German Nazi party. These lines not only proclaim one race's superiority but justify its right to domination.

It is easier to see ethnocentricity in other nations, especially if they have been our enemies, than in ourselves. Certainly, you can think of many quotations or popular sayings that express American ethnocentricity. It is the kind of thinking that Bob Dylan mocked in the ironic title and refrain of his song "With God on Our Side."

Religiocentrism is another form of ethnocentricity; in this case a total identification is made with a particular religious tradition or ideology. Again, the implicit assumption is that "we are right and everyone else is wrong; there is only one correct religious viewpoint and that is ours."

> "All any couple needs to have a happy marriage is to be good Christians."

> "In Islam we know that women are morally crooked because they came from Adam's rib. It is best for a girl not to come into existence, but being born she had better be married or buried."

Finally, in recent times two newer concepts describing self-centered viewpoints have come into being: *androcentrism* and *anthropocentrism*. The women's movement has drawn attention to the prevalence of androcentric (male-dominated) thinking, whereas the animal rights proponents and environmentalists have pointed out our pervasive anthropocentrism (human centeredness).

Discovery Exercise

Identifying Political and Social Points of View

Read the following passages and notice how they express very different viewpoints based on different concerns, values, and priorities. See if you can assign each a political or social label, such as "radical left," "feminist," and so on.

1. "I never burned my bras in the sixties. But I wish I had." (*Ms.* magazine)

2. "*The Race to Save Our Earth* was written to excite students about alternative technologies and to encourage their participation in creative solutions to global problems." (*Solar Mind: Holistic Approaches to Technology & Environment*)

3. "It will be our own actions, our own ideas, our own well-designed laws, our own politicians that will end the feet dragging of AIDS funding, the raping of health options, the assurance of full civil rights and jobs for people, and an environment safe from violence . . . of bigotry." (*Frontiers*)

4. "There is a cultural war going on in America led by the elite of academia, the media, and the judiciary which has been infected with a philosophy of moral relativism that encourages and promotes abortion, homosexuality and other crimes and aberrations." (Rep. William Dannemeyer quoted in *San Francisco Examiner*)

5. "Black realists have little faith in the American justice system and believe armed, physical retaliation against racists who kill and abuse Blacks, then escape justice, is a just, viable option." (James Strong, *The Final Call*)

6. "Let's assassinate the CIA." (*Nation*)

Answers

1. feminist
2. environmentalist
3. gay or liberal
4. fundamentalist right
5. black Muslim
6. radical left

Discuss these questions in writing or in class:

1. Which quotes were the most difficult for you to identify?
2. How did you identify your choices?

3. Do you feel confident of your ability to identify political points of view?

4. If you disagree with any of these labels, explain why.

CATEGORIZING TODAY'S POLITICAL AND SOCIAL VIEWPOINTS

Today's students often find it both frustrating and confusing to understand, use, and apply the labels "left" and "right" to categorize shifting world patterns of political, social, economic, and religious values (see Figures 8.1 and 8.2). Perhaps this is because, as some political scientists maintain, the use of the left-to-right spectrum as a paradigm (model of reality) to explain viable political positions is now obsolete. It was derived, they say, from the period of the French, American, and industrial revolutions, which conceived oppositions between monarchies and democracies, between more and less authoritarian control, and between open markets and free trade versus social protection from the market system's inequities.

Other models or viewpoints, besides the left-to-right spectrum, have been offered, such as the two-axis model depicted in Figure 8.3. This model has the advantage of including perspectives that do not fit on the single-axis left-to-right paradigm, such as anarchism, populism, libertarianism, and environmentalism. A horseshoe arrangement, shown in Figure 8.4, makes other relationships apparent, as, for instance, some shared characteristics of the far right and far left.

In the United States, it is also not easy for us to determine any clear distinctions between the Democratic and Republican parties.

> Unlike other developed democracies, the United States does not have a parliamentary political system in which voters cast their votes for parties. Parties in most countries have distinct commitments to differing national programs, differences easily discerned by voters. Citizens voting in those countries know that when they cast their ballots for a party's candidate they are voting for particular policies. In the United States, voters cast ballots for individual candidates who are not bound to any party program except rhetorically, and not always then. Some Republicans are more liberal than some Democrats, some libertarians are more radical than some socialists, and many local candidates run without any party identification. No American citizen can vote intelligently without knowledge of the ideas, political background, and commitments of each individual candidate. (Ben H. Bagdikian, *The Media Monopoly*, 1983, p. 176. Used with permission of the author.)

And to make this even more complicated, we also have difficulty defining many of the terms used to describe the range of views within any one

Figure 8.1 The Left-to-Right Political Spectrum

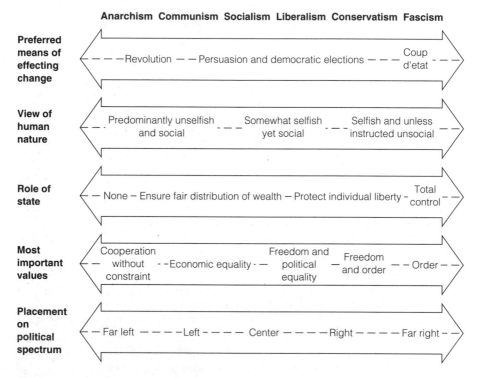

Figure 8.2 Traits of Political Systems on Left-to-Right Spectrum

Adapted from Kay Lawson, *The Human Polity: An Introduction to Political Science.* Boston: Houghton Mifflin, 1985, p. 118. Used with permission of the publisher.

party. The meanings of the words *liberal, conservative, radical left,* and *radical right* can shift from one decade to another. In the 1930s, Franklin Roosevelt's New Deal proposal for Social Security was called radical Jewish socialism. Today Social Security is a conservative American institution. Since the late 1960s, views have shifted around so many new issues that we now have the new left, the neoliberals, the new right, the neoconservatives, and the far right. As for the more familiar terms *conservative* and *liberal,* their more traditional definitions seem to contain inconsistencies when applied to contemporary issues. For instance, if one defines a *conservative* as one who wants to conserve existing wealth, values, and traditions, one

(Hamiltonian: favors nationalization, global interdependence, government-corporation cooperation)

(favors equality and collective control)

(favors liberty and private control)

(Jeffersonian; populist, green perspective [peace and environmentalism]: favors liberty and equality, small cooperatives, community self-reliance)

Figure 8.3 The Two-Axis Model of Political Views

From Michael Marien, "The Two Post-Industrialisms and Higher Education," *World Future Society Bulletin*, May 1–June 1982, p. 20. Used with permission of World Future Society.

nevertheless finds conservatives wanting to minimize government responsibility for the conservation of natural resources. And if one defines a *liberal* as open to changes in the status quo, one finds liberals strongly objecting to the constitutional amendments proposed by conservatives. Finally, how one defines all these terms, whether *liberal, conservative, radical left,* or *radical right,* depends on one's own ideology and perspective within the whole political spectrum.

The professed neutrality of the American mass media is perhaps another reason that it is so difficult to categorize viewpoint today in America. Our largest city newspapers, national radio programs, and television networks generally claim to be objective and nonideological. This situation differs from European countries, where party newspapers, representative of individual parties, interpret the news and issues on the basis of their ideologies. In such countries a person might sit down to breakfast to read a dialogue on topical issues among newspapers with such titles as the *Socialist News, Christian-Democrats,* the *Catholic World,* the *Independent,*

LEFT WING Communist–Socialist–Leftist Radical/Revolutionary		RIGHT WING Capitalist
Chinese Communism *Castro Cuba* *U.S. Marxists* Egalitarian philosophy, gov't collectivization of property; one party	*Common Radical Traits* Military govt's, political violence, totalitarian structures, persecution of dissent, genocide, racism, worship of leader, and state dictatorships of individuals and/or bureaucracy	*Nazi Party Germany* *Fascist Italy* *Ku Klux Klan* Racial supremacists David Duke, Tom Metzger
	Democratic Socialism (Europe mainly) Welfare state, gov't regulation of major industries, protection of poor and consumers, income tax, constitutional democratic gov't	*U.S. Far Right* For God, Constitution, family, military; Jesse Helms, Pat Buchanan
U.S. New Deal Liberal Democrats (Roosevelt to Johnson) Gov't spending to stimulate economy and employment; social security, welfare		*Neoconservatives* Strong military stance
New Left Opposition to war; active for civil liberties: Rainbow Coalition, gays, feminists, Jesse Jackson		*Old and New Wealth* *Conservatives* Fords, Rockefellers, Bush; strong corporate influence on government; protection of wealth; gov't deregulation, antifederalism
Neoliberals Less gov't handouts; for conservation of energy and resources; for greater corporate taxation, cutting defense budget, public job and health programs		*Conservative Democrats* *Conservative Republicans*
Progressives and Environmentalists Progressive grassroots politics lacking a party; for peace, global perspectives on ecology, human rights, conservation of resources, local activism for problem solving		*Libertarians* Capitalist; for least gov't regulation of economy and private life; for least intervention in affairs of other nations

Figure 8.4 The Horseshoe Model of Political Views

Green Peace, and the *Nazi Hope.* Here no reader could wonder about a viewpoint's source, its stands on issues, or its sponsors. Moreover, in comparing such papers, the reader is constantly reminded that reports of historical events and issues are *not* realities in themselves but are *interpretations* from different viewpoints.

In the United States, our mainstream newspapers, radio shows, and television shows do not reflect this country's full diversity of opinion or include much expression of extreme or minority views. Nevertheless, a trip to a neighborhood library can offer a very wide selection of nonmass-media publications that are identified by their social, religious, or political affiliations. Reading these small newspapers and magazines can help you develop your own sense of what constitutes right-wing opinion or left-wing opinion or whatever. Moreover, for the purposes of critical thinking, it can be quite stimulating to become acquainted with a wide spectrum of views on contemporary social and political issues.

CORE DISCOVERY WRITING APPLICATION

First Option: Observing Viewpoints in Magazines

Go to the library and select one magazine you have never read before. It need not be current, which is advantageous, since most libraries allow you to check out back issues. The purpose of this exercise is to engage in critical reading *by not identifying with a viewpoint but by standing outside it with objective awareness.* Specifically, you are to (1) study an unfamiliar viewpoint, (2) observe how it frames information, (3) infer who controls the magazine, and (4) infer what readers it seeks to influence.

Study your publication, and write your notes about it in the following order:

1. *Magazine name and date.*

2. *Cover page:* Describe the cover in sufficient detail so someone else might visualize it. What image, symbols, or words first attract your attention? What would motivate a person to reach for the magazine on a newsstand? What other details do you notice on closer inspection? What mood does the cover convey? Let the cover affect you while observing how it achieves this effect.

3. *Table of contents:* Study what subjects this magazine covers. Read a few of the articles. What slant does it take on life? What seems to be its values and interests?

4. *Advertising:* Study all the advertisements. Describe the types of advertisers, the products, and the way they are presented.

5. *Audience:* Does this publication seem to be written for a particular political, social, or ethnic group? See how much information you can

infer about its readers from the magazine's topics, advertisements, and language.

Write up your notes on these five items in a report. Attach to your report either the magazine itself or a photocopy of its cover and table of contents. Be prepared to give an oral summary of your work to the whole class or a small group.

Scoring for First Option: Observing Viewpoints in Magazines

1. Choice of magazine whose unfamiliarity poses some challenge.

   10 points

2. Description conveys the cover, its impact, and its calculated effort to attract readers through mood, choice of images, symbols, words, and topics. The writer does not soak up its effects (or become hypnotized) but remains a critical observer.

   20 points

3. Table of contents not just listed; discussion shows thoughtful attention to the details that give evidence of the magazine's interest, slant on life, values, and ideology.

   20 points

4. Advertisements: specific examples are given to show the types of advertisers, the types of products and how they are presented. Speculations are offered about what the ads suggest about the values of the magazine and its readers.

   20 points

5. Audience: thoughtful conclusions are drawn about the social, political, and educational level of the readers.

   20 points

6. No distracting errors of spelling, punctuation, sentence use, word use.

   10 points

CORE DISCOVERY WRITING APPLICATION

Second Option: Determining Political or Social Viewpoint and How It Shapes Content

This library research assignment offers you a chance to become more familiar with the wide and shifting range of political and social viewpoints in the United States today. A sampling of the magazines listed here will show you the characteristics of each: their ideology, values, rhetoric, tastes, and editorial voice. This assignment may be done individually or in pairs. From the list that follows choose one magazine if you work alone, two if you have a partner. Make your selections from what you find in your library. Browse through the periodicals rack for current issues as well as the stacks for back issues or for those magazines no longer published.

Because you may be unaccustomed to recognizing magazines' viewpoint, some publications are listed under political and social headings here. You are encouraged to browse, using this list as a guide, in order to get a sense of their different values and slants on life. And you are encouraged to question these labels or find new magazines that you can categorize on your own.

Marxist

Monthly Review
People's World

Democratic Socialists

In These Times
Dissent
New Politics
Socialist Review

Christian Left

Sojourners
The Other Side
Christianity & Crisis
National Catholic Reporter

Liberal

Atlantic Monthly
Harper's
American Prospect
The Washington Spectator
Ebony

Progressives or Left Liberal

The Nation
Village Voice
Z Magazine
Mother Jones
New Internationalist Tikkun
(Jewish progressive)

Feminist (center to left liberal)

Ms.

Conservative Center

Town and Country
Wall Street Journal
Barron's
U.S. News & World Report
Time
Newsweek
National Review

(*continues*)

Neoliberal

The New Republic
Washington Monthly

Environmentalist

Green Letter
Earth Island Journal
Earth First!

New Age

In Context
Utne Reader
Yoga Journal
Brain/Mind Bulletin
East West Journal

Libertarian

Reason
Business Week

Neoconservative

Commentary
(American Jewish sponsored)
Policy Review
(Heritage Foundation)

Conservative Right

Chronicles of Culture
Conservative Digest
Armed Forces Journal
American Opinion
(John Birch Society)
Christian Crusade Weekly
Moral Majority Report
Christian Beacon
Plain Truth
Your Heritage News

Fascist

Soldier of Fortune
Spotlight
The Citizen
Cross and the Flag
Freedom
White Power

Summary of Objectives

To review, this exercise has three purposes: (1) to make you more familiar with the wide range of political and social viewpoints available in U.S. magazines; (2) to extend your knowledge of the range of debate, commentary, and information available both in and outside mainstream publications; (3) to experience the way alternative viewpoints can challenge your assumptions and stimulate your thinking.

Instructions

1. Go to the library and select one unfamiliar magazine of some challenging intellectual content; *it should be so unfamiliar that you will need to use your abilities to observe and infer in order to grasp its viewpoint.* (Your magazine choice need not be current. You can usually check out back issues from the library.) Do not select the kind of magazines you usually see in the supermarket, like *Time, Life, People, Newsweek,* or a sports, trade, home, or beauty magazine.

2. Describe the magazine's cover so that others can imagine what it looks like. How do its images and words affect you? What feelings does it stimulate in you? What would motivate someone to buy it?

3. Identify the magazine's social and political viewpoint. Who owns the magazine? Give your evidence.

4. Study the table of contents. Look at the range of subjects offered. Read some articles. What can you infer about the slant and mood, purpose and values of this magazine?

5. Describe some advertisements and generalize about which sponsors sell their products in this magazine. What social class would they appeal to? What kinds of advertisements are missing?

6. In a few sentences, give an example of the language used in one article. For what readers at what level of education does it seem to be written?

To follow up on this assignment in class, bring your magazine with you. Read or summarize your work to others in small groups. When you have finished, recommend one paper from your group to be read aloud or summarized for the class. Discuss what you learned from this assignment.

Student Writing Example

FORBES MAGAZINE, October 10, 1995

Diane Syverud

Viewpoint: Corporate Conservative

This magazine cover brings you right into the office, eye to eye, with a friendly middle-aged man who conveys corporate success and importance. His eyes are blue and friendly, his face freckled, and his hair thin; he wears a white starched shirt (as only dry-cleaners can do it); his jowls are a little choked by his prominent red tie, which has a magical kind of diamond pattern of raised gold tilelike squares. The solid gold wedding band on his ring finger suggests solid conservative values. His self-assured smile seems to say, "You can approach me, you can trust me. I'm successful!" The cover appears to be targeting those who want to know the secrets of corporate power and success.

The letters of the title *Forbes* are white and thick, partially obscured by the head of the man. Teasers at the top of the magazine read, "Marketing via the Internet" and "Old Scam, New Name," followed by "Biggest Mistake Investors Make—Are You Guilty?" and "Playing Virtual Gold." These enticements to read the articles inside seem to be aimed at a business audience of people who want to spend their leisure time reading but also learning how to profit. To the right of the man are two captions: in small white letters, "People Say GE Has Problems" and underneath in large black letters, "What's Jack Welch Smiling About?" I then realized that the cover figure is Jack Welch, the CEO of General Electric. Then I noticed that the smaller white letters appear to deemphasize that there could even be a problem, while the large black caption feels more solid, suggesting the situation is stable.

Table of Contents

The articles seem to be designed for upper-echelon readers with money to spare and look after. The article "Rent a Cop" explains how affluent people buy police protection. (Also, it subtly suggests that if you don't have the money to buy protection, you don't deserve it.) Articles appealing to new pastimes for the rich include "Harvey's Casino Resorts" and "Playing Virtual Golf." Serious business is taken up with "Politics as Usual" and "Biggest Mistakes Investors Make." The categories in the table of contents, such as Money and Investing, International Marketing, Management, and Corporate Strategies, reinforce my belief that this magazine is specifically geared toward the affluent big business giants—or those who would like to be. Their political leanings are reflected in an article titled "Taking the Fifth," which refers to the "ridiculous spending projects of the liberals." Obviously, this magazine is not written for a liberal audience.

Advertising

The first impression I got from the advertising was that it reflected sexist attitudes. For readers who appear to be white, upper-echelon, conservative, big-business males, women are portrayed as submissive to or less than men. For example, in one ad, a woman is shown in a low-cut, white, tight miniskirt, squatting in white high heels while holding on her lap a large wooden plaque. She has long blonde hair, and her face is drawn, like a tired Marilyn Monroe. Another picture shows several professionally dressed women in dark blue suits, seated and surrounded by standing men. Yet another picture shows a feminine woman standing like a quiet accessory in admiration of a white-uniformed ship's captain.

In the ads, persons of color are portrayed as male athletes or as shabby coal miners worried about pension plans, while Asians seem to be mirroring the white businessman image. The products advertised include ultra-expensive cars, car phones, first-class airfare packages; a full-page glossy ad promotes English gin. The message these ads conveys to me is that if you read *Forbes,* you too can someday drive fancy cars, fly first class, and deserve fine English gin at the end of your day.

Language

I would like to examine an article called "Virtual Golf." This article exclaims that the "electronic golf club is both an instructional tool and a smart toy!" It informs the reader that the total cost for a home set-up of Virtual Golf can be under $4,000 "with no green fees, carts, or caddies." What a deal! Many of us can't afford golf clubs, much less a virtual golf game. But this article implies that any successful businessman won't be able to resist this opportunity. It describes a cardiologist who "is an admitted golf fanatic who settles for electronic golf when his schedule or the weather keep him off the real course. He has taken pains to make the electronic links in his sunken living room as realistic as possible." The language here is middlebrow; the reader could have either a high school or college education. There is no humor here or objectivity about the values involved; it seeks to attract readers who want to be admired for their possessions but also seen as sportsmen.

It's not surprising to me that *Forbes* magazine is considered the voice of corporate America!

Used with permission of Diane Syverud.

Scoring for Second Option: Determining Political and Social Viewpoint and How It Shapes Content

1. Selection of magazine suitable for this assignment, as instructed, of an unfamiliar viewpoint with intellectual substance. Not a mainstream news or trade or home or glamour magazine.   10 points

2. Description of magazine cover follows instructions by describing detail that supports generalizations about its intention, the imagery and language used, and the feelings it stimulates. It does not get lost in trivia like describing bar graphs.   20 points

3. Makes thoughtful analysis of table of contents, arriving at some supported inferences about the range, slant, and focus of the magazine.   20 points

4. Shows thoughtful assessment of the advertising by following instructions to discover which advertising sponsors and products appear, which are missing, and   20 points

what demographics they seem to
be designed for. How might these
advertisers influence magazine
policies?

5. Follows instructions for analysis   10 points
   of language used, giving an
   example and speculating on the
   audience for which it is intended.

6. Is able to describe this magazine's   10 points
   viewpoint or place it on the
   political or social spectrum, giving
   reasons for doing so.

7. No distracting errors of spelling,   10 points
   punctuation, or sentence
   structure.

NEWS FRAMING

When we get into the habit of seeing information as a creation of view-point, we bring a more critical perspective to what is known as the daily news. We begin to wonder *who* decides *what* is news? Are they noble truth seekers dedicated to public service? A book such as *How to Watch TV News* (by Neil Postman and Steve Powers) says no in answer to this last question, casting doubt even on the assumption that the intention of any news media is to keep you informed. The media's purpose, these authors maintain, is to keep you entertained and sell you products:

> You may think that a TV news show is a public service and a public utility. But more than that, it is an enormously successful business enterprise. . . . The whole package is put together in the way that any theatrical producer would proceed, that is, by giving priority to show business values. (p. 161)

The authors then go on to say that acquiring media literacy means taking the time to inquire about the viewpoint, or the economic and political interests, of those who run TV stations:

> Keep in mind that other professionals—doctors, dentists, and lawyers, for example—commonly display their diplomas on their office walls to assure their clients that someone judged them to be competent. . . . But diplomas tell more than station "owners" and news directors and journalists tell. Wouldn't it be useful to know who these people are? Where they come from? What their angle is? And, especially, where they stand in relation to you? (p. 163)

Used with permission of Dan Perkins.

Learning the identity of the owners of any given TV network (as well as magazines or newspapers) has become a challenge in this decade of rapid media mergers. It can require ongoing research to learn what combinations of business conglomerates (including banks, insurance companies, industries, publishers, and individuals) control which newspapers or television stations or which of these media groups are merging with still other media groups. Some of the potential ramifications of information control by these monopolies are depicted in the Tom Tomorrow cartoon above.

The introduction of the Internet has shown us the enormous range of creative expression, debate, data access, and data sharing possible when information is not controlled. It has brought us viewpoints that have never been imagined, much less heard before. Yet, the Internet has not supplanted our newspapers and television and radio news because of their ubiquity and convenience. And even though we do not always know who censors and shapes this information, we can use our skills of observation and inference making to filter what we read and hear and to exercise more selectivity. The Core Discovery Writing Application that follows is designed to introduce you to the concept of *news framing* and the skills of news-framing analysis to help you better evaluate what you read. A news frame is the creation of editors, who represent the policies and values of the publishers, owners, and advertisers. The frame reflects decisions made about what stories go on the front page, how they will be arranged, which will have pictures, which will be short, which long, which sensationalized, which minimized. When we analyze the frame, we bring our active awareness to newspaper layout, story prominence, headline language, choices about which information is played up and which is played down, what information is missing. We look at the calculated creation of its context. Frame analysis habits teach us not to get lost in our reading but to remember to take the cues of viewpoint into account.

CORE DISCOVERY WRITING APPLICATION

Observing How a Newspaper Frames Its Information

This exercise might be adapted for the whole class to use on the same newspaper or with a variety of newspapers.*

1. Each student should bring the same paper to class for this exercise. On the same day, or a second day, students should bring a range of different papers. They could be *USA Today*, the *Wall Street Journal*, a local city newspaper, and a big city newspaper.

2. Study the front pages of each. What subject was chosen for the main headline? How was the headline worded? What were the subjects of stories accompanied by pictures? What stories were given less prominence? What are the differences in depth of treatment?

3. Now study the inside pages. Which news stories are given less prominence in each? What stories do not appear in some papers? How do the editorials differ? How do the advertisements differ?

4. Choose one news item that appears in each to compare. Consider the following items:
    (a) Which stories carry bylines?
    (b) Does the story show slant or balance, giving more than one point of view?
    (c) Are opinions and judgments mixed in with the facts?
    (d) Does the headline accurately reflect the article's data and conclusions?

*The author is indebted to Ralph H. Johnson and William Dorman for their lectures on how to teach frame analysis.

PROBLEM SOLVING

UNDERSTANDING A VIEWPOINT

The film *The Killing Fields* was based on the experiences of *New York Times* correspondent Sidney Schanberg. It is an account of his friendship with Cambodian Dith Pran, who was his *Times* assistant when Cambodia was invaded by the Khmer Rouge in 1975. Schanberg managed to escape, but Dith Pran had to stay behind in a country where two million people were to be massacred or to die of starvation or disease.

Four years later Dith Pran walked to freedom over the border into Thailand. He remarkably survived by thoroughly understanding the viewpoint of the communist Khmer Rouge. Knowing that he would be killed immediately if they suspected his association with Westerners, he cut his hair, threw away the dollars Schanberg had given him, and disguised himself in the dress, manner, and language of a working-class taxi driver. He survived by pretending to be ignorant. "I did not care if they thought I was a fool," he said.

Question

1. Dith Pran solved the problem of surviving by finding a disguise his enemy could accept. He fully understood their viewpoint. Can you describe a problem that you solved by understanding another's viewpoint?

---

5. What can you infer about the different values of each newspaper that resulted in the framing of each newspaper?

CHAPTER SUMMARY

1. Critical thinking means learning to recognize viewpoints and how they shape the content of any message.

2. Viewpoints—like assumptions, opinions, and evaluations—can be either consciously or unconsciously assumed.

3. We communicate best when we are aware of our own viewpoint (see it objectively as relative) and can understand and assume the viewpoints of others as well. For a writer, it is especially important to be able to anticipate the viewpoints of potential readers.

BUILDING ARGUMENTS

VIEWPOINTS

Much has been said of the want of what you term Civilization *among the Indians. Many proposals have been made to us to adopt your laws, your religion, your manners, and your customs. We do not see the propriety of such a reformation. We should be better pleased with beholding the good effects of these doctrines in your own practices than with hearing you talk about them, or of reading your newspapers on such subjects. You say, "Why do not the Indians till the ground and live as we do?" May we not ask with equal propriety, "Why do not the white people hunt and live as we do?"* (Old Tassel of the Cherokee tribe, 1777)

Exercise

1. What argument is Old Tassel refuting?
2. Given what you know about U.S. history from 1777 to the present, was Old Tassel's viewpoint heard or understood by the white men?
3. How can you explain that Old Tassel could describe and compare the two opposing viewpoints while the white men only saw their own?
4. Write an argument in which you explain a viewpoint that has not been heard or understood. (This could be personal, political, or social.)
5. Write a dialogue with an exchange of arguments between two viewpoints. Decide whether they will be able to hear one another and modify their opinions or not.

4. Unconscious viewpoints include the egocentric, ethnocentric, religiocentric, androcentric, and anthropocentric.

5. Political and social labels are based on the recognition of stable or predictable ideologies, values, and policies. At present our political and social differences are not easy to define in terms of a left-to-right spectrum.

6. In periodicals we find a wider range of viewpoints than in the mass media.

7. Periodicals can express viewpoints through symbols as well as words. Evidence of viewpoint can be seen in the selection of and emphasis on topics, and in advertising.

CHAPTER QUIZ

Rate each of the following statements as *true* or *false*. Rewrite any false statements to make them true.

_____ 1. Viewpoints can be either consciously or unconsciously assumed.

_____ 2. To be exterior to one's own viewpoint is to see it objectively as just one viewpoint among many.

_____ 3. Ethnocentrism means being absorbed in one's personal viewpoint without being able to put oneself in other people's shoes.

_____ 4. "The Jewish people are God's chosen people" could be interpreted as an example of religiocentrism.

_____ 5. In wartime, people tend to become more and more ethnocentric in their attitudes, expressing ideas that righteously affirm their own national superiority.

_____ 6. A *reactionary* viewpoint is one that advocates major political, social, or economic changes in order to return to an earlier, more conservative system of the past.

_____ 7. A *conservative* viewpoint believes it is often necessary to change the political, economic, or social status quo to foster the development and well-being of the individual.

_____ 8. A *liberal* viewpoint defends the status quo against major changes in the political, economic, or social institutions of a society.

_____ 9. So-called radical groups, whether right or left, want extreme, drastic, or fundamental changes in the status quo.

_____ 10. We communicate best when we can hear or anticipate the viewpoints of others and are objective about our own.

_____ 11. News framing is the shaping of information by newspaper editors based on marketing considerations as well as their publisher's policies and values.

Composition Writing Application

Essay Comparing and Contrasting Two Viewpoints

This essay will build on the research you did in a magazine writing application. In that exercise you observed, recorded characteristics, and made inferences about information to determine viewpoint, values, and objectives. You also personally evaluated this information. Mentally, you classified, categorized, compared, and contrasted and inferred cause and effect.

In this essay you are to make your classifications, comparisons, and contrasts more explicit. Here are the parameters for your work:

1. *Form and length*: Essay of four typed pages.

2. *Topic*: Comparison of two viewpoints, their values and ideologies, as expressed in two magazines from the same month and year. Limit your topic by focusing on (a) the same issue or controversy (for instance, tax reform, the nuclear debate, or a public personality) as discussed in both periodicals; or (b) a report of the same event; or (c) the magazines' subjects of advertising and approach to advertising (one could limit this even more, for instance, by comparing the liquor ads in *Ms.* to those in *Time* or *Esquire*); or (d) tone of the magazines, or their attitudes toward life: optimistic, paranoid, pessimistic, suffering and angry, conspiratorial, superficial, and so on.

3. *Thesis*: The thesis should represent the inferences you make about the values and ideologies of each one as indicated by its tone, its implied attitudes toward life, its interests, the readers it appeals to, and anything else that you find to be distinctive.

4. *Evidence and support*: Give concrete examples from the materials you are using to show the sources of your inferences about the values and ideology of each viewpoint.

5. *Structure*: Comparison (how alike) and contrast (how different). One strategy is to describe one magazine or newspaper fully according to subject (such as all the liquor ads) in several paragraphs, followed by several paragraphs treating all the liquor ads in the other magazine. Another option is to choose one part of your subject (such as all the beer and wine ads) and to compare one magazine to another on this part, then to move on to the hard liquor ads, comparing both magazines again in one paragraph. With either strategy, both your thesis and conclusion should bring both periodicals together in one or several generalizations stating what this comparative study has shown you.

Peer Review

Follow up in class by reading your papers to one another in small groups. Bring your magazines to class for your group to examine as you read. Work with partners to rate one another on the extent to which the parameters were observed. Rate what is outstanding about the essay.

Reading

WHITE BUCKS AND BLACK-EYED PEAS: COMING OF AGE IN WHITE AMERICA

Marcus Mabry

Marcus Mabry, at age twenty-eight, published his autobiography. He majored in English and French literature at Stanford, attended the Sorbonne, and has worked as a journalist for the *Boston Globe* and for *Newsweek* in Paris. This reading is the preface to his book, *White Bucks and Black-Eyed Peas* (New York: Scribner, 1995).

I was born in 1967. The year before Martin Luther King was assassinated. One of **1** the riot years. I started school in the post–Civil Rights Era of the 1970s. For the eight years I was in high school, college and graduate school, Ronald Reagan was president of the United States. I belong to a class of African-Americans who came of age in the 1990s. I belong to that minority within a minority that is college-educated—and that minority within *that* minority that is male. We are almost a class unto ourselves: twenty-something, black, professional and bound for success.

We are both a testament to American opportunity and a bellwether of Ameri- **2** can turmoil. Our brief history has been one of contradictions and compromises. Individually, we have greater professional opportunities than any preceding generation of African-Americans. Yet, by many measures, black people collectively are worse off relative to white Americans today than they were before the Civil Rights "revolution."

Part of a famously nonactivist generation, we helped push the U.S. Out of **3** South Africa and pried open the canon of Great Works. Although we are the most assimilated and the most integrated black Americans ever, we seem to find true community only among ourselves. We seek to make it, but we want to "stay black." We want white Americans to understand our culture, but not expect us to educate them: "It's a Black Thang, You Wouldn't Understand." We want to be judged by a colorless standard, but we proudly affirm our racial identity.

As we have been trying to unearth the men and women we are, America has **4** been trying to figure out what to make of us. While we have been learning to play the white corporate game, the rules have been in flux. Poll after poll has shown that while white Americans say there should be equality between the races, they believe that today it is white Americans who have less opportunity to find a good job or attend a first-rate college.

By the time we "arrived," white Americans were already wondering if they had **5** not given African-Americans too much. After college, companies hired us because of affirmative action, or merit. They promoted us because of quotas, or merit. And they resented us for being there.

Meanwhile, we have become increasingly separated from the masses of African-Americans, people who live in distant neighborhoods where we venture only for a haircut. Many of our parents had already worked their way into the middle, even upper middle, class. Many had not. Most of us who trickled up from the ghetto and into the buppie (black urban professional) elite—through hard work, the remnants of government programs for the poor, or a combination of both—left our mothers and fathers and brothers and sisters down there when we went off to good white schools and colleges. **6**

We saw some of them slide deeper into the poverty pit as the post-industrial economy wiped out well-paying blue-collar jobs. We saw our old neighborhoods sink from being "poor, but proud," into a numb despair, brooding and violent by turn. We saw the cohesion and solidarity fade from black America, as we broke into open class warfare between ourselves. Buppies loathing welfare mothers. Professionals crossing the street to avoid the brother on the sidewalk. And women wondering where all the men had gone. **7**

Our generation never knew the America that had crafted a rough consensus on racial equality or how to achieve it. Never buoyed by the hopes and promise of the Civil Rights Era, we were not disappointed when the dream was never realized. But the realization that despite our individual opportunity, the dream would never come true for most black people, made us cynical and pessimistic. While *I* was doing well, *we* were doing worse. And, yet, even the Talented Tenth had no abiding faith that tomorrow would be better. **8**

My trek from AFDC to the Sorbonne is not meant to speak for all our experiences. No one person could; there are too many roads from there to here, even while there are too few. Each offers its own twists and turns, sacrifices, successes and sorrows. But like African-Americans of any generation when I speak of "me," I have to speak on "us." As much as blacks lament our unending travails in America, we, more than any others, are dependent on America for our very identity. This nation is not only the crucible of our suffering; it is the forge which bore us. **9**

I cannot understand my present without exploring our past. White people often ask me how I escaped poverty when so many poor black males do not. I usually answer luck. I might add Uncle Sam with his Aid to Families with Dependent Children (AFDC), food stamps, Medicaid, Head Start, college grants and Perkins loans—all of which benefited me. But if reasons to explain why I am "an exception" are needed, then the first two are my grandmother and my mother. One planted me firmly in this world. The other taught me to reach for the heavens. My grandmother rooted me in reality, through her staunch loyalty to an unjust existence and her faith that life was its own reward. My mother taught me the power of dreams through her endless pursuit of experience and wonder. My story is only their story come to fruition, the seed of three generations of African-American promise that, until me, for myriad reasons, failed to germinate. **10**

Policy wonks, social engineers and politicians—liberal and conservative—debate whether government aid or family values will elevate poor Americans from **11** nihilism to productivity, from hopelessness to self-sufficiency. There is no magic formula, of course—three parts bootstrap and one part handout—that will guarantee a fair opportunity for the disadvantaged. I believe that without my grandmother and my mother's energetic involvement in my development, I would not be writing this book. Their determination that I succeed carried me so far from poverty. At the same time, without taxpayers' dollars I would not have been empowered with the tools—knowledge, role models and a good diploma—to free myself from the cycle of low income and low achievement. If my mother and my grandmother were the heart and mind that propelled a poor black boy toward success, then that aid was the essential lifeblood that nourished them.

My journey took me from poverty to prep school; from New Jersey to Africa,   12
Europe and Asia, and from assistant custodian on the government's now-defunct summer jobs program to *Newsweek's* correspondent in Paris. The prep school from which I graduated with distinction is the same one where one of my grandmothers worked as a cook. I am proof that even today the cliched American dream can come true for boys who start off in the world poor and black—even after crack, Rodney King, Pat Buchanan; even for a member of "an endangered species."

The American ideal is meritocratic success through individual effort. But follow-   13
ing the societal directive, instilled from our elite prep schools and our prestigious universities, is not easy. In order to achieve, we all make sacrifices. But for African-Americans, brothers in particular, this truism appears deceptively facile—especially for those of us who travel from poverty to success. While working-class Irish-Americans or Italian-Americans may face similar alienation from the families they leave behind, they do not hazard their group identification. In our quest for accomplishment, and in our success, poor African-Americans risk our families, our racial identity, our very selves.

In this book, I describe the events and people that shaped me. I was twenty-   14
five years old when I began writing. I will be twenty-eight when the book is published. I do not intend to answer all the questions that my life to this point has raised; I am still unsure of many of the answers myself. And I find they change over time. Just as I have constantly grown in my ability to understand myself and the events and people that touched my life, so does my voice change in the course of this narrative: from passive observer to active participant, from self-centered to societally-oriented, from naive to contemplative. Do not read this memoir for conclusions. This is quite evidently not a life story, but the story of the beginning of a life.

The book deliberately begins and ends with my family because, at this early   15
point in my journey, one important lesson I have learned is that more than the acceptance of any community of strangers—black or white—it must be in the support and acceptance of those I love that I find my sense of belonging, my place in the world.

I am ever grateful to my God, my family, my nation, my mentors and my   16
teachers, and to the generations of African-Americans who died so that I might live

free. Still, I must reckon the price I paid for the privilege of living in two worlds—one black and poor, one white and affluent—from the friction within my family to the questioning of my own personhood. The price of success seemed betrayal. I carry with me the scars of "making it": the uncomfortable and embarrassing dependency of my family, the feelings of "tomming" and the constant balancing act between everyone and everything, white and black.

Study Questions

1. Describe in one paragraph how Marcus Mabry characterizes his viewpoint (for example, his generation, social class, ethnic group, and political perspective).

2. How is his viewpoint familiar to you and how is it foreign?

3. What does he say is his predicament?

4. What is his view on affirmative action?

5. What does he say will be the themes and limitations of his autobiography?

For Further Reading

Bagdikian, Ben. *The Media Monopoly*. Boston: Beacon Press, 1983. See Chapter 1, "The Endless Chain"; Chapter 2, "Public Information as Industrial By-product"; Chapter 10, "Democracy and the Media."

Blyskal, Jeff, and Marie Blyskal. *PR: How the Public Relations Industry Writes the News*. New York: Morrow, 1985.

Gingrich, Newt, and Dick Armey. *Contract with America*. New York: Random House, 1994.

Henwood, Doug. *The State of the USA Atlas: The Changing Face of American Life in Maps, Graphics*. New York: Touchstone, 1994.

Herman, Edward S., and Noam Chomsky. *Manufacturing Consent*. New York: Pantheon, 1988.

Jensen, Carl. *Censored: The News That Didn't Make the News, the 1995 Project Censored Yearbook*. New York: Four Walls Eight Windows, 1995.

Lee, Martin, and Norman Soloman. *Unreliable Sources*. New York: Lyle Stuart, 1991.

Postman, Neil, and Steve Powers. *How to Watch TV News*. New York: Penguin, 1992.

Project Vote Smart. *Voter's Self-Defense Manual; U.S. Government: Owner's Manual*. Corvallis, Oreg.: Center for National Independence in Politics (annual publication).

Stauber, John, and Sheldon Rampton. *Toxic Sludge Is Good for You! Lies, Damn Lies, and the Public Relations Industry*. Monroe, Maine: Common Courage Press, 1995.

Tannen, Deborah. *You Just Don't Understand: Women and Men in Conversation*. New York: Ballantine, 1990.

Weiss, Michael J. *Latitudes and Attitudes: An Atlas of American Tastes, Trends, Politics, and Passions*. New York: Little, Brown, 1994.

Periodicals

Extra, a newsletter published eight times a year by Fairness & Accuracy in Reporting. It examines examples of conservative bias or media exclusion of left perspectives, as seen from the left perspective.

Mediawatch, a monthly newsletter giving examples of liberal bias as seen from the conservative perspective.

Internet

The Institute for Global Communications (IGC) whose networks—Peacenet, EcoNet, LaborNet, and ConflictNet, and Internet Gopher—provide a wealth of information not available in the mainstream media. Address: gopher://gopher.econet. apc.org/

Texts Offering Opposing Viewpoints for Study

Ideas in Conflict. Gem Publications, 411 Mallalien Drive, Hudson, Wisc. 54016.
Taking Sides. Duskin Publishing Group, Inc. Slice Dock, Guilford, Conn. 06437.

OBJECTIVES REVIEW OF PART II

When you have finished Part II, you will understand

- The concepts and complexities of assumptions, opinions, evaluations, and viewpoints.
- How these concepts are mental experiences.
- How they are problematical when confused with facts.
- How a viewpoint frames information.
- Some varieties of conscious and unconscious viewpoints.

And you will have practice in developing these skills:

- Recognizing the mental formation of assumptions, opinions, evaluations, and viewpoints.
- Checking for assumptions, reexamining opinions, evaluations, and viewpoints for their strengths and limitations.
- Identifying underlying assumptions and value assumptions in discourse.
- Separating opinions and evaluations from facts.
- Recognizing opinions and evaluative words.
- Using observing and inferring to identify characteristics of social and political viewpoint.
- Analyzing the news frame.

PART III
Forms and Standards of Critical Thinking

CHAPTER 9

Argument:
What's a Good Argument?

Used with permission of Ben Dib.

Fighting may be easier than arguing, but even fighting can't proceed when viewpoints and ideologies become entangled. This chapter shows you how to disentangle before the fighting starts or, better, how to make fighting unnecessary. You will be learning about arguments as supported claims, focusing on their structure in order to better read, judge, and write them.

At the end of this chapter are several writing applications that will take research time to complete. If you are assigned one of these, you can begin your research now while also completing your study of the remaining chapters in this book. You may write a take-home final research paper or an argumentative essay that calls for all the knowledge and skills you gained from completing this book.

Discovery Exercise

Reading and Judging Arguments

Read the six points of view offered here on a controversial subject. Then answer the questions that follow in writing.

Viewpoint 1

None of us here at U.S. English [an organization whose goal is to make English the official language of the United States] wants the newcomers to deny their roots, or even to lose their native tongue. To remember, and celebrate, the folkways, the festivals, the food of the old country . . . enriches the variety of American life. . . . But the day that the immigrant's native tongue becomes the first language of any community or—God forbid—a State, the American experiment will be on its way to breaking up into a collection of feuding German republics, with several Quebecs in our future.

Alistair Cooke, author, broadcaster, member of Board of Advisors for U.S. English. From an undated promotional newsletter.

Viewpoint 2

As you know, I have been outspoken in my opposition to the English Only move-ment. I have pledged to veto any bill that came before me calling for establishing English as the official language of our State. It appears my opposition to this legis-lation has led U.S. English to concentrate on destroying the outstanding bilingual education programs offered by school districts throughout New York State.

Bilingual education has been extremely successful in helping students to learn English. In fact, a national study conducted by the U.S. Department of Education found that students in bilingual classes had more success in learning English than students in English only immersion classes.

Mario M. Cuomo, governor of New York State. Letter to Tom Sobol, commissioner of education for New York State, July 27, 1989.

Viewpoint 3

But the point of officializing English is to strengthen our common bond, not to obliterate our individual identities. For millions of Americans, ethnicity and lan-guage are linked. Communicating in an ancestral tongue is a means of maintaining ties with the past. . . . Ethnic diversity is one of the greatest strengths of the United States. English should be our official language, but it should not be our only language.

Barbara Mujica, associate professor of Spanish, Georgetown University. *Dallas News*, 24 June 1989.

Viewpoint 4

Our nation and the English language have done quite well with Chinese spoken in California, German in Pennsylvania, Italian in New York, Swedish in Minnesota, and Spanish in the Southwest. I fail to see the cause for alarm now.

Sen. John McCain, R-Ariz. From *Time,* December 5, 1988.

Viewpoint 5

We must stop the practice of multilingual education as a means of instilling ethnic pride, or as a therapy for low esteem, or out of elitist guilt over a culture built on the traditions of the West. With all the divisive forces tearing at our country, we need the glue of language to help hold us together. And if we want to ensure that all of our children have the same opportunities alternative language education should stop, and English should be acknowledged once and for all as the official language of the United States of America.

Sen. Robert Dole, R-Kans. Debate on *MacNeil-Lehrer Newshour,* September 5, 1995.

Viewpoint 6

I support making English the official language of the country because I want to keep America one nation, one people. And quite frankly, thoughtful people all across the spectrum, whether it's Arthur Schlesinger all the way to Bob Dole and Newt Gingrich, people like the *New Republic* and Cato and Heritage, all are supporting this initiative, because we see today America breaking into groups. And as Woodrow Wilson said, "America is not a nation of groups. America is a nation of individuals."

Rep. Toby Roth, R-Wisc. *MacNeil-Lehrer Newshour,* September 5, 1995.

Viewpoint 7

The problem is that there is nothing that's wrong that needs fixing. I'm a bilingual person. I was born in Puerto Rico an American citizen. I'm a member of Congress. I'm speaking to you in English. I speak to other people in Spanish at times. . . . I would say all parents who come to this country want their children to speak English. In fact, when Hispanics sit around the dinner table and the issue of language comes up, it's not about a plot to undo the English language. It's usually about the fact that the children and grandchildren no longer speak Spanish. . . . English is the language accepted by all immigrant groups. . . . But when you say it has to become the official language, you are making a political statement, and you're making a statement against certain segments.

Rep. Jose Serrano, D-N.Y. *MacNeil-Lehrer Newshour,* September 5, 1995.

Study Questions

1. How would you describe each of the viewpoints given here?
2. What is the basic position, pro or con, taken by each? How do you know this position?
3. Take one viewpoint for analysis. What reasons are given to support its position?
4. Which do you find to be the most persuasive?
5. How did you decide?

CRITICAL ANALYSIS OF ARGUMENTS IN READING

As you will remember from Chapter 2's discussion of word precision, good critical reading does not begin with criticism but with accurate comprehension of the material. Accurate comprehension stems from an attitude of mental receptivity that faithfully records the message, which can be especially difficult when those values do not agree with your own. In the different viewpoints on English Only that opened this chapter, you may well have found yourself reading carefully those opinions you liked and skimming over those you didn't. This first stage of patient receptivity can be as challenging as the critical phase that follows. But, as stated earlier, it is not possible to be skeptical and receptive at the same time. When critical analysis begins too soon, it can interfere with making an accurate reading of the material. And a criticism of an argument based on an inaccurate reading is a waste of time.

KNOWING WHAT QUESTIONS TO ASK

The critical phase of reading, as distinct from the receptive phase, is a time for questioning and evaluating content. Once you have absorbed and understood the content, you can ask five basic questions in making your examination:

1. What viewpoint and what values or interests have shaped this argument?
2. How is the argument structured in terms of reasons and conclusion?
3. Is it an argument? Or is it a report? Or is it a combination?

4. What is the issue of controversy?

5. What are the strengths and weaknesses of this argument?

We will consider these questions one by one, except for the last question on an argument's strengths and weaknesses. The standards you need to understand in order to answer the last question are taken up in Chapters 10 and 11.

WHAT VIEWPOINT, INTERESTS, AND VALUES SHAPED THIS ARGUMENT?

Your study of Chapter 8, "Viewpoints," made the importance of this question meaningful to you. As a result, you might have approached the opening Discovery Exercise in this chapter by giving as much attention to each quotation's viewpoint as to its content. You might have first read the names and credentials beneath each statement, then read the argument, then reconsidered the argument in light of the speaker's title and associations. You might have made inferences about their values, motives, and beliefs. You would have begun by asking the first question of critical reading: *What viewpoint, values, and interests shaped the content of this argument?*

HOW IS THE ARGUMENT STRUCTURED IN TERMS OF REASONS AND CONCLUSIONS?

In the chapters that follow, you will be learning more about argument form and standards in both inductive and deductive reasoning. You will learn that with induction, we usually use this form:

Data

Data

Data

Data

Hypothesis or generalization → conclusion

And with deduction we used this form (the syllogism):

Major Premise

Minor Premise

Conclusion

Yet, these structures serve only as artificial models, abstracted from the arguments we hear and use throughout a day. We do not speak in syllogisms or expect to read them in newspaper editorials or hear them in presidential debates on television or from a used-car salesman. However, in order to argue, we have to know what point we want to make and how it can be supported. And when we hear the arguments of others, we need to be able to size up these components very quickly, abstracting the argument's core from the form in which it appears. Thus, when reading the English Only arguments earlier in this chapter, you may have sensed that some of them were better reasoned than others, but you may not have been really sure how to explain why or why not.

The next few pages offer a method for explaining whether an argument is well reasoned or not. This method can also make the construction of arguments easier. This method is known as the analysis of arguments in terms of *reasons* and *conclusions*. The main advantage of this method is that it applies to both inductive and deductive arguments. The term *reasons* can be used to include both the premises of deduction and the factual evidence of induction and the term *conclusion* to include inductive hypotheses as well as deductive conclusions. This portion of the chapter will offer a great deal of practice in identifying and analyzing arguments in terms of their reasons and conclusions. And the final research writing assignment will challenge you to demonstrate this skill.

Identifying the Conclusion of an Argument

The key to understanding any written argument is finding its conclusion. Although a conclusion is generally defined as a summary statement that comes last in any kind of spoken or written statement (or *discourse*), an argument's conclusion is not necessarily an ending point or summary but a statement of a kind of thesis, or decision, or judgment. Usually, but not always, it is also a statement that one wants to convince others to believe.

In the formal reasoning of induction and deduction, a conclusion is the *last* step in a reasoning process. In everyday spoken or written argumentation, a conclusion may be stated *at any time* during the argument—or never stated at all but only implied.

Inductive

Yesterday I was happy singing.

Last week I was happy singing.

Everytime in my life I sing, I feel happy.

Conclusion: Singing makes me happy.

Deductive

Singing makes me happy.

I am singing.

Conclusion: I am happy.

(Statement) I would rather sing than do anything else.

(Implied) Singing makes me happy.

Conclusions, however, need not be single or separate but may be arrived at in rapid succession, one leading to another and another. If, for instance, your pleasure in singing led you to join a college chorus, that decision could have been based on several prior conclusions such as "I want to sing with others" and "I prefer a college chorus to a church choir." Considered as an argument, your final conclusion could have been based on a series of *reasons* such as the following: (1) the chorus has a good musical reputation; (2) the tuition cost is low; (3) the sign-up for the semester is next week. Thus, in an argument, a conclusion is the bottom line, which carries with it a sense of finality. And the reasons are the thinking considerations that lead to this point of decision.

However, even though we can *feel* our own conclusions, it is not always that easy to find them in written arguments, where the reasons may also sound like conclusions.

> Those who watched the Democratic convention in July 1988 may remember that it was the first at which the nominee gave his acceptance speech in two languages. [reason in form of evidence leading to next reason] Years from now, we may well remember this event was a turning point, a time and place at which the seeds of disunity were still more deeply planted across the land. [reason supporting the implied conclusion]

In this case, both reasons offered could have served as conclusions in another context. But here they support a conclusion that is not stated: I am in favor of "official" English.

Conclusions can sometimes be easily recognized by the so-called inference indicator words that precede them. Such indicator words include the following: *therefore, so, in fact, the truth of the matter is, in short, it follows that, shows that, indicates that, suggests that, proves that, we may deduce that, points to the conclusion that, in my opinion,* and *the most obvious explanation is*.

1. *The truth of the matter is* that "official" English is based on xenophobia.

2. *In my opinion* "official" English will help, not hurt, immigrants.

3. *It all goes to show* that the United States is becoming like Germany in the 1930s, where arguments for the purity of the Aryan race and the German language were made with the same reasoned logic as those being made for English Only today.

Identifying Reasons

Reasons are statements of opinion, propositions, premises, or statements of evidence offered to explain, justify, or support conclusions.

1. I am not in favor of "official" English. [conclusion] *Such laws would oppress minorities.* [reason] *Such laws would create problems where there are no problems.* [reason]

2. "*But the point of officializing English is to strengthen our common bond, not to obliterate our individual identities* [reason]. . . . English should be our official language, but it should not be our only language." [conclusion]

When we are giving our *own* reasons for an argument, they are self-evident. But it is not always easy to distinguish the reasons from the conclusions offered in someone else's argument. Yet, we must do this if we are to know exactly what another is trying to prove and whether the reasons given are adequate support. This means we have to take the argument apart, and the best strategy for analysis is to find the conclusion first and thus extricate it from the whole. This method is rather like finding the leader of a group with whom to communicate rather than trying to talk to everyone in the group at once. Thus, once we find the conclusion, the reasons are simply what remain.

Another technique for finding reasons is to look for the so-called inference indicator words that often introduce reasons: *because, first . . . second, since, for, for one thing, in view of the fact that, for the reason that, is supported by, for example, also.*

1. "I am in favor of officializing English [conclusion] *first because* it would avert cultural separatism [reason] *and secondly* because this would make us stronger as a nation." [reason]

Exercise

Identifying Reasons and Conclusions

In the following statements, underline the conclusions and number the reasons:

1. I am going to become an engineer because I see more advertisements in the newspapers for engineers than for any other profession.

2. By the study of different religions we find that in essence they are one. All are concerned with revelations or breakthrough experiences that can redirect lives and empower them toward good.

3. I am not pro-abortion at all. I think that people nowadays use abortion as an easy form of birth control. It's also against my religion.

4. Guns kill people; that's why handguns should be banned.

5. Deep fat frying can greatly increase the calories of foods such as fish, chicken, and potatoes. Therefore, it is better to bake, boil, or steam foods.

6. "It is important that individual citizens equip themselves with a baloney detection kit to determine whether politicians, scientists, or religious leaders are lying—it's an important part of becoming a citizen of the world." (Carl Sagan)

7. America should put a freeze on immigration. Its first duty is to take better care of its own disadvantaged, poor, and unemployed.

8. Marijuana laws are lenient in California and will probably not be changed. This is because those with the strongest economic interest— the commercial growers—would be out of business. After all, it's the third largest agricultural business in the state of California.

9. The U.S. policy on the use of chemical weapons is to protest their production by other nations while producing them ourselves. This is supported by the content of our negotiations on the one hand and our military budget allocations for binary nerve gas on the other.

10. I don't drink because alcohol gives me a brief high followed by a longer depression.

More on Distinguishing Reasons from Conclusions

Discovering the structure of arguments in general reading can involve some complexities that take a little practice to untangle. For instance, sometimes the conclusion is not stated at all but merely implied. In the fourth viewpoint on officializing English, Senator McCain's disapproval of the idea is stated only in terms of his reasons.

> Our nation and the English language have done quite well with Chinese spoken in California, German in Pennsylvania, Italian in New York, Swedish in Minnesota and Spanish in the Southwest. I fail to see the cause for alarm now.

Here the implied conclusion of the senator's statement, "I am opposed to officializing English," is obvious. In some arguments, however, the missing conclusion may be more difficult to formulate.

If you spend a billion dollars on retail trade, you generate 65,000 jobs. If you spend it on education, you generate 62,000 jobs; on hospitals, 48,000 jobs; on guided missiles and ordinance, 14,000 jobs. When you move money from the Department of Education to the Pentagon, for instance, or from a state like Michigan which would spend it on education, you are destroying jobs at about a three to one ratio.

Marion Anderson, testimony before special congressional ad hoc hearings on the full implications of the military budget, January 1982; quoted by Ronald Dellums in *Defense Sense*.

In this case the speaker's conclusion might be stated as *"Contrary to popular belief, defense destroys more jobs than it creates."*

Sometimes a series of conclusions can be offered as reasons for an implied conclusion. In the following quotation, the speaker is offering a parody of the reasons given in the Preamble to the Constitution for the creation of that Constitution. These conclusions serve as his argument's reasons.

The arms race does not form a more perfect union. The arms race does not insure domestic tranquility. The arms race does not provide for the common defense. The arms race does not promote the general welfare. And finally, the arms race does not secure the blessings of liberty to ourselves and to our posterity.

Bishop Walter F. Sullivan, testimony before special congressional ad hoc hearings on the full implications of the military budget, January 1982; quoted by Ronald Dellums in *Defense Sense*.

Conclusions do not always appear at the end of an argument: sometimes they appear in the beginning, as in newspaper headlines.

Lifeline Banking Idea Unlikely to Take Hold at Banks

Aside from the heated debate over whether the nation's banks, like public utilities, should have to provide low-cost, low-use "lifeline service" to the poor, there's some doubt about whether they would, and more about whether they will.

Oakland Tribune, October 22, 1984.

Sometimes a conclusion appears in the middle of a series of statements.

Groups such as Public Advocates may be asking for the impossible or for something no longer possible, ignoring valid possibilities already in place. *Nevertheless, banks might be wise to move faster in coming up with special services not just appropriate, but actively promoted for low-income groups.* [conclusion]

One reason might be the good of society. Those who live a cash-only life cost everyone time and money. It costs Pacific Bell $1.98, for example, to process a cash payment personally delivered and only 9 cents to process a mailed-in check.

Another reason suggested is the good of the bank, which could enjoy some public relations advantage in offering special services for the poor.

Oakland Tribune, October 22, 1984.

As we stated earlier, the first problem to address in analyzing arguments is to identify the conclusion, separating it from the reasons given in its support. This action prepares the way for us to question whether or not the reasons are adequate to support the conclusion. Indeed, we cannot answer such questions until we have unveiled the structure of the argument and clearly identified for study the conclusion and reasons offered. Obviously, we need to determine clearly *exactly what the author is claiming to prove* before becoming involved in a reaction of agreement or disagreement. By identifying the conclusion, we know the author's exact position on an issue. We may agree or disagree with this position—but first we must know what it is. If we should mistake one of the reasons for the conclusion, we may find ourselves going off on a wrong track in our analysis and rebuttal. But once we have identified the conclusion, we can easily determine the reasons and isolate them for examination.

The other advantage of learning how to identify conclusions and reasons is that it enables us to refute or dismiss arguments that are fallacious. Such a process of elimination allows us to spend more time with arguments that can really instruct us or challenge our thinking. Moreover, when we are writing our own arguments, we have a clear structural model to keep in mind that will help us build and test our arguments at their core.

Exercises

More Practice in Identifying Reasons and Conclusions

Analyze the following arguments by underlining the conclusions, or by supplying the conclusion in writing if it is only implied. Note that sometimes a conclusion may be part of a sentence, or the conclusion may be offered alone without any reasons attached.

1. Frequent snacks of high-energy food are not harmful to backpackers. Indeed, hikers are found to have more energy and less weariness if they snack every hour.

2. Broadcast television is not appropriate in the courtroom. The relentless pressure of the media threatens the balance between the First Amendment's press freedom and the Sixth Amendment's fair trial rights.

3. "Whereas birth is a cause for celebration, death has become a dreaded and unspeakable issue to be avoided by every means possible in our modern society. Perhaps it is that death reminds us of our human vulnerability in spite of all our technological advances." (Elisabeth Kübler-Ross)

4. The current welfare system is a powerful force driving illegitimacy because it pays mothers more for each child and denies benefits to fami-

lies with two parents. If women were denied support for illegitimate children, they would be discouraged from having more.

5. There's nothing like the taste of fresh, hot brownies. Bake your own the easy way with Brownlee's Brownie Mix! (advertisement)

6. No doctor should have the right to allow a patient to die. No doctor is God.

7. Videos are a good way to entertain children. You can control what they watch, and there are many worthwhile films to choose from.

8. Life is fast-paced in Japan, but its citizens do not have as high a rate of coronary heart disease as those in the northeastern cities of the United States. This may be because their culture does not associate hard work with competitiveness the way ours does.

9. Since the 1920s, sperm counts have declined among American men. The underlying causes are uncertain, but the factors of stress and toxic chemicals are being considered.

10. If only 1 percent of the car owners in America did not use their cars for one day a week, they would save 42 million gallons of gas a year and keep 840 million pounds of CO_2 out of the atmosphere.

11. Homelessness should not be tolerated. If we allow people to live in the streets, we contribute to their abandonment. Nor is building more shelters the answer. Real solutions must address the causes by providing affordable housing, job training, income assistance, health care, substance-abuse treatment, and child care.

12. Because of their greater use of prescription drugs, women turn up in hospital emergency rooms with drug problems more frequently than men. (FDA consumer report)

13. "English as the language of international pop music and mass entertainment is a worldwide phenomenon. In 1982, a Spanish punk rock group, called Asfalta (Asphalt), released a disc about learning English, which became a hit. The Swedish group Abba records all its numbers in English. Michael Luszynski is a Polish singer who performs almost entirely in English." (*The Story of English*, Penguin Books, 1986)

Exercise

More Practice with Longer Arguments

Underline the conclusions and number the reasons given in the following arguments:

1. "Contrary to popular perception, immigrants are less likely to collect welfare than native-born residents. They also create more jobs than

they take and contribute more in taxes than they cost in public services. In California, they helped build Silicon Valley, resurrected the apparel industry, and could help lift the state of California out of its worst recession since the Great Depression through their ties to the burgeoning trade markets of the Pacific Rim." (Philip Pak Woo. *San Francisco Focus Magazine*, November 1994).

2. "With proper government policies, immigrants are a blessing. We saw this with earlier waves of immigration, as America absorbed and assimilated tens of millions of foreign immigrants of every language, religion, and ethnicity. By 1900, some 20 percent of America's total population was foreign-born, and an additional 10 percent arrived in the following decade. Today's immigration rate is only a fraction of this level. Millions of impoverished, poorly educated Jews, Slavs, and Italians became proud and productive Americans through a public school system that emphasized English language skills and American culture, and a society that provided economic opportunity rather than government entitlement." (Ron K. Unz, Republican primary candidate for California governor. *Policy Review*, November 1994)

3. "Immigration is not a neutral factor in the maintenance and creation of welfare. It fosters and expands constituencies of the poor, who, not unnaturally, favor the extension of welfare programs from which they benefit. In 1990 the welfare-participation rate of immigrants as a whole was 9.1 percent; that is, 1.7 percentage points higher than that of Americans as a whole." (John O'Sullivan, editor. *National Review*, November 1994)

4. "Washington is asking Californians not only to tolerate four million illegals but also to school them, look after their health, and pay them unemployment benefits. . . . So it's time for voters to stop putting up with this situation. Because the burden of immigration is greater than our resources to cope with it." (William F. Buckley Jr., editor. *National Review*, November 1994)

CORE DISCOVERY WRITING APPLICATION

Writing a Short Persuasive Argument: A Letter of Complaint

This assignment is about power. It is a practical opportunity to restore some power that you may have lost. This will take the form of writing an effective argument in a letter of complaint. In this letter, you will not only describe an injustice but communicate clearly what you want done about it.

The Steps

1.   Address the letter to a specific individual: to a friend, a parent, an elected official, a landlady, a newspaper editor. In short, address it to someone who has some power to do something about the situation. It may take some research to determine who this person is, but that is part of the assignment.

2.   As you outline your letter, state exactly in neutral (nonblaming) terms (a) what the situation is, (b) what is unfair about it, and (3) what you want from the other person now. Your final paragraph should serve to keep the two of you connected by asking for reactions, a call, an appointment, or an agreement by a suggested time.

3.   Use reasoning and evidence to support your case. Make your conclusions straightforward and simple. Be clear about what you want.

4.   Your letter should be one to two pages typed; use a business letter format.

Writing Preparation

In choosing your topic, select a situation that feels genuinely unjust and unfinished to you, one that you have not been able to handle in a way that you would like. The more emotion you feel on the subject, the greater the challenge will be to formulate an effective, well-reasoned argument. When we feel very angry, sad, or apathetic, it is difficult to think clearly or make ourselves heard. Yet, writing and revising to work through your emotions can bring you to clarity and power so that you will be able to present your case effectively. If at the beginning you feel overwhelmed by feelings, write them out or hit some pillows until you blow off steam. When you feel more collected, you can compose your argument. After you have finished your first draft, reread it, asking yourself whether your purpose was to make the other party feel ashamed, guilty, or wrong. These objectives may make you feel better but will not help you be heard. When made to feel guilty, people usually become afraid or defensive and are not open or likely to cooperate to change or amend a situation. Use neutral language, and be quite specific about how you see the problem and what you want understood or done, but respect both yourself and the person you are addressing. Rephrase as requests any demands you have made that are within the range of the other party's capacity for acceptance and accomplishment.

Peer Review

To follow up on this exercise in class, exchange your letter or essay with a partner and do the following:

1.   Underline the conclusion and circle the reasons.

2. Answer these questions on a sheet to attach to your partner's work:

   (a) Which reasons clearly support, justify, or explain the conclusion? Which do not?

   (b) Are more reasons needed? Explain.

3. If any portion is not clear to you, circle it and ask your partner to explain it to you.

When you receive your work back, consider the comments. If you cannot agree with the critique, seek another partner and go through the same process verbally. If you find the criticisms helpful, revise your work accordingly.

If this exercise stimulated your interest in making yourself heard to achieve change, you may be interested in reading the publication *Tell It to Washington: A Guide for Citizen Action, Including a Congressional Directory*. Pub. no. 349. Available from the League of Women Voters of the U.S., 1730 M Street NW, Washington, D.C. 20036.

Scoring for Letter of Complaint

1. Letter is addressed to a specific person who has the power to do something about the situation.	10 points
2. Organization is simple and clear, describes the situation, the complaint, and is requesting a specific action.	10 points
3. Request made that is clear and possible to fulfill.	10 points
4. Conclusion is clear; sufficient and adequate reasons are given.	10 points
5. Topic chosen involves challenge of self-control. (Not a routine letter as returning a defective product.)	20 points
6. Language does not blame, make guilty, or cause defensiveness.	10 points
7. A final connecting statement is made, requesting, but not demanding, a response within a stated period of time.	10 points
8. No distracting errors of punctuation, sentence structure, spelling.	20 points

---

ARGUMENTS AND REPORTS: DIFFERENT PURPOSES, STRUCTURES, AND STANDARDS

Report	Argument
Purpose: To inform	**Purpose:** To persuade
Structure:	**Structure:**
1. Data presented and/or explained.	1. Assertion of principal claim, thesis, or conclusion.
2. Support for data's accuracy and veracity offered in the forms of corroborating evidence independent studies examples expert testimony records surveys, polls, investigations statistics analogies	2. Support of reasons for conclusion. Includes all items on left as well as appeals to feelings and values such as justice, purpose, meaning, consistency, harmony, unity, responsibility.
3. Different hypotheses that interpret this data may be offered; one hypothesis might be supported with recommendations, but mood is one of openness.	3. Clearly committed position with effort to win agreement.
4. Summary of findings.	4. Summary repeats why this position is correct.
Standards:	**Standards:**
Objectivity	Clarity about claims
Verifiability	Adequate and convincing support
Reliability	Cogent reasoning
Rigorous scientific standards	Fairness of presentation

Discovery Exercise

Distinguishing Arguments from Reports

The following article is a *report* that explains some facts about an event and an issue. Read it and answer the question that follows.

Changing Our National Anthem

Rep. Andrew Jacobs, D-Ind., has introduced a bill that would change the national anthem to "America the Beautiful." He says that both musicians and the general public agree that "The Star-Spangled Banner" is just too difficult to sing correctly. However, although everyone might agree with him on this score, winning public support for the change might not be so easy. According to a recent telephone poll conducted by *Time* magazine, 67 percent were against this replacement.

The idea of changing our national anthem is a controversial proposal. Why is this a report on the subject and not an argument?

The following is an *argument* and not a report. Read it and then write down what makes it an argument.

> I am in favor of replacing "The Star-Spangled Banner" with "America the Beautiful." Our present anthem, with its incredible range of octaves, makes it difficult even for an opera singer to perform. As a result, most of us can only hum along. Moreover, the content of the lyrics is antiquated, hard to remember, and warmongering. "America the Beautiful" spares us all these problems.

Define *argument* and *report*.

IS IT AN ARGUMENT
OR A REPORT OR BOTH?

Because reports and arguments are each evaluated by different criteria in critical reading, it is essential to recognize the difference between them. The main purpose of *reports* is to offer information; this can be done through relating events or by offering facts or findings. Reports follow the rules of inductive reasoning. *Arguments*, on the other hand, only *use* information to reason toward an objective—to explain an idea, to justify it, or to persuade others to accept it. A report can relate an event, as in the first example, "Changing Our National Anthem"; it can offer findings, by interviewing supporters and detractors; and it can offer a hypothesis to predict what the final outcome may be.

But as often as not, a report leaves the conclusions up to the reader. It does not argue to prove a point. *One cannot, therefore, analyze a report as though it were an argument.*

This distinction may not always be so simple, however, because there are also *arguments disguised as reports*. These are particularly prevalent in many of the so-called newsmagazines that publish "reports" that are so slanted in their language, selection of information, and emphasis that they actually function as disguised arguments. Compare the following report to the example on page 266.

Oh, Say Can You Sing It?

> To put audiences out of their pregame misery, many stadiums resort to canned versions of error-free performances of ["The Star-Spangled Banner"]. . . . But a

taped version takes away the thrill of victory and the agony of defeat inherent in every live performance, as well as the singers' inalienable right to get it wrong.

Time, February 12, 1990, p. 27.

Reports and arguments are not always entirely separate entities. Often, we find the two combined, with report information serving as evidence or reasons to back up an argument.

> Today Rep. Andrew Jacobs, D-Ind., introduced a bill that would change the national anthem to "America the Beautiful." He'll never get very far with that idea. We have enough trouble hanging onto our traditions, and, for better or worse, "The Star-Spangled Banner" holds too many of our shared memories for us to part with no matter how difficult it may be to sing.

Class Discussion

Identify the following as either reports or arguments, or as mixtures of both. Remember that an argument usually tries to persuade others to accept an idea by justifying and explaining it. A report simply presents the facts and suggests hypotheses, records conclusions made by several sources, or even lets the readers draw their own conclusions. Slanted reports, on the other hand, seek to sway others.

1. "Americans receive almost *2 million tons* of junk mail every year. About 44% of the junk mail is never even opened and read. Nonetheless, the average American still spends 8 full months of his or her life just opening junk mail." (*50 Simple Things You Can Do to Save the Earth*, Earthworks Press, 1989)

2. "Conservation to some people once implied sacrifice, deprivation and lower living standards. Now even many of them recognize that *conserving energy is the cheapest, safest, cleanest and fastest way to avoid future energy crises.*" (Sen. Alan Cranston, D-Calif., newsletter to constituents, November 1984)

3. "Too often the American economic system is looked upon as being a kind of battlefield between two opposing sides—consumers and the business/industrial community. This is a misguided but widely held viewpoint. *It is wrong to believe that consumers are at the mercy of business and industry.* The individual consumer is sovereign in the free market economy. . . . All of us are part of free enterprise, and what is good for business is good for the consumer." (Robert Bearce, "Free Enterprise," *Your Heritage News*, May 1984)

4. "Handguns caused about 10,000 deaths in the U.S. last year. The British, with a quarter the population, had 40. In 1978, 18,714 Americans were murdered, nearly two-thirds with handguns. In that year there were more killings with pistols and revolvers by children ten and under

in America than the British total for killers of all ages. In Japan, with half the U.S. population, the 1979 total of crimes involving handguns was 171; in West Germany it was 69.

"Americans seem unable or unwilling to acknowledge the simple truth that nations such as Australia, Britain, Canada, Japan, Germany, and Sweden have strict gun control and far less mayhem. It cannot be a coincidence." (Christopher Reed, "The Age," *Worldpress*, May 1984)

5. *Noriega's Surrender*
"Noriega was a mere shadow of the machete-waving, gringo-hating dictator who once vowed that the Americans would have to kill him to get him out. . . . But Noriega, the master of psychological warfare, met his match in . . . a wily Spanish priest who persuaded the fugitive to put his faith in due process." (*Newsweek*, January 15, 1990)

6. *Making Suicide Pay*
"There is finally good news for Mr. Milo Stevens, the 26-year-old incompetent who botched a suicide attempt in 1977 during which he launched himself into the path of a New York Transit Authority subway train. He has won a $650,000 negligence settlement and is still free to try again." (*American Spectator*, March 1984)

7. "[In Sweden researchers] reviewed medical records of 500,000 people covering the years 1960 through 1985 comparing cancer rates and long-term proximity to power lines and magnetic-field exposures. Conclusion: The risk of leukemia for children who lived near power lines was two to four times greater than for youngsters who lived at a distance from the power lines." (*San Francisco Chronicle*, March 8, 1993)

WHAT IS THE ISSUE OF CONTROVERSY?

Arguments are based on *issues*. An *issue* is a controversial problem that evokes different arguments pro and con. Examples of controversial issues are U.S. involvement in the U.N., the death penalty, and tough drug sentencing. Different *debate questions* might arise around each issue, such as

Should the United States pay its debts to the U.N.?
Should the United States withdraw from the U.N.?

These questions center around proposed solutions. Sometimes the cause of a controversy is put up for debate. On the issue of binge drinking by college athletes, a causal debate question might be phrased,

Is liquor advertising conditioning athletes and their fans to drink?

When we read arguments about issues, the questions debated may not be explicit and may require some thinking for the reader to articulate. In the last exercise, numbers 2, 3, and 4 were arguments about energy conservation, consumer protection, and handgun control. In none of these examples was the debate question stated. If formulated, the questions might be

2. Is conserving energy the best way to avoid energy crises?
3. Are consumers at the mercy of business and industry?
4. Should the United States have stricter handgun controls?

You will note that these debate questions are all expressed in neutral terms, which requires a careful choice of words free of biased connotations. Take, for instance, the last debate question. It is prefaced by the word *should*, which offers the matter up to arguments pro and con; the word also implies that opinion and values are relevant. The phrase "stricter handgun controls" is a neutral expression, although one side might prefer to get rid of "the gun mayhem," while the other side might prefer "take away our constitutional rights to defend ourselves." The debate question needs to be formulated in a way that engages the interest of both sides yet does not take sides.

Class Discussion

Read the following arguments and for each (1) state the issue and (2) formulate the debate question:

1. "They're [the major media] ethnocentric. They seldom focus on how revolutions, natural disasters, military coups affect the people where these events happen. They focus on how it affects 'American interests.'" ("An Interview with Jeff Cohen," head of FAIR [Fairness & Accuracy in Reporting], Newsletter, 1989)

2. "I have heard the questions often. Have you no sense of social obligation? the Liberals ask. Have you no concern for people who are out of work? for sick people who lack medical care? for children in overcrowded schools? Are you unmoved by the problems of the aged and disabled? Are you *against* human welfare? The answer to all these questions is, of course, no. But a simple 'no' is not enough. I feel certain that Conservatism is through unless Conservatives can demonstrate

and communicate the difference between being concerned with these problems and believing that the federal government is the proper agent for their solution." (Barry Goldwater, "The Welfare State," from *The Conscience of a Conservative*, 1960)

3. "The State is a means to an end. This end is the preservation and advancement of a community of physically and spiritually homogeneous living creatures." (Adolph Hitler, *Mein Kampf II*)

4. "Happiness begins when we happen to think for ourselves in the light of truth regarding people, places, and conditions. We are unhappy when we let or enlist other people to do our thinking for us." (Rev. William Duby, *Church of the People*, November/December 1992)

5. "Some people would like you to believe that we can prevent suffering simply by legalizing physician-assisted suicide. The Physician-Assisted Death Proposition is not that simple. It's riddled with flaws and loopholes." (argument opposed to Proposition 161 in *California Ballot Pamphlet*, 1992)

6. "A national anthem is like the Constitution: one should not change it as one changes one's shirt, particularly when the change is dictated by fashion." (unidentified opinion on editorial page, *San Francisco Chronicle*, November 30, 1989)

WHAT ARE THE STRENGTHS
AND WEAKNESSES OF THIS ARGUMENT?

To make a list of standards for judging the strengths and weaknesses of an argument would mean reviewing most of the material covered in the past several chapters of this text. These seven questions summarize such standards:

1. Are the reasons adequate to support the conclusion?

2. Is the reasoning sound—are the premises true and the reasoning valid?

3. Are there any hidden premises or assumptions crucial to the argument?

4. Are any central words ambiguous?

5. Are there fallacies in its reasoning? (You will learn how to use this question in the next chapters.)

6. Is any important information or evidence omitted?

7. Is any information false, contradictory, or irreconcilable?

All but the final three questions have already been discussed in this text. Fallacies will be explained in the next chapters. What follows now is an explanation of the last two questions.

Detecting Missing Information

Detecting missing information is not so difficult when we are familiar with the basic facts about a subject. In the final exam research assignment to follow, you will be asked to analyze two different points of view on a subject of controversy. As you research this assignment, you will gradually accumulate a sense of all the facts that this controversy entails. As this knowledge increases, so will your ability to judge how different arguments use this information: which information is given the most emphasis, which is minimized, and which is omitted altogether.

It is not this easy, however, to detect missing information in arguments about unfamiliar subjects. Here we have to depend on our ability to observe, read carefully, and ask questions. Looking for the most important missing elements under three categories—missing definitions, missing premises and conclusions, and missing information—can be helpful.

These categories, which also function as standards, have already been discussed in this text. The importance of definitions was stressed in the second chapter, where you learned how their absence confuses argumentation as well as general understanding. In the chapter on deductive reasoning was an explanation of missing premises and conclusions. In your work on photograph description and on report writing, you encountered the problems caused by missing pertinent information, which could also be described as missing data.

Figuring out where data are takes active concentration and thinking. Because data are invisible when missing, their absence has to be detected with the searchlight of questions and imagination. Sometimes the absence of essential information can only be traced through the confusion we feel while reading. For instance, consider the following advertisement:

> *Our highest rate for five years. Guaranteed.* Now for a limited time only you can lock into our highest rate for up to five years with an Iowa Federal five-year C.D. If you're retired, think about what this could mean. You won't have to worry about dropping interest rates for a long time. And it's FSLIC insured. Completely safe.

If you don't feel tempted to rush right down to invest, you might realize that the actual interest rate is never mentioned. And here you are being asked to "lock into" it for a period of five years! Thus, it may be true after all that you won't have to worry about dropping interest rates: you may spend more time regretting missing the higher ones. To forget to read carefully for missing information may result in later being unhappily reminded of the adage "Let the buyer beware."

Class Discussion

What questions would you ask of the writers or speakers who said the following?

1. *Weight problem?* You've tried every kind of diet, exercise, pills and if you do lose a pound or two, it's back in no time. Everybody offers their advice, which is even more frustrating. Your weight problem is taking over your life. At our Health Spa, health specialists will work to take your weight off for good. Call us. Toll free. Georgetown Hospital Health Spa.

2. You are invited to my twenty-first birthday party. Prizes will be given for those who arrive Friday evening exactly at 7:07 P.M. in the Sigma Delta Dormitory lounge.

3. He hit me first.

4. Oh, honey, by the way, my former boyfriend came into town today and gave me a call.

5. I have to go out now and take care of some business.

6. The government should subsidize tobacco growers more than it does. If American tobacco growers are unable to meet production costs, they will be forced to quit growing tobacco, and we will be entirely dependent on foreign sources. Besides, tobacco farmers are making lower profits today than they were ten years ago.

7. Our religion forbids sexual misconduct.

8. *Nuclear Power Is Cheaper Energy for Tomorrow*
    "The price of electricity from fossil fuel plants will always depend heavily on the cost of fuel, which is unpredictable. The cost of nuclear fuel is more stable; its supply is within our control; and there's plenty of it. As a nuclear plant's construction costs are paid for, its lower fuel costs *hold down* the price of the electricity. Eventually, the lower cost of fuel more than makes up for the higher cost of construction." (advertisement, U.S. Committee for Energy Awareness)

Detecting False, Contradictory, or Irreconcilable Information

A final subject for critical concern is the detection of false information or false assertions in an argument. As critical readers, we cannot hold court hearings to prove lies, but we can remember to watch for any discrepancies or contradictions that might suggest the presence of lies. A sound argument that is both true and well reasoned does not contain contradictions.

Of course, the distinction exists between contradictions based upon insufficient thinking (as discussed in "Inconsistencies and Contradictions" in Chapter 11) and contradictions denoting an imperfect structure of lies. However, for our purposes as critical thinkers, ascertaining the distinction is not usually the issue. What matters is to recognize that whenever contradictions appear, the argument or claim is unsound. The argument, at best, has to be placed "on hold" mentally, awaiting further evidence or study.

And this policy applies not only to discrepancies found in arguments but to inconsistencies between words and action, between evidence and denials, between different testimonies, between differing accounts of facts, between claims and consequences, and between what we are told and what we know to be true. In any case, no discrepancy ever appears with the label "discrepancy" marked clearly on it; its detection results only from alert perception and thinking.

Reading

WOMAN AWARDED $25 MILLION IN SUIT AGAINST IMPLANT MAKER

A jury yesterday awarded $25 million in damages to a Houston woman who said   1
she developed an autoimmune disease from ruptured silicone-gel breast implants
made by a subsidiary of Bristol-Myers Squibb Co.

In the biggest damage award against a manufacturer of silicone implants to   2
date, the Harris County jury ruled in favor of 45-year-old Pamela Jean Johnson in
her suit against Medical Engineering Corp.

Previous cases have gone to trial in federal court. In April, a federal judge in   3
San Francisco upheld a $7.3 million damage award to a woman whose implant
ruptured.

Johnson, who had sought $64 million in damages, charged that silicone leaked   4
from two sets of implants, attacked her immune system and caused various illnesses, forcing her to undergo a partial mastectomy.

Bristol-Myers Squibb, whose stock tumbled $3.875 to close at $67.375 on the   5
New York Stock Exchange after the ruling, said it will appeal the verdict.

Johnson smiled broadly and then broke into tears as Judge Don Wittig read the   6
verdict to a packed courtroom. The judge will issue a final ruling on the jury's verdict
on January 11.

The trial, which began December 10, was the first in Texas for a product liabil-   7
ity case against a maker of silicone-gel breast implants.

Johnson's lawyer, John O'Quinn, told reporters that the verdict sent a message   8
to breast-implant manufacturers. "The message is you have to put safety first,
ahead of profit. Human health is too important to market products that have not
been proven to be safe," he said.

Similar lawsuits have been filed across the country by women who say they   9
have suffered illnesses stemming from breast implants that ruptured.

An estimated 2 million implants have been provided to 1 million to 1.3 million   10
women in the United States since they were introduced in the mid-1960s by Dow
Corning Corp., a joint venture of Dow Chemical Co. and Corning Inc.

The implants were taken off the market in January after the Food and Drug   11
Administration called for a voluntary moratorium. The FDA has since limited their
use to cases involving women with medical needs who take part in scientific studies.
The action followed reports that the implants have caused arthritis-like diseases,
debilitating skin conditions and possibly cancer.

Johnson received her first implants in 1976. They ruptured and were removed   12
in 1989. Another set of implants made by Medical Engineering was in-
serted but removed the same year when they ruptured. A third set, made by another company, was removed this year, according to her attorneys.

Johnson's attorneys charged that the Bristol-Myers subsidiary, which began   13
making silicone implants in 1972, told doctors that silicone gel would not leak from
the devices even if the shell ruptured and that it would not harm human tissue.

The company's attorneys argued that the implants met all applicable federal   14
regulations and that Johnson's illnesses were related to drugs she took, mainly for
heart problems.

From *San Francisco Chronicle*, December 24, 1992. Used with permission of Reuters.

Study Questions

1. Assuming the information given in this article is accurate, describe the contradictions you find here.

2. Do you think the women who sued the breast-implant manufacturers might have been more cautious about using these products if they had been trained in critical thinking skills?

3. Discuss any consumer or political situations you are aware of that involved injury claims resulting from the acceptance of information later shown to contain discrepancies, contradictions, and falsehoods.

CHAPTER SUMMARY

1. The critical reading of arguments is an active endeavor that requires involvement, interaction with questions, and evaluation.

2. The questions asked in the critical reading of arguments are
    (a) What viewpoint or values shaped this argument?
    (b) Where is the conclusion of this argument? What reasons support it?
    (c) Is it an argument or a report or both?
    (d) What is the issue of controversy?
    (e) What are the argument's strengths and weaknesses?

3. The analysis of arguments in terms of their reasons and conclusions applies to both inductive and deductive arguments. Reasons include data, evidence, and premises, while conclusions include those deductively drawn as well as hypotheses.

4. The conclusion of an argument is the last step in a reasoning process. However, it may be stated at any time during an argument or not at all.

5. Reasons support conclusions. They may be generalizations that could function as conclusions in another context. Once the argument's main conclusion is uncovered, the identification of generalizations as support becomes clear.

6. Arguments state and defend a claim. Usually they also attempt to persuade. Arguments disguised as reports slant the facts and language toward a bias.

7. Reports that only relate events or state facts cannot be analyzed as though they were arguments.

8. An issue is a selected aspect of a topic of controversy upon which positions may be taken either pro or con. Issues are stated in neutral terms often beginning with the word *should* and ending with a question.

9. The following questions can serve as guidelines for analyzing the strengths and weaknesses of arguments:
    (a) Are the reasons adequate to support the conclusion?
    (b) Is the reasoning sound?
    (c) Are there any hidden premises or assumptions?
    (d) Are any central words ambiguous?
    (e) Are there fallacies?
    (f) Is any important information missing?
    (g) Is any information false, contradictory, or irreconcilable?

Take-Home Final Research Exam: An Assignment Due at the End of the Course

The purpose of this research exam is to allow you to demonstrate all the knowledge and skills you learned while studying this book. These skills are being able to

1. Isolate a controversial issue.

2. Do research to find two arguments from two different sources representing two different viewpoints on one debate question related to the same issue.

3. Identify the political and social orientation of a viewpoint.

4. Select a complete argument, either in full or extracted from a larger article, in order to analyze its structure, strengths, and weaknesses according to standards learned in this text.

5. Objectively compare, evaluate, and summarize all arguments before drawing your own conclusions.

6. Follow instructions and communicate your findings clearly.

General Instructions for the Research Take-Home Final

Choose one topic of recent controversy that interests you. Browse in the library; study magazines and newspapers representing all points of view to stimulate your thinking. Once you have selected your topic, narrow it down to one issue related to that topic. For instance, if you were interested in the subject of women in the military, you would work with only one issue expressed in the debate question "Should women serve in combat?" Select and photocopy two different arguments representing two different social or political positions on your chosen issue. These arguments should be short, not more than six paragraphs. If you want to excerpt the argument from a longer article, photocopy the whole article and put a border around the section you will analyze. Newspaper editorials and letters to the editor can also serve as short arguments. If you are working on a political topic, find two different views, such as liberal and conservative, from two different published sources. If you chose a sociological issue, such as physician-assisted suicide, find two different perspectives such as a physician's view, a minister's view, and/or a relative's view.

Photocopy each argument on a separate sheet of paper and attach them to your paper. Then begin your analysis by following the questions in the four parts that follow.

Take-Home Final Analysis Questions (Considered separately for each argument)

Write the debate question on the title page followed by the table of contents.

Part I: The Argument

List the following information at the top of your page:

1. The title
2. Title of the article or argument, magazine or newspaper
3. Date of publication
4. Argument or argumentation in a report. (Remember this assignment is not suitable for a simple report.)

Part II: Basic Outline of Argument

Beneath this information, write your critique in outline form, using these points:

5. Label the viewpoint politically or socially.
6. State the argument's conclusion. *(You may have to put this in your own words.)*
7. List the reasons given in the argument to support this conclusion. (This may best be done in your own words. Do not oversimplify or omit significant reasons. But also do not quote every line or material that you do not understand as a substitute for trying to understand it.)

Part III: Critique Questions

Review the argument according to the criteria given next. Discuss each fully and systematically. Remember, this is not just an exercise in finding flaws; you may find much in the argument to commend.

8. How is the argument structured? Describe and evaluate the way it is put together. Notice, above all, whether the conclusion is clear and whether sound and sufficient reasons are offered in its support.
9. Are any central words in the argument ambiguous or prejudicial?
10. Does the argument contain any fallacies? If so, provide examples.
11. Does the argument make any hidden assumptions? How do they affect the argument?

12. Is any important information missing?

13. Is any information false, irreconcilable, or contradictory?

Part IV: Final Summary Comparing the Two Arguments

On a final page, summarize the two arguments. Do you find contradictory evidence in them? Which viewpoint do you find the more persuasive and why? (Note that you are not being asked to defend your own viewpoint on this issue but only to show why you find one to be the more persuasive argument.)

Format

Follow your instructor's directions for format. You might put it together in a simple notebook of four to six pages of analysis, plus the photocopied pages, a title page, and table of contents page, for about ten pages in all. Take pride in giving your work a professional appearance.

Scoring for Take-Home Final Research Exam

1. Two different arguments (not reports) from two different authors addressing the same issue and taken from two different publications.   20 points.

2. Follows the format required; photocopies are attached.   10 points

3. Conclusion and reasons correctly identified; all reasons are listed.   20 points

4. Accurate and insightful critique that addresses: 42 points (7 points each)
    analysis of argument structure
    ambiguous and prejudicial words
    fallacies of reasoning
    hidden assumptions
    missing information and/or false information
    any other pertinent characteristics

5. Final summary that compares the two and chooses the better argument.   8 points

---

Readings

IT'S A GRAND OLD FLOG
Stephanie Salter

These two readings give arguments for and against corporal punishment. They are based on a 1994 incident in which Michael Fay, an American citizen in Singapore, was caned as punishment for vandalism. Read each argument carefully, then analyze each separately, using the questions that follow the readings.

> *America should be taking lessons from Singapore on how to prevent crime. Hold the line. Don't give in.*
>
> —*Letter to Singapore's U.S. Embassy*

In the name of a cleaner, safer, nicer United States, the American people have 1
spoken. In letters and faxes to the government of Singapore. In telephone calls to Rep. Tony Hall, D-Ohio. In electronic telephone surveys and TV polls.

The people have spoken, and they say they want blood. 2

Literally. The blood of an 18-year-old fellow citizen named Michael Fay. 3

Last September, Fay and some teenage pals vandalized several cars in Singa- 4
pore with spray paint and eggs. Some of Fay's friends stole a few traffic signs, too, and left them with Fay as mementos of the spree.

Fay was the first of nine youths to go before a magistrate. The other trials are 5
pending. According to Singapore law, which says vandalism is equal to rape, robbery and extortion, Fay was sentenced to four months in prison, a $2,215 fine and—most important—six lashes on his bare buttocks with a yard-long rattan cane.

A week ago, an appeals court upheld Fay's sentence. Now, only clemency from 6
the president, Ong Teng Cheong, can avert the caning.

As any American who watches two minutes of news should know by now, 7
caning is no Hardy Boys trip to the woodshed. Administered by a martial arts expert, the lashes come one on top the other. The cane is dipped in a chemical that ensures pain and permanent scarring.

The first lash splits open the flesh. The second often brings on shock. The third, 8
unconsciousness. The time between strokes can be as long as 60 seconds. A doctor, on site, revives the recipient to consciousness for each lash.

Blood loss can be profuse. 9

Amnesty International classifies caning as "cruel, inhuman and degrading pun- 10
ishment violating the Universal Declaration of Human Rights and international conventions on torture." The U.S. State Department condemned it in a 1993 human rights report.

The American people do not care about Amnesty International, the State De- 11
partment or permanent scars.

They want Michael Fay's blood.   12

"The vast majority" of letters and calls to the Singapore Embassy in Washing-   13
ton say they want blood. The letters to Hall, Fay's former congressman, "are pre-
dominantly opposed" to his efforts to spare Fay the caning.

In an *Examiner* phone-in poll last week, 3,801 people—74 percent of the   14
callers—said they wanted Michael Fay's blood.

A fax from a San Francisco man said, "They ought to have that law here, and   15
if they did, I can guarantee you we would all have cleaner Muni buses to ride."

Yes, for every graffiti-covered bus in San Francisco, Michael Fay's flesh must be   16
opened and his blood spilled.

For every senseless homicide on the streets of Chicago, every rape in Atlanta,   17
every mugging in Philadelphia, every stolen car stereo in Lexington, Ky., every
tagged storefront in Fresno, the American people need Michael Fay's blood.

They need it for the L.A. riots, for the rising number of teenage pregnancies,   18
the high school dropout rate, the divorce rate, the increasing incidence of venereal
disease, the breakdown of the nuclear family, the attack on traditional values and
for Beavis and Butthead.

"If we had caning here in American schools, I bet children would listen to the   19
adults and have respect for them. I say go for it!" a woman told the *Dayton Daily
News* in its phone poll about Fay. "Cane every single one who doesn't have respect
and I bet they'll learn real quick."

Really? Never mind that the population of the United States is much larger and   20
more diverse than Singapore's, which is 77 percent ethnic Chinese and 14 percent
Muslim Malays. Never mind that, even though Singapore's crime rate is decidedly
lower than ours, its number of death sentences rises each year.

Never mind that the Singapore government—a dictatorship in democracy's   21
clothing—has done away with such basic tenets of U.S. justice as trial by jury.

To the Ohio woman and all Americans eager to see Michael Fay beaten, his   22
blood—and plenty more—is the magic elixir for our national woes. Such twisting,
leaping logic typifies the disproportionate anger and vengeance that is being aimed
at this young man.

So, because this is more about blood lust than anything, give America blood—   23
big-time, Yankee style. In the name of a cleaner, safer, nicer U.S., let the networks
and CNN, Fox and MTV (we want to deter youth from crime after all) broadcast
the caning live.

All across this permissive country of ours, we can watch as 18-year-old Michael   24
Fay is stripped naked and buckled into a wide leather belt that protects his internal
organs and lower back from damage. Then we can see his arms and legs get
strapped to an X-frame stand.

With screams as soundtrack, we can watch each lash land, his flesh open and   25
his red American blood flow to atone for a nation's sins.

April 18, 1994.
Used with permission of the *San Francisco Examiner*.

SINGAPORE VS. SAN FRANCISCO

Dear Editor:

Your misinformed posturing on behalf of Michael Peter Fay is absurd (editorial, 1 "Singapore, spare the cane," April 3). After two years of residence in Singapore, he should have been fully aware of the consequence that his disregard for the law would bring.

As a frequent visitor to Singapore, I can assure you that the laws are clearly 2 enumerated and the Singaporean reputation for enforcement is universally understood.

When I survey my graffiti-covered neighborhood, I see places where people 3 routinely litter and have little regard for common courtesy. The streets are never cleaned. Neither residents nor shopkeepers seem to take any interest in cleaning them.

To do my marketing, I must run the gauntlet of lunatics and beggars who line 4 the streets and haunt the ATMs. I am hesitant to ride public transportation, fearing encounters with the wild animals masquerading as children. It is an area where people go about with eyes downcast, fearing any confrontation. I live in one of the more desirable areas of San Francisco. This is barbaric.

I cannot help [but] contrast it with images of Singapore. There, the streets are 5 safe and spotless, the children respectful, ordered and well behaved. Public transportation is efficient, inexpensive and safe. No madmen lurk in doorways or sleep in the streets.

The people are warm, outgoing and justifiably proud of their society and its 6 discipline. They understand that certain sacrifices must be made by individuals for the safety and security of the whole society.

I would trade some of my purported freedom for the chance to live in a safe, 7 sane and civilized country.

Perhaps it is time we reclaim our own society by enacting laws that will serve 8 as deterrents to crime, and carrying them out impartially and with purpose. Your eagerness to let Fay go because he "looks scared" is at the very core of the increasing disregard for law and order in our society.

Slapping people on the wrist and letting the insurance companies fight it out 9 is our way of dealing with such transgression. In extreme measures, we send people to prison where they can hone their criminal skills and sharpen their ability to manipulate the legal system. Freedom and sympathy in our country is [sic] accorded to perpetrators of crimes, not the victims.

The epidemic of crime in the United States and our total inability to control it 10 is hardly a recommendation for any country to accept our advice in matters of jurisprudence.

Any sanctions the U.S. could impose would be laughable and ineffectual. We 11 would be best served by requesting that the Singapore government send our country some advisors to help us achieve some measure of dignity and order here as they have so admirably done in Singapore.

Fay's mental and physical pain will be amply compensated by the book, movie 12 and talk-show contracts that will surely follow.

San Francisco
April 11, 1994

Used with permission of the *San Francisco Examiner*.

Chapter Summary Practice Exercise

The Analysis Questions

You will notice that most of the questions provided here also appear in the instructions for your take-home research final on pages 276–278. This practice exercise is intended first of all to help you review and integrate the skills taught in this chapter. Moreover, if you are assigned the take-home research final, this exercise will help prepare you for that assignment. One student's analysis of the readings about Michael Fay appears in the *Instructor's Manual*. After you have completed this exercise, your instructor may show it to you on transparencies or photocopy so the class can discuss it.

Practice Exercise Instructions

Working alone or with a partner or group, write an outline that analyzes the argument of each reading. Do this by answering each of these questions:

1. What is the debate question addressed by both arguments? (Remember that corporal punishment is a topic involving many issues.) Write down your statement of the debate question on a title page. Now begin your analysis by making a separate outline that answers the six remaining questions.

2. What is the viewpoint of the writer? Label or discuss.

3. What is the conclusion of the argument? Quote or summarize.

4. What reasons do the writers give in support of their conclusions? Number and summarize each, using quotes as needed.

5. Do you find any words central to the argument that are ambiguous (not clearly defined) or that convey hidden evaluations, bias, or prejudice through their connotations? Quote and discuss each.

6. Is any essential information missing in the argument?

7. Do you find any information that seems to be false, inconsistent, or irreconcilable?

Composition Writing Application

Writing an Argumentative Research Essay

Here is an opportunity for you to express and defend your own view on the issue you researched for your take-home final. Write an argumentative essay following these steps:

Preparation

1. Write out fully your own viewpoint on the issue that you researched for the take-home final project. Write freely without self-censorship for as many pages as it takes to exhaust what you have to say.

2. Now shape your principal claim into a thesis, taking care to choose your key terms carefully. Use clustering as needed.

3. Leaving wide spaces between each statement, outline your support for this thesis in terms of claims and/or evidence. If it is a deductive argument, write out its syllogism. If it is inductive, note your hypotheses.

4. Consult your research notes to see what might be pertinent to use. Add notes to your outline about where this information could be included to document or support your argument. Also use your own experience or any additional research you discover you need to support your thesis.

5. As you write and revise your outline, note where you need to acquire more evidence or examples and where you already have enough material to write eight to ten typed pages.

6. Keep your outline before you as you write. Tack it up on the wall. Read and reread it to make sure that each part of the essay relates to your thesis. Revise it as needed.

Writing the First Draft

7. Now start to flesh out the skeleton of your outline. Introduce your subject, stating the issue in your first paragraph. Explain why this issue interests you and why it should be of interest to the reader. You might summarize some of the different positions taken on this issue. Then state your position—your thesis or principal claim. Also provide any definitions necessary to explain how you are using your terms.

8. As you write, seek to be as clear as possible. Guide your readers so that they can know exactly what you are doing at each step as you pursue your argument. Read your work aloud to friends to discover what they need to hear to understand you.

9. In the second paragraph or paragraphs give an argument to defend your principal claim, clearly stating your premises and conclusion as well as your evidence.

10. In the paragraph that follows, state any major objection or objections that others might have to your argument. You can counter these with further arguments or evidence.

11. If you think of further criticisms that might be made of your counter-argument, reply to these.

12. As you continue to write your draft, decide at some point whether you can fully support your original thesis or whether you might need to modify it. If this should occur, go back to your outline and revise accordingly.

Final Touches

13. When you have finished your final draft, find another good listener. Notice where you are not understood or where, in explaining, you find that you need to say more in writing.

14. Rewrite your work as necessary to improve coherency and correct errors.

15. Use the MLA format* and include a bibliography of your sources at the end.

16. Present your essay in a form that shows pride in your work.

*The Modern Language Association's style guide.

CHAPTER 10

Fallacies:
What's a Faulty Argument?

Reprinted with permission of the Copley News Service, San Diego. Copyright 1985 San Diego Union.

I f the senator depicted in the cartoon on this page were to use a mass mailing to convince his constituents of an absurdity, how do you think the argument would read? What signs suggest the defense of a lie? What clues reveal an unfair argument? How do you know when public consent is being "manufactured" or manipulated? We will consider some of these questions as we study these fallacies of reasoning.

You will find over 20 fallacies discussed in this book. Each has a different name to illustrate a different reasoning error, an error that may be accidental or may be intentional. Each sidesteps the work of constructing a well-reasoned argument. Since remembering all of these fallacies at once can be difficult, they will be presented to you in two segments, beginning with this chapter. To further aid your understanding and recall, they have been classified into four major groups, three of which (presented in this chapter) are called fallacies involving trickery. The fourth group, fallacies of inductive reasoning, appears at the end of Chapter 11.

Discovery Exercise

Recognizing Fallacies

Environmental zealots threaten four industries in California—agriculture, mining, timber, and construction—and the people will no longer tolerate what the zealots are doing to the ability of Californians to make a living. The zealots can shut down the American economy. (Rep. William Danne-meyer R-Calif.)

1. Does this statement appeal to your own bias or not?
2. Is the argument fair and well reasoned?
3. What exactly is right or wrong about the argument?
4. If you are familiar with some fallacies, do any of the following apply: poisoning the well, slippery slope, bandwagon, slanted language, appeal to fear, hasty generalization, use of ambiguous wording?

FALLACIES OF TRICKERY

A fallacy is a deceptive argument. (The Latin word from which fallacy is derived, *fallacia*, means deceit or trick.) Such an argument may appear on the surface to be reasonable, and it can even be persuasive, but its reasoning is faulty. This may be due to confusion; it may also be due to an intent to manipulate. When it is deliberate, it fans the smoke of fear, pity, or prejudice, it distracts from the issue, plays with language, assumes what it should prove. In this chapter you will learn to recognize and avoid such errors or tactics by studying the fallacies of trickery.

Trickery with Language

word ambiguity

euphemisms

prejudicial language

equivocation

Trickery with Emotions

appeal to fear

appeal to pity

appeal to false authority, popular wisdom, and bandwagon

appeal to prejudice: personal attack and poisoning the well

Trickery with Distraction

red herring

straw man

pointing to another wrong

circular reasoning

FALLACIES INVOLVING TRICKERY WITH LANGUAGE

Four Fallacies Involving Ambiguity

Fallacious arguments involving ambiguity use words with multiple meanings or connotations as though they had only one meaning or connotation. Of course this can happen unintentionally, but it can also be intentional. A good argument makes careful word choices. It wants to persuade, but to persuade fairly on the basis of a clear understanding. A faulty argument seeks to win an agreement that may be based on word confusion. It can choose ambiguous words to deceive, to ward off questioning, to incite prejudice, to hide the weaker aspects of the argument. The four varieties of ambiguity we will consider here are word ambiguity, euphemisms, prejudicial language, and equivocation.

Word Ambiguity. Word ambiguity occurs when a central word is never defined or is left unclear. "We should treat *drug* use as a private right that harms no one but the user." Here, what is meant by *drug* is left undefined. The unperceptive reader will make assumptions or guess. The reader trained in critical thinking will stop and ask questions. Does the author mean hard drugs or just medications and stimulants? If the questions are not answered, the thoughtful reader will have to dismiss the argument altogether. Consider some further examples:

> And where are all the jobs that welfare mothers are supposed to get? Even a burger joint wants you to work evenings and weekends, times when there is *virtually no* child care.

Here, the words *virtually no* are ambiguous. Does this mean that child care is scarce or that it is unreliable or unavailable? A better argument would mention the prohibitive costs of child care for a single mother on a minimum wage. The writer may want to convey that single working mothers need more, and not less, assistance, but she makes her argument ineffective by not using her words with precision.

> School prayer will not help as long as students are taught immorality, e.g., basic condom training. Returning to teaching students *basic morality* will help. If public schools insist on teaching immorality, parents must have the choice to send their children to a school that teaches *fundamental morality*.

Here, the writer defines *immorality* as public education in the use of condoms. However, it is not clear what the writer means by "basic morality" or "fundamental morality." a lack of education in contraceptives? sex only in marriage and only for procreation? the Golden Rule? With this information missing, a thoughtful reader cannot take the argument seriously.

Class Discussion

The ambiguous words are in boldface in the material that follows. Discuss why they are ambiguous and how this affects the argument.

> Writing in the February 15, 1993, *Forbes* magazine, Leslie Spender and *NR* Senior Editor Peter Brimelow came up with what is still, to the **great disgrace** of academic economists, the only **serious** estimate of affirmative action's cost to the economy: some $115 billion in **direct and indirect expenditures** in 1991. (Editor, *National Review*, March 1995)

> A recent summary of over 200 studies, published in 1990, offers convincing evidence that the observation of violence, as seen in standard everyday television entertainment, does affect the **aggressive behavior** of the viewer. (Leonard D. Eron, Harvard School of Public Health, panel discussion, May 1992)

> There is something intrinsically **anti-American** about the way Al Gore flagellates the U.S. over its environmental policies. (Rush Limbaugh)

Ambiguous words are often chosen by advertisers to lure buyers into projecting their own desires and hopes on advertising claims. For advertisers, the advantage of this approach is that they can later deny responsibility for the buyer's interpretations. Such ambiguities may take the form of such "weasel words" as *helps*, as in "Helps prevent cavities," or *as much as*, as in "Saves as much as 1 gallon of gas." A few other familiar weasel words appear in the following ads:

1. Save on typewriters from a leading maker! SALE! SALE! $200! Made to sell for $495! (Here the word *sale* only tells you the store has something to sell. Perhaps it was overpriced in the first place.)

2. Women's coats—$54. A $75 value. (The word *value* is relative. Perhaps the store bought the coats especially for the sale and set the previous value arbitrarily.)

3. These blouses have the feel of silk. (That an item has the *feel* of silk does not mean it is silk.)

4. Come see our sheepskin-look seat covers. (Remember, they are not saying that the items *are* sheepskin.)

Class Discussion

Identify the ambiguous words in the following sentences by underlining the words and stating how they function for persuasion:

1. All ingredients in this ice cream are natural and nutritious.
2. These pies are made from locally grown cherries and have that old-fashioned country taste.
3. Ace aspirin provides relief up to eight hours.
4. Ida Insect Spray helps fight mosquitoes.
5. Tony's Tonic helps you feel and look ten years younger.
6. You can save as much as 1 quart of oil a day.
7. Wear a jacket that has the feel of leather.
8. Cults enslave people.
9. The federal government has too much power.
10. You should be willing to do anything for love.
11. Prayer in the schools would be the start of something big.

Euphemisms. The word *euphemism* comes from the Greek word meaning good voice, or to use words of good omen. Euphemisms are inoffensive words used in place of others that might be considered distasteful or offensive. Some familiar euphemisms are *remains* for corpse, *bathroom* for toilet. New euphemisms crop up all the time, like *motion sickness* for nausea or *revenue enhancement* for taxes. As well as helping maintain polite social atmosphere and dispensing with inconvenient feelings, euphemisms also can be used for political propaganda.

In political life, euphemisms perform the task of public relations: neutral words camouflage actions, things, or events that are unacceptable in light of professed values. The result is a distortion of truth and meaning. In George Orwell's novel *1984*, such distortions of language are grimly parodied in his creation of a state built on the slogans "War Is Peace," "Freedom Is Slavery," "Ignorance Is Strength." Here the government ministries include the Ministry of Truth (which produces lies and propaganda), the Ministry of Love (which practices imprisonment, brainwashing, and torture), and the Ministry of Peace (which concerns itself with war).

Politicians use double-talk when they speak of "disinformation" to describe lies planted in media releases, "contributions" for taxes, "investment" for spending, and "deficit reduction" for tax and spending increases. Government employees also create phrases that might be called "neutralized terms." These euphemisms are distributed to military officers for public use. They serve as code words that sanitize military actions that might raise uncomfortable questions and offend our professed national values.

Neutralized Term	Conventional Term
Ziploc or body bags	plastic container for corpses
acceptable losses	number of our own soldiers expected to die in battle
friendly fire	shooting our own soldiers by mistake
police action	unproclaimed act of war
unconventional warfare	combat methods violating Geneva Convention agreements
combat stress disorder	nervous breakdown of soldier from battle trauma
antipersonnel weapon	explosive with a casing designed to maim people in a large area
hot zone	area exposed to nuclear fallout or biological or chemical agents
rigged or amped out	describes soldier who has taken narcotics or amphetamines
black ops	officially unsanctioned activities such as kidnapping or assassinating enemy leaders

List some of the value assumptions that lie behind the neutralized terms in this list.

Class Discussion

1. In the novel *1984*, George Orwell predicts the development of a totalitarian government that will purposefully corrupt language in order to control thought. Do you feel that the use of the kind of political double-talk we just focused on actually deceives Americans, or do you think these expressions are generally recognized with humor?

2. In the last decade a number of new words have been introduced into our language. Those who regard these words as ludicrous label them "politically correct." These new word substitutions proclaim the values of feminists, environmentalists, and the progressive left. Read the list and explain how they differ from the list of neutralized terms. Where are the euphemisms in this list?

Conventional Term	Politically Correct Term
paper	processed tree carcasses
eggs and milk	stolen nonhuman animal products
white skin	melanin impoverished
lumberjack	tree butcher
housework	unwaged labor
housewife	domestic incarceration survivor

Prejudicial Language.   We touched on slanted language earlier when we discussed connotative words in the chapter on evaluations. To refresh your memory, note the use of language in the following two headlines:

> <u>Cultic</u> America: A Tower of Babel. They tend to be small, scattered and <u>strange</u>. (*Newsweek*, March 1993)

> The Government's <u>Propaganda War Against</u> the American Indian Movement (*EXTRA*! October / November 1992)

What are the connotations of the underlined words and phrases, and what purpose do they serve in terms of persuasion? (What associations, for instance, do we have with the word *cultic*? How are we affected by the biblical and war metaphors?)

Compare the two headlines to the translations below. Do they give the same message? Would they attract readers as readily?

> New Religions in America: A Crisis of Separation Without Understanding. The groups tend to be small, scattered and unfamiliar to us.

> The Government's Conflict with the American Indian Movement.

Read the following quotations for signs of a bias:

> "America's dirty little war in El Salvador has so far been limited to thin transfusions of money and material as well as moral support for murderous regimes." (*Mother Jones*, June / July 1983)

> "During his career, Saddam Hussein has transformed himself into numerous expedient political persona, including a revolutionary, a party henchman, an Iraqi strongman, a devout Moslem, and a Pan-Arabish messiah. His mercurial ruthlessness, combined with his domestic terror tactics, his xenophobia, and his political acumen have enabled him to become the absolute ruler of Iraq." (*Congressional Quarterly*, 1991)

Some of the words chosen in these examples are not necessarily inaccurate, but they do require acceptance of a bias. No supporting evidence or argument is provided in these quotes. The task for the critical reader is to be aware of word choices and to observe rather than react to the persuasive emotional power that word connotations carry. If claims are more loaded with evaluative terms than with facts or valid arguments, we might infer that the argument was not thoughtfully constructed or that the evidence was weak and therefore omitted. But we must also take into consideration how journalists and politicians tend to use highly connotative words to rivet readers' attention.

Class Discussion

Which of these do you find to be well-reasoned arguments and which are arguments that seek to persuade chiefly through the use of slanted words?

1. "Dear Editor: The nursery rhyme 'Little Red Riding Hood' has a new twist. The Hood, also known as Hillary Rodham Clinton, has the wily Willie Wolf, her husband and co-president, on a long leash. Hillary Hood has Willie Wolf trained to obey her every whim, including the hiring of cabinet members, which must bear her stamp of approval. It didn't take too many commands on the part of Hillary Hood for Willie Wolf to propose a plan to take from the rich and middle class, through heavy taxes, and give to the poor. Thus Hillary Hood soon may have Willie Wolf taking her name as he wants to be known as Robin Hood." (Letter to Editor, *San Francisco Chronicle*, February 13, 1993)

2. "**'Save the Forest' Hype Is Just a Fad.** America's obsession with the Amazon reveals more about ourselves than it does about the rain forest. These aren't much different from earlier jungle fantasies; in both cases, the jungle played a role as our opposite. When we believed in science and progress, the jungle was a primitive, bewildering, even terrifying green hell. But the greenhouse summer of 1989 triggered a growing fear that humanity will not survive without the mysterious forces embodied in the last of the great wild lands." (Jon Christensen, *National Catholic Reporter*, January 26, 1990)

3. "**Government and Greed Destroy the Forest.** Look at the balance sheet. Clearing the Amazon produces hardwoods which are essential for nothing. Dams flood the forest to generate electricity to make aluminum for throw-away cans. Iron ore is dug out of the ground to be sold at throw-away prices. Diseased cattle stroll about farting their greenhouse gases into the atmosphere to pander to a particular dietary preference in the cities. Rivers are polluted with deadly mercury to produce gold that is smuggled out through Uruguay to languish in the vaults of Swiss banks. The mass of the people of the Amazon are corralled into poverty, fearing for their lives. Indigenous people are persecuted to the verge of extinction. Can it really be for this that the greatest forest on earth is being made to disappear?" (David Ransom, *The New Internationalist*, May 1991)

Equivocation. The word *equivocation* comes from the Latin word meaning equal voice. In general, to equivocate is to use ambiguous words purposely in order to mislead or deceive or hedge. "Equal voice" is giving the same voice accent to saying something meaningless as to saying something meaningful. Often we hear this when a person confronted with accountability for an event uses the phrase "to the best of my knowledge" to deny that something did occur or did not occur, implying both (1) "I know everything," and (2) "I could be wrong." Another evasion is the phrase "as far as I know," which can serve the same purpose. Still another is "not that I can recall."

Equivocation can also take the form of going through the formal rhythm of answering questions with words that could only be translated as "quack, quack, quack, quack, quack."

> HE: "Do you love me?"
>
> SHE: "If I didn't, would I be here with you now?"
>
> HE: "But will you marry me?"
>
> SHE: "I will marry you when—everything considered—marriage is a commitment that needs careful consideration and responsibility."

In logic, equivocation has a different and more specialized meaning from that just described. It means drawing an unwarranted conclusion from premises containing a term that *shifts* in its meaning within the argument. A classic example of an argument using equivocation reads as follows: Only man is rational. No woman is a man. Therefore no woman is rational. Here there is a shift between the use of the word *man* in the sense of *human* and the use of the same word to mean *male*. Because of this lack of consistency, the conclusion is unsound.

Class Discussion

Some of the following examples of equivocation are old familiars from textbooks on fallacies. Show that you can identify the key equivocal words here by underlining them. Write out, for comparison, the definition of each word used twice, to show their differences. Then explain how these words create elusive shifts within the argument.

1. The laws of gravitation and motion must have a lawmaker for the simple reason that they are laws and all laws have a lawmaker.
2. People say that sexism and racism are forms of discrimination. But what is wrong with discrimination? We discriminate all the time in our choices of food, homes, and friends.
3. Business is business.
4. Sick children should stay in bed, right? Well, I am sick of school!
5. In a cartoon, Margaret Heckler, a former health and human services secretary, is shown looking unhappy in a press conference with the president. He has just requested her resignation so that she can take a position as ambassador to Ireland. The president commends her for being "one of this administration's greatest assets, far and away."
6. "The streets are safe in Philadelphia, it's only the people who make them unsafe." (Frank Rizzo, mayor)
7. "Nature is cruel. It is our right to be cruel as well." (Adolf Hitler)

FALLACIES INVOLVING TRICKERY
WITH EMOTIONS

As you learned from Chapter 7, "Evaluations," a sure sign of a poor argument is one smothered in a sauce of evaluative words. The positive and negative connotations of evaluative words can quickly trigger emotions of bias. If the emotion is strong enough, the reader will not even notice the lack of supportive reasons. Fallacies involving emotional trickery appeal to fear, pity, popular wisdom, false authority, and prejudice. They seek to persuade by exploiting weaknesses instead of trusting and inviting conscious consideration and consent. They can be insidiously effective in clouding any further rational discussion on an issue. As techniques, they stress material irrelevant to the argument that will make their position hold more dramatic interest. They are used in politics and advertising as propaganda ploys familiar to us all. Indeed, they are so familiar, most of us have even learned to tolerate and live with them. Moreover, in this age of hype and hucksterism, when ideas usually have to enter into sales competition in order to come across, even writers who can construct sound arguments may feel that they have to turn the volume up to be heard.

All of this does not mean that any argument that includes expression of feeling or emotion is invalid. Usually we are not aroused to construct arguments unless motivated by feelings. To be sane on many topics is to feel clear anger, indignation, or grief. However, a fallacious argument is not always clear about its emotional involvement, which might be so great that the argument cannot evolve coherently. If this happens, the writer might be even more tempted to manipulate by composing an argument that would arouse a feeling response in others to agree with his or her own feelings. A fallacious argument constructed on this basis cannot appeal to reason or to rational feeling but instead appeals to fear, pity, respect for authority, need for popularity, prejudice, and the wish to libel.

Emotional Appeals to Fear and Pity

Appeals to fear and pity are staples of commercial advertising. An appeal to fear or pity may be justified in many circumstances, but an argument becomes fallacious when it depends upon this appeal to carry it. Moreover, the attempt to arouse such feelings can be designed to prevent others from ever noticing the lack of a sound argument. The following examples may serve as familiar reminders of the use of appeals to fear.

1.   "What your best friends won't tell you . . ."
2.   (Picture of a frantic traveler who has lost her traveler's checks.) "Next time be safe with our fast call-in service."

3. (Picture of man in hospital bed in a state of shock after seeing his bill.) "Did you think one insurance coverage plan was enough?"

4. (Picture of burglars breaking into a house.) "Are you still postponing that alarm system?"

Class Discussion

The use of an appeal to anger is not usually listed among types of fallacious arguments; using this type of appeal to arouse others out of a state of indifference is often assumed to be legitimate in argumentation. Listed here are some appeals to fear, pity, and anger. Read the arguments and decide which you think are fallacious (in that the situation is exaggerated) and which you feel are appropriate calls for fear, anger, or pity. Again, this may depend on your personal values. Defend your answers.

1. "Berkeley, California has become a police state as police presence has increased from 12 cops to 40 to 60 on any given weekend night. Cops are everywhere, on foot, bicycle, motorcycle, undercover, and in both marked and unmarked cars. The police mobile substation, a menacing blue bus with smoked windows, cruises the area for added effect. Sinister jump squads, followed by a paddy wagon, keep tensions high by making quick arrests." (*Copwatch Report*, Fall 1992)

2. "Loretta Fortuna wants out. Sickened by odors wafting from the red toxic pools near her home, angered by the political battleground she's had to maneuver, grief-stricken by two miscarriages within a year and perpetually worried for the health of her two small sons, she finally had enough. Fortuna has spent the past year waging a campaign on behalf of her family and neighbors to get a leaking waste dump near her home cleaned up. But now she has decided to move elsewhere, a disheartened casualty of a frustrating battle. The Gloucester Environmental Management Services landfill . . . is one site among 1,175 toxic nightmares nationwide waiting to be cleaned up." (Robert J. Mentzinger, *Public Citizen*, May / June 1990)

3. These are our beliefs. During your life you can accept them or not. If you do, you will be saved. Otherwise you will go to hell for eternity.

4. "Last summer [1988], American farms suffered multibillion dollar crop losses from a devastating drought. Thousands of square miles of dry forests went up in smoke as fires raged uncontrollably. Entire communities were left homeless and destitute in the wake of hurricanes Gilbert and Helene. And smog blanketed many cities as a mass of hot air hovered over the country. 'It must be the greenhouse effect,' was the comment made over and over again by members of Congress. Media coverage had sensitized most Americans to the peril posed by the unchecked growth of greenhouse gas emissions, and the unpleasant

weather seemed to be a preview of what we can expect if global climate models are accurate in their predictions." (Claudine Schneider, *Issues in Science and Technology*, Summer 1989)

5. "'We are God in Here . . .' That's what the guards in an Argentine prison taunted Grace Guena with as they applied electrical shocks to her body while she lay handcuffed to the springs of a metal bed. Her cries were echoed by the screams of other victims and the laughter of their torturers." (Appeal letter from Amnesty International USA)

6. Smokers know they are plague victims and suspect they may be carriers. So they puff on their butts behind a closed office door, and indulge their health-nut friends by abstaining from cigarettes during the dinner hour—which without a nicotine fix, seems to stretch on for days." (Richard Corliss, *Time*, April 11, 1994)

7. "Alarmed by a comet's violent collision last year with the planet Jupiter, scientists warned yesterday that speeding asteroids and comets could inflict far more damage on Earth than previously thought, perhaps even disrupting the climate and causing millions of deaths. . . . Among the ideas presented were the use of super-powerful spacecraft and well-timed nuclear explosives to pulverize potential invaders from outer space or to nudge them away from their Earth-bound orbits. . . . The meeting . . . is sponsored by the U.S. Department of Energy, NASA, and the Air Force Space Command." (*San Francisco Chronicle*, May 23, 1995)

8. "The consequences of the Democratic health care plans will be ruinous, tax increases, job losses, less money in your pocket to spend the way you want to spend it." (Political advertisement, 1994)

Appeal to False Authority. This is an argument whose chief or only support is a false, or questionable, authority. The argument is not upheld by sound reasons but by the alleged endorsements by individuals who lack credentials or expertise on the question at hand.

Buzz Bonanza, star of stage and screen, prefers Tasty Toothpaste.

The president of the United States says that brushing your teeth once a week is enough.

A false authority can also be vague:

Doctors say you should brush your teeth every day with Florident.

Experts agree you should use an electric toothbrush.

Inside sources at the White House say the president doesn't like to brush his teeth.

The argument that relies on false authority can also take the form of appeal to tradition, to popular wisdom, and to bandwagon.

Here are some examples of the appeal to the authority of tradition:

If you want to be a real American, own a Ford and drink Coca-Cola.

You have to go to law school. Every oldest child in this family for the past four generations has gone to law school.

New Englanders don't complain about hardships.

False authority can also reside in popular wisdom:

If you have any doubts about the status of American health care, just compare it with that in the other industrialized nations! Ask anyone you know from a foreign country where they would most like to be treated if they had a medical emergency. Ask them which country is the envy of the world when it comes to health care. (Rush Limbaugh)

Sometimes the claim is made that popular wisdom lies in a mass momentum. If a herd is headed in one direction, that must be the right direction. This subvariety of the false authority is known as *the bandwagon fallacy*. An argument that appeals to the comfort of joining the crowd and coming over to the winning side is also fallacious. It is another version of an appeal to authority: this time the authority is a vague group or mass of others. It also promises the exhilaration of being swept up in an irrepressible momentum of instinctive wisdom.

Here are some examples of appeals to the bandwagon:

1. Don't vote for Proposition 9. The polls show it will lose 5 to 1.
2. Everyone else does it; why can't I?
3. Last year over 10 million people switched to Buckaroo Trucks!
4. Buddy Springs! America's Beer!
5. Millions of Americans are now buying personal computers for their children. Give your children a head start in school with their personal home computer today!
6. Join the Pepsi Generation!

In all these forms of appeals to false authority, you will notice conclusions unsupported by reasons. What appears instead is a subtle pressure to trust bogus authorities or to trust conformity. While a good argument lays its logical reasons on the table with evidence available for questioning and verification, an appeal to false authority suggests one should not trust one's own reasoning but depend on those vague others who know better.

However—and this is most important to remember—the existence of false authority *does not mean that a good argument should avoid using and quoting authorities*. One the contrary, authorities with relevant expertise provide sound support for reasons and are used routinely to make claims credible and convincing.

The first comprehensive study of the geographic skills of America's youngsters shows they are "getting the message that they are part of a larger world," Education Secretary Richard Riley said yesterday. "We're not at the head of the class yet, but it's a good start," said National Geographic Society President Gilbert Grosvenor in releasing the results of National Assessment of Educational Progress tests. Nearly three-quarters of the 19,000 students tested in the first national study of geographic knowledge showed at least a basic understanding of the subject, the Education Department reported. (Associated Press, October 18, 1995)

In this example you will notice that each claim is attributed to an authority. If you, as the reader, are in doubt about the qualifications of Richard Riley and Gilbert Grosvenor to offer opinions, at least you have enough clues for further research. When you are composing your own argument, choosing suitable authorities with relevant expertise on your topic can be a more complex task. So-called experts may have credentials, but you must also consider their track records; furthermore, you might want to know whether other authorities agree or disagree with them. In summary, authority citation can offer impressive support for an argument, but assessing the authority requires research knowledge and judgment.

Class Discussion

Explain how the following statements are different kinds of appeals to authority. Which are fallacious? Which legitimate?

1. My doctor says that I should take a nap every afternoon.

2. A 10-year study by leading scientists has found that Tuff toothpaste prevents decay in 4 out of 5 cases.

3. Buzz Bonanza, star of stage and screen, drives a Macho Motorcycle.

4. I read it in the newspapers.

5. Interviewer: "Vice President Quayle, do you feel domestic assault rifles should be banned?" Quayle: "My viewpoint is always in agreement with the president's. And I am sure that if he felt we should have a ban on them, we'd have one."

6. "Women have babies and men provide the support. If you don't like the way we're made you've got to take it up with God." (Phyllis Schlafly)

7. "President Clinton's plans to revive the recession-battered economy all hinge on the assumption that government policy can reliably control the destructive cycles of boom and bust. Recent research released by the prestigious National Bureau of Economic Research claims that even with all the expertise of modern economists at their disposal, government policy makers are hardly any better at stabilizing the economy than they were before World War I. The National Bureau is a

private non-profit institution whose judgments on when recessions begin and end are accepted as official by nearly all economists and government agencies." (*San Francisco Chronicle*, November 16, 1992)

8. For over a quarter of a century our teachers have been committed to the idea that the best way to teach students is to withhold criticisms and build self-esteem. But both Alfred Binet, the father of intelligence testing, and Sigmund Freud, the father of psychoanalysis, described the development of self-criticism, which we learn from the criticisms of others, as the essence of intelligence.

Appeal to Prejudice: Personal Attack and Poisoning the Well

Prejudice is a complex feeling: a mixture of envy, fear, and resentment. To become prejudiced means you have adopted an attitude of rejection. Arguments that seek to incite prejudice may do so in order to spare the hard work of constructing a sound argument, for once prejudice is transmitted, those infected with the virus will not even notice the argument's faults. There are two basic fallacious appeals to prejudice. The first uses the strategy of personal attack.

Personal Attack. This fallacious argument is a familiar campaign strategy. Also known under the Latin name of *ad hominem*, it uses the hand-grenade tactics that leave smoke screen to hide the lack of an argument. It uses frontal attacks, such as abusive name calling, or rear attacks, such as innuendo. This is a fallacious argument because the criticisms of the person are irrelevant to the issue. The trick is to stir up prejudice quickly so that the irrelevance will be overlooked.

Poisoning the Well. Another variety of personal attack is called poisoning the well. When poison is poured into a small portion of a well, all its water is contaminated, and no one dares drink from it. Thus, when a person, idea, or cause is discredited at the outset, people will not want to hear more about it. All neutrality and openness will be lost. Consider this example:

> Of all the screwball, asinine, muddle-headed letters I have ever seen from this newspaper's readers, the one from Detroit advocating the legalization of drugs takes the cake.

Poisoning the well can also be more subtle:

> This president, who has never worn a uniform, announced today that he would send our troops overseas.

Poisoning the well functions like gossip:

> Senator Smith, known as the "waste-fill senator" because of the tons of propaganda he mails from his office, made a speech in favor of increasing immigration quotas before Congress today.

This is a fallacious argument. Even if Senator Smith deserves a bad reputation for his mailings, he might be able to make a well-informed, persuasive speech on immigration quotas. If it could be shown that he bought extravagant amounts of paper from paper mill lobbyists who exploited immigrant labor, such information might make this criticism relevant. But as this argument stands, his "waste-fill" reputation is beside the point.

Poisoning the well can be directed not only against individuals but also against ideas or collective groups like the news media:

> The news media has been sounding the alarm lately, loudly decrying the terrorists, tax-evaders, and assorted huddled masses poised to overrun us. These racist and alarmist stories are in sync with the message from Washington. (Kelly Gettinger, *Progressive*, August 1993)

Class Discussion

Which of the following are examples of poisoning the well?

1. School prayer is a silly idea cloaked in religious freedom and pious language because it runs counter to common sense.
2. "Senators Bob Dole and James Exon are in deep shit, and they're shoveling it your way. Between their overblown speeches and half-baked legislative proposals, these two have spun out of orbit and into some kind of moralistic black hole. This tweedledum and tweedledee duo is trampling the Constitution while raising the level of Congressional hypocrisy to nosebleed heights." (Brock N. Meeks, *Wired*, September 1995)
3. "**Cultic America: A Tower of Babel**. If the cult watchers are to be believed, there are thousands of groups out there poised to snatch your body, control your mind, corrupt your soul. Witches' covens, satanic rituals, Krishna consciousness, fanatic fundamentalists, black and white supremacists, New Age cosmic crazies—few are armed but most are considered dangerous. They'll seduce you and fleece you, marry and bury you." (*Newsweek*, March 12, 1993)
4. "'Many companies charge drivers more than twice as much as other companies for identical insurance coverage . . .' That's the word from the California Department of Insurance following a new State survey on automobile insurance rates." (ad from 20th Century Insurance)

FALLACIES USING THE TRICKERY
OF DISTRACTION

Four other fallacies—the red herring, pointing to another wrong, using a straw man, and circular reasoning—can be classified in many ways, but what they all have in common are tricks for diverting attention away from the issue at hand. Some, like red herring and pointing to another wrong, distract attention from the central issue to another. The straw man makes a false representation of an opponent's position, pretends it is an accurate depiction, and then destroys it. Circular reasoning creates an illusion of logical support. Such fallacious arguments can be the most difficult to identify when their ploys of distraction are effective. They are both challenging and fun to study.

Red Herrings

The term *red herring* comes from a ruse used by prison escapees. Because dogs were given prisoners' belongings to smell, then told to follow the scent, the prisoners would smear themselves with herring in the hope that the strong odor would throw the dogs off track. The red herring throws us off track into irrelevancies, diverting our concentration from the question at hand. Take this example:

> Marijuana smoking is not all that harmful. I would feel safer in a car with a driver under the influence of marijuana than one under the influence of liquor any day.

Here, the claim to be examined is that marijuana is not all that harmful. However, instead of offering support for this claim, the writer draws our attention to the question of the relative safety of a driver under the influence of marijuana versus one under the influence of alcohol. This is an entirely different issue, which easily leads into a discussion of their relative effects on reflexes and perception. Meanwhile, the first claim either is forgotten or may be assumed to have been proved.

The red herring can be the most difficult of all fallacious arguments to detect when it actually proves a point but a point that is not the one being addressed. It can even create a contradiction, as in this argument:

> VETERAN: "We should not send American troops to Bosnia. No American life is ever worth being shed on foreign soil."
>
> INTERVIEWER: "But didn't you fight in World War II when American soldiers died both in Europe and Asia?"

VETERAN: "Well, that war was fought because one man was trying to control the world. Hitler took over Europe and his allies controlled the East."

Another red herring tactic is to make one claim while pretending to support it with another claim, whereas neither claim actually has been supported.

I cannot understand why the environmentalists feel it is harmful to cut down the redwood forests. This work provides a good living to loggers and their families.

Here, no reasons are given for why it is not harmful to cut down the redwoods. Nor is the word *harmful* clarified. The writer never considers who is being harmed or for how long. Nor is there mention of the lumber company's responsibility and profits. Instead, the writer uses the ambiguous phrase "good living to the loggers," suggesting images of innocent loggers thrown out of work, thus opening the path to a long diversion.

Here is another, more familiar bumper-sticker example of the same fallacious argument:

Guns don't kill people. People do.

Class Discussion

Study the following examples of red herring arguments. Write out (1) the issue and (2) the diversion.

1. Guns are not America's major problem, or even high on the list of our problems. Cars, cancer, accidents in the kitchen all kill far more people than guns do. It is not *guns* that we should be frightened of but the effects of poverty, lack of education, a judicial system that sends criminals and psychopaths back out into the streets. Guns are not a solution, but they are not the problem, either!

2. TV can't be harmful to children, because it occupies their attention for hours and keeps them off the streets. (taken from S. Morris Engel's *With Good Reason*, St. Martin's Press, 1982)

3. Those who are so ferociously involved in Mothers Against Drunk Driving would better spend their time in working with A.A. to help alcoholics.

4. Why are you always nagging at me about the way I drive?

Pointing to Another Wrong

The technique of pointing to another wrong is also called two wrongs make a right. Again, it introduces an irrelevancy, or an irresponsibility, however you choose to see it, into an argument. It is an attempt to justify an action

considered objectionable by appealing to similar instances that went unnoticed, unjudged, or unpunished.

Consider these examples of pointing to another wrong:

1. Student to instructor: "Why are you getting after me for being late to
   class? You never say anything to that pretty woman who comes late to
   class every day."

2. Motorist to police officer: "Why are you giving me a ticket for going the
   wrong way on a one-way street? Didn't you see that red sedan I was
   following doing the same thing?"

3. So what if I don't separate the cans and newspapers out from the garbage for recycling. I don't have that much time. Neither do most other
   people.

4. The politically correct people will tell you that Columbus brought oppression, slavery, and genocide to the peaceful Indians. But Indians
   committed as many atrocities against the white people as well as
   against one another.

5. Why do you complain about cruelty to animals in scientific experiments? Look at the way animals are cruel to one another. Have you
   ever seen the way lions bite into the necks of zebras, rip open their
   insides, then eat their hearts and entrails?

Straw Man

Another fallacious argument is called a straw man because it constructs a
false and faulty replica of an argument that it opposes, then knocks it down
as easily as one could disperse a shape made of straw. It is a fallacious
argument that first misrepresents, oversimplifies, exaggerates, and caricatures an opponent's position, then it demolishes it. This tactic succeeds
when those who hear it forget that the creation is not the same as the
original argument.

> Those who are in favor of national health care want to give us army-style med-
> icine. If the government starts running health care for us, we'll find ourselves
> waiting all day in barracks full of sick people, while the doctors are shuffling
> through piles of red tape in their offices and leaving for home by the time our
> turn arrives.

The straw man argument might also pick out a trivial aspect of an idea,
cause, or person, claiming that this part is essential to the whole. It raises
this objection as though it alone were an essential reason for acceptance or
rejection.

> I can't respect Hindus because they wear those red spots painted on their
> foreheads.

Class Discussion

Consider these examples and decide whether they contain the straw man technique:

1. When you support picketing, you are supporting a conspiracy to commit extortion through disruption of business, intimidation, and slander. I have no sympathy for strikers who always have the option of going to work for someone else if they don't like the compensation or conditions offered by their employer. I feel they have no right to force the employer to change employment policy to suit them. Why does hiring people to do a specific job, for specific pay, force the employer to practically adopt the employee, catering to him or her from the cradle to the grave? It must be stopped and the extortionists jailed for long terms.

2. I am bewildered by those who support the "three strikes and you are out" law. This tough position denies all possibility for change in people. With it, we turn our backs on these people, saying they can never get better. Thus, we buy into a cycle of hate and fear in a total rejection of love and compassion, locking ourselves up in our houses of fear just like we lock up the prisoners in our prisons.

3. I congratulate the police chief for granting concealed weapons permits. He rightly believes the public, when educated in firearms safety, can be empowered to defend themselves. And I congratulate him for his courage in standing up to those cops and public officials who believe the public cannot handle the freedom of responsibility of firearms, freedom of speech, and freedom of assembly.

4. DOCTOR: "You need to get more exercise. Why don't you walk to work?"
    PATIENT: "I can't do that doctor—I work at home!"

Circular Reasoning

Another argument that is fallacious because it neglects to provide support for its conclusion is circular reasoning. In most of the other cases the support was inadequate, but this case offers no support at all. Circular reasoning simply asserts its conclusion, then reasserts it again, sometimes in different language. This change in language may give the effect of providing a reason, but it is going in circles. It also has another name: begging the question. However, it may be easier to remember by the term *circular reasoning* because it does just that by saying "*A* is true because *A* is true." Here are some examples:

> Taxing inheritances is justified because people should pay a tax on money they have been given by their families.

Here, the first half of the sentence is repeated in different words in the second half, as though the second half were a supporting conclusion.

> Running is good for your health. If you want to be healthy, you should run.

Circular reasoning claims to offer an acceptable inference when the inference actually is missing.

> Adultery and fornication are wrong. Therefore, it follows that contraception is wrong.

Here, the gap between the first claim and the second is huge. If we agree that adultery and fornication are wrong, why is contraception also wrong? To make a good argument, we have to provide more links of explanation, to show the second claim follows logically from the first.

Class Discussion

See if you can find the circular reasoning in these examples:

1. Movie stars are intelligent. If they weren't intelligent, they wouldn't be movie stars.
2. Kerosene is combustible. Therefore, it burns.
3. Concealed weapons should be discretionary. After all, people should have the right to conceal their guns if they wish.
4. To curse is immoral because it is wrong.
5. Elect Wallace Brown supervisor—a Gulf War pilot.
6. The budget given the Pentagon by Congress again exceeded military requests by a few billion dollars. Isn't it obvious that when we have the best-funded defense in the world, we will have the best defense in the world?
7. WILLIAM BENNETT: "Martin Luther King said what degrades humans is unjust, what uplifts them is just. Is there any doubt that TV talk shows degrade people?"
   TALK SHOW HOST: "I have 4½ million viewers. Are you going to tell them that they can't watch my show any more?"

CHAPTER SUMMARY

1. Word ambiguity uses undefined and vague words in an argument, seeking advantage in the use of key words that could be interpreted in more than one way.

2. Euphemisms are words that mask meaning by enveloping a less acceptable idea in positive or neutral connotations. The use of euphemisms is fallacious in an argument when the goal is to mislead or to disarm objections.

3. Prejudicial language persuades through the use of loaded words that pretend to convey objective information.

4. *Equivocation*, in the general sense of the word, creates a verbal smoke screen that seems to be saying something while saying nothing. As a fallacy in logic, equivocation draws an unwarranted conclusion from an argument that contains a term with more than one meaning under the pretense that it has only one meaning. This shift in meaning occurs between the premises and the conclusion.

5. Appeals to fear and pity persuade through emotion, avoiding both a rational presentation and a rational analysis of the argument.

6. Appeal to false authority seeks to influence others by citing phony or inappropriate authorities. This authority might be a person, a tradition, or conventional wisdom.

7. Appeal to bandwagon is another example of the appeal to authority. But in this case, the authority is an amorphous mass, offering the exhilarating momentum of the herd instinct. This fallacious argument is also called mob appeal.

8. Personal attack uses abusive language or name calling against a person connected with the issue as a substitute for reasoning.

9. Poisoning the well seeks to prejudice others against opponents or their ideas, preventing their positions from being heard. This technique seeks to remove the neutrality necessary for listening and to implant prejudice instead.

10. The red herring is a ploy of distraction. It brings up one issue, then minimizes or diverts attention from it by emphasizing other issues that are irrelevant. Those following this line of argument will soon find themselves off the track.

11. The straw man is an argument that misrepresents, oversimplifies, or caricatures an opponent's position; it creates a false replica, then destroys the replica, claiming it is a true representation. The straw man also invalidates ideas, by raising trivial objections as though they were crucial.

12. Pointing to another wrong is also called two wrongs make a right. This ploy says, "Don't look at me; he did it too!"

13. Circular reasoning is the assertion or repeated assertion of a conclusion with the insistence that the conclusion is a reason.

CHAPTER QUIZ

Identify the following arguments either as *NF* for *not fallacious* or by the name of one of the types of fallacious arguments defined in this chapter. In some cases, you may find that more than one fallacy applies; choose the one you feel to be the most appropriate. Be prepared to defend your answers.

_____ 1. It was announced today that our troops, who have been shelled for some weeks now in Lebanon, have made a *strategic transfer* to their ships offshore of that country.

_____ 2. You want this office to function as a team. But we don't have a room big enough in this building to house all of us at the same time. Therefore, we can't do it.

_____ 3. I wouldn't give money to the American Civil Liberties Union if I were you. Do you want to support an organization of Nazis? Why, they once defended the rights of the American Nazi party!

_____ 4. Children are supposed to have rights like everyone else, aren't they? Well, then I am right in not wanting to go to bed.

_____ 5. Five million people have already seen this movie. Shouldn't you?

_____ 6. Why do I think the president's program is sound? Because the polls show that the vast majority supports it.

_____ 7. By a margin of 2 to 1, shoppers prefer Brand X to any of the leading competitors. Reason enough to buy Brand X.

_____ 8. What if your bank fails and takes your life savings? Buy diamonds—the safe investment.

_____ 9. Repressive environmentalists and economic zero-growthers have attacked the Environmental Protection Agency. Those stop-all-progress destructionists have nothing under their thick skulls.

_____ 10. A spokesman for a chemical industrial firm, when charged and fined for disposing of toxic wastes in the lakes of Illinois, protested, "Thousands of other industries are doing the same thing."

_____ 11. Good thinking depends on clear perception.

_____ 12. Democrats are captives of an antigrowth dinosaur mentality that offers nothing for the future but repeating their failed past. If the big spenders get their way, they'll charge everything on your Taxpayers' Express Card.

_____ 13. There is *virtually no tar* in these cigarettes.

_____ 14. We need to strike a blow to stop illegal aliens. It has been estimated that illegal aliens are costing our taxpayers in excess of $5 billion a year. Should our senior citizens be denied full health care benefits, should our children suffer overcrowded classrooms in order to subsidize the costs of illegal aliens?

_____ 15. In Ethel Rae Cosmetics we don't call ourselves "salespeople" but "teachers." We teach people how to take better care of their skins.

_____ 16. Using hidden notes on a test is not unethical; our professors wouldn't be where they are today if they hadn't done the same thing.

_____ 17. Maybe I do cheat on income tax, but so does everyone else.

_____ 18. Those people so fanatical about protesting in front of the nuclear plants would be better involved in voter registration and voter education.

_____ 19. Don't support the American Civil Liberties Union. They want nothing but criminals' rights.

_____ 20. You can't trust the newest generation of Republicans. They are monsters created by Newt Gingrich to use assault language on their political enemies, to imitate his style of being combative and intimidating.

_____ 21. There are plenty of people out there on the streets waiting to get your job. If you go on strike, you may find yourself out there with them.

_____ 22. Elijah Jones was the tenth victim of police brutality this year. Arrested for murdering his two children in a fit of insanity due to the pressures of his ghetto existence, he had hoped, on release from a mental institution through the help of the drug Thorazine, to make a new life for himself. But Sunday he was shot down mercilessly by the pigs when he attacked a police officer after robbing a liquor store.

_____ 23. The *natural* way to relieve muscular pain is through our vitamin ointment. It *relieves* pain from burns, stiff neck, backache, swelling, and so forth.

_____ 24. Ice cream may provide some nutrition but lots of fats and calories too. To save my heart and health, I avoid eating ice cream.

_____ 25. American educators, in a recent survey, unanimously agreed that longer school days, more homework, and longer school years would only penalize children and not necessarily result in better learning.

_____ 26. The president of the United States says that the problems of illiteracy can be solved only by longer school days, more homework, and longer school years.

_____ 27. In China, Europe, and Brazil, efforts are being made to defuse the population time bomb that adds one billion people every decade.

For Further Reading

Barry, Vincent, and Joel Rudinow. *Invitation to Critical Thinking*. 2nd ed. New York: Holt, Rinehart & Winston, 1990.

Damer, T. Edward. *Attacking Faulty Reasoning*. 2nd ed. Belmont, Calif.: Wadsworth, 1987.

Engel, S. Morris. *With Good Reason: An Introduction to Informal Fallacies*. 5th ed. New York: St. Martin's Press, 1994.

Hurley, Patrick J. *A Concise Introduction to Logic*. 5th ed. Belmont, Calif.: Wadsworth, 1994.

Lutz, William. *Doublespeak*. New York: HarperPerennial, 1989.

Perkins, Ray. *Logic and Mr. Limbaugh*. Chicago: Open Court, 1995.

Shulman, Max. "Love Is a Fallacy." In *Tall Short Stories*. Erik Duthie (ed.). New York: Simon & Schuster, 1959.

Solomon, Norman. *The Power of Babble: A Politician's Dictionary of Buzz Words and Doubletalk for Every Occasion*. New York: Lauren, 1992.

CHAPTER 11

Inductive Reasoning and Inductive Fallacies: How Do I Reason from Evidence?

"I forget . . . What are we making again?"

© 1984. Reprinted courtesy of Bill Hoest and Parade Magazine.

The kids in this cartoon are not following an architectural drawing or a definite mental plan but are working by trial and error. Creating as they go along, sometimes forgetting their original plan, their reasoning is haphazard and unsystematic.

Inductive reasoning is a method used to discover new information or to supply missing information. We could use it to guess what the kids are building. And the kids could use it to learn that nails alone will not keep the structure standing. When we use inductive reasoning, we observe, test, and check things out in some systematic fashion.

Inductive reasoning is useful when an examination of all data would be an impossible or impractical task. For instance, through samplings or extrapolation we could estimate how many voters nationwide favor a particular candidate, how many needles there are in a haystack, or how many stars there are in the universe.

This chapter is about inductive reasoning. Although inductive reasoning might be called an open-ended method of learning and discovering, it is not hit and miss, or trial and error but has its own rules for arriving at answers. And it can be fun.

Discovery Exercises

Defining Key Terms

Using at least two dictionaries, write down definitions of the following words:

1. induction
2. reasoning
3. empirical
4. scientific method
5. inductive reasoning

Answering a Survey on Test Performance

Write your answers to the following questions in preparation for discussion. Take notes, also, on the way in which you must reason in order to reply.

1. Do you consistently do well on school tests?
2. Think of a time when you made a high score on a challenging test. What steps did you go through to prepare yourself mentally, physically, and in actual study?
3. Think of a time when you did poorly on a challenging test. How did you prepare? What did you fail to do?
4. What insights did you gain through answering these questions?
5. Do you think this information might be applied to improve your test performance in the future?

Now discuss the following questions in class:

1. Explain how you were reasoning in order to answer these questions. Was this inductive reasoning?
2. How was this reasoning similar to, or different from, the way you worked mentally to describe the vegetables and fruits in the first chapter.

LOOKING AT INDUCTIVE REASONING

In this last exercise, as well as in the descriptive work you did earlier in the book, you used inductive reasoning. In this work, you first sensed, observed, and gathered data, then drew inferences about patterns, configurations, and meanings. This method of gathering data and letting it speak for itself is also called *empirical* research or the *scientific method*. It was the approach, you will remember, used by Samuel Scudder.

In the descriptive exercises you completed, your main concern was with developing the discipline of careful observation without preconceptions or prior judgments. At this point, we are going to look more abstractly at the nature and structure of inductive reasoning in order to learn more about the rules devised to obtain the most reliable results.

Induction comes from the Latin *in* = in, and *ducere* = to lead. Induction leads reasoning from evidence about *some* members of a class to form a conclusion about *all* members of that class. This can be done through sensory observation, enumeration, analogous reasoning, causal reasoning, and from pattern recognition. We have already explored sensory observation at some length; we will now define and explain the other modes of inductive reasoning.

ENUMERATION

Induction can be based on enumeration, which includes simple counting as well as statistical analysis of data from a controlled sampling. With numerical information, sometimes a trend can be predicted, or *extrapolated*, from that point on. If you have a car that has run without any repairs for six years, and then suddenly you have one or two major repair problems every six months, you can extrapolate a trend that may well continue until all parts are replaced. The process of such reasoning can be formally demonstrated by a series of sentences followed by a line separating the evidence from a conclusion drawn about it.

Here are two examples:

This can of Chock Nuts contains exactly 485 peanuts.

This second can of Chock Nuts contains exactly 485 peanuts.

This third can of Chock Nuts contains exactly 485 peanuts.

(Therefore) all cans of Chock Nuts must contain exactly 485 peanuts.

I got shoes.

You got shoes.

All God's chillen' got shoes.

In the second example, the sampling might be said to be insufficient to warrant the conclusion, but the song carries a wonderful feeling anyway.

ANALOGIES

Inductive reasoning can also be based on analogies. An analogy is the comparison of something familiar to something unfamiliar in order to find or explain a common principle. To argue inductively through analogies is to proceed on the assumption that if two things are similar in some respects, they are probably similar in other respects.

Here are two examples of analogous reasoning.

1. Bats are blind and yet by using reflected sound can move without hitting obstacles. By analogy, the development of sonar devices for blind humans might also help them move safely through public places.

2. Ben Franklin proved by a simple experiment that materials of different colors absorb heat differently. He put squares of cloth of different colors on some snowbanks and left them in the sun. In a few hours he noticed that a black piece had sunk into the snow the deepest, lighter-colored pieces less, and a white piece not at all. From this Franklin reasoned that dark colors absorb the sun's heat more readily than paler ones, which reflect part of the sun's radiation. By analogous reasoning, he decided that people who live in tropical climates should wear white clothing.

DISCOVERY OF PATTERNS

Inductive reasoning seeks to discover patterns in the evidence that suggest a configuration, a tendency, or a trend that could explain or give a name to the entire situation or problem. In this case, the evidence might be called the *parts* and the explanation the *whole*. In medicine, the name given to the whole is called the *diagnosis*.

For example, a child is brought to the doctor with the following symptoms: fever, cough, and eye inflammation. Small red spots with white centers are found on the insides of her cheeks. The doctor says that if a rash appears first on her neck and then on the rest of her body within three to five days, with a diminution of the fever, then he can be sure of a diagnosis of common measles. In the experience of this doctor and his colleagues, this pattern of symptoms has always indicated common measles and nothing else. In this situation, therefore, the doctor uses induction to diagnose what may become common measles—provided all these symptoms do appear and no others. Other symptoms, or the lack of all these symptoms, could suggest another diagnosis.

CONCERN WITH CAUSES

Induction, as well as other forms of reasoning, seeks causes to explain events. For instance, on the simplest level of using induction to determine causation, you could reason thus:

> When I put on a red dress I get attention.
>
> When I don't wear red, I don't get attention.
>
> **Wearing red must get me attention.**

Sometimes causes can never be fully determined but are expressed in the form of speculations or hypotheses. In October 1985 a humpback whale, later affectionately called Humphrey, made an unprecedented visit to San Francisco Bay and from there to the Sacramento River Delta region, where he remained for twenty-four days. It took $50,000 and the combined efforts of many individuals to persuade him to return from the brackish water of the delta to the safety of his natural habitat in the ocean. The press reported a great many speculations about the cause of his visit and reluctance to leave. They included (1) he was feeding on the wealth of fish he found there; (2) he was insane or suicidal; (3) he was confused and lost; (4) he was plagued by parasites and moving into fresh water to kill them; (5) "he" was a "she" and pregnant, seeking a place for birthing.

Class Discussion

Inductive reasoning, whether using enumeration, analogies, pattern recognition, or guesses about causation, has its own rules or standards for producing the most reliable or probable conclusions. See if you can discover whether the following examples use inductive reasoning correctly or poorly. Give your reasons for your evaluation in each case.

1. The leaves on our maple tree turn red in October.
   Some years it is cold in October, and some years it is warm through October. No matter what the temperature, our tree always turns in October.

   October makes the leaves of maple trees turn red.

"Miss California already, don't you, Humphrey . . . ?"
Used with permission of the *Minneapolis Star and Tribune*.

2. I always get a cold after I go swimming.
   I only get a cold when I go swimming.

   The cause of my colds is swimming.

3. The last ten times I flipped this coin, it came up tails.

   The next time I flip it, it is certain to be tails.

4. I get nervous when I drink coffee.
   I get nervous when I drink tea.
   I get nervous when I drink cola.

   All drinks make me nervous.

5. Jules and Jim like the same dogs.
   Jules and Jim like the same foods.

   Jules and Jim must like the same people.

6. My lover promised to come see me at 8:00 P.M.
   I have waited until 4:00 A.M.

   He is not coming.

7. When I stopped smoking, I gained 10 pounds. Smoking keeps my weight down.

8. My wife and I know how beneficial fresh garlic can be to health, but we worried about the smell. Then we found a solution. We chop up pieces of garlic and put them inside a banana to share just before going to bed. Afterward I have never noticed any garlic on the breath. Even the next morning, there is no garlic smell. We believe we have discovered a cure for garlic breath.

9. I had a wart that was protruding and sore. I decided to try vitamin E. I applied the oil about two or three times a day, and in less than ten days the wart was gone. This proves that vitamin E cures warts.

HYPOTHESES

A conclusion derived from inductive reasoning is called a *hypothesis*. You found a number of them in the story of Humphrey the whale. In the example you just read about warts, the hypothesis was that vitamin E cures warts. Thus, a hypothesis is a theory, or a working assumption, used consciously as a vehicle for finding more facts or evidence. The conclusions given in all the preceding examples, whether correctly reasoned or not, were hypotheses. Thus, the conclusion derived from inductive reasoning is characteristically a tentative one. Indeed, such an inductive generalization can be less certain than the evidence itself.

The discovery of more evidence always requires that the hypothesis be tested again, when it may have to be revised or even discarded. The discovery of even one counterexample challenges the truth of a hypothesis. In the case of the claim for vitamin E as a cure for warts, if one other person faithfully applied vitamin E two or three times a day but still had a wart six months later, this alone would challenge the claim that vitamin E is a cure for warts. However, neither case could be considered as proving or disproving the claim of a cure because these "experiments" lack *control of variables*. Moreover, the sampling of only two people is obviously insufficient evidence.

To repeat, a conclusion derived from the inductive process is a hypothesis. Only after time and continuous testing can a hypothesis be established as a final conclusion or as a fact. This was true, for instance, of the discovery that a vaccination could prevent smallpox. It took the interweaving of many hypotheses and many tests to establish this fact, which when put into practice has now eradicated the disease.

The following two examples show how hypotheses serve as imaginative guides for inductive reasoning and become modified or reinforced through their interaction with the emerging evidence.

1. When a child developed a high fever and complained of pains in the kidney area, a kidney infection was diagnosed by the doctor (first hypothesis). However, an examination of the child's mouth and throat revealed enlarged and swollen tonsils (new evidence), and it seemed more likely at this point that the fever and kidney pains were due to the infected tonsils (new hypothesis).

2. In the eighteenth century Europeans began to experiment with the nature of electricity. The similarity between lightning and electric sparks was observed, and it was conjectured that lightning was simply a big electric spark. Ben Franklin decided to test this hypothesis. Using analogous reasoning, he noticed that lightning and electric sparks were similar in color and in shape, that they traveled at about the same speed, and both killed animals. Franklin published a proposal suggesting that a "sentry box" be built on a high tower with a man inside on an insulated platform who would draw sparks from passing clouds with a long pointed iron rod (test for a hypothesis). Before Franklin got around to trying out this experiment himself, it was conducted in France, and it was proved that clouds are electrified (proof of the hypothesis). Franklin then found a way to verify his hypothesis again, using his well-known kite experiment. He fixed a sharp-pointed wire to the top of a kite, then knotted a large iron key between the kite string and a length of ribbon used for insulation. When a storm cloud passed by, Franklin saw the fibers of the kite string stand on end and drew a spark from the key with his knuckle (second proof of the hypothesis in an experiment conducted under different conditions).

Identifying a Hypothesis

In the following example, underline the hypothesis. Also circle the statement that shows a plan to test the hypothesis and the statement that indicates the hypothesis was disproven.

> A study of high school students in ten major U.S. cities showed that four out of every five were *not* coffee drinkers. It was conjectured that this statistic could be due to the fact that our TV commercials show only older people or married couples drinking coffee. A new advertising promotional scheme was planned showing teenagers enjoying coffee at athletic events, during class breaks, and at lunch hour to see if it might change this ratio. One year and $4 million later, another study was conducted that showed four out of five American high school students still were not coffee drinkers.

Class Discussion

Here are four examples of inductive reasoning that include hypotheses. Read and underline the hypothetical statements, and discuss whether you find adequate support for these hypotheses. Can you imagine other, more likely hypotheses that might better explain some of these situations? What form of inductive reasoning does each case use? Does it use analogies, extrapolate and predict from patterns, speculate about cause and effect, or gather data and statistics?

1. A study of high school students in ten major U.S. cities showed that four out of every five were not coffee drinkers. It was conjectured that this statistic could be due to TV commercials showing only older people drinking coffee. A new advertising promotional scheme was devised to seek to change this ratio by showing teenagers enjoying coffee at athletic events, during class breaks, and on dates to see if it might change this ratio.

2. I have been wearing a wool knitted cap for the past ten years. People think it is strange, but it has kept me from having sore throats. Before I started wearing the cap, I had sore throats all the time. But since I started wearing it, I have not had any.

3. Japanese government officials and auto industry spokesmen said American drivers might be having trouble with their Japanese-made seat belts because their cars are too dirty. They reported finding animal hair in American cars, pieces of food, and soft drink drippings. In Japan, people do not drink or eat in their cars or even wear shoes. This explanation for the faulty seat belts (whose release button gradually became brittle and would not lock securely) came in response to reports that federal safety officials in the United States were planning to recall and repair defective seat belts in nine million cars. The Japanese manufacturers said that they had received no complaints in Japan about the 4.79 million vehicles on the road with the same seat belts. (Summarized from an article in the *San Francisco Chronicle*, May 23, 1995)

4. World bicycle production increased to more than 110 million units in 1994. The trend has been rising steadily since 1970. Bikes have been found to be speedier and more efficient than cars in gridlocked U.S. cities for couriers, pizza deliverers, police, and paramedics. Developing countries, where bikes have long been popular, are also finding new uses for bikes, such as in San Salvador where they are used for trailer towing. The potential for their further growth is great. They hold promise of becoming a valuable, environmentally friendly means of transportation. (Data summarized from *Vital signs 1995*)

STATISTICS AND PROBABILITY
IN INDUCTIVE REASONING

Inductive reasoning can work with statistical samplings (a form of enumeration) and make predictions on the basis of an estimate of probabilities. For example, the payoffs for betting on the winners of horse races are determined by inductive reasoning. Suppose you read in the papers that today at Green Meadows racetrack the following horses will run with the odds as listed: Post Flag 9.90 to 1; Bru Ha Ha 3.40 to 1; Plane Fast 6.80 to 1; En-Durance 5.20 to 1. These odds are based on the Racing Association's estimates of each horse's chance of winning. Bettors who pick winners will be paid a multiple of the first number in each of these odds for each dollar bet.

The field of mathematics known as statistics is a science that seeks to make accurate predictions about a whole from a sampling of its parts. Probability and statistics have yielded some basic rules for evaluating the reliability of conclusions drawn by inductive reasoning from statistical samplings. For the purposes of our introduction to the subject, there are five basic rules:

1. The *greater* the size of the *sample* (or number of study subjects), the greater is the probability that that sample is representative of the whole of a *class* (or group it is supposed to represent).

    The results of a survey of the coffee-drinking habits of students in one high school based on questioning only ten students would obviously not be as reliable as the results of a survey of the whole student body. However, samplings are made for the sake of convenience or necessity, and the same information can be extrapolated for a full population when some rules for size, margin of error, and random selection are followed. These rules are taught in the study of statistics. Yet, without knowing all these rules, you can still estimate that a survey of ten students could not speak for a whole high school, or one high school for all U.S. high schools.

2. The *more representative* the sample is of a class, the more likely it is that accurate conclusions will be drawn about the class from the sample.

    In a poll seeking a representative sampling of menopausal women in Illinois, the most representative respondents would probably be Illinois women between the ages of forty and sixty. Less likely to be representative would be women under the age of thirty. Moreover, a survey limited to women in their forties would also not be representative, nor would a survey of women in the city of Chicago only.

3. One *counterexample* can refute a generalization arrived at through inductive reasoning.

   If you complain that your friend *always* comes late and is *never* reliable, and then one day your friend arrives early, you have a counterexample that refutes your generalization.

4. If statistical evidence is offered, it should be offered in *sufficient detail* to permit verification. Sources or background material about the researchers should also be cited so others can determine their reputation and independence from vested interests in the study's outcome.

   In the following example, consider the vague references to "independent laboratory tests" as well as to the research data used to support the claims:

   FATOFF has been proven to cause weight loss. After years of research and expensive experimentation, an independent *laboratory* with *expertise* in biotechnology has finally uncovered a naturally occurring substance that can be taken orally in tablet form. Now it is being made available to millions of overweight men and women who are losing as much as 10 lbs. a month. It has taken over *15 years of research and over 200 medically documented studies* to produce FATOFF. But there is only one catch: FATOFF is expensive to produce.

5. When polls are taken, it is important to know not only whether a *reputable organization* or agency (such as Gallup, Roper, or Harris) took the poll but also the *exact formulation* of the question.

Compare the following questions:

1. Do you favor a constitutional amendment that declares, The English language shall be the official language of the United States?

2. English is the language of the United States by custom, although not by law. In order to avoid the political upheavals over language that have torn apart Canada, Belgium, Sri Lanka (Ceylon), India, and other nations, would you favor legislation designating English the official language of the United States?

The first question might elicit quite a different response than the second. When you hear or read about polls, be sure to see if the exact wording of the question is given so that you can analyze it for bias. Also, do not accept without question results from polls identified only vaguely as "a recent poll." If the pollster's name is given, consider whether it was an independent source or a source filtering information to represent its own political or commercial interests. You need to be able to determine whether the source was unbiased and whether the results are verifiable.

Class Discussion

The following examples offer statistical evidence. Rate the statistics given in each as *reliable* or *not reliable* and then state what rule or standard you used in making your judgment.

1. *Study Shows Major Role of Alcohol in Crime*
   "More than half of jail inmates convicted of violent crimes had been drinking before committing the offenses, the government said yesterday. . . . A report by the Bureau of Justice showed that more than half of convicted jail inmates who admitted they had been drinking said they felt 'pretty drunk' or 'very drunk' just before committing the crimes for which they were convicted.

   "Altogether, 54 percent of 32,112 people convicted of violent crimes had been drinking, the survey said. . . .

   "Nearly seven out of ten people convicted of manslaughter—68 percent—had been drinking before the offense, while 62 percent of those convicted of assault had been drinking. The survey found that 49 percent of those convicted of murder or attempted murder had been drinking.

   "The findings were based on personal interviews with a random sample of 5,785 jail inmates convicted of crimes from some 400 local jails around the country. The sample was designed to be representative of the more than 223,500 people housed in the nation's 3,338 local jails during the time of the survey in 1983." (Associated Press; reported in the *Oakland Tribune*, November 4, 1985)

2. "I would guess that the average office female makes 509 visits to the lavatory to a male's 230, and spends 10.7 minutes there to a male's 2.5. What management is going to put up with this 'primp time' featherbedding at equal pay?" (Edgar Berman, guest columnist, *USA Today*)

3. "It was May 1971 when Russell Bliss, a waste hauler, sprayed oil at Judy Piatt's stables in Moscow Mills, Mo., to help control the dust. A few days later hundreds of birds nesting in the stable's rafters fell to the ground and died. Soon, more than 20 of her cats went bald and died, as did 62 horses over the next three and a half years. Piatt herself developed headaches, chest pains and diarrhea, and one of her daughters started hemorrhaging. In 1974 the federal Centers for Disease Control in Atlanta identified the culprit as dioxin and traced it to Bliss's oil, which contained wastes from a defunct hexachlorophene plant that had paid him to dispose of it. Bliss, it turned out, had sprayed the waste-oil mixture on horse arenas, streets, parking lots and farms throughout the state, leaving what state Assistant Attorney General Edward F. Downey called 'a trail of sickness and death.'" (*Newsweek*, March 7, 1983)

Working from Facts to Inferences to Hypotheses

Follow these steps in this assignment:

1. Skim through books that list facts, such as *The Information Please Almanac, The Book of Lists, the People's Almanac, Statistical Abstracts of the United States.*
2. Find a group of related facts on one subject and write them down.
3. Draw all the inferences you can that would explain what these facts mean. Write them down as a list of potential conclusions.
4. From these select one conclusion that seems to you to be the most likely hypothesis to explain the facts' meaning.
5. Discuss this hypothesis and list what further facts you would need to determine whether or not it is true.
6. Make this a short essay assignment of one to two pages.
7. Title your paper with a question your hypothesis seeks to answer.
8. Make your thesis the answer to that question.

Student Writing Example

WHY FEWER INJURIES IN HOCKEY THAN OTHER TEAM SPORTS?

Shamma Boyarin

The Facts

Team sport injuries reported in U.S. hospitals in 1980*:

    463,000 injuries related to football
    442,900 injuries related to baseball
    421,000 injuries related to basketball
    94,200 injuries related to soccer
    36,400 injuries related to hockey

*(Source: Susan Baker. *The Injury Fact Book*. Lexington, Mass.: Lexington Books, 1984)

Why Were Fewer Injuries Related to Hockey Reported?

Potential Conclusions or Hypothesis

1. Hockey is a less dangerous sport.
2. People who play hockey are tougher and less likely to go to the hospital with injuries.

3. Hockey is a less popular sport, so fewer people are injured.
4. Hockey is more safety conscious than other sports.

Discussion

On the basis of my knowledge of all five sports, I would say that hockey is the most dangerous. And this factor of danger leads to three practices that make hockey different from the other team sports:

1. Hockey players, even nonprofessionals, are more likely to wear protective gear.
2. The rules of hockey are designed to prevent unnecessary injuries as much as possible. Referees enforce these rules more rigorously than in other sports.
3. Because it is a very tiring game, players are allowed to rest more often. A player with a minor injury can rest more and not aggravate the injury.

Because of these precautions, I do not think that the first two hypotheses are likely. As for the third, hockey may be a less popular sport, and this may contribute to the smaller number of injuries, but I don't think this can account for its dramatic difference from the rest. I do not think that hockey is a less popular sport than soccer, which reported nearly three times as many injuries. Therefore, I select the final hypothesis as the most likely reason for fewer injuries in hockey, namely, *hockey's players and officials are more safety conscious.*

Supporting Argument for the Thesis

I don't know how many people injured in hockey were in fact wearing protective gear, or how many of the injuries could have been prevented by such gear, so I can't prove that protective gear prevented injuries. I also don't know how many games with injuries were official games following strict rules. After all, a player injured in a neighborhood game can step out whenever he feels like it. Also the word *related* is vague. Does this include bystanders? Is a baseball fan hit in the stands with a baseball included in "baseball-related injuries"?

During the 1994 football game between Atlanta and San Francisco, two players started fighting. Their teams were penalized, but they continued playing. If it had been a hockey game, both players would have been thrown out of the whole game. Since hockey has such a violent reputation, the referees are more strict with brawling players. Finally, I can compare hockey to what I have read about injuries in football. Last year, *Sports Illustrated* ran an article on head injuries in professional football. The magazine pointed out that many injuries could be prevented by changing the rules a little, as well as by putting an extra shell on players' helmets. They cited one player who said that wearing such a shell did not hinder his performance. However, the NFL has not adopted these suggestions, which seems to indicate my theory is correct: there are fewer injuries in hockey because its players and officials are more safety conscious.

Used with permission of Shamma Boyarin.

Scoring for Working from Facts to Inferences to Hypotheses

1. Minimum of two pages.   10 points
2. Title includes questions your   10 points
   hypothesis seeks to answer.
3. Group of related facts listed taken   10 points
   from identified source.
4. Imaginative list of (more than   20 points
   three) inferences that could be
   drawn from these facts.
5. Further facts needed to determine   10 points
   reliability of hypotheses listed.
6. Adequate support for argument   30 points
   defending hypothesis.
7. No distracting errors of spelling,   10 points
   punctuation, sentence structure.

SUMMARY: INDUCTIVE REASONING

1. Inductive reasoning is the process of thinking that you used in describing a fruit or vegetable in Chapter 1, when you began by not knowing the identity of the object.

2. The inductive method is the same as the scientific method used by Samuel Scudder.

3. Induction reasons from evidence about some members of a class in order to form a conclusion about all members of that class.

4. Induction can be done through sensory observation, enumeration, analogous reasoning, causal reasoning, and from pattern recognition.

5. A conclusion derived through inductive reasoning is called a hypothesis and is always less certain than the evidence itself.

6. Inductive reasoning is used as a method for obtaining information when it would be impossible to examine all the data available. This is done by taking statistical samplings or by making extrapolations.

7. The five basic rules for evaluating the reliability of hypotheses based on statistical samplings are as follows:

   (a) The greater the size of the sample, the greater is its probability of being representative of the whole of a class.

   (b) A sampling must be representative in order to lead to reliable results.

   (c) One counterexample can refute a generalization arrived at through inductive reasoning.

   (d) Statistical evidence should be offered in sufficient detail for verification.

   (e) When evaluating the results of polls, it is important to examine both the polling agency and the polling question for bias.

Quiz: Inductive Reasoning

Rate the following statements as *true* or *false*. Justify your answers.

_____ 1. Inductive reasoning is also known as the scientific method.

_____ 2. You know that some fish with sharp teeth are predatory. You have to decide quickly whether the fish swimming around you with sharp teeth might also be predatory. Your decision will be based on what is known as analogous reasoning.

_____ 3. You could use inductive reasoning to put together a picture puzzle if all the pieces were available, even if there were no box cover to show what the whole picture would look like when it was finished.

_____ 4. There is a contest to guess how many gumballs are in a jar. You can use inductive reasoning to figure this out.

_____ 5. Inductive reasoning could help you cook a new dish by carefully following instructions from a cookbook.

_____ 6. Inductive reasoning can extrapolate reliable predictions from only one or two examples of a phenomenon.

_____ 7. Counterexamples can test or refute theories or generalizations.

_____ 8. A hypothesis is a theory that can lead to new facts and discoveries, but the hypothesis itself is not a certainty.

_____ 9. Statistical evidence is always reliable regardless of the attitudes of the people who research and present the information.

_____ 10. *USA Today* conducted a random survey of 1,217 people in one week and found that 43 percent said the United States could win a nuclear war. This finding shows us that the United States could win a nuclear war.

FALLACIES OF INDUCTIVE REASONING

In studying the material and completing the exercises in the first part of this chapter, you developed some standards for inductive reasoning and saw some examples of fallacious inductive reasoning. Now we will more clearly define some of the fallacies to which inductive reasoning is subject:

1. the hasty generalization
2. the either-or fallacy
3. the questionable statistic
4. inconsistencies and contradictions
5. the loaded question
6. the false analogy
7. false cause
8. the slippery slope

The Hasty Generalization

The hasty generalization is the fallacy that occurs most often in inductive reasoning. A hasty generalization is a conclusion reached prematurely without sufficient study of the evidence. Often the haste is motivated by feelings too strong to allow for a fair and objective survey of the data.

1. I waited half an hour for him to get dressed. All men are really more vain than women.
2. Everyone that I talked to in my neighborhood said that they had guns. This whole town is armed.

In these two cases, the sampling was too small to justify the conclusions made. Seen objectively, the irrationality of such claims is self-evident, yet in the heat of conviction, they can carry some persuasiveness.

Sometimes hasty generalizations are based on biased or careless interpretations of the data: "I read recently in a survey of medical students that it cost them, on the average, $30,000 each to get through medical school. This means that only the wealthy can still make it into the medical profession." This is a hasty generalization because there is no data about the financial status of the students and no information about the percentage who have scholarships or loans. An assumption is made and the data interpreted to fit the assumption.

To avoid hasty generalizations, be very careful in your use of the words *all, every, everyone,* and *no.* These are all *quantifiers.* Test to see if what you actually mean are the *qualifiers* such as *in this case, in some cases,* or *it appears* or *seems* or *suggests that*. A careful use of quantifiers and qualifiers can often make the difference between an accurate statement and a fallacious one.

Class Discussion

Which of the following are hasty generalizations?

1. Most poor black people who live in cities are anti-Semitic. That's because their landlords are Jewish.

2. Every woman in the military that I ever met was a lesbian. They are all either lesbians or about to become lesbians.

3. Because Asian students are now becoming the majority ethnic group accepted for math and science studies into West Coast graduate schools, this suggests that Asians may be either genetically gifted in abstract thinking and/or culturally encouraged in it.

4. "Americans like to feel that they are leaders—particularly in areas of science and social programs. Yet a recently released National Academy of Sciences report tells us that we are decades behind Europe in the development of contraceptives. . . . Europeans have many more forms of birth control available, including contraceptive implants, injectable contraceptives and other approaches that are easier to use, work longer and fail less often." (*San Francisco Chronicle*, February 15, 1990)

The Either-Or Fallacy, or False Dilemma

An argument that presumes that there are only two ways of looking at a situation—or that only one of two choices can be made—when actually other alternatives do exist, is guilty of the either-or fallacy, or false dilemma. Sometimes these false dilemmas appear in those frustrating questions on personality assessment tests:

1. When you see a friend coming toward you on the sidewalk, do you rush forward to greet the person or do you cross to the other side of the street?

2. Do you act impulsively rather than deliberately?

3. Do you have only a few friends or a large circle of friends?

More often, false dilemmas appear in poll questions: "Are you for or against abortions?" Such questions are convenient for tabulation purposes but do not allow for weighed discriminations that reflect actual opinion. When confronted with either-or questions, a thoughtful person is faced with another dilemma: that of refusing both choices or of compromising with an answer that plays into the questioner's assumption and bias.

The false dilemma is often an assertion of an argument that oversimplifies or seeks to intimidate:

1. Live free or die.
2. America. Love it or leave it.
3. When you have a headache, all you can do is reach for aspirin.
4. Are you with me or against me?
5. When we outlaw guns, only outlaws will have guns.
6. The Cougar convertible: you'll either own one or want one.

In each of these cases, the dilemma is built into the argument, simplifying the situation to fit premeditated terms or assumptions. Sometimes, as in these slogans and commercial appeals, this is an intentional ploy to negate resistance. More often, false dilemmas are based on convictions strong enough to suppress any willingness to think the problem through carefully. To seek to persuade through the use of false dilemmas is to try to force others to agree to an oversimplification.

Here is an example of such an oversimplification: "Mothers of young children can either have careers or stay at home. But they can't expect both to have careers and to raise happy children." This argument is based on many assumptions. The first is that the children are happier with the mother at home. Another is that the father's part is unimportant. And many alternative possibilities are not considered by the speaker. What if a mother has a business in her home? What if she is so successful in her career that she has to work only 10 hours a week? What if she is a single parent who must work but who runs a janitorial service in which her children also work with her? A false dilemma assumes that there is only one choice, when imaginative thought could produce many more options.

Class Discussion

Analyze the false dilemmas just given and offer reasons for your agreement or disagreement with designating them as such.

The Questionable Statistic

Inductive reasoning requires some knowledge of statistics and how statistics can be used or misused as evidence. As you learned earlier, to evaluate whether statistics are used fairly, you need to look for such things as the size of the sample, whether it was representative and random, whether a margin for error was considered, and what the margin was. These are only some of the basics involved in assessing the reliability of statistics. The fallacy of the questionable statistic refers to confusion or deception in the use of statistics, even to the point of citing figures that would be impossible to obtain.

Recall this use of statistics, quoted earlier: "I would guess that the average office female makes 509 visits to the lavatory to a male's 320, and spends 10.7 minutes there to a male's 2.5. What management is going to put up with this 'primp time' featherbedding at equal pay?" In this case, the author is lightly mocking the use of statistics, implying that even if the actual figures are not this exact, everyone knows that his claims are true. But he does not offer either genuine statistics or evidence for his claim of the "primp time featherbedding" motive.

When statistical claims are false or deliberately misleading, they are not always easy to detect unless we have a knowledge of the subject or of the laws of statistics. A sure warning sign is *unattributed figures* or figures given without citing their source, purpose, and methods of calculation.

> Why isn't alcohol illegal? It has the same rate of addiction (10 percent) as cocaine.

In this case, a critical thinker would want to know how *addiction* is being defined, how this figure was derived, who conducted the study, and whether this 10 percent figure was quoted out of context.

Here is another example, also unattributed, with a flashing red light attached:

> Illegal aliens cost American citizens $5 billion a year.

First, the word *cost* is undefined; what expenses does this term cover? Second, "illegal aliens" refers to undocumented immigrants who live underground: how were they found? Whoever made this statement should have been prepared either to answer these questions or not make this claim at all. The figure cited here borders on what is called *an unknowable statistic*.

Here is a clearer example of guesswork:

> If we legalize drugs, drugs would become much cheaper, at least one-fifth the cost. Then five times as many people would buy them. Then we would have five times as many addicts, and instead of 100,000 addicted babies born to addicted mothers each year, we would have a million.

The chief weakness of this argument is that it is based on the assumption that if drugs were legal, they would be less expensive. From there, the figure of "at least one-fifth the cost" seems to be drawn out of a hat. Next are repetitions of *five*, concluding with the dreadful statistic of one million addicted babies. The argument commits the fallacy of the unknowable statistic, not once but four times, seeking to establish as factual guesswork calculations for a hypothetical situation with too many variables and unknowns.

Sometimes it does not take much reasoning to recognize that the statistics quoted could not have been gathered. Consider these examples:

Two-thirds of all thefts are never detected.

One-third of all fires are intentionally set.

Loss in federal taxes from those who barter instead of paying cash for goods is one billion dollars annually.

Class Discussion

What questions would you ask about the statistics used in the following statements?

1. Only 106 of an estimated 895 cases of rape that occurred in New England last year were reported.
2. "If it is elitist to say that 30 percent of the American people are dumb in the sense of uninstructed, then I'm an elitist. But it's true." (William F. Buckley Jr.)
3. It is a known fact that people use only 10 percent of their actual potential.
4. "If the *Roe* v. *Wade* decision remains in force until the beginning of the twenty-first century, our nation will be missing more than 40 million citizens, of whom approximately 8 million would have been men of military age." (from "It's 'Life for a Life'" quoted in "Notes from the Fringe," *Harper's* magazine, June 1985)
5. One-third of all inmates admitted to mental hospitals are pretending insanity, having cleverly fooled everyone, including their doctors.

Inconsistencies and Contradictions

Inconsistencies and contradictions appear in both inductive and deductive reasoning. To say "All men are equal, it is just that some are more equal than others" is to reason deductively with two contradictory premises. In this case, one of the premises has to be false. The following student description of a photo, based on inductive reasoning, contains inconsistencies and contradictions. What observations do you find here that would seem to contradict the conclusion found in the topic sentence?

> This photograph shows two students seated on a bench reading in a school library, while in the foreground a woman bends down on the floor to change her baby's diapers. A stack of books about yoga appears on a bench to her right. She must have put them down there on her way to the checkout counter. One

curious thing is that all the library books appear to be new paperbacks, and none have call numbers written on their spines.

In this example the writer has backed herself into a corner. How can she explain a library of all new paperbacks uncoded for shelving or borrowing purposes? And isn't it unusual for a student to bring her baby with her to a school library? And do most libraries have benches by the shelves for browsing? These inconsistencies should at least challenge her to reconsider her hypothesis that the photograph shows a school library. Doing this, of course, would mean throwing out a carefully worded paragraph and starting all over again. But exercising such discipline in the name of truth is what it takes both in science and good writing. Thus, an alert response to contradictions can lead us to truth.

Contradictions often appear in political reasoning. Sometimes they can be detected within statements, sometimes between different articles or speeches, and sometimes between statements and actions. If you want to please as many people as possible, discrepancies often become the consequence. Here are two examples of contradictions within statements:

1. "Of course I cannot approve of hecklers disrupting my opponent's speeches. However, I would also say that in a democracy, they also have the right to be heard as much as the speaker."

2. "At present the administration is gently prodding Israel toward peace talks with Jordanian and Palestinian negotiators. U.S. officials are trying to clear the way for a $1 billion U.S. arms sale to Jordan for advanced fighter planes, anti-aircraft defenses, and other military equipment. The arms sale has been made contingent on Jordan's agreement not to use them except in self-defense."

The first example illustrates what is more commonly known as double-talk. Obviously, in a democracy no one can be heard if speakers are capriciously interrupted by others. This is also known as the fallacy of misapplied generalization: all people who want to speak should be allowed to speak in a democracy. Hecklers are people who want to speak. Therefore, hecklers should be permitted to (prevent others from speaking in order to) speak themselves.

The second example describes foreign policy decisions that seem to run counter to one another's purposes. The reader wonders how the United States can persuade Israel to agree to peace when the United States has already announced its intention to arm Jordan, Israel's neighboring adversary, with a billion dollars' worth of military equipment. One wonders how the United States can expect to exercise any control over Jordan's interpretation of the word *self-defense*. And finally, one wonders what the U.S. government is doing in the weapons sales business.

Class Discussion

List the contradictions you find in the following examples.

1. I love mankind, it's just that I can't stand people.

2. "The Nuclear Regulatory Commission has imposed strict penalties for employees at nuclear plants found to be stoned from illicit drug use on the job; but no penalties were prescribed for workers discovered to be drunk at the nuclear controls. Asked about the more lenient approach to alcohol, an NRC spokesman said: 'The implications are less horrendous.' But a meltdown by any other name . . ." (David Freudberg, KCBS Radio, February 16, 1990)

3. "China will no longer classify as secret the new national laws that local citizens and foreigners are obliged to obey, China's official newspapers reported yesterday." (*New York Times*, November 9, 1989)

4. "Capital punishment is our society's recognition of the sanctity of human life." (Sen. Orrin Hatch, R-Utah)

5. "The more killing and homicides you have, the more havoc it prevents." (Richard M. Daley, mayor of Chicago)

The Loaded Question

Loaded questions occur often in polls, as discussed earlier, in order to create a bias toward a certain answer: "Do you believe pornography should be brought into every home through television?" We are all familiar with the loaded questions "Have you stopped beating your wife?" and "Are you still a heavy drinker?" In such cases, the guilt is assumed and not proven, and a reply to the question traps the respondent into either an admission of guilt or a protest that could be interpreted as a guilty defense. Loaded questions are related to the fallacy of circular reasoning (begging the question), where conclusions are asserted without evidence or premises to support them.

Class Discussion

Which of the following are loaded questions and which are not?

1. What can we each do to end the spread of violence in America?
2. Where did you hide the murder weapon?
3. When are you going to stop asking me so many silly questions?
4. Are you going to be good and do what I say?
5. Do you want to see America destroyed by corporate take-overs?

6. What do you think about the new brain research that says that emotional stability is more important than IQ in determining success in life?

7. Forty-three percent of U.S. grade school children are reading below grade level. Why? Is this because they are not learning phonics?

8. Do you feel honest, law-abiding citizens have the right to defend themselves with a firearm if their lives are in danger?

9. Would you hand over to the secretary of the treasury, or to some other unelected bureaucrat, your constitutional right to own guns?

The False Analogy

As you learned earlier, an analogy is a form of reasoning in which two things are compared to one another and shown to have a ratio. (The word from which *analogy* is derived, the Greek *analogos*, means according to ratio.) A good analogy often compares some abstract principle that is difficult to understand to a concrete familiar experience in order to make the abstract principle clearer. A good or sound analogy must compare two things or ideas that have major parallels in the aspects under consideration. If one uses the analogy of a pump to explain the heart, the heart does not have to physically look like a metal pump with a handle, but it should at least function on the same principles. Here is an analogy taken from physics about the nature of subatomic particles: "If you wish to understand subatomic particles, think of them as empty space that is distorted, pinched up, concentrated into pointlike ripples of energy." Here the appearance is the essential parallel that permits a visualization of something invisible to us.

In a false analogy, however, important differences that may invalidate the "logic" of the analogy are either overlooked or willfully disregarded. How do we identify a false analogy? A recommended technique is to first write out the equation that the analogy offers and then list characteristics of the compared items in two columns headed Similarities and Differences. Study the following example:

> *Claim*: "There is no convincing evidence to show that cigarette smoking is harmful. Too much of anything is harmful. Too much applesauce is harmful." (cigarette manufacturer)
>
> *Equation*: too much cigarette smoking = too much applesauce

When we see the equation, we sense that something is not right here. For a further check, make a list of the similarities and differences between each. If the differences far outweigh the similarities, you have a false analogy.

Similarities	Differences
1. ingested into body	1. one ingested through lungs first and is not digestible
	2. one a food, other not a food
	3. one addictive, other not
	4. both don't affect body and consciousness in same way
	5. no evidence applesauce causes cancer, but evidence that cigarette smoking does

Discovery Exercise

Evaluating Analogies

Use the procedure just demonstrated to analyze the analogies that follow:

1. "There are no grounds for the claim that the incidence of lung cancer is higher in this county because of the presence of our oil refineries. Cancer can be caused by all kinds of things. People don't stop eating peanut butter because it causes cancer, do they?" (biologist working for an oil refinery)

2. Who is the endangered species? The spotted owl or the loggers of the Northwest?

3. We welcome immigrants because our country needs them the way old soil needs new seeds.

4. Nature is cruel. It is our right to be cruel as well. (Adolf Hitler)

Class Discussion

Rate the following examples as either good analogies or false analogies and tell why:

1. Drug testing of employees could be an infringement of civil liberties but is necessary for the preservation of law and order. For the sake of survival, we often have to agree to the invasion of privacy and to limitations on free speech. Baggage and passengers must pass through metal detectors before boarding aircrafts. It is illegal to joke about explosives or guns when passing through security to board an airplane.

2. "People and politicians, who really . . . don't know enough about the issue of acid rain have been brainwashed by the media and environmentalists into believing that we, in Ohio, are the primary cause of the decay. The biggest killers of human life in the U.S. are automobiles, cigarettes and alcohol. Yet none of these products have been banned.

Americans, and no Americans more than we in the coal fields, want to see a healthy and safe environment for all generations to come, but we just cannot accept legislation such as this without a scientific basis." (Rep. Douglas Applegate, D-Ohio, speaking against a House bill to require federally mandated emission limitations on the largest sources of sulphur dioxide)

3. "If you take a piece of meat and throw it in a pack of hungry dogs, they are going to kill each other over it. If you don't have any opportunities available to you, and something that can make you easy money [selling crack cocaine] comes up, what are you going to do?" (Paris, Oakland rap artist)

4. Measuring a country's health by measuring its gross domestic product is rather like measuring a person's health by how much medical care he buys. Thus, a person who just had bypass surgery and cancer radiation treatments would be considered healthy.

False Cause

Inductive reasoning is used to speculate about cause or to determine cause. The criminal justice system uses inductive reasoning to gather evidence to determine guilt or innocence. Faulty reasoning about causality can result in the arrest and conviction of an innocent person or the release of a guilty person. A trial presents evidence to the jury as support for causality in a crime.

False cause is a fallacious argument that insists on a causal connection between events that cannot reasonably be connected, or that interprets causation in an oversimplistic manner. Sometimes false cause reasoning can be ludicrous, as may be seen in the little Sufi teaching stories about Nasrudin excerpted here. These old stories, designed to provoke and teach good thinking habits, are best when read aloud. Read them now, and discuss how the fallacy of false cause appears in each instance:

Nasrudin was throwing handfuls of crumbs around his house.
"What are you doing?" someone asked him.
"Keeping the tigers away."
"But there are no tigers in these parts."
"That's right. Effective, isn't it?"

"When I was in the desert," said Nasrudin one day, "I caused an entire tribe of horrible and bloodthirsty Bedouins to run."
"However did you do it?"
"Easy. I just ran, and they ran after me."

Two men were quarrelling outside Nasrudin's window at dead of night. Nasrudin got up, wrapped his only blanket around himself, and ran out to try to stop the noise. When he tried to reason with the drunks, one snatched his blanket and both ran away.

Used with permission of Chronicle Features.

> "What were they arguing about?" asked his wife when he went in.
> "It must have been the blanket. When they got that, the fight broke up."

From Idries Shah, *The Exploits of the Incomparable Mulla Nasrudin*. New York: Dutton, 1972. Reprinted with permission of The Octagon Press, Ltd., London.

Blaming the wrong target is one kind of false cause. More frequent are those false causes that vastly oversimplify a situation, such as scapegoating. The term *scapegoating* refers to the ancient practice of offering ritual sacrifices for the appeasement of some god or some person or persons. Although we may now think sacrificing maidens on altars to the gods is barbaric, scapegoating rituals still abound in our personal, political, and social lives. In this Toles cartoon, we see the absurdity of blaming and punishing one person for TV violence.

Another version of false cause is known in Latin as *post hoc ergo propter hoc*, meaning "after this, therefore because of this." The post hoc fallacy reasons in a childlike way that because one event happened after another event, the second was caused by the first.

> First my cat ate a mouse, and then she got the measles. The mouse gave her the measles.

Used with permission of the Universal Press Syndicate.
© 1994 *The Buffalo News*.

The court decided that since he ate Twinkies before he committed the crime, he could not help himself.

Sometimes arguments center around causal reasoning that debates the question of what came first: the chicken or the egg? Nasrudin, in the excerpts, had the capacity to confuse us with his own confusion, as in making his running away from the Bedouins the cause of their running after him. Sometimes we find arguments that propound both the chicken and the egg position about causality, as in these two:

> The violence on the home screen follows the violence in our lives. (Del Reisman, president, Writers Guild of America)

> [Violence on TV is definitely a cause of the growing violence in our lives.] It presents violence as an appropriate way to solve interpersonal problems, to get what you want out of life, avenge slights and insults and make up for perceived injustices. (Leonard D. Eron, professor of psychology)

Finally, all the examples of causal reasoning discussed here could be questioned for their assumption that causality is linear, with one effect always resulting from one cause. More recently, science has begun to use *systems thinking* to study causality in a manner that is ecological, taking the widest perspective of context, interrelated parts, and cycles. Systems thinking recognizes how the wolf's predator role is actually essential to the health of the deer. Systems thinking sees the folly of attempting to protect the deer by killing off the wolves, which leads in turn to an overpopulation of the deer, overgrazing, and eventually mass deer starvation. Systems thinking avoids the fallacious reasoning that results from the assumption and insistence on linear causality.

Class Discussion

False or questionable cause is a fallacy that is often found in political arguments. Analyze the following statements. Decide if you agree or disagree that they are examples of the fallacy of false cause and state why.

1. "As a white nation, we wish to survive in freedom in our own fatherland, and we demand to be governed by our own people. South Africa must retain the fatherland given us by God." (Andries P. Treurnicht, leader, far-right conservative party, South Africa; speech reported in *Los Angeles Times*, May 28, 1986)

2. The corruption of American youth has been caused by rock and roll music. Its rhythms and lyrics, together with the role models provided by its singers and musicians, have encouraged experimentation with drugs and promiscuity.

3. Malnutrition has been largely eliminated in China, which is quite an achievement for a country that supports one in five of humankind. This has been accomplished by intensive land use, the recycling of wastes, widespread irrigation, and abundant human labor.

4. Americans buy Japanese cars, cameras, and stereos because they are unpatriotic. An ad campaign appealing to their patriotism could reverse this trend.

5. State-sponsored affirmative action, bilingual education, and multiculturalism are promoting dangerous levels of ethnic group tensions and conflicts.

The Slippery Slope

The slippery slope is another fallacy that deals with causation. In this case the claim is made that permitting one event to occur would set off an uncontrollable chain reaction. In politics this is also called the domino theory: if one country falls, so will all the rest like a line of dominoes. This argument was often given as a reason that the United States should stay in Vietnam: if Vietnam fell to the communists, China would take over the rest of Asia.

The same argument was also cited for the U.S. presence in El Salvador: if El Salvador fell to the guerrillas, so would all of Central America and Mexico, thus jeopardizing the whole Western hemisphere. Although these were predictions of a possible scenario, as arguments they were fallacious in that they urged agreement on the basis of logic for a position that contained many variables and unknowns.

Here are three examples of arguments built on the fallacy of the slippery slope:

1. If you offer people unemployment insurance, they will become lazy and expect the government to support them for life.

2. Sex education in the schools leads to promiscuity, unwanted pregnancies, and cheating in marriages.

3. "If you teach critical thinking in an Indian university, the young people would go home and question, then disobey their parents. Their families would quarrel and break up. Then they would question their bosses and everyone else. The next thing you know the whole country would fall apart." (comment made by a University of Bombay professor)

Class Discussion

Which of the following arguments are slippery slopes?

1. The U.S. Constitution guarantees the right to bear arms. It doesn't spell out what type of armed weapons—it says "the right to bear arms." If the legislators start with the banning of assault weapons, where will it end? One day it might be illegal to own a knife. If our rights are taken away one by one, we are really no better off than in a communist state with Big Brother looking over our shoulder at every move we make.

2. "A widely acclaimed and disturbing study out of the University of Vermont has shown a 'decline in emotional aptitude among children across the board.' Rich and poor, East Coast or West Coast, inner city or suburb, children today are more vulnerable than ever to anger, depression, anxiety—a massive emotional malaise. The result is that boys who can't control their emotions later commit violent crime; girls who can't control emotion don't get violent, they get pregnant." (Daniel Goleman, author of *Emotional Intelligence*. New York: Bantam, 1995)

BUILDING ARGUMENTS

INDUCTION

The first of May 1779, the troops under General John Sullivan commenced their march but did not arrive at Wyoming until the middle of June. . . .

The village was immediately set on fire, and the rich fields of corn were cut down and trodden underfoot. On the first of September, the army left the river, and struck across the wilderness. . . .

Once or twice the Indians threatened to make a stand for their homes, but soon fled in despair, and the army had its own way. The capital of the Senecas, a town consisting of sixty houses, surrounded by beautiful cornfields and orchards, was burned to the ground and the harvest destroyed. . . . The fourth day it reached a beautiful region, then, almost wholly unknown to the white man. . . . As the weary columns slowly emerged from the dark forest and filed into this open space . . . they seemed suddenly to be transported into an Eden.

The tall, ripe grass bent before the wind—cornfield on cornfield, as far as eye could reach waved in the sun—orchards that had been growing for generations, were weighted down under a profusion of fruit—cattle grazed on the banks of a river, and all was luxuriance and beauty. . . . All about were scattered a hundred and twenty-eight houses—not miserable huts huddled together, but large airy buildings, situated in the most pleasant spots, surrounded by fruit trees, and exhibiting a civilization on the part of the Indians never before witnessed.

Soon after sunrise immense columns of smoke began to rise the length and breadth of the valley, and in a short time the whole settlement was wrapped

SUMMARY: FALLACIES OF INDUCTIVE REASONING

1. Hasty generalization is the fallacy of basing a conclusion on insufficient evidence.

2. The either-or fallacy, or false dilemma, is an argument that oversimplifies a situation, asserting that there are only two choices, when actually other alternatives exist.

3. The questionable statistic is the statistic that is either unknowable or highly suspect.

in flame, from limit to limit; and before night those one hundred and twenty-eight houses were a heap of ashes. The grain had been gathered into them, and thus both were destroyed together. The orchards were cut down, the cornfields uprooted, and the cattle butchered and left to rot on the plain. A scene of desolation took the place of the scene of beauty, and the army camped that night in a desert.

The next day, having accomplished the object of their mission, Sullivan commenced a homeward march. . . . The thanks of Congress was presented to Sullivan and his army for the manner in which they had fulfilled their arduous task. (Joel Tyler Headley, *Washington and His Generals*, 1859 [an account of the 1779 tragedy of Cherry Valley and Wyoming in New York State when President George Washington ordered troops to secure the frontier against the Iroquois in case they should be influenced by the English to attack Americans])

Exercise

1. Is this a neutral report? Is it an inductive argument?
2. Does the choice of words suggest the author's sympathy was more on the side of the Indians?
3. Does the author draw a conclusion about the significance of this event or does he leave it up to the reader?
4. Do you think he is using irony in the last sentence?
5. Tell a story that is an inductive argument. Your conclusion can be stated, implied, or left up to the reader.

4. Inconsistency in evidence is the fallacy of offering evidence that contradicts the conclusion.

5. The loaded question is the use of a biased question that seeks to obtain a predetermined answer.

6. The false analogy is a comparison of two things that have some similarities but also significant differences, which are ignored for the sake of the argument.

7. False cause is the fallacy of insisting on a causal connection between events without reasonable evidence to support the claim.

8. The slippery slope is the fallacy of claiming that permitting one event to occur would lead to a chain reaction that could not be stopped. It urges agreement on the basis of logic for a position that involves many variables or unknowns.

PROBLEM SOLVING

INDUCTIVE REASONING

He had just been graduated from college. . . . In the long summer afternoons, he sits in the orchard which still stands near the old gray stone house; on one memorable day, an apple falls with a slight thud at his feet. It was a trifling incident which has been idly noticed thousands of times; but now, like the click of some small switch which starts a great machine in operation, it proved to be the job which awoke his mind to action. As in a vision, he saw that if the mysterious pull of the earth can act through space as far as the top of a tree, of a mountain, and even to a bird soaring high in the air, or to the clouds, so it might even reach so far as the moon.

Questions

1. What problem did Newton solve?
2. How did he go about it?
3. Explain how he used inductive reasoning and a hypothesis.

From L. T. More, *Isaac Newton: A Biography*. New York: Scribner's, 1934.

Quiz: Fallacies of Inductive Reasoning

Identify the following arguments either as *NF* for *not fallacious* or by the name of one of the fallacies of inductive reasoning covered in this chapter.

_____   1. All riders on the buses in a Boston suburb now pay for their rides with special credit cards. All buses are equipped with electronic scanners that record account number, route, time, and date. The American public is being conditioned for the complete Big Brother totalitarian surveillance of the future.

_____   2. When survivors emerged from the earthquake ruins, they said the quake was due to the anger of the gods.

_____   3. "Any regulations that dampen corporate profits in the oil and coal industries will backfire because environmental preservation depends heavily on the health of the U.S. economy. The richer the U.S. is, the more it can help poorer countries with their pollution problems." (representative of a coalition for oil and coal users)

_____   4. A woman college graduate can expect, over a lifetime, to make $1,600,000 less than her male counterpart.

_____ 5. Is it raining outside today?

_____ 6. "More than any other time in history, mankind faces a crossroads. One path leads to despair and utter hopelessness. The other, to total extinction. Let us pray we have the wisdom to choose correctly." (Woody Allen, "My Speech to the Graduates")

_____ 7. Are you still getting into the movies without paying?

_____ 8. You can either be an artist or make money but not both.

_____ 9. I want a pleasant, quiet place to study.

_____ 10. Are you still fooling around with that guy?

_____ 11. My wife left me with the kids; which goes to show you, all women are no good!

_____ 12. People shouldn't allow their children to read books written by cult leaders any more than they should allow them to eat contaminated food.

_____ 13. The reason that we lost the war in Vietnam was because of the treasonous protests going on here at home.

_____ 14. If the baseball players start using drugs, then so will the managers, and the next thing you know all the games will be fixed and baseball will no longer be a real American sport.

_____ 15. One of the major causes for the rapid growth of the European population in the 19th century was the improvement of medical knowledge.

_____ 16. Inmates at the county jail grow 120 tons of produce each year from their organic garden. Although this food is given away to soup kitchens and sold to gourmet restaurants, the prisoners are not allowed to eat any of the garden-fresh food themselves. When the inmates asked to have their usual canned, frozen, and dried food diets supplemented with their garden vegetables, they were informed by the director of food services that the jail kitchens were not set up for the preparation of fresh food. He added, however, that from time to time some of the garden vegetables were obtained for the staff dining room at the jail.

_____ 17. "Is two months' salary too much to spend for something that lasts forever?" (ad for diamonds)

_____ 18. I was turned down in two job interviews. I guess I just don't have what it takes.

_____ 19. The cause of the failure of the banks is the lack of faith of the American people in them.

_____ 20. Women, like rugs, need a good beating occasionally.

Composition Writing Application

Detecting Fallacies in an Argument

This is an assignment that you can begin now and complete when you have finished the fallacies of deductive reasoning in the next chapter.

So far, you have been examining fallacies in examples abstracted from the context in which they appear. The purpose of this assignment is to give you the opportunity to search for fallacies in an argument, to extract them, and to discuss the manner in which they affect the argument as a whole. This is a research assignment. *You will need to find a short argument: a good source for short arguments that often contain fallacies is letters to editors.* Comb newspapers and magazines for your choice, and photocopy it to accompany your analysis. Your parameters will be as follows:

1. *Topic*: Fallacies in an argument.
2. *Approach*: Critical analysis.
3. *Form*: Exposition and argumentation. Identify the fallacies involved and explain whether they affect or do not affect the soundness of the argument.
4. *Length*: Two typed pages, plus a one-page photocopy of the argument.

Reading

THE FAILURE OF OBJECTIVITY

William Broad
Nicholas Wade

How many of you have been told that your intelligence was a fixed, inherited trait and that there was little you could do to change it? This erroneous idea, which held sway over American and British education for decades, was based on a fraudulent study. How Sir Cyril Burt misused the scientific method to make his claim, and how scientific method was used to uncover fraudulence in Burt's research, is the subject of this excerpt. Both authors work for the *New York Times*. Broad is a science reporter, and Wade is an editorial writer.*

Cyril Burt, one of the pioneers of applied psychology in England, was a man of   1
brilliance and great culture. He became professor of psychology at University College, London, and was the first psychologist to receive a knighthood for his services.

*Notes to the original reading have not been included here.

The American Psychological Association gave him its Thorndike prize in 1971, the first time that the high honor had been awarded to a foreigner. When he died, the same year, the obituaries proclaimed him "Britain's most eminent educational psychologist" and even "dean of the world's psychologists." "Everything about the man," wrote Arthur Jensen of Stanford University, "—his fine, sturdy appearance; his aura of vitality; his urbane manner; his unflagging enthusiasm for research, analysis and criticism; . . . and, of course, especially his notably sharp intellect and vast erudition—all together leave a total impression of immense quality, of a born nobleman."

But the man who impressed Jensen with his nobility of intellect possessed a 2 grievous intellectual flaw: he was a cheat. He invented data out of whole cloth to support his own theories and confound his critics. He used his mastery of statistics and gift of lucid exposition to bamboozle alike his bitterest detractors and those who acclaimed his greatness as a psychologist.

What was more remarkable still, Burt attained a great part of his eminence in 3 the field of IQ testing not because of any thoroughgoing program of research, of which he did little worth the name, but through his skills of *rhetoric*. If a real scientist is one who wants to discover the truth, Burt was no scientist, because he already knew the truth. He used the scientific method with great effect, but not as an approach to understanding the world. In Burt's hands the scientific method can be seen most clearly for its utility as a purely rhetorical device, a method of argument with which to assume a position of moral superiority, to pretend to greater learning or diligence. According to his biographer L. S. Hearnshaw, "He was fond of accusing his opponents of basing their criticisms 'not on any fresh evidence or new researches of their own, but chiefly on armchair articles from general principles.' 'My co-workers and I,' on the other hand, were engaged in on-going research. It was a powerful argument with which to belabor the environmentalists; but to sustain it there had to be co-workers, and these co-workers had to be currently engaged in data collection." But there were no new data, and no co-workers. The lonely and embattled Burt sat in his armchair, summoned both data and co-workers from the vasty deep of his tormented imagination, and clothed them so well in the semblance of scientific argument that the illusion fooled all his fellow scientists for as much as thirty years.

Burt's work was influential, in different ways, on both sides of the Atlantic. In 4 England, he served as a consultant to a series of blue-ribbon committees that restructured the English educational system after the Second World War. The crux of the new system was a test applied to children at the age of eleven, the results of which determined their assignment to a higher- or lower-quality education. The 11+ exam, as it was called, was based on the assumption that a child's educability and future potential can fairly be assessed at that age. Burt cannot be held responsible for the 11+ exam, which was the decision of many people, but his persuasive insistence that intelligence is more than 75 percent a fixed, inherited ability was certainly influential in shaping the climate of opinion among English educators from which the 11+ was born.

The 11+ exam and the selective system of education that was based on it 5 began to come under heavy attack in the 1950's, after Burt had retired from his professorship at University College, London. To defend his theory against the critics, Burt started to publish a series of articles in which striking new evidence for the hereditarian view was produced. The new evidence, Burt explained, had mostly been gathered during the 1920's and 1930's when he was the psychologist for the London school system. It had been updated with the help of his co-workers, Miss Margaret Howard and Miss J. Conway. The pearl of Burt's impressive IQ data was that derived from separated identical twins, the largest single such collection in the world. With the same heredity but different environments, separated identical twins afford uniquely ideal subjects for testing the interplay of the two effects on intelligence. Burt's data on twins and other kinship relations "were widely quoted, widely accepted as valid, and were among the strongest piece of evidence for the preponderantly genetic determination of intelligence," says Hearnshaw.

In 1969, after the 11+ had been abolished and England's selective education 6 replaced with a comprehensive system, Burt published an article purporting to document a decline in educational standards. The intention of the article was clearly to influence educational policy.

Meanwhile, the authority and crispness of Burt's new twin data was attracting 7 the eager attention of hereditarian psychologists in the United States. Arthur Jensen made considerable use of Burt's findings in his 1969 article in the *Harvard Educational Review*, a furiously debated tract in which he argued that since the genetic factor determines 80 percent of intelligence, programs of compensatory education addressed to lower-class black and white children were useless and should be scrapped. Burt's twin data were relied on even more heavily by Richard Herrnstein of Harvard in his September 1971 article in *The Atlantic* arguing that social class is based in part on inherited differences in intelligence. "The measurement of intelligence," the Harvard psychologist proclaimed in his widely influential article, "is psychology's most telling accomplishment to date." Pride of place was given to Burt's twin studies.

When Burt died in October 1971, at the age of eighty-eight, his theories were 8 at the peak of their influence in the United States, even if educational policy in Britain had turned away from them. His oeuvre crumbled only after his death, and the collapse was quite sudden, because the edifice was a mere façade of scholarship. The man who had eyes to see the emperor's outrageous state of undress was Leon Kamin, a Princeton University psychologist who had never ventured into the IQ field until a student urged him to read one of Burt's papers in 1972. "The immediate conclusion I came to after 10 minutes of reading was that Burt was a fraud," says Kamin.

Kamin noticed first that Burt's papers are largely innocent of the elementary 9 trappings of scholarship, such as precise details of who had administered what tests to which children and when. This peculiar vagueness is evident in Burt's first major summary of his IQ and kinship studies, an article published in 1943, and continues thereafter. But in Burt's twin studies, Kamin spotted something much more serious.

Burt published the first full report on the IQ of his separated identical twins in   10
1955, when he claimed to have located twenty-one pairs. A second report in 1958
mentioned "over 30" pairs, and the final accounting in 1966 cited fifty-three pairs,
by far the largest collection in the world. The correlation between the IQ scores of
the separated twins, Kamin noticed, was given as 0.771—*in all three studies.* For a
correlation coefficient to remain unchanged, to three decimal places, while new
members are added to the sample on two occasions, is highly improbable. But it
was not the only case. The correlation in IQ of identical twins reared together stuck
at 0.944 through three sample sizes. All together there were twenty such coinci-
dences in a table of sixty correlations. Kamin summarized his study of Burt's work
in a book published in 1974. His review was biting, ironic, and devastating. He
concluded, in words that will always be part of the history of psychometrics, "The
absence of procedural description in Burt's reports vitiates their scientific utility. . . .
The marvelous consistency of his data supporting the hereditarian position often
taxes credibility; and on analysis, the data are found to contain implausible effects
consistent with an effort to prove the hereditarian case. The conclusion cannot be
avoided. The numbers left behind by Professor Burt are simply not worthy of our
current scientific attention. . . ."

Despite the unchallenged statements published by Kamin and Jensen two   11
years earlier, the actual charge of fraud evoked spasms of indignation from psychologists on both sides of the Atlantic. The very suggestion, said Herrnstein, "is so
outrageous that I find it hard to stay in my chair. Burt was a towering figure of 20th
century psychology. I think it is a crime to cast such doubt over a man's career."
Hans Eysenck, a leading IQ expert at the Institute of Psychiatry in London, wrote to
Burt's sister that the whole affair "is just a determined effort on the part of some
very left-wing environmentalists determined to play a political game with scientific
facts. I am sure the future will uphold the honour and integrity of Sir Cyril without
any question."

In effect, the task of deciding exactly what had gone wrong was left to Leslie   12
Hearnshaw, professor of psychology at the University of Liverpool. Hearnshaw, an
admirer of Burt's, had given the eulogy at his funeral, as a result of which he had
been commissioned by Burt's sister to write a biography. To his growing amazement as he continued his research, Hearnshaw found that Burt had indeed invented
data in several of his crucial papers. "As I read Burt's correspondence I was surprised, and shocked, by his contradictions and demonstrable lies—lies which were
not benign, but clearly cover-ups," Hearnshaw says. The evidence from Burt's detailed personal diaries showed that he had not carried out the research he claimed
to have done. "The verdict must be, therefore, that at any rate in three instances,
beyond reasonable doubt, Burt was guilty of deception," his official biographer
concluded.

Published in 1979, Hearnshaw's study of Burt is a sympathetic and subtly   13
drawn portrait. It shows a man of great gifts, but with a pathological streak in his
character that found expression in his jealous treatment of critics, rivals, and even
former students. Introverted, private, ambitious, there was a duality in Burt's nature

that allowed his talents to be bent to demeaning ends. His twin data are at least partly spurious, Hearnshaw believes, because he could not have added twins to his collection after his retirement in 1950, yet the papers of 1958 and 1966 state this to be the case. Burt may once have worked with the elusive Misses Conway and Howard, but not in this period: he had no co-workers and did no research. For the same reason, his paper of 1969 purporting to document a decline in educational standards over the period 1914 to 1965 must also be fictitious, at least in part. The third case of proven falsification, in Hearnshaw's view, lies in Burt's claim to have invented the technique of factor analysis. Although Kamin suspects that possibly everything Burt did was fraudulent, right from his first research paper in 1909, Hearnshaw believes that the earliest work there is any reason to doubt dates from 1943. "From 1943 onwards Burt's research reports must be regarded with suspicion," he concludes.

"The gifts which made Burt an effective applied psychologist," observes   14
Hearnshaw, ". . . militated against his scientific work. Neither by temperament nor by training was he a scientist. He was overconfident, too much in a hurry, too eager for final results, too ready to adjust and paper over, to be a good scientist. His work often had the appearance of science, but not always the substance." How could a man who had only the appearance of being a scientist rise to the height of his academic profession, to the senior chair of psychology in Britain? If science is a self-policing, self-correcting community of scholars, always checking one another's work with rigorous and impartial skepticism, how could Burt get so far and stay undetected for so long?

If Burt's fraud is taken as starting in 1943, he remained undetected for thirty-   15
one years, until Kamin's book of 1974. For psychology as a discipline, the point is not so much that the fraud itself passed unnoticed, but that the glaring procedural and statistical errors—there for whatever reason—were not picked up earlier. During the sixteen years that Burt was editor of the *British Journal of Statistical Psychology*, numerous articles signed by pseudonyms (such as Conway) appeared and in unmistakably Burtian style heaped praise on Burt and criticism of his opponents. At least from 1969 onward, his data occupied a central position in controversy, in a subject that is presumably no less rigorous than other disciplines. Why did journal editors and referees not require that he report his results in scientific form? Why did scholars reading his papers not spot the flaws? . . .

The most plausible answer . . . is that many scientific communities do not   16
behave in the way they are supposed to. Science is not self-policing. Scholars do not always read the scientific literature carefully. Science is not a perfectly objective process. Dogma and prejudice, when suitably garbed, creep into science just as easily as into any other human enterprise, and maybe more easily since their entry is unexpected. Burt, with the mere appearance of being a scientist, worked his way to the top of the academic ladder, to a position of power and influence in both science and the world beyond. He used the scientific method as a purely rhetorical tool to force the acceptance of his own dogmatic ideas. Against such weapons, the scientific community that harbored him was defenseless. Against rhetoric and ap-

pearance, the scientific method and the scientific ethos proved helpless. Against dogma disguised as science, objectivity failed.

From William Broad and Nicholas Wade, *Betrayers of the Truth: Fraud and Deceit in the Halls of Science*. New York: Simon & Schuster, 1982. Copyright © 1982 by William Broad & Nicholas Wade. Used with permission of Simon & Schuster, Inc.

Study Questions

1. Why is this reading called "The Failure of Objectivity"?
2. Why do these authors say that Burt was not a scientist?
3. Explain Burt's influence on the origin of the English 11+ exam and the significance it had for English schoolchildren for over a decade.
4. Who was Arthur Jensen and how did he use Burt's data?
5. Who first realized that Burt was a fraud? What circumstances and data brought him to this conclusion?
6. Who confirmed Kamin's findings and how?
7. Why, according to the authors, did Burt remain undetected for so long in a scientific community?
8. What main purpose, do you think, shaped this essay?

For Further Reading

Brown, Lester, Nicholas Lenssen, and Hal Kane. *Vital Signs, 1995: The Trends That Are Shaping Our Future.* New York: Norton, 1995.

Caney, Steven. *Invention Book.* New York: Workman, 1985.

Folbre, Nancy. *The New Field Guide to the U.S. Economy.* New York: New Press, 1990.

Huff, Darrell, *How to Lie with Statistics.* New York: Norton, 1954.

Jacoby, Russell, and Naomi Glauberman, eds. *The Bell Curve Debate.* New York: Random House, 1995.

Roberts, Royston M. *Serendipity: Accidental Discoveries in Science.* New York: Wiley, 1989.

CHAPTER 12

Deductive Reasoning:
How Do I Reason from Premises?

Used with permission of Chronicle Features,
San Francisco.

In this cartoon the cook is using deductive reasoning to ponder his dilemma. He wonders if his first premise—that "the cook always goes down
with the ship"—is really true. The pattern of his reasoning goes like this:

(All) cooks go down with their ships.

I am a cook.

(Therefore) I will go down with the ship.

Deduction begins with principles and seeks to apply them to specific situations. In this case, we can wonder whether the cook will let this form of
reasoning dictate his destiny or whether he will use his instincts and jump.

This chapter will guide you through some of the basics of deductive
reasoning so that you can recognize deductive reasoning in your own
thoughts and those of others. It will introduce you to some of the basic
vocabulary and standards of deductive reasoning and show you how deduction and induction interplay in our daily reasoning. But please remember that this chapter is only the briefest preliminary to the complex subject
of logic, which needs at least a semester of course work to comprehend.

Discovery Exercises

What Is Deductive Reasoning?

Using at least two dictionaries, look up the terms *deduction, deductive,* and *reasoning.* In your own words, what is deductive reasoning?

Evaluating Deductive Arguments

Study the following short deductive arguments. Which of these seem to you to be based on good reasoning and which do not? Explain the basis for your decision in each case.

1. America believes all people should be free. Therefore, whenever America intervenes in the politics of other countries, it is in order to make them free.
2. God made men to serve women. Therefore, men should obey their women.
3. Warts are caused by touching toads. This child has a wart on her finger. This child has touched a toad.
4. "The Supreme Court's Miranda ruling (giving defendants the right to have a lawyer present during questioning) is wrong and only helps guilty defendants. Suspects who are innocent of a crime should be able to have a lawyer present before police questioning. But the thing is you don't have many suspects who are innocent of a crime. That's contradictory. If a person is innocent of a crime, then he is not a suspect." (Attorney General Edwin Meese, quoted in the *Oakland Tribune*, October 6, 1985)
5. If she had been the last person to leave the house, she would have locked the door. However, the door was unlocked. Therefore, she was not the last person to leave the house.
6. If the temperature goes below freezing, the orange crop will be lost. The temperature went below freezing. The orange crop will be lost.

Now write down your answers to the following questions in preparation for class discussion:

1. Which of the preceding arguments contain statements that are false?
2. In the examples with the false statements, are the inferences nevertheless reasonable?

3. Are there any that may contain true statements but seem illogical in their reasoning?

4. Are there any that contain statements that are true and seem well reasoned?

5. Can you infer any rules for deductive reasoning from what you have learned here?

ABOUT DEDUCTIVE REASONING

Deduction is the subject of formal logic. It is called *formal* because its main concern is with creating *forms* that serve as models to demonstrate both correct and incorrect reasoning. Unlike induction, where an inference is drawn from an accumulation of evidence, deduction is a process that reasons from a series of carefully worded statements, each proceeding in order from the one before. These statements are about relationships between classes, characteristics, and individuals. The first statement is typically about all or some members of a class: "All crocodiles are reptiles." The second statement identifies something or someone as either belonging or not belonging to that class: "Coco is a crocodile." At this point, the two statements lead to an inference that becomes the conclusion: "Coco is a reptile."

Compared to the inductive method, which always remains open to more discoveries that could alter the conclusion, deduction proceeds toward an inevitable conclusion within a closed framework. A conclusion reached through deduction is not a hypothesis: its objective is not to generalize about evidence but simply to draw a conclusion based on the preceding statements. In our example, since Coco has been identified as a crocodile, then she *must* be a reptile.

Deduction begins with a generalization ("All crocodiles are reptiles") often derived by induction. In this case, the generalization that all crocodiles are members of the reptile family is a conclusion based on inductive observations repeatedly confirmed. Deduction also works with generalizations not necessarily derived from inductive reasoning. For instance, it can begin with a belief: "All crocodiles are sacred animals." Indeed, deduction starts with any statement that makes a claim. And a claim, which is an assertion that something is true or that it exists, can be worked with logically, whether it is true or not. This is possible because *deduction's main concern is not with sorting out evidence for truth but with studying the implications of a generalization applied to a specific situation*. Its focus is on logic, or the rules of reasoning.

Consider, for instance, the logic of the following belief:

All sacred animals should be worshiped.

The crocodile is a sacred animal.

The crocodile should be worshiped.

Here the conclusion naturally follows from the claims made. Logic can work with claims such as these—or any kind of claim—because it regards them all as *assumptions*. The truth of a statement is important in logic, but when a logician wants to gauge truth, he or she uses memory and experience, not the sampling and testing of the inductive method. Moreover, a logician finds it intriguing that false statements can be made to follow one another reasonably:

All crocodiles are spiders.

All spiders have wings.

All crocodiles have wings.

The purpose of deductive logic is to help us reason well with the information we *have* rather than to *research* information. It offers us models, guidelines, and rules for correct reasoning that can lead us to reliable conclusions with that information. Thus *logic*, by definition, is the science of reasoning or the science of inference.

One major barrier to understanding logic is its technical vocabulary. This vocabulary is needed to identify the components of deductive arguments and to convey its rules for correct usage. However, for the student, the initial task of mastering this terminology can become so formidable that it can prove to be an obstacle to understanding what the subject of deductive logic is all about. The definitions that follow should give you a basis for understanding.

THE VOCABULARY OF LOGIC

The following are key terms in logic: *proposition, argument, reasoning, syllogism, premise* (major and minor), *conclusion, validity, soundness*. We will define and discuss them one at a time.

Argument

In logic, the term *argument* does not mean a quarrel, as in everyday language. *Argument* in logic refers to a series of statements that support claims within a logical structure. Arguments appear in both deductive and inductive forms. As we have seen before, deductive arguments involve one or more statements (claims, assertions, or *propositions*) that lead to a conclusion:

> All people who flirt are showing interest in someone.
>
> She is flirting with me.
> _____
>
> **She is showing interest in me.**

Inductive arguments also establish claims through reasoning, but in this case, the claims are based on experiences, analogies, samples, and general evidence. Compare the following example to the preceding deductive argument:

> This woman seeks me out whenever she sees me having my lunch on the lawn. She comes over and sits next to me. She asks for a sip of my coffee. She teases me and makes me laugh a lot.
> _____
>
> **She is interested in me.**

Reasoning

Both arguments use reasoning to arrive at a conclusion. *Reasoning* can be defined as the drawing of conclusions, judgments, or inferences from facts or premises. Deductive arguments start with one or more premises and then investigate what conclusions necessarily follow from them.

> If I flirt back, she will encourage me further.
>
> I will flirt back.
> _____
>
> **She will encourage me further.**

Sometimes these premises appear in long chains of reasoning:

> (1) If I am nice to her, she'll think I'm flirting. (2) And if she thinks I'm flirting, she'll come on to me. (3) And if she comes on to me, I'll have to reject her. (4) And if I reject her, she'll be hurt. (5) I don't want her to be hurt.
> _____
>
> **Therefore, I won't be nice to her.**

Syllogism

Logic arranges deductive arguments in standardized forms that make the structure of the argument clearly visible for study and review. These forms are called *syllogisms*. We do not speak in syllogisms, which sound awkward and redundant, but they are useful constructs for testing the reliability of a deduction according to the rules of logic.

Premises and Conclusion

A syllogism contains two statements, or premises, and a conclusion. The first statement is called the *major premise* and the second is called the *minor premise*.

Major premise: No flirts are cross and mean.

Minor premise: This man is cross and mean.

Conclusion: This man is not a flirt.

In deduction, the reasoning "leads away" (Latin *deductus*) from a generalization about a class to identify a specific member belonging to that class—or it can lead to a generalization about another class. In the preceding deductive argument, the major premise states a generalization about the class of flirts: none is cross and mean. Then it determines through reasoning that a specific individual does not belong to that class: *because* he is cross and mean, he *must* not be a flirt. Between the word *because* and the word *must* lie the inference and the logic. Such reasoning can be checked for reliability by outlining the argument in the strict form of the syllogism.

Validity and Soundness

The standards used for testing reliability are based on some specific rules that determine an argument's *validity* and *soundness*. A deductive argument is said to be valid when the inference correctly follows from the premises:

All fathers are males.

Jose is a father.

Jose is a male.

Here, because Jose is a member of the class of fathers, and all members of that class are males, Jose must be a male. Even if we only assume these premises are true, it is entirely reasonable to infer that he is a male. We do not have to ponder the matter any further. Thus, we have a valid argument whose conclusion cannot be false.

Invalid reasoning might proceed like this:

All fathers are males.

Jose is a male.

Jose is a father.

In this argument, the first two premises do not lead to this conclusion. The conclusion may be true or it may not be true. But we cannot make that determination from this line of reasoning. Even if we are certain that all fathers are males and that Jose is a male, we still cannot infer from these premises alone that Jose is a father. The conclusion could be false. Therefore, this argument is invalid.

Now, another rule in deductive logic involves the standards carried by the definition of the word *sound*. *A deductive argument is sound if the premises are true and the argument is valid*. A sound argument uses true premises and correct reasoning to arrive at a conclusion that must be true. By this definition, the first argument is sound because its premises are true and its reasoning valid, leading to a conclusion that cannot be false. And the second argument, although it has true premises, is not sound because the reasoning is invalid, leading to a conclusion that could be false.

So far, so good. Yet there are some other complexities. An argument can be valid *even though the premises are not true*:

All men are fathers.

All fathers are married.

All men are married.

Here is another example:

All fathers are baseball fans.

All baseball fans like beer.

All fathers like beer.

Thus, the logician makes a distinction between the truth or falseness of statements in an argument and the validity of the entire argument. The term *sound* is used to signify that an argument is valid and the premises are true. The rule for determining soundness is that if the premises are both true and the argument is valid, the conclusion must also be true.

To summarize, deductive argument is structured or cast into a unit that allows the application of standards to information acquired through reasoning. With this basic understanding of the vocabulary of logic, we can now consider in greater detail the unit of deductive argumentation—the syllogism.

SYLLOGISMS AS STANDARDIZED FORMS

To review, syllogisms consist of claims that can be either true or false. A syllogism asserts a relationship between the terms (classes or individuals) given in the premises and the conclusion. Standardized forms for phrasing the premises have been developed to show us whether the reasoning fits into the deductive reasoning framework; these forms also make reasoning errors clearly visible. Five of these standardized forms for expressing premises are as follows:

1. All _____ are _____.
2. No _____ are _____.
3. Some _____ are _____.
4. Some _____ are not _____.
5. If _____, then _____.

You will notice that in the first four forms, each of the blanks offers space for a noun or noun phrase and each is connected by forms of the verb *to be* expressed in the present tense. This simplification allows a reduction of everyday language into verbal mathematics, thus making the task of argument analysis much easier.

Compare the following translations from natural to standardized language:

Natural Language

1. Ice cream always tastes sweet.
2. Cats never take baths.
3. Some airlines have lower fares.
4. If she is over seventy, she must be retired.

Standardized Language

1. All ice cream food is sweet food.
2. No cats are animals that take baths.
3. Some airlines are lower-fare transport.
4. If she is a person over seventy, then she is a retired person.

Discovery Exercise

Practice in Constructing Syllogisms*

1. Rephrase each of the following sentences into a standard major premise. Then see if you can add a minor premise and a conclusion.

---

*For the style and method used in these exercises, I am indebted to Matthew Lipman's *Philosophical Inquiry: An Instructional Manual to Accompany Harry Stottlemeier's Discovery*. 2nd ed. Published by the Institute for the Advancement of Philosophy for Children, Upper Montclair, N.J., 1979.

(a) All horses have exactly four legs.

(b) Everybody's got needs.

(c) All coal miners are poor.

(d) Many eighteen-year-olds are college students.

(e) No eight-year-old is a college student.

(f) Lead is poisonous.

(g) If he's late, he'll be sorry.

2. Fill in the blanks in the following sentences so that all the syllogisms are valid:

(a) All horses are mammals.
All _____ are animals.

All horses are animals.

(b) All horses are living things.
All living things are things that reproduce.

All _____ are things that reproduce.

(c) No horses are creatures that sleep in beds.
This creature is sleeping in a bed.

Therefore, this creature is _____ .

(d) If today is Tuesday, this must be Belgium.
This is _____.

This must be _____.

3. Choose the correct answer in each of the following cases:

(a) All beers are liquids.
It therefore follows that:
(1) All liquids are beers.
(2) No liquids are beers.
(3) Neither (1) nor (2).

(b) Florida is next to Georgia.
Georgia is next to South Carolina.
(1) Florida is next to South Carolina.
(2) South Carolina is next to Florida.
(3) Neither (1) nor (2).

(c) Ruth is shorter than Margaret.
Margaret is shorter than Rosie.
It therefore follows that
(1) Ruth is shorter than Rosie.
(2) Margaret is shorter than Ruth.
(3) Ruth is taller than Rosie.

WHAT SYLLOGISMS DO

The logician has a number of purposes for phrasing arguments in syllogisms: (1) to find out exactly what is being said and thus to be able to judge whether each statement is true or false; (2) to discover and expose any hidden premises; and (3) to find out if one thought follows logically from another. Let's look at each of these purposes in greater detail.

What Is Said and Is It True?

Of course he is cheating on his wife. Doesn't he always come home late?

You will sense that something is wrong with this statement, but where do you begin? First, translate it into a syllogism that exposes the argument's structure:

All wife cheaters are people who always come home late.

He is a person who always comes home late.

He is a wife cheater.

In this case, the syllogism reveals a stereotype or hasty generalization in a *hidden major premise*. The words *all* and *always* make the claim in this hidden premise false. We could easily point out exceptions, such as "wife cheaters" who are punctual or loyal mates who work late. But in addition, *wife cheater* is an ambiguous term. What actions constitute wife cheating? The second premise also contains the vague terms *always* and *late*, which could be exaggerations. What does *late* mean? one minute or four hours? *Late* according to one person's expectations or according to a mutual agreement? Then there is the vague term *always*. If the person accused came home early only once, the generalization would not hold. Thus, although the reasoning may be valid, the argument's use of vague terms and false generalizations makes it unsound.

Now, let's consider another example. Take the statement, "Our guest is Japanese. We had better cook rice rather than potatoes for dinner."

No Japanese is a potato eater.

Our guest is Japanese.

Our guest is not a potato eater.

The syllogism shows the reasoning is valid, but again the major premise, which had been hidden, is revealed as too broad a generalization to be true, leading to an uncertain conclusion. Therefore, the argument is unsound.

Here is another example. You may have seen this claim on billboards: "Milk is good for everybody." Because the billboard supplements this claim with attractive happy people, you may well conclude that you should remember to drink more milk. However, a syllogism will reveal some hidden aspects in this claim worth studying. Nevertheless, this will not be easy to do because of the ambiguity of the word *good*. *Good* has at least two meanings in this context: healthy and tasty. But a syllogism cannot function with words that have double meanings. (See the fallacy of equivocation.) In poetry, double meanings are effective. But in arguments, double meanings can be manipulative because they encourage assumptions and escape accountability. (You say you are going to sue us because milk made you sick? But did we say *healthy*? No! We meant *tasty*!)

Suppose you assume that *good* means healthy; you write out the syllogism thus:

> People who drink milk are people made healthy.
>
> I am a person who drinks milk.
> _____
>
> **I am made healthy.**

If you assume that the premises are true, the reasoning is valid. But when you want to know whether the argument is sound, you must ask questions to test the truth of the generalization in the major premise. Are there exceptions that would challenge its universality? What if my brother is allergic to milk? What about nutritionists who say that cow milk is good only for cows? The syllogism exposes an unsound argument because it contains a false generalization.

Is There a Hidden Premise?

A major advantage of using syllogisms is that they reveal hidden premises—as you found in the major premises of the preceding examples. Consider the following further examples in which questionable hidden premises appear in both the minor premises and conclusions.

1. Senator Jones is a Democrat. Expect him to tax and spend.
    All Democrats are taxers and spenders. (hidden premise)
    Senator Jones is a Democrat.
    _____
    Senator Jones is a taxer and spender.

2. Do I think he's sexy? Well, he drives a truck, doesn't he?
    All those who drive trucks are sexy. (hidden premise)
    He drives a truck.
    _____
    He is sexy. (implied conclusion)

In the second example, both the major premise and the conclusion are hidden or implied. This often happens in advertising slogans: "The burgers are bigger at Burger John's." As a syllogism, this reads

Bigger burgers are better burgers. (hidden premise)

Burger John's burgers are bigger.

Burger John's burgers are better. (hidden conclusion)

You should buy Burger John's burgers. (additional hidden conclusion)

Does One Thought Follow Logically from the Other?

Here the logician is concerned with validity. Does one thought follow logically from the other? Does the inference drawn in the conclusion make sense?

If you are a suspect, then you are questioned by the police.

You were questioned by the police.

You are a suspect.

Here, even if both the premises were true, the conclusion could still be false. (Maybe you were a witness or questioned about something else.) The argument is invalid because the conclusion is not implied by its premises. The illogic of the reasoning here can be recognized intuitively, but its exposure in the syllogism shows how it is illogical

The next argument is obviously valid:

She is either married or single.

She is married.

Therefore, she is not single.

If the two premises are true, logic compels us to accept the conclusion as true. The inference follows: it makes sense. The syllogism makes this even clearer to us.

Exercise

Reviewing the Vocabulary of Logic

Work with a classmate to write down the definitions you can remember of the following words: *logic, reasoning, deductive* and *inductive reasoning, proposition, premise* (major and minor), *conclusion, argument, syllogism, true statement, valid argument, sound argument, hidden premise, hidden conclusion.* When you have finished, compare your definitions with the

"Of course if $\int_{r}^{x} \sqrt{}^4 \, du = \lim\limits_{a\to\infty} \sum\limits_{i=1}^{n} \left(\dfrac{1}{n^x}\right)^4 \cdot \dfrac{x}{n}$, *we're sunk."*

From *I Paint What I See*. Copyright © 1971 by Gahan Wilson. Used with permission of Simon & Schuster, Inc.

chapter summary on pages 366–368. If there is a discrepancy, or if any of the definitions are still unclear to you, review the text discussion until you can explain the term to your partner.

SUMMARIZING INDUCTIVE AND DEDUCTIVE REASONING

Inductive and deductive thinking are not isolated modes. They interweave in our minds constantly throughout the day as we confront both serious and mundane problems. Suppose you have an apartment in the Boston suburb of Needham and commute to Boston University downtown. You

COMPARING INDUCTIVE AND DEDUCTIVE REASONING

Inductive Reasoning	Deductive Reasoning
Specific to general (usually, not always).	General to specific (usually, not always).
Purpose is to reach a conclusion for testing and application.	Purpose is to reach a conclusion that cannot be false.
Discovers new laws.	Applies known laws to specific circumstances.
Thinking guided by theories, observation, research, investigation. Data are collected and analyzed. Sudden insights and unexpected discoveries can occur.	Thinking makes inferences about the relationship of claims.
Tests verify measure of truth in terms of reliability, accuracy, applicability, replicability.	Truth of premises is assumed or determined by reasoning.
Conclusion is a *hypothesis* or statement of probability.	Conclusion is final.
Indicator words that show this is a hypothesis: *probably, improbable, plausible, implausible, likely, unlikely, reasonable*.	Indicator words that show this is a conclusion: *necessarily, certainly, absolutely, definitely*.
Even if the premises are true, the conclusion is only probable and could even be false. More data or major changes could call for further testing.	If the premises are true, or assumed to be true, and the reasoning valid, the conclusion cannot be false.

have a car, but you prefer to commute by the T train. You made this decision by reasoning deductively:

All public trains are faster than car transport.

I want faster-than-car transport.

————————————————————————————————

I will take public trains.

This reasoning stands you in good stead for some months. However, one
morning you arrive at the station to find an unusually large crowd of people
waiting there. You wonder what this means. Are there fewer trains today?
Has there been an accident? Will we all be delayed? You form hypotheses

through inductive reasoning. You seek to test each hypothesis by searching for more information from those waiting. But all they can tell you is that their expected train has been delayed. Therefore you reason deductively:

> Delayed trains are unpredictable in schedule.
>
> This train is delayed.
> _____
>
> **This train is unpredictable in schedule.**

Then you reason inductively again. You need to decide whether to wait or go home and get your car. You weigh the unknown factor of when the train will arrive against the time it might take to go home, get your car, and drive through heavy traffic. You decide that, although the delayed train *may* make you late, your driving by car will *certainly* make you late. And so, on the basis of your estimate of time and probability, you choose to wait in the station. Since you made this decision carefully, you will not get upset if the train is delayed for yet another half hour. And you can be glad you did not impulsively run home to get your car without thinking the matter through, only to feel your blood pressure go up when you found yourself stuck in traffic with the train passing you by. You made a conscious decision to take the consequences with responsibility.

In college we study deduction and induction separately both for convenience and because of their different structures and standards. But whether we are aware of that or not, in our thinking we move back and forth between the two modes all the time. Yet, taking conscious notice of how our thinking moves between the deductive and inductive mode has considerable advantages; we then can purposely direct our thinking to the mode that is more appropriate. This awareness also allows us to use the different standards of the two modes to evaluate what we are doing. Thus, we have a greater probability of arriving at better decisions. And even if we are disappointed with the results of our decisions, at least we know that we made a conscious choice that we can learn from.

Composition Writing Application

Writing a Deductive Argument

Write a deductive argument within the following parameters:

1. *Topic*: Application of an aphorism, or wise saying, to life.
2. *Approach*:
   (a) Explain the aphorism.
   (b) Define its terms.
   (c) Illustrate it.
   (d) Choose to agree, disagree, or both.

DEDUCTIVE REASONING

I would agree with St. Augustine that "an unjust law is no law at all." . . . How does one determine whether a law is just or unjust? A just law is a man-made code that is out of harmony with the moral law. To put it in the terms of St. Thomas Aquinas: an unjust law is a human law that is not rooted in eternal law and natural law. Any law that uplifts human personality is just. Any law that degrades human personality is unjust. All segregation statutes are unjust because segregation distorts the soul and damages the personality. It gives the segregator a false sense of superiority and the segregated a false sense of inferiority. Segregation, to use the terminology of the Jewish philosopher Martin Buber, substitutes an "I-it" relationship for an "I-thou" relationship and ends up relegating persons to the status of things. Hence segregation is not only politically, economically, and sociologically unsound, it is morally wrong and sinful. Paul Tillich has said that sin is separation. Is not segregation an existential expression of man's tragic separation, his awful estrangement, his terrible sinfulness? Thus it is that I can urge men to obey the 1954 decision of the Supreme Court, for it is morally right, and I can urge them to disobey segregation ordinances, for they are morally wrong.

Questions

1. What was King's problem at that time?
2. How does King attempt to solve his problem?
3. Which terms does he define and why?
4. Notice how he draws major premises from statements made by authorities and then reasons from these premises. Write out one syllogism that he uses to advance his claims.

From Martin Luther King, Jr., "Letter from the Birmingham Jail," 1963.

---

3. *Form*: Exposition and argumentation—explain, justify, and persuade through logic, reasoning, and example.

4. *Length*: Concise two pages.

5. *Subject*: Choose your own aphorism or select one of the following:

   (a) "The most savage controversies are about those matters as to which there is no evidence either way." (Bertrand Russell)

   (b) "Man is a social animal who dislikes his fellow men." (Delacroix)

   (c) "Competition brings out the best in products and the worst in people." (David Sarnoff)

(d) "Failure is when you stop trying."

(e) "People get the kind of government they deserve."

(f) "Prejudice is never easy unless it can pass itself off as reason." (William Hazlitt)

(g) "Life was meant to be lived, and curiosity must be kept alive. One must never, for whatever reason, turn his back on life." (Eleanor Roosevelt)

(h) "The unleashed power of the atom has changed everything save our modes of thinking and thus we drift toward unparalleled catastrophe." (Albert Einstein)

(i) "Even though a situation is catastrophic, that still does not mean it has to be taken seriously." (Austrian saying)

(j) "People are basically of two kinds: those who lean and those who lift." (unknown source)

(k) "When two persons quarrel, always both are in the wrong." (the mother of the sri Aurobindo Ashram, India)

CHAPTER SUMMARY

1. Deductive reasoning is the process of starting with one or more statements called premises and investigating what conclusions necessarily follow from these premises.

2. Deduction is the subject of formal logic, whose main concern is with creating forms that demonstrate reasoning.

3. Logic has its own technical vocabulary. The following is a summary of the definitions of key terms:

Argument   An assertion with statements that support it.

Claim   Assertion or statement that maintains that something is true or false that is put forward for questioning and testing.

Conclusion   The last step in a reasoning process. It is a statement of decision or judgment based on evidence and reasoning. In logic, a conclusion is an inference derived from the premises of an argument.

Hidden Premise or Conclusion   A premise or conclusion that is not stated but implied in an argument. When the argument is cast in a syllogism, the missing premise or conclusion is expressed.

Hypothesis   A theory, explanation, or tentative conclusion derived through inductive reasoning based on a limited view of facts or events. A *working hypothesis* can be used as a guide for further investigation to

BUILDING ARGUMENTS

DEDUCTION

Great Spirit, my Grandfather, you have said to me when I was still young and could hope, that in difficulty I could send a voice four times, once for each quarter of the earth, and you would hear me.

Today I send a voice for a people in despair.

. . . To the center of the world you have taken me and showed the goodness and the beauty and the strangeness of the greening earth, the only mother, and there the spirit-shapes of things, as they should be, you have shown me, and I have seen. At the center of the sacred hoop you have said that I should make the tree to bloom.

With tears running, O Great Spirit, my Grandfather—with running eyes I must say now that the tree has never bloomed. A pitiful old man, you see me here, and I have fallen away and done nothing. Here at the center of the world, where you took me when I was young and taught me; here, old I stand and the tree is withered, my Grandfather.

Again, and maybe the last time on earth, I recall the great vision you sent me. It may be that some little root of the sacred tree still lives. Nourish it, then, that it may leaf and bloom and fill with singing birds. Hear me, not for myself but for my people; I am old. Hear me, that they may once more go back into the sacred hoop and find the good road and the shielding tree.
(Black Elk, shaman of the Oglala Sioux, 1912)

Exercise

1. Can a prayer or prophecy be a deductive argument?
2. Write out the syllogism behind the reasoning of the first statement (major premise, minor premise, and conclusion). Also write out the syllogism behind the narrator's reasoning about the sacred hoop.
3. Write a deductive argument in which you make a claim about Black Elk's prayer. Support it with premises and draw a conclusion.

Speeches of the Native Americans offered in this series were taken from Virginia Irving Armstrong, *I Have Spoken*. Athens, Ohio: Swallow Press / Ohio University Press, 1989.

see if it leads to new facts or verification. Many hypotheses can be used and discarded one after the other until one is found that explains and aligns all the data and stands up to all testing and verification.

Inductive reasoning   The process of noting particular facts and drawing a conclusion about them.

Logic   The science of reasoning; also called the science of inference.

Premises   Statements, evidence, or assumptions offered to support a position.

Propositions   Claims, statements, or assertions used in an argument. They can be either premises or conclusions and either true or false statements.

Reasoning   The act or process of arriving at conclusions, judgments, or inferences from facts or premises.

Sound   A sound argument is one in which all the premises are true and the reasoning is valid.

Syllogism   The formalized structure of a deductive argument, usually written, in which the conclusion is supported by two premises. (Greek *syllogiz* = to reason)

True   Corresponding to reality.

Valid   A valid argument is one in which the reasoning follows correctly from the premises to the conclusion. An argument can be valid without the premises or conclusion being true.

4. The standardized language of syllogisms allows a reduction of everyday language into verbal mathematics.

5. Syllogisms allow logicians to determine what is being said, to identify hidden premises, and to find out if the argument makes sense.

6. Deductive and inductive reasoning are not isolated pursuits but are mentally interwoven both in major and mundane problem solving.

Chapter Quiz

Rate the following statements as *true* or *false*. Justify your answers.

_____ 1. A premise is a reason given to support a conclusion.

_____ 2. Syllogisms are used in logic because logicians like to make their knowledge arcane, or hidden and secret.

_____ 3. Logic is less concerned with truth than with whether one statement follows reasonably from another.

_____ 4. Reasoning occurs only in deduction—not in induction.

_____ 5. A generalization reached through induction can become a premise used in a deductive syllogism.

_____ 6. "All homeowners are taxpayers. He is a property owner. Therefore, he is a taxpayer." This is a valid argument.

_____ 7. "Bloodletting reduces fever. This patient has fever. This patient needs bloodletting." This syllogism shows valid reasoning although both premises may not be true.

_____ 8. "White-skinned people are superior to dark-skinned people. Therefore, it is the manifest destiny of white-skinned people to rule dark-skinned people." No country would ever accept such fallacious reasoning as this.

State whether the reasoning in each of the following syllogisms is correct or incorrect:

9. If the two parties agree, then there is no strike.
   The two parties agree.
   _____
   Therefore, there is no strike.

10. If the two parties agree, then there is no strike.
    There is no strike.
    _____
    Therefore, the two parties agree.

11. If the two parties agree, then there is no strike.
    The two parties do not agree.
    _____
    Therefore, there is a strike.

12. If the two parties agree, then there is no strike.
    There is a strike.
    _____
    Therefore, the two parties do not agree.

After you have decided, compare your answers to those given here. Explain why these answers are correct.

9. correct   10. incorrect   11. incorrect   12. correct

Reading

THE DECLARATION OF INDEPENDENCE
Thomas Jefferson

Based on a clear line of deductive reasoning, this great historical document written in 1776 is also an enduring work of literature. Jefferson begins by stating some "self-evident truths," or axioms, which set off a revolution and formed the ideological basis for the laws of a new government. Study this document as a structure of reasoning. Outline the whole into four parts. What is the function of each part?

When in the Course of human events, it becomes necessary for one people to 1
dissolve the political bands which have connected them with another, and to assume among the powers of the earth, the separate and equal station to which the
Laws of Nature and of Nature's God entitle them, a decent respect to the opinions
of mankind requires that they should declare the causes which impel them to the
separation.

We hold these truths to be self-evident, that all men are created equal, that 2
they are endowed by their Creator with certain unalienable Rights, that among
these are Life, Liberty and the pursuit of Happiness. That to secure these rights,
Governments are instituted among Men, deriving their just powers from the consent of the governed. That whenever any Form of Government becomes destructive of these ends it is the Right of the People to alter or to abolish it, and to institute
new Government, laying its foundation on such principles and organizing its powers in such form, as to them shall seem most likely to effect their Safety and Happiness. Prudence, indeed, will dictate that Governments long established should not
be changed for light and transient causes; and accordingly all experience has
shewn, that mankind are more disposed to suffer, while evils are sufferable, than to
right themselves by abolishing the forms to which they are accustomed. But when
a long train of abuses and usurpations, pursuing invariably the same Object evinces
a design to reduce them under absolute Despotism, it is their right, it is their duty,
to throw off such Government, and to provide new Guards for their future security.
Such has been the patient sufferance of these Colonies; and such is now the necessity which constrains them to alter their former Systems of Government. The history
of the present King of Great Britain is a history of repeated injuries and usurpations,
all having in direct object the establishment of an absolute Tyranny over these
States. To prove this, let Facts be submitted to a candid world.

He has refused his Assent to Laws, the most wholesome and necessary for the 3
public good.

He has forbidden his Governors to pass Laws of immediate and pressing im- 4
portance, unless suspended in their operation till his Assent should be obtained;
and when so suspended, he has utterly neglected to attend to them. He has refused
to pass other Laws for the accommodation of large districts of people, unless those
people would relinquish the right of Representation in the Legislature, a right inestimable to them and formidable to tyrants only.

He has called together legislative bodies at places unusual, uncomfortable, and 5
distant from the depository of their public Records, for the sole purpose of fatiguing
them into compliance with his measures.

He has dissolved Representative Houses repeatedly, for opposing with manly 6
firmness his invasions on the rights of the people.

He has refused for a long time, after such dissolutions, to cause others to be 7
elected; whereby the Legislative powers, incapable of Annihilation, have returned
to the People at large for their exercise, the State remaining in the mean time
exposed to all the dangers of invasion from without, and convulsions within.

He has endeavoured to prevent the population of these States; for that purpose 8 obstructing the Laws for Naturalization of Foreigners; refusing to pass others to encourage their migrations hither, and raising the conditions of new Appropriations of Lands.

He has obstructed the Administration of Justice, by refusing his Assent to Laws 9 for establishing Judiciary powers.

He has made Judges dependent on his Will alone, for the tenure of their offices, 10 and the amount and payment of their salaries.

He has erected a multitude of New Offices, and sent hither swarms of Officers 11 to harass our People, and eat out their substance.

He has kept among us, in times of peace, standing Armies without the Consent 12 of our legislatures.

He has affected to render the Military independent of and superior to the Civil 13 power.

He has combined with others to subject us to a jurisdiction foreign to our 14 constitution, and unacknowledged by our laws; giving his Assent to their Acts of pretended Legislation:

For Quartering large bodies of armed troops among us: 15

For protecting them, by a mock Trial, from punishment for any Murders which 16 they should commit on the Inhabitants of these States:

For cutting off our Trade with all parts of the world: 17

For imposing Taxes on us without our Consent: 18

For depriving us in many cases of the benefits of Trial by Jury: 19

For transporting us beyond Seas to be tried for pretended offences: 20

For abolishing the free System of English Laws in a neighbouring Province, 21 establishing therein an Arbitrary government, and enlarging its Boundaries so as to render it at once an example and fit instrument for introducing the same absolute rule into these Colonies:

For taking away our Charters, abolishing our most valuable Laws, and altering 22 fundamentally the Forms of our Governments:

For suspending our own Legislatures, and declaring themselves invested with 23 power to legislate for us in all cases whatsoever.

He has abdicated Government here, by declaring us out of his Protection and 24 waging War against us.

He has plundered our seas, ravaged our Coasts, burnt our towns, and de- 25 stroyed the Lives of our people.

He is at this time transporting large Armies of foreign Mercenaries to compleat 26 the works of death, desolation and tyranny, already begun with circumstances of Cruelty & perfidy scarcely paralleled in the most barbarous ages, and totally unworthy the Head of a civilized nation.

He has constrained our fellow Citizens taken Captive on the high Seas to bear 27 Arms against their Country, to become the executioners of their friends and Brethren, or to fall themselves by their Hands.

He has excited domestic insurrections amongst us, and has endeavoured to   28
bring on the inhabitants of our frontiers, merciless Indian Savages, whose known rule
of warfare is an undistinguished destruction of all ages, sexes and conditions.

In every stage of these Oppressions We have Petitioned for Redress in the most   29
humble terms: Our repeated Petitions have been answered only by repeated injury.
A Prince, whose character is thus marked by every act which may define a Tyrant,
is unfit to be the ruler of a free people.

Nor have We been wanting in attentions to our British brethren. We have   30
warned them from time to time of attempts by their legislature to extend an un-
warrantable jurisdiction over us. We have reminded them of the circumstances of
our emigration and settlement here. We have appealed to their native justice and
magnanimity, and we have conjured them by the ties of our common kindred to
disavow these usurpations, which would inevitably interrupt our connections and
correspondence. They too have been deaf to the voice of Justice and of consan-
guinity. We must, therefore, acquiesce in the necessity, which denounces our Separation, and hold them, as we hold the rest of mankind, Enemies in War, in Peace
Friends.

We, therefore, the Representatives of the United States of America, in General   31
Congress, Assembled, appealing to the Supreme Judge of the world for the recti-
tude of our intentions, do, in the Name, and by Authority of the good People of
these Colonies, solemnly publish and declare, That these United Colonies are, and
of Right ought to be Free and Independent States; that they are absolved from all
Allegiance to the British Crown, and that all political connection between them and
the State of Great Britain, is and ought to be totally dissolved; and that as Free and
Independent States, they have full Power to levy War, conclude Peace, contract
Alliances, establish Commerce, and to do all other Acts and Things which Independent States may of right do. And for the support of this Declaration, with a firm
reliance on the protection of divine Providence, we mutually pledge to each other
our Lives, our Fortunes and our sacred Honor.

Study Questions

1. In the first sentence it is stated that people are entitled by "the Laws of
    Nature and of Nature's God" to separate and equal stations. What does
    this mean? Is there any evidence offered to back this claim?

2. Outline the deductive reasoning offered in the second paragraph.
    Which truths does Jefferson claim to be self-evident? What is the pur-
    pose of governments? From where do they derive their power?

3. How does Jefferson anticipate the argument that this kind of reasoning
    would allow people to overthrow governments "for light and transient
    causes"?

4. What are some of the complaints listed by Jefferson to justify a declaration of independence from England? Are some more evaluative than factual?

5. In the last paragraph, in the name of what authorities does he make the declaration?

6. The reasoning in this document opens with a deductive framework citing self-evident truths. Do you think the recognition of such truths preceded the abuses listed or were they born out of them?

For Further Reading

If you want to know more about logic, the following texts are suggested:

Cederbloom, Jerry, and David W. Paulsen. *Critical Reasoning*. 3rd ed. Belmont, Calif.: Wadsworth, 1991.

Hurley, Patrick J. *A Concise Introduction to Logic*. 5th ed. Belmont, Calif.: Wadsworth, 1994.

Kahane, Howard. *Logic and Philosophy*. 4th ed. Belmont, Calif.: Wadsworth, 1982.

Seech, Zachary. *Open Minds and Everyday Reasoning*. Belmont, Calif.: Wadsworth, 1993.

Thomas, Stephen. *Practical Reasoning in Natural Language*. 2nd ed. Englewood Cliffs, N.J.: Prentice-Hall, 1981.

OBJECTIVES REVIEW OF PART III

After you have finished Part III, you will understand

- Why arguments are supported claims.
- How reasons differ from conclusions.
- What questions to ask in analyzing arguments.
- Why fallacies make arguments deceptive.
- Definitions and examples of twenty-two fallacies.
- The forms and standards of inductive and deductive thinking.
- The concepts of empirical reasoning, scientific method, hypothesis, probability, and causal reasoning.
- The basic vocabulary of logic.
- The functions of the syllogism.
- The differences between deductive and inductive reasoning.
- How inductive and deductive reasoning interplay in our thinking.

(continued)

OBJECTIVES REVIEW OF PART III (continued)

And you will have practice in developing these skills:

- Identifying conclusions and separating them from reasons.
- Identifying reports and separating them from arguments.
- Articulating the question at issue.
- Analyzing arguments.
- Writing a persuasive argument under the pressure of strong feelings.
- Researching and preparing your take-home final.
- Evaluating deductive arguments for validity and soundness.
- Identifying hidden premises.
- Applying different standards to inductive and deductive reasoning.

PART IV
Creating with Critical Thinking

CHAPTER 13
Research Skills
How Can I Create Knowledge?

CHAPTER 14
Problem Solving
How Can I Create Solutions?

CHAPTER 13

Research Skills:
How Can I Create Knowledge?

"Notice all the computations, theoretical scribblings, and lab equipment, Norm. . . . Yes, curiosity killed these cats."

Cartoon by Gary Larson. Used with permission of Universal Press Syndicate.

Too much curiosity could kill any cat. This cartoon illustrates the frustration and exhaustion of undirected investigation. Chapter 13 offers a plan for research paper writing designed to help you meet your deadline without killing yourself. It reviews the kind of thinking needed to meet the four trials of research: (1) knowing what a research paper is and what you are supposed to do; (2) narrowing your topic to a thesis that can be adequately supported; (3) staying in charge of your sources without being overwhelmed by them; (4) following a schedule that gives you the flexibility you need.

This chapter does not try to tell you all you would ever need to know about research. Instead, it puts you to work in *researching how to research*. Two exercises lead you to a research paper assignment that should not only challenge your research skills but enable you to practice and demonstrate everything you have been learning about critical thinking.

Discovery Exercise

Knowing What a Research Paper Is and What You Are Supposed to Do

For this exercise you (or you and your partner) will need two dictionaries and an English handbook. If you do not have a handbook, ask your instructor to put several on reserve in your college library.*

When you have these reference materials before you, write down their definitions of the following words:

research paper	claim
subject	support
topic	documentation
thesis	plagiarism
thesis statement	quote
thesis sentence	paraphrase
controlling idea	summary
working thesis	outline
issue	

Class Discussion

Answer these questions in writing in preparation for class discussion:

1. Did you find that your sources agreed in their definitions of all these terms? Were there differences?
2. How did you find *research paper* defined in your sources?
3. Does a research paper only investigate and explain ideas, or does it also engage in evaluating, problem solving, and arguing about issues?
4. Did you find the terms *subject, topic,* and *issue* to be used interchangeably? Did some authors say to move from the subject to the topic, whereas others said to move from the topic to the subject?
5. Were *thesis* and *controlling idea* and *thesis statement* and *thesis sentence* used interchangeably?

---

*Some useful sources are *The Little Brown Handbook*, 6th ed., by H. Ramsey Fowler and Jane E. Aaron (HarperCollins, 1995); *Harbrace Handbook* by John C. Hodges and Mary E. Whitten (Harcourt, 1984); *The Prentice-Hall Guide for College Writers* by Stephen Reid (Prentice-Hall, 1989).

6.   What is documentation and what is its purpose?

7.   How confident are you of your ability to quote, summarize, para-
     phrase, and outline one written paragraph? Do you need to ask for
     more practice in doing any of these?

8.   Are you confused about any of the terms you were asked to define?

LEARNING THROUGH DEFINING: UNDERSTANDING THE RESEARCH PAPER'S CHALLENGE

Before we can think clearly about a subject, we need to have a clear understanding of its terminology. How do we arrive at this understanding? By
making a serious study of any word that we're not sure about. This is the
practice you have been encouraged to follow through exercises at the beginning of every chapter in this book. In your dictionary and handbook
study of the words related to research skills, the task of achieving clarity
may have been more difficult than you had first anticipated. You may have
been surprised to find a lack of definition agreement and uniformity. The
words *subject, topic,* and *issue* are sometimes used interchangeably as synonyms and sometimes given distinct meanings. Similarly, *thesis, thesis statement,* and *controlling idea* may represent three different concepts or one.

  This lack of vocabulary precision tends to hinder, rather than assist,
the primary thinking task involved in research paper writing: that of *narrowing* the essay's focus. Because a paper with too broad or narrow a focus
leads to a failed endeavor, we may end up doing a lot of work for nothing.
Even a fifty-page paper with wonderful language, examples, ideas, great
typing, and no sentence errors will not pass muster without a clear thesis
governing an essay that is adequately supported.

  The irony is that the thinking needed to accomplish this essential maneuver of narrowing down is not very difficult. All that is necessary is to
assign clear definitions to a vocabulary that can instruct you in what to do.
Agreements about these definitions can lead you through this first trial of
research paper writing.

What Is a Research Paper?

You probably discovered from your definition studies that *research* is derived from the middle French *recercher* meaning to seek out or search
again. When we research something, we inspect more closely something
that interests us: we study it, ask questions, investigate, gather facts and
opinions about it, then evaluate this information for truth and accuracy.

Research papers are written not only by students for college courses but also by professionals, career men and women, and laypeople. These are the reports or studies that we read or hear about in the news every day. A group of citizens, protesting plans to build a waste-burning plant in their neighborhood, goes before the city council to read from an environmental impact study. A governor quotes an engineering firm's report of freeway earthquake hazards as the basis for his plea for more renovation funds. A high school graduate lands a job on a newspaper after writing a report on topics of interest to potential youth readers. In each of these cases, a written report helped individuals attract attention and influence decisions.

The written form of the research paper depends on its audience and its purpose. If it is meant merely to give an account of a subject and explain it, its form is called *expository*. If its author chooses to argue for a position on a subject, its form is *argumentative*. (Some sources say that a research paper uses *only* exposition, whereas others do not insist on this limitation.) You wrote your first expository essay in Chapter 2, an essay of definition, in which you defined, explained, analyzed, and clarified the meaning of a word. As expository essays, research papers are much longer, ranging from ten to five hundred pages.

Another characteristic of a research paper is that it uses outside sources to explain, support, or authenticate its ideas, which are clearly documented in the paper. A research paper cites its sources—or accurately notes such data as names, titles, publication information, and page numbers—for three reasons: (1) as proof of fact or authority; (2) to give credit where credit is due, clearly separating the writer's ideas from ideas from other sources; (3) to enable the reader to verify this information and study the subject further.

Narrowing Down: Moving from Subject to Topic to Thesis

The term *subject* describes the largest class of information or ideas from which your *topic* is selected. In the example research paper that you will find at the end of this chapter, the final selected *topic*, "Driving Under the Influence: The Long-Term Picture," was derived from the following *subject* headings:

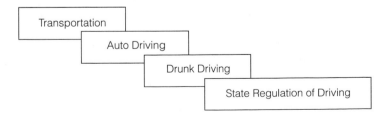

Transportation
Auto Driving
Drunk Driving
State Regulation of Driving

For a college student in search of a topic suitable for a fifteen-page research paper, deciding to write on any of these subjects would be naïve. It would be unwise to tackle a subject area so large that it would require several years' research and a book-length manuscript to cover adequately. Here the standard of *adequately* is crucial. A college research paper is not a scrapbook or a random collage of encyclopedia and magazine articles. It is an essay that thoroughly explains, argues, or proves the writer's single main idea. All sources used are subservient to this one purpose. To take on too large a subject, such as Auto Driving, would lead to only superficial treatment. Therefore, differentiating a subject from a topic is important in the first stage of your preparation.

Topic is what essentially becomes the title of your paper. It is the final subclass of your subject, although it still provides a kind of superior heading or umbrella for your thesis. In the example research paper, the topic given in the title extends the subcategory boxes as follows:

Driving Under the Influence in Minnesota

The Long-Term Picture

The term *issue* means a topic that is in dispute, a debatable question that elicits propositions pro and con. Here, the implicit issue is "Is drunk driving a critical problem in Minnesota?" A narrower, more controversial issue is "Should Minnesota permanently revoke the license of anyone cited for drunk driving?"

The word *thesis* was defined earlier as the idea that the essay intends to prove. In the example paper, the thesis is "Drunk driving in the state of Minnesota is a critical problem that must be more strongly addressed by state and local governments." Because the thesis controls the entire content of an essay of any length, it is also called the *controlling idea*.

The terms *thesis statement* and *thesis sentence* come from one academic tradition that says the thesis should be stated in a single declarative assertion. Although this tradition is often ignored by professional writers, stating the thesis clearly in the first paragraph provides a good test of focused thinking both for the writer and the reader. It clarifies the paper's intention as well as its limitations and organization. Furthermore, it serves as an organization and research guide.

Again, as with the topic sentence, how the essay reads is different from the way in which it is conceived and researched. To be objective, research cannot begin with a conclusion (and your thesis is your conclusion) but usually begins with a hunch, working thesis, or hypothesis. This working thesis also guides the organization and direction of your research, which can be revised as your evidence indicates. You may decide to change your thesis after calibrating whether you have taken on too broad or too narrow a topic. You might have decided first to limit your study to drunk driving arrests in downtown Virginia, Minnesota, only to discover there were too few arrests there to be typical of the area; this could mean that you have confined yourself to too narrow a topic. Or you may have initially intended to prove that drunk driving was *not* a critical problem in Minnesota, only to have your evidence completely change your mind and your thesis.

The final formulation of the thesis continues the narrowing process. Here we find a progression to three more subcategories:

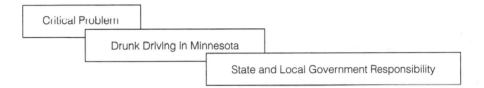

The Working Outline

Once the working thesis has been formulated, we can develop from that a *working outline*. This outline can be revised on a daily basis, depending on the evidence discovered, together with the revision, if any, of the thesis.

In the example paper, the final outline became a list of recommendations. These recommendations also inform the reader of the essay's organizational outline: the need for stronger enforcement, more severe punishment, and more education. Here three categories appear under the heading Recommendations:

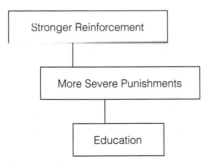

Summary of the First Trials of Research Paper Writing

Once you know what a research paper is, have chosen its subject and topic, and have sketched out a working thesis and working outline, you have finished the first major thinking maneuvers required by research paper writing. This task may take fifteen minutes to two days. It can save you hours and hours of needless labor spent on the selection of a topic or thesis too broad for adequate coverage or too narrow for treatment in the number of pages assigned.

Discovery Exercise

From Subject to Working Thesis to Working Outline

1. Choose one of the following words as a subject area word or supply one of your own: *jeans, cars, Japan, shoes*.

2. Make a cluster with this word, discovering your associations connected with it.

3. Diagram in boxes, as above, a topic for this subject, then a working thesis and working outline suitable for an eight-page essay. (Allow yourself first to play with several topics and theses before you make your final selection.)

4. Repeat this process with another subject word, working until you can do this rapidly and confidently.

5. Finally, narrow one topic one step too far, so that there wouldn't be enough information about it for an eight-page essay.

SORTING OUT THE RESEARCH PAPER TERMINOLOGY

A research paper, or any kind of essay, consists of two parts: *the claims* and *the support*. Understanding these terms clearly can make the organization of a paper seem quite simple. When we state the thesis, we are making a *claim, which is an assertion that something is true or false*. We can do this with a neutral, detached attitude or with an argumentative attitude. We can combine both attitudes in the claim that drunk driving is a critical problem in Minnesota. We then make further claims in the form of recommendations for changing this situation.

Support is defined as the information, evidence, facts, inferences, opinions, or arguments given to uphold a claim. As good professional writers know, claims asserted without support will not impress a critical reader. The best writing *shows* rather than *says*, convincing through the power of its evidence. There are also standards for the quality of evidence: support needs to be both sufficient and credible, as well as authoritative, recent, primary, and unbiased. Thus, in the example research paper, the effective use of primary sources—such as interviews, a survey, and government reports—provides convincing support for the thesis claim. The longer the paper, the more support is required.

Documentation is also a hallmark of the research paper; supplying it requires time and work not only in the research stage but in the final writing. In the example, the Modern Language Association (MLA) style of citation is evident in the bibliography and in the parenthetical references to authors and dates. This research paper example shows you how the final product evolved from keeping careful records about names, dates, titles, and publication data. Learning how to do this is not difficult, but it needs to begin in the earliest stage of your work, not the night you start writing your paper when the library may be closed.

A Review Before the Research and Writing Begin

If we review the definitions just covered, we can see a kind of checklist for preliminary organization of a research paper:

1. Am I clear about what is meant by a research paper?
2. Am I starting with a subject, topic, or thesis? Given the number of pages I must write, how far must I narrow down in order to arrive at a working thesis? (For this answer, clustering, mapping, diagramming, or preliminary research may be needed.)
3. What claims or arguments could I make on this topic? Can I find sufficient material in local libraries or from other data sources to support my topic? Or do I have the problem of selecting from too much material?
4. Will my purpose be mainly to explain, analyze, define, clarify, or argue my thesis?
5. Do I understand how to document my sources? Do I have a system for keeping a clear record of my notes and sources?

STAYING IN CHARGE AND ON SCHEDULE

Midway in their research paper writing, many students begin to feel overwhelmed by their source materials. They compare themselves unfavorably to those authors who demonstrate both professional authority and writing skills. Or they may feel uncertain about how to evaluate which information would best support their thesis. If these doubts continue, such students may shift from being writers to being "data dumpers" who merely compile information for the reader to organize. The best remedy for this tendency is self-recognition in its early stages followed by a conference with the instructor.

Data dump papers can also result from too much time spent in the practice of writing out notecards by hand. This tradition, still the stock-in-trade recommendation of all English handbooks, developed before the invention of the photocopy machine and laptop computer. Certainly it is important to have a clear method for keeping careful records of supportive information, quotations, citations, and bibliographies; however, with time limitations, making a notebook of photocopied materials can be more efficient than writing out everything by hand, including summaries or paraphrases that may not even be used in the final product. Photocopying can save more time for the actual composing process, and in this writing stage, the work of selecting and shaping source materials for quotation, paraphrase, or summary can be done more realistically. Investing less time in the note-taking process could also make it less tempting for students to claim to have paid their dues by only collecting research. The rule for research writing is to keep your own thinking and objectives in charge of your source materials. *Your* thinking creates the essay, not your sources. After all, research writers were not meant to be file clerks or collage artists!

A research writer is also not a plagiarist. What this word means also requires honest definition and discussion among students and instructors. A question in the exercise that follows will give you an opportunity to do just that. Plagiarism can also be related to the feeling of being overwhelmed by sources; it can result from assuming that one's own ideas are not as significant as those in print, from not understanding ideas as property, from not knowing when and how to quote, from not knowing how to paraphrase or summarize properly. Research writing truly challenges the writer to understand the nature of ideas and how to use them with integrity.

Planning a reasonable writing schedule that can expand for the unexpected is the last major trial of research paper writing. This means starting early and working on a regular basis before the final pressure develops. This is a familiar resolution, rarely kept. Although a short essay might blossom from time pressure, research writing's thinking, investigating, and checking for details proceed better when not hurried. The problem is that when you are hurried, you may find yourself unable to handle unexpected problems, like having to revise your thesis to fit some new evidence, or having to go out to the library one more time for additional research.

Altogether, passing the trials of research writing requires that you know yourself. Even the advice written for you on these pages will probably not offer you much help. *Information or advice that is given to you, even when thoroughly understood, is far harder to remember and use than what you discover for yourself*. The following exercises are offered with this principle in mind. They provide a preliminary research project designed to help you acknowledge what you know and to motivate you to learn what you do not know. Both exercises are optional. Look through the questions, confer with your instructor, then decide if you need to go through all or some of them. Then proceed to the Composition Writing Application instructions to begin your research paper essay.

Discovery Exercises

A COLLABORATIVE LEARNING OPPORTUNITY

Research About Writing a Research Paper

Research paper writing might be quite new to some of you, whereas for others, instruction on this subject has been offered every year since junior high school. How much do you know and how much have you applied? This is a survey designed to help you take an honest look at yourself, to recognize what you need to know, to remember where you have succeeded, where you failed, what you might adapt to improve. Answer these questions in writing. If possible, use them for class discussion with your instructor.

1. Your instructor has given you one month in which to choose your topic, do your research, and write a fifteen-page paper. Into what stages would you divide your work and how many days would you give to each stage?

2. What methods do you use for deciding on a topic or issue?

3. When do you formulate your thesis: before, during, or after your research?

4. Your instructor might suggest that you build a cluster, try looping, or use freewriting to get going on a subject. Do you understand what each of these terms means? How well do they work for you?

5. Your instructor asks you to do both primary and secondary research. Define each and give examples to show how you have used both.

6. You need a system for keeping a good record of your notes. What method have you used in the past? What could improve it: a laptop computer, notecards in a card box, a research notebook? What are the advantages of each? Which system would you like to know more about?

7. When you are doing research, do you write down your own ideas as they come, or do you wait until you have collected all your sources first?

8. When you write a research paper, do your sources tend to overpower you, like a car without a driver? What do you do when this starts happening?

9. When do you outline your paper? Do you always stick to that same outline, or do you keep revising it depending on what new ideas or research have turned up?

10. Do you use your outline to show you what claims or support may be missing, what is irrelevant, or what may be overemphasized?

11. What do you have to do to get yourself down to the actual writing of a paper?

12. After you finish your first draft, can you manage your scheduling to allow yourself a one- or two-day interval of rest, so that you reread what you have written with a fresh perspective? Do you ask others to let you read it aloud to them? (Having a listener not only helps both of you detect errors and gaps in communication but can also provide you with insights to write into your revision.)

13. Can you allow enough time before the due date to proofread for errors, check for complete bibliographical information, and rewrite a final draft if necessary?

14. Give a definition and example of plagiarism.

Peer Review

Bring your survey answers to class to share with small groups of six to eight people or with the whole class. See if you can classify what you have to say under the following:

1. Ideal scheduling for the stages of writing; dealing with time pressures.

2. Moving from subject to topic to thesis.

3. Keeping good records of your research.

4. Staying in control through your purpose as writer.

5. What causes students to plagiarize?

Research About Gathering Research: How Much Do You Know?

The following questions may require about an hour in the library. Work with a partner or alone as your instructor decides.

1. How can you use the library to help you decide on a topic? After you have chosen your topic, what plan do you follow in using the library to help get information?

2. Does your library have card catalogues, or is it computerized? What questions do you have about using either system?

3. If you were writing on drunk driving, would you look in the encyclopedia first? Why or why not?

4. If you were writing on Abraham Lincoln's childhood, would you look in the encyclopedia first?

5. Suppose you decide to write on drunk driving and want to start with a bibliography of readings to study. Where would you turn for this information?

6. What is microfilm, what is it used for, and how does it differ from microfiche?

7. The *Readers' Guide to Periodical Literature* covers two hundred popular mass-circulated magazines and journals. Your library may have *Info-Trac.*; its software offers several larger indexes, including a general periodicals index of seven hundred periodicals. In book form, many specialized indexes also exist, such as the *New York Times Index* and *Consumers Index*. Study at least three indexes that are new to you, and write down what you learned about working with each.

8. Does your library carry newspaper, periodical, and book review abstracts? How can this information help you in research?

9. Your instructor says you should use the MLA style of documentation in your paper. Where would you find information about this format to guide you? Would you need this information only while doing the final draft of your paper, or would you need it as you compile your research?

10. If you are given an appointment of only 15 minutes in which to interview some authority on your research topic, how would you prepare yourself?

11. List other sources in addition to the library and personal interviews that could give you information about a topic.

Peer Review

Bring your survey answers to class for discussion in small groups. Summarize, orally or in writing, your results using the following:

1. This is what I learned about how the library can help me in my research.

2. This is the source I will consult to follow the MLA style of source citation.

3. This is the way in which I will keep my notes in order to maintain a good record of information and citations.

4. Aside from the library, these are the other sources I could use for gathering research information.

Composition Writing Application

Writing a Research Paper Using Both Primary and Secondary Sources—A Collaborative or Independent Project

This chapter centers around one assignment that can be done individually or collectively. It requires that you take a conscious look at investigative or research skills, working with both primary and secondary sources. The assignment begins with a research proposal that must be approved by your instructor before you get too far into the project itself.*

Your Research Proposal

1. Select a topic about which you (or your partner) know something and want to know more.

2. Build clusters that show your thinking associations on this topic.

3. List the types of people who may have an interest in reading about this topic (see Figure 13.1).

4. List places, events, and people you might observe to gather information about your topic.

5. List people you might interview for information about your topic. Select people with a wide range of experiences, knowledge, and opinions. (Check phone books, newspapers, libraries, and other people for potential sources.)

6. Prepare a set of open-ended interview questions (not just questions to which one might answer *yes* or *no*).

7. List potential sources of printed information.

8. List other sources.

Research Project Requirements

1. One page of personal observations on this subject for each writer of the project paper. These may be interwoven in your final essay or attached in separate narrative form.

2. A minimum of two interviews. You may have more. Summaries of these interviews should be attached to your final essay.

---

*The author is indebted to Sue Sixberry, English instructor at Mesabi Community College, who designed this assignment, gave permission for its adaptation, and supplied the student research paper on pp. 390–401, which is used with permission of Donna Schley and James Kochevar.

Figure 13.1 Cluster on DUI
Used with permission of Donna Schley.

3. Three printed sources. At least two of these must be of different types (for example, books, pamphlets, newspapers, magazines). In your paper you must use MLA format to document your sources. Photocopies of the materials used must be attached to your final paper.

4. The length of the essay itself should be a minimum of seven typed double-spaced pages.

(continues p. 402)

DUI: THE LONG-TERM PICTURE

Donna Schley
James Kochevar
English 112

Table of Contents

I. Introduction: Background of the Issue

On May 3, 1980, Cari Lightner, age thirteen, was struck and killed by a drunk driver. This was the second time a drunk driver had hit her. The first time both she and her twin sister were injured as car passengers, although not seriously. This time Cari was walking with a friend to a school carnival; a car jumped the curb, hit her from behind, and threw her 125 feet through the air. Then amid the cries, shrieks, and the dust, the driver sped off. Cari died an hour later. After four days, the driver of the car was arrested and charged with felony manslaughter, felony hit-and-run, and felony drunk driving. Adding to the anguish she already felt, Cari's mother discovered that when the driver hit Cari, he was out on bail for a hit-and-run committed just two days earlier. Moreover, she discovered that he had been arrested for drunk driving four times before and that he had a valid California driver's license when he was arrested (Harakas C4).

II. Thesis: Organizing Claim and Three Supporting Claims

Although the above incident happened in California, many similar episodes have happened in our state. <u>Drunk driving in the state of Minnesota is a critical problem that must be more strongly addressed by state and local governments.</u> The need for stronger enforcement, more severe punishment, and education is essential.

1

III. Need for
Stronger En-
forcement.
Support for
Claim

The recent heightening of public awareness in the problem of drunk driving has led to a recognition of the need
for stronger enforcement. In a recent interview, Anthony

A. Current
Procedures

Delzotto, the chief of police in Gilbert, Minnesota, stated that
this trend has naturally caused law enforcement officials to
be more conscientious in their dealings with drunk driving.
In turn, public awareness has caused some drivers to alter
their drinking and driving habits. Delzotto admitted that the
number of drunk driving arrests in Gilbert has decreased in
the last two years, a fact he attributed to stronger emphasis
on enforcement over the past five years (Delzotto interview,
1988).

B. Problems
Inherent in
System

However, according to Robert Flood, deputy court
administrator in Virginia, Minnesota, arrests have been on
the increase in recent years. Flood points out that although
more arrests are helping to address the problem, this practice only scratches the surface of this enormously complex
issue (Flood interview, 1988). Law enforcement and safety
officials estimate that on any typical Friday or Saturday
night, there are between 20,000 and 30,000 drunk drivers
on Minnesota roads (Mn. Dept. Pub. Safety 1). Flood estimates that of these 20,000 to 30,000 drunk drivers, only 200
are arrested for driving under the influence. He says this is

2

due to the limited number of officers on duty in relation to the number of drunk drivers as well as to the time it takes to process an arrest. Basically, by the time an officer makes an arrest, processes it, and returns to make further arrests, most drunk drivers have already left the highways for the evening (Flood interview, 1988).

C. Suggested Improvements

One suggested solution has been to add more officers during peak hours. This, however, would make only a small improvement, as one officer is able to make only one or two arrests per evening and the cost of hiring 20,000 to 30,000 officers would be prohibitive (Flood interview, 1988). This is not to say that officials should discontinue stricter enforcement. By continuing to emphasize the importance of not drinking and driving, officials strengthen their own position and prevent complacency in the public at the same time.

IV. Need for More Severe Punishments. Support for Claim

Along with the need for stronger enforcement, the need for more severe punishments has also become accepted. Currently in Minnesota, if a person is convicted of a DUI, he/she may be imprisoned up to 90 days or fined up to $700 or both.

A. Current Minnesota Penalties

A person may have his/her driver's license revoked for not less than 30 days. If the violation involves injury or death, the individual could be imprisoned, fined, and/or receive at least 90 additional days of revocation (Mn. Dept. Pub. Safety 4).

3

These penalties may vary; some are stronger, some weaker. In Virginia, Minnesota, District Court Judge Donovan Frank sees the severity of the problem and strongly feels the need for more stringent punishment. For the typical first-offender DUI arrest, Frank gives the maximum penalties, plus two years of probation. However, on the condition that the offender attend the DUI clinic, the sentence may be reduced and the imprisonment stayed (Frank interview, 1988).

B. Dilemma of Repeat Offenders

Within the whole DUI picture, the major problem seems to be that of repeat offenders. Even though the penalties and costs of a DUI conviction increase with every violation, there continues to be a high rate of repeat offenses. According to Frank, that rate is as high as 25 percent of the first-time offenders. He further states that 90 percent of all repeat offenders are chemically dependent. Therefore, along with strong penalties, treatment for these dependencies is essential (Frank interview, 1988).

C. Case for Change

Several different organizations have made many efforts to strengthen the laws against drunk driving. Although these efforts have succeeded to a certain extent, further legislation is required. Some of the newer ideas for punishment include the use of bumper stickers that carry the message that drunk driving is wrong or that the offender is a drunk

4

driver, identification of drunk drivers by their license plates, mandatory jail sentences for first-time offenders, automatic jail sentences at the time of arrest, and the overall strengthening of fines and penalties (Frank interview, 1988). In view of the fact that some countries have mandatory death penalties for first-time offenders, none of the proposed suggestions seems too severe.

V. Need for Education. Support for Claim

Over and above the need for stronger enforcement and the need for more severe punishment, the real need appears to lie in the area of education. Some of the current programs

A. Current Programs

used to educate people on the problems of drunk driving include the use of advertising in all forms of media, the dissemination of information by organizations such as Mothers Against Drunk Driving and Students Against Driving Drunk, the use of DUI clinics, and the educating of young people in drivers' training classes.

B. Environmental Attitudes

But are we educating early enough and/or thoroughly enough? According to the Search Institute in Minneapolis, Minnesota, 61 percent of twelfth graders report driving after drinking once or more during the "last 12 months" (Search Institute 2). A survey of 77 people conducted by these writers in the Iron Range area of northeastern Minnesota found that 95 percent of the respondents were aware

5

of the penalties for a DUI, yet 49 percent of them continue to drink and drive (Appendix). The tradition of drinking and driving is an old one in the Iron Range, and the reasoning behind stricter laws and enforcement may still not be fully recognized. Interestingly enough, however, another 49 percent plan ahead by providing for a sober driver when they go out drinking. This, at least, would indicate that recent efforts to educate the public on this matter have had some effect (Appendix).

C. Seeking Social Responsibilities

According to Robert Flood, 65 people are killed each day on U.S. highways as a result of drunk drivers. Is this acceptable? Most people would say that even one unnecessary death is one too many. When this number of people are killed in a plane crash, immediate cries go out to make the airlines safer. Yet, most deaths caused by drunk drivers go unheeded (Flood interview, 1988). So where does the responsibility lie? Does it lie with our government officials, with our law enforcement officials, or with society as a whole? The aforementioned survey revealed that 18 percent of the people think that the penalties are too strict already (Appendix). This would appear to indicate that nearly one out of five people think that either drunk driving is all right and that the killing of 65 people a day on U.S. highways by drunk

6

drivers is acceptable, or that drunk driving is not a serious enough problem to address with stricter enforcement and higher penalties. At the very least, this would suggest the need for more segments of society to take responsibility for the problem. A massive public education drive is needed. The issues of drunk driving should be discussed in grade school and high school health classes, become a more comprehensive part of drivers' education, and find more emphasis in alcohol abuse counseling. It should be a subject for discussion in political campaigns, be featured in public service announcements and at health fairs, and involve the participation of multiple civic and grassroots organizations. More Americans need to look squarely at the statistics of an average of 25,000 alcohol-related U.S. traffic fatalities a year that includes 8,500 teenagers dead. An additional 40,000 are disfigured (De Vore 11). All of us need to ask ourselves how we could have come to accept so much needless suffering.

VI. Summary and Conclusion

Yet, ultimately the issue of drunk driving is so pervasive and complex that solutions will not quickly be found nor will they be comprehensive in their scope. But it is critical that we continue to seek answers to the problem. It is important that we strive for stronger enforcement and more severe punishments. But the most important thing we have to do is

7

educate the public. Only through education will we be able to effect the kind of long-term change of attitude that results in long-term change in behavior.

Herbert Spencer of Alcoholics Anonymous summed it up best when he said, "There is a principle which opposes all information, which is proof against all argument, and cannot fail to keep man in every last ignorance--that principle is contempt prior to investigation" (1976). Here the word <u>contempt</u> seems not only to include the idea of scornful indifference but the denial that has made us tolerate an intolerable problem for too long.

VII. Opinions

Opinion
James Kochevar

This research paper, aside from its intention (to learn how to conduct research and how to write a research paper), has taught me many new things. Of all people, I, a recovering alcoholic, should be aware of the consequences of drunk driving. Although I have never had a DUI myself, I certainly have driven drunk. I've had several accidents because of my drinking and have driven many times in a "black out," not remembering a thing the next day. Although it's been over six years since my last drink, I guess that I've become rather complacent regarding my responsibilities in this matter.

8

Only once have I offered to drive someone home who had been drinking. Moreover, I have never taken any action to help any of the organizations concerned with this matter, to help further their causes. To sum up what I've learned about this problem, I would have to say I learned that just because I no longer drink or drive drunk doesn't mean that I'm immune to those who do.

Opinion
Donna Schley

As a result of conducting the research on the problems of drinking and driving, I have discovered how really severe this problem is. Before doing this research project, I was an occasional drunk driver. Seeing the severity of this widespread problem, I have vowed to myself that I will never again drive drunk. I also plan to share my thoughts with my friends. By pitching in and helping, I hope to save one or more lives. I have never taken someone else's life because of my carelessness or stupidity. Nor do I ever want to. I hope more of the public soon will be as enlightened as I have been.

9

In April 1988, seventy-seven individuals were asked the
following questions at Mesabi Community College and in
some Iron Range, Minnesota, bars.

Appendix--Survey

1. Do you drink and drive?

    yes 38 (49%)   no 39 (51%)

2. Do you and your friends plan ahead for a sober driver
    when you go out drinking?

    yes 38 (49%)   no 39 (51%)

3. If not, when you have had too much to drink do you let
    someone else drive if they ask?

    yes 64 (83%)   no 13 (17%)

4. Are you aware of the penalties for a DUI?

    yes 73 (95%)   no 4 (5%)

5. Have you ever been arrested for a DUI?

    yes 8 (10%)   no 69 (90%)

6. Were you ever convicted?

    yes 7   no 1

7. How many DUI arrests have you had?

    7 had 1   1 had 2

8. How many convictions have you had on these arrests?

    6 had 1   1 had 2   1 had 0

10

9. Do you predict that you will get arrested again?

   yes 2   no 6

10. Do you feel the laws are strict enough? Too strict?

    yes 36 (47%)   no 27 (35%)   too strict 14 (18%)

11. Have you ever been involved in an accident while you were under the influence of alcohol or any other substance?

    yes 13 (17%)   no 64 (83%)

12. Were there any injuries? Any fatalities?

    yes 4   no 9

IX. Bibliog-
raphy

Bibliography

Delzotto, Anthony. Chief of Police in Gilbert, Minnesota. Personal Interview. 19 Feb. 1988.

De Vore, S. "The Deadly Combination of Drinking and Driving." Current Health Sept. 1988: 11–13.

Flood, Robert. Deputy Court Administrator in Virginia, Minnesota. Personal Interview. 18 Feb. 1988.

Frank, Donovan. District Court Judge in Virginia, Minnesota. Personal Interview. 18 Feb. 1988.

Harakas, Margo. "One Mother's Furious Fight." Palm Beach Post 26 July 1981: C4.

Minnesota Department of Public Safety. Drinking Drivers Lose: Minnesota DUI Laws. DDL 4321.

Search Institute. Highlights from 1983 Minnesota Survey Drug Use and Drug-Related Attitudes. 1983.

Spencer, Herbert. Alcoholics Anonymous. Third Edition. New York City: Alcoholics Anonymous World Services, Inc., 1976.

11

5. This essay must have a title page, a table of contents, and a bibliography.

6. Use an expository or argumentative style, or a mixture of both, as your instructor recommends.

Bibliography of Sources for MLA Documentation Rules

Aaron, Jane E. "Documenting Sources: MLA Style." Chapter 49, *The Little Brown Compact Handbook*. New York: HarperCollins, 1993.

Beene, Lynn, and William Van De Kopple. "Documenting Your Research Paper by MLA or APA Format." Chapter 45, *The Riverside Handbook*. Boston: Houghton Mifflin, 1992.

Fowler, H. Ramsey, and Jane E. Aaron. "Documenting Sources" (Chapter 37) and "Two Sample Research Papers" (Chapter 38). *The Little Brown Handbook*. 6th ed. New York: HarperCollins, 1995.

CHAPTER 14

Problem Solving:
How Can I Create Solutions?

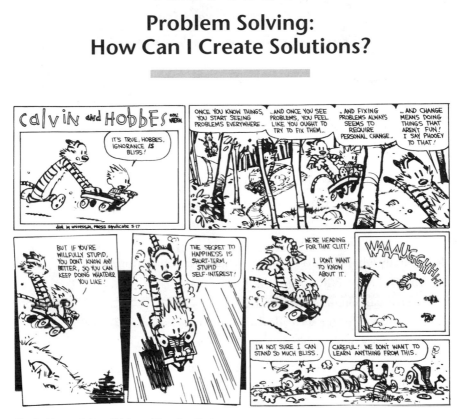

Used with permission of Universal Press Syndicate.

E ven if you end up a wreck, why learn from the experience? Understanding problems takes a lot of mental work. The purpose of this
chapter is to help you find adventure and creativity instead of just
work.

If you have been studying the boxed problem-solving series throughout
the text, you already have learned how each chapter's concept applies to
thinking about problems. This chapter on problem solving has been written in such a way that you can refer to it at any time during the study
of this text. You can use it to focus in depth on the subject as well as
to discover how problem solving brings critical and creative thinking
together.

Discovery Exercises

A COLLABORATIVE LEARNING OPPORTUNITY

What's a Problem?

Using the dictionary,

1. Write down a dictionary definition of the word *problem*.
2. Now write down a different definition of your own.

What Do We Know About Problems?

1. Make a list of five problems in your own life.
2. Make a list of five problems in public life.
3. Select a problem to work with.
4. Exactly what is in conflict with what in this situation?
5. Are there any other causes of the problem?
6. List some potential solutions.
7. For each solution, write down its advantages and disadvantages.
8. Now, what new problems might each solution create?

Discuss what you have written in small groups. Did you learn anything new about the nature of problems by doing this?

PROBLEM ANATOMY: FINDING THE CONFLICT

Problems don't go away by themselves.

Putting things off only makes them worse.

These two familiar sayings reflect some common wisdom about problem solving. We all know the energy drain of postponing dental appointments, bills, or exam preparation—all of which remain problems until we put our thinking to work on them. Problems provoke thinking. And to solve them we need both critical thinking to analyze the situation and creative thinking to generate solutions. When we generate solutions, we go beyond the usual range of our imaginations and invent something new. We discover or achieve something that may surprise us. Einstein said that "a problem cannot be solved at the level of consciousness it was created." Problems require us to grow in our understanding. They show us when we are not interacting successfully with the world; they prod and test us to move beyond our limitations, to bring something new into being, to achieve more than we thought we could.

One simple definition of a problem is an undesirable situation that endures. A child who is late to school every day for three months is a problem, as is an apartment-complex neighbor who keeps his television at top volume, or an old car that keeps running up repair expenses. In each case, there is an unwanted situation that will not go away by itself. Both thinking and action are needed to effect change, since precipitous action alone can lead to even greater problems. Punishing the child severely could result in further behavior problems, yelling at the neighbor could lead to a fight, and buying a new car could mean debts. Before we act, we need to know how to think through our problems effectively and quickly.

One technique for faster problem solving is to ask three questions:

1. What exactly is the problem?
2. Who has the problem?
3. What conflict is making this problem persist?

Let's take the case of the chronically tardy child. On the surface, the problem is a classroom disrupted by someone arriving a half hour late each day. Let's say also that neither the teacher nor the parents are able to reason with the child or persuade or force her to arrive on time. The problem consists of two oppositions:

Teacher's intention for order *versus* Child's unknown intention

Here, it is useful to look for problem ownership. It is a problem for the teacher, who, along with the other students, is inconvenienced by an interrupted class. It is also a problem for the parents, who don't want to feel they can't control their child. But the continuing hassles over tardiness do not seem to be a problem for the child. And the adults remain baffled because no matter what tactics they use or threats they make, they cannot get the child to see it is a problem. As the situation drags on, the parents and teacher begin to see the conflict in terms of a bad child versus good adults:

Bad child *versus* Good teacher and parents

Such an analysis of the conflict would then lead to further deteriorations in their relationships, causing conflicts in more areas. However, if the child were to be closely questioned by a neutral outside party who did not assume the child was bad and hopeless, that person might discover that tardiness was the child's way of getting some needed (although negative) attention:

		Teacher and parent's
Child's need	*versus*	nonrecognition of that need

Such a discovery of the underlying and actual conflict could then lead to more effective solutions, such as more satisfying ways of giving time and positive interest to the child. Here, their mutual creativity has to be invoked.

Exercise

Problem Ownership and Conflict Factors

Consider the following problems to see if you agree that it is helpful to identify the owners of each problem as well as the opposing conflicts. List the owners and draw arrows to show the oppositions.

1. When the mother comes home after her night class, she finds that her children have not fed their animals as they promised. The dog is whining, the cats are jumping on the sink, and the hamster is gasping for water.

2. Some refugees from Cuba arrive by boat in Florida. The immigration officers put them in jail.

3. You miss your bus and have to drive to school. You have trouble finding a parking space, which makes you late for a test. Your instructor glares at you and says, "You'll have to do the best you can in the time remaining."

4. The government of Brazil is alarmed by the severe drop in the tourist industry. Vacationers who had come to the beach in Rio de Janeiro were being attacked by thousands of poor people from the surrounding ghettos. The government raises $4 million to hire public relations specialists from the United States to restore Brazil's image.

By analyzing problems in terms of ownership and the conflict of purposes and intentions, we can also look for cause without judging the wrongness or rightness of either party. Indeed, such an evaluation may be not only a distraction but an irrelevance; worse, it may lead to problems of enemy making. Let's look at both a personal and public problem in these terms.

Suppose a husband buys a new car with high monthly payments. When he comes home with the car and tells his wife, she gets very angry about his having made a purchase that could wreck their monthly budget. She shakes her fist and calls him a spendthrift. Then he shouts back, "And you're a skinflint!" She threatens to leave him. He gets upset. Here, what was not a problem to the husband (financing the car) is a problem to the wife. She becomes alienated from him when he cannot see it as a problem and conveys her outrage with a threat. Thus, she succeeds in giving him a problem he can feel: the loss of their relationship. In this situation, the car is not the problem. Nor is either spouse wrong; the problem could be a conflict between preferences for unilateral versus bilateral financial decisions:

His unilateral preference   *versus*   Her bilateral preference

If they cannot recognize the source of the conflict but focus on the car or who's wrong, they might try to solve the problem by getting a divorce—a solution that would create more losses and more problems.

Ownership and conflict can also be recognized in a public problem. A chemical company, which makes large contributions to a mayor's reelection campaign, dumps its waste into the city river. A citizens' group goes to see the mayor in protest, but the mayor takes no action. For the citizens, the problem is what the chemical company is doing and what their elected mayor is not doing. They become so angry that some of them petition for the recall of the mayor and a boycott of the chemical company. For the mayor and chemical company, the problem is the agitation of the citizens. They call them fanatical environmentalists. But the core of the problem lies in a conflict of values and needs. The citizens, because they value the long-term health and welfare of the community, have the intention of keeping the river unpolluted. The chemical company values profits and, to that end, has the intention of finding a convenient and inexpensive method for getting rid of its wastes. The mayor has the more complex problem because he needs campaign contributions from the chemical company but also needs the votes of the citizens. And his problem is to create a new way to reconcile all these aspects.

Exercise

What Is at Conflict?

In the blanks provided, diagram what oppositions are in conflict in each of the following situations:

1. You want to lose weight, but you hate diets and exercise.

   _____

2. You want to break up with your boyfriend, but you are afraid you won't find anyone else.

   _____

3. You need to find a new apartment since your rent has been raised. But your current apartment is the only one available just a block from school, a convenience you really like.

   _____

4. Your instructor speaks more rapidly than you can take notes. When you ask her to slow down, she does for a short time, then picks up speed again.

   _____

5. You are enjoying being with a group of friends watching the Boston Red Sox play baseball. Suddenly, you feel something hit your back, and you turn around to see a woman sitting a few rows up throwing peanuts at you. You laugh and turn around, only to be hit again. You don't know her and can't figure out why she singled you out. You wonder what to do to make her stop.

   _____

Class Discussion

Compare notes on the exact nature of the conflicts you find in each of these cases. Do you find opposing intentions can exist within one person? Are both sides necessarily recognized? Finally, given the discovery of the specific nature of these conflicts, what solutions might be feasible? Would any of these solutions create new and possibly greater problems?

DETERMINING CAUSE

- In the early nineties, a lawsuit was filed against Ozzy Osbourne for producing a song called "The Suicide Solution," which was said to have precipitated the suicides of two teenagers. It then became a

In the disposal of toxic waste, this method is still the cheapest...

.. and simplest way to get rid of the problem.

Used with permission of Clay Bennett.

court matter to decide whether there was a direct causal link between the events.

- An individual in Boston decided to commit suicide by throwing himself in front of a subway train. When he survived the accident, he sued the subway system for negligence and won.

- A private citizen paid several thousand dollars to place a full-page ad in a city newspaper urging everyone to vote out incumbent members of Congress in 1992 since every incumbent was dishonest.

- When the Iran–Contra scandals broke, upper-level government officials claimed they knew nothing about it. Some lower-level officials were fired or sent to jail.

- After the Los Angeles riots, there were a number of speculations as to the causes:
  (a) The initial media reports attributed the violence to (1) the widely aired videotape of Rodney King's beating; (2) the Rodney King

Used with permission of L. J. Kopf.

verdict that condoned police violence; (3) the all-white jury of an all-white community; (4) the failure of police to respond initially and strongly.

(b) The vice president announced that the underlying cause was the decline of family values.

(c) A presidential spokesman said the social programs of the Democrats caused the riots.

(d) A representative of Free Our Beaches said the cause was the people's lack of access to nature, which made them crazy.

(e) A Korean-American sociology professor said it was a local breakdown of humanity, civility, and the system—resulting in anarchy.

(f) An unemployed welder said the cause was a buildup of frustration from lack of jobs.

Class Discussion

1. Look at these just cited instances as problem solving through finding and blaming the cause. What do you find to be familiar yet troublesome about each of these cases? Does the fallacy of false cause apply to any of these cases?

2. Consider some current social problems such as: failing banks, public health costs, unemployment, and city crime.

   (a) Choose one and make a cluster of all your associations on the problem.
   (b) In each case, list those people or groups who recognize this as their problem. Then make diagrams to show exactly what *conflict or conflicts* appear in each problem.
   (c) Drawing on this information, list what you infer could be the *causes* of the problem.

ALTERNATE APPROACHES TO PROBLEM SOLVING: A TOOL KIT

Four approaches to problem solving are guided by questions. While both the rational approach and the fact-finding approach apply the laser of rational-analytical thinking, the last two, the goals and lateral thinking approaches, apply intuition and a holistic approach. While the solutions reached through the rational and fact-finding approaches may seem familiar, those created from the goals and lateral thinking approaches may be novel and original.

Rational Approach

This approach applies the laser of rational-analytical thinking. It asks five questions:

1. What exactly is the problem?
2. What conflict holds it in place?
3. What choices are there for solutions?
4. What are the advantages and disadvantages of each choice?
5. What seems to be the best choice?

Study Questions

1. Working individually, take up one of the problems you listed in the Discovery Exercises. Take it through the six steps and see what happens.
2. Write down the advantages and disadvantages of this approach. Do you think it could be useful for some situations and not others? Specify which.

Fact-Finding Approach

Fact finding is another methodical approach to problem solving. It asks six questions:

1. What exactly is the problem?
2. What conflict holds it in place?
3. Is some crucial information about this situation missing? (List or cluster to find out.)
4. How can I get this information?
5. Is there any information about this situation not available?
6. Once I have assembled more information, does it give me a different view of the problem and some potential solutions?

Class Discussion

1. Think of a problem that you solved by finding more information. (If you did the fact-finding writing report in Chapter 3, use this example.)
2. What are the advantages and disadvantages of this approach? Do you think it could be useful for some situations and not others? Specify which.

Goals Approach

> There is a difference between problem-solving to make something go away and creating an action to bring something into being. You will always have a new problem if you do not know how to create what you want. And *creating* is no problem. (Robert Fritz, *The Path of Least Resistance*)

In his book *The Path of Least Resistance*, Robert Fritz describes how the team members of his Technologies for Creating organization worked with some villages in Uganda that were suffering from the aftermath of war. The villagers needed help in solving severe problems of human and livestock diseases, no hospitals or social services, repressive politics, poverty, and general hopelessness. The team did not offer aid or address each problem in turn but instead trained people to use their innate wisdom to transform the quality of life in their communities. In workshops, participants identified each problem, then reflected on how they wanted their lives and communities to be. *The main focus was on what they wanted, rather than what they didn't want*. From there they went into action. When they agreed they wanted clean water in one village, they met, found the spring to be built and protected, and created eight new wells. The youth of one village built a school and a road; the women of another village dug a fishpond for fish farming. One leader noted that the people were having fun and loving what they were doing because they were doing it for their own development. Another stated, "We have learned new things in agriculture, health, and nutrition. But above all, we have learned to live together, and rise above our differences."

Questions to Apply in Using the Goals Approach

1. How is this situation short of what I really want?
2. What is the larger goal that I really want?
3. What is in the way of my achieving that goal?
4. What action can I take now toward that goal?

Class Discussion

Think of a personal or public problem. What solutions have been tried to make the problem go away? Would this problem disappear or seem insignificant if a larger goal were envisioned? (Use group brainstorming or clustering to discover the goal.) What immediate steps could be taken toward that goal?

Lateral Thinking Approach

An architect had finished building a cluster of apartment buildings surrounded by lawns. The last problem was to design walkways from one apartment to the other and to the parking lot, tennis courts, and playground. She had two assistants. One was a vertical thinker who drew up sidewalks along the perimeters of each building and in geometric lines to each of the public locations. The other was a lateral thinker who proposed that they put in no sidewalks for 6 months but only seed the lawns. Then after 6 months, once foot traffic had found its own most convenient paths through the grass, the sidewalks would be laid along these paths.

It does not seem possible to give step-by-step instructions for thinking laterally because its very nature is intuitive and playful rather than vertical and rational. Lateral thinking is more like living with a cat. If you want its attention, you cannot command it but must coax it. Lateral thinking cannot be ordered to appear, but it can be invoked when offered attention, respect, and the tease of curiosity. It is not even easy to explain what it is and how you gain it. At the end of Chapter 5, Edward de Bono illustrates his definition of the term by telling a story. He has developed many exercises designed to evoke lateral thinking's appearance so that we may recognize and cultivate it as a skill. One of these simple exercises is called PMI (for Plus Minus Interesting), adapted here for your use.

Using the Lateral Thinking Approach. The most effective way to use these questions is to work with them in small groups, using rapid-fire listing or brainstorming without censorship. But they can also be tackled alone by using clustering. For the best results, study the middle questions for no more than 6 minutes each. (If done in class, several groups can be formed, each competing to make the longest list while being timed by the instructor. Then the results may be read and compared before continuing to the next question.) *While going through these steps, note when your mind shifts into new and unexpected insights, for this experience is also the product of lateral thinking.*

1. What exactly is the problem?
2. What is negative about it? (Brainstorm or cluster for 6 minutes.)
3. What is positive about it? (Brainstorm or cluster for 6 minutes.)
4. What is neither positive or negative but just interesting about this problem? (Brainstorm or cluster for 6 minutes.)
5. Does this problem involve any underlying assumptions?
6. Does the problem look different now? Do new solutions seem possible?

Study Questions

1. Supply an example of a problem you solved by lateral thinking.
2. Take a problem from your initial Discovery Exercises list. Use the questions, brainstorming, or clustering to find a lateral solution.

Composition Writing Application

A COLLABORATIVE LEARNING OPPORTUNITY

The Problem-Solving Paper: A Research Assignment

The outline that follows is intended to help you organize your paper. Whether you are working individually or as a team, sketch out your answers to the first nine items for instructor approval prior to writing the paper:

1. State the problem.
2. Briefly describe the history of the problem.
3. Whose problem is it?
4. Exactly what factors are at conflict in this problem?
5. What do you think are the causes of the problem? (Give your own analysis as well as that of at least three other sources.)
6. What solutions have been tried or proposed? (Try to find at least three.)

7. What are the advantages or disadvantages of each? (Consider actual or predictable results, missing information, unexamined assumptions.)

8. Is there an innovative or novel way of looking at this problem? (Your own analysis mainly, but you can cite other sources also.)

9. Which problem-solving approach do you feel would be the best for solving this problem and what steps could be taken to implement it?

10. Support your claims with reasoning and evidence.

11. Use the MLA style of notation to make clear your use of sources, whether in direct quoting, paraphrasing, or summarizing.

12. Give a bibliography of all sources consulted.

Problem-Solving Paper Guidelines

1. *Form*: An analytical report and/or analytical and/or argumentative essay with a thesis.

2. *Organization*: A paper that identifies the problem, describes its history, analyzes its components, and suggests solutions.

3. *Length*: Ten pages typed or whatever length is needed to adequately develop its thesis.

4. *Sources*: Use the MLA style of notation with a list of Works Cited.

5. *Suggested Topics*: Affordable Housing, Gun Violence in Schools, Voter Apathy, Health Care, The Ozone Layer, The Disappearance of Animal and Plant Species, The Junkyard in Space, Job Retraining, Creating Community Support in Cities, Schools of the Future.

For Further Reading

Ackoff, Russell L. *The Art of Problem Solving*. New York: John Wiley, 1978.

Adams, James. *Conceptual Blockbusting*. New York: Norton, 1979.

De Bono, Edward. *Children Solve Problems*. New York: Penguin, 1972.

———. *Serious Creativity*. New York: HarperBusiness, 1992.

———. *Teach Your Child How to Think*. New York: Penguin, 1993.

Fritz, Robert. *The Path of Least Resistance*. New York: Fawcett Columbine, 1989.

Gordon, Thomas. *T.E.T. Teacher Effectiveness Training*. New York: David McKay, 1974.

Thompson, Charles. *What a Great Idea!* New York: HarperPerennial, 1992.

OBJECTIVES REVIEW OF PART IV

When you have finished Part IV, you will understand

- The concepts and skills of research paper writing.
- The definition and anatomy of problems.
- How unrecognized conflicts hold problems in place.
- How to use some tools and strategies for problem solving.
- How poorly conceived solutions and faulty identification of causes create new problems.

And you will have practice developing these skills:

- Establishing and following a research procedure.
- Getting the information you need.
- Using MLA citations.
- Writing a research paper based on primary and secondary sources.
- Producing a research paper individually or collaboratively.
- Identifying ownership and conflict factors in problems.
- Selecting an appropriate approach for solving a particular problem.
- Solving problems with creative thinking.
- Writing a problem-solving research paper.

Index